THE ASSOCIATION FOR SCOTTISH LITERARY STUDIES
NUMBER THIRTY-EIGHT

ELIZABETH HAMILTON

THE COTTAGERS OF GLENBURNIE

AND OTHER EDUCATIONAL WRITING

*

THE ASSOCIATION FOR SCOTTISH LITERARY STUDIES

ELIZABETH HAMILTON

THE COTTAGERS OF GLENBURNIE

AND OTHER EDUCATIONAL WRITING

Edited by

PAM PERKINS

GLASGOW

2010

*

First published in Great Britain, 2010
by The Association for Scottish Literary Studies
Department of Scottish Literature
University of Glasgow
7 University Gardens
Glasgow G12 8QH

www.asls.org.uk

Hardback
ISBN: 978-0-948877-85-8

Paperback
ISBN: 978-0-948877-86-5

A catalogue record for this book
is available from the British Library.

The Association for Scottish Literary Studies acknowledges
support from the Scottish Arts Council towards
the publication of this book.

Typeset by AFS Image Setters Ltd, Glasgow
Printed and bound by Bell & Bain Ltd, Glasgow

Contents

Acknowledgements

I would like to thank Margery Palmer McCulloch for her helpful suggestions when I first submitted the proposal for this edition and the anonymous ASLS reader for the detailed and thoughtful comments on the text. I am also grateful to Kirsteen McCue for both encouragement and practical advice at all stages of this project and to Vanessa Warne and Cliff Eyland for reading and commenting on drafts of the introduction. Much of the research for the edition was carried out at the National Library of Scotland with funding from the Social Sciences and Humanities Research Council of Canada; without access to those collections, this edition could not have been completed.

Note on the Texts

I have used the first edition of 1808 as my copy-text for the *Cottagers of Glenburnie*, following Hamilton's spelling and punctuation, though I have silently corrected some inconsistencies in Hamilton's use of quotation marks in reported dialogue. The book was republished in numerous cheap editions throughout the first half of the nineteenth century, often with some abridgement and occasionally even with minor changes to the title. The second and subsequent editions published during Hamilton's life, for example, appeared as *The Cottagers of Glenburnie: A Tale for the Farmer's Inglenook*, while later editions were called simply *The Cottagers of Glenburnie: A Tale* (London, 1839) or *The Cottagers of Glenburnie: A Scottish Tale* (in a non-dated Edinburgh edition). The only substantive change to the content made during Hamilton's lifetime was the addition of the letter describing the later fate of the MacClarty family, which appeared in editions published from 1810 onwards, though (like the prefatory letter to Hector Macneill), it was omitted from some of the cheaper editions published later in the century. The transcription here is from the 1810 (fifth) edition of the novel. My sources for the other works by Hamilton are as follows: *Memoirs of the Life of Agrippina*, the first edition of 1804; *Letters on the Elementary Principles of Education*, the third edition (1803); and *Letters Addressed to the Daughter of a Nobleman*, the second edition of 1806. Further information on the publishing history of these works is provided in the individual headnotes.

Introduction

Two hundred years ago, when it was first published, *The Cottagers of Glenburnie* became an immediate critical and popular success, notwithstanding its uncompromisingly didactic subject matter. Its author, Elizabeth Hamilton, had already written two satirical novels, a handbook on education, and an ambitious study of classical history, but it was this tale of Scottish peasant life that made her one of the best-know women writers of her day. Yet by the middle of the nineteenth century, it had slipped from the status of a modern classic to a work considered suitable mainly for children and the lower classes, and by the opening of the twentieth, it had all but disappeared from the canon. In reading the book today, it is useful to consider how it slid, in little more than a generation, from being praised by some of the most sophisticated and influential readers of the day to being handed out as an improving tract for slum-dwellers. In doing so, one might better understand its place not just in the literature of Romantic-era British women reformers, such as Hannah More and Mary Leadbeater, but also, and more generally, in the early nineteenth-century Scottish canon. Although Hamilton herself made some deprecating comments about the limited aims of the work in her private correspondence, *The Cottagers of Glenburnie* is as thoroughly grounded in her life-long interest in educational theory as any of her more overtly ambitious books on the subject, and part of the intention of this edition is to place the novel in the wider context of Hamilton's literary and educational writing. While only four of her nine books are represented here, the selections chosen suggest some of the range and scope of her work. *Letters on the Elementary Principles of Education* (1801) was the most successful of Hamilton's non-fiction, and it contains the clearest and most full presentation of her educational theories. *Memoirs of the Life of Agrippina, Wife of Germanicus* (1804) undertakes to demonstrate the validity of some of those theories through the use of historical narrative, while *Letters Addressed to the Daughter of a Nobleman* (1806) is an attempt to make Hamilton's ideas accessible to an audience of children, much as *Glenburnie* reaches out to a working-class readership. Taken together, these works emphasize the ways in which, despite its ostensibly simple plot and style, *Glenburnie* brings together the political and social concerns of so many of Hamilton's women contemporaries in England and Ireland with the Scottish enlightenment interest in theories of the mind and of moral education on which Hamilton drew throughout her career.

There is no doubt that Hamilton impressed her own contemporaries with both the intellectual content and – perhaps even more dramatically – the supposed practical impact of *Glenburnie*; tributes to the book and its influence dot both the major and the minor literature of the day. The novelist and travel writer Elizabeth Isabella Spence, for example, apparently found her thoughts turning immediately to Hamilton when, during a Scottish tour in 1811, she caught a glimpse of cottage life at Craigbarnet, near Glasgow, and she reported with some distaste on the unappealing appearance of the village's mud and thatch cottages, disfigured as they were by "a dirty puddle for ducks" by the door, "a littered entry, and no path-way to approach it by. It is," she concludes austerely, "with too much truth, Mrs Hamilton describes the want of neatness in the Scotch peasantry." A little later in her journey, she found herself thinking of Hamilton once again, as some ladies with whom she was walking scolded a peasant woman for not washing her child's face: the woman's "reply was literally what Mrs Hamilton says, '*She can'd na be fashed*' – that is, she could not take the trouble, – alleging at the same time, as an excuse, it would be *a' ane*, soon as dirty again."[1] Yet if three years after the publication of *The Cottagers of Glenburnie*, middle-class tourists such as Spence were looking at rural Scottish villages as an unattractive, real-life illustration of Elizabeth Hamilton's novel, it appeared that matters had changed considerably only a few years later. When Spence went back to Scotland in 1816, she was gratified to find that

> poverty and dirt no longer excited disgust. The visible change for the better, is most grateful to the eye, and pleasant to the feelings, in the progress of improvement. The neat cottages of the poor are now built of good substantial stone of the country, finished with

slate, instead of thatched roofs, and sashed windows, which admit the light of heaven. The dunghill before the door has disappeared, and rural gardens, with fruit-trees and flowers, embellish the walls. How greatly are the lower class indebted to Mrs Hamilton, for the 'Cottagers of Glenbervie:' [sic] which has tended to effect such a happy change amongst that community of people, that must ensure not merely comfort, but health.[2]

The change is, admittedly, partly geographical, as in the second passage, Spence is describing the villages of the northeast coast, but her phrasing implies that the alteration is more a matter of time than place – cottages *now*, not *here*, are made of stone. In the five years since Spence last visited Scotland, and in the eight years since its publication, *The Cottagers of Glenburnie* had, Spence implies, quite literally transformed the country.

The idea that a single, short work, written in deliberately simple style, could produce in less than a decade a complete revolution in matters as varied as personal hygiene, vernacular architecture, and even agricultural practice, might appear hyperbolic at best, and comically naïve at worst. Yet even if one is sceptical about the supposed transformation of the Scottish working classes that Spence claimed to have observed in the decade following the publication of *The Cottagers of Glenburnie*, she was not the only writer of the day to credit Hamilton's novel with a practical reformist effect. As early as February 1809, Maria Edgeworth was sending a copy of the novel to her aunt, Margaret Ruxton, commenting that "I think it will do a vast deal of good, and besides it is extremely interesting, which all *good* books are not."[3] Eighteen months later, in a letter to Anna Laetitia Barbauld, she was musing on the effect that Mary Leadbeater's *Cottage Dialogues* (1811) might have in Ireland, and hoping that they would be "for Ireland, what the Cottagers of Glenburnie are for Scotland [...] I do not pretend to say that the dialogues are equal in humour or ability to Mrs Hamilton's book, but I think they will do as much good in this country as her's did in Scotland."[4] The perception of the book's influence on working-class Scottish life persisted until late in the century: in an 1871 overview of Scotland's

women poets, Sarah Tytler and J. L. Watson commented
that Hamilton "wrote 'The Cottagers of Glenburnie' with a
will, for the benefit of her humbler countrywomen. To her
credit and to theirs, the tale did wonders in remedying the
evil she condemned – the fatal *vis inertia* of 'I canna be
fashed,' which lingers, now, chiefly as a tradition of darker
ages."[5] Whether or not anybody ever in fact changed the
ways they kept house or planted their gardens as a result of
reading *The Cottagers of Glenburnie*, it is clear enough that
at least some of Hamilton's contemporaries and successors
wanted to believe that what they saw as improvements in
working-class Scottish cultural practice in the early decades
of the nineteenth century were more or less directly attri-
butable to the impact of her book.

This early nineteenth-century tendency to see *The
Cottagers of Glenburnie* as a peculiarly influential and successful example of reformist literature is not merely a curiosity
of reception history – an indication of the surprising contemporary impact of a now more-or-less forgotten novel –
but also points to some of the reasons that the book might
have suffered the dramatic fall from critical favour that left
it all but forgotten and unread for much of the twentieth
century. As Edgeworth's comment to her aunt implies,
there is a tendency to be suspicious of books that are supposed to be good for us, and particularly when such
books are directed towards a supposedly uncultivated readership, the easy assumption is that the didactic elements
will overpower more sophisticated literary or intellectual
pleasures. Hamilton herself encouraged this idea in letters
to friends around the time of the publication of her novel,
explaining to one Dr S–, for example, that

> [h]ad I thought it worthy your perusal, I should have
> sent a copy; but in fact it is intended for a very differ-
> ent order of readers, and was written solely with a
> view to shame my good country folks into a greater
> degree of nicety with regard to cleanliness, and to awa-
> ken their attention to the source of corruption in the
> lower orders.[6]

She is similarly deprecating in the dedicatory epistle head-
ing the book itself, modestly insisting that the novel possesses none of the "genius" of "The Skaith of Scotland"

(1795), Hector Macneill's joylessly moralistic verse tale of once-virtuous peasants ruined by drink. This sense that the novel is little more than a dramatized conduct book for the working classes might also have been reinforced by its critical reception, both at the time of its publication and in the twentieth century. Francis Jeffrey, for one, suggested in an otherwise warmly approving review that perhaps the book might be improved by cutting out everything that didn't pertain directly to the feckless MacClarty family and their upwardly mobile foils the Morisons (see Appendix). More recently, and much less warmly, Gary Kelly has argued that the programme that Hamilton's Mrs Mason advocates involves a heavy-handed repression of traditional working-class and Scottish folkways and their replacement by an anglicized culture shaped by middle-class values.[7] This is a reading that leads him to a far more negative view of the book than Jeffrey's, but different as the two critics are in their assessment of the novel, they share the assumption that at heart, the book is a manual for working-class self-improvement.

In this view, *The Cottagers of Glenburnie* is primarily a Scottish version of Hannah More's *Cheap Repository Tracts* (1795-98) – a link that Hamilton herself makes in her dedicatory epistle to Macneill – or, as Edgeworth suggests, an anticipation of Leadbeater's attempts to improve the Irish working classes. Of course, in many respects, that is precisely what the book is, and part of the reason for the renewed interest in it at the beginning of the twenty-first century is the new critical attention paid to such writing by scholars such as Anne Mellor.[8] Yet, as Hamilton also implies in the epistle to Macneill, she expected to attract readers beyond More's working-class audience, and Jeffrey's and Edgeworth's enthusiastic praise for the book's literary merits – in addition to its social utility – suggests that, notwithstanding Hamilton's modest comments to Dr S, she was able, at least initially, to reach out to a sophisticated readership as well as to the unskilled readers who are the book's most obvious target audience. Nor is this point suggested only by the book's early reviews. In its obituary notice for Hamilton, *The Scots Magazine* took for granted that "all our readers" would know the book,[9] an assumption supported by the casual allusions made to the novel by other writers for a generation or so after Hamilton's death. Travellers in places as far-flung as America, the Rhine Valley, and India made Glenburnie a form of shorthand for evoking rural squalor, while reviewers up to the middle of the nineteenth century used the book as a standard against which to evaluate subsequent works on rural and working-class life – often suggesting that later writers failed to measure up.[10] The unluckily named James Hamilton, for example, was the subject of an eviscerating 1848 review, in which the reviewer noted acidly "that Mr Hamilton, in his domestic sketches, and lessons, aims at being compared with *Mrs Hamilton*, the celebrated writer of the '*Cottagers of Glenburnie*.'" Unfortunately, the reviewer continues, it is only "in his own mind, that he inherits this lady's power of shrewd perception and graphic narration."[11]

Yet by the second half of the century, *The Cottagers of Glenburnie* seems to have been slipping out of the adult and middle-class canon. When, in 1856, Henry Cockburn published his reminiscences of the early nineteenth-century Edinburgh literary scene, he relegated the novel to a second or third tier of literary merit, commenting that it was the "dirt" of the MacClarty family "on which almost solely the book lives."[12] More to the point, perhaps, while the novel was reprinted throughout the century, its publishing history suggests that it was increasingly assumed to be most relevant to children and the poor. It is, for example, included in an 1887 list of Girls' Own Library publications promoted as being "Suitable for School Prizes."[13] Likewise, an undated edition (*The Cottagers of Glenburnie: A Scottish Tale*) owned by the National Library of Scotland is bound with a number of other works for children, including the *Memoir of a Pious Child* and *Roman History in the Way of Question and Answer*, by "A Lady". The 1859 Chambers edition (*The Cottagers of Glenburnie, with a Memoir of the Life of the Author*) states explicitly that it is "peculiarly suited by its price for popular use" and that the aim of this new edition is to convey "into still more minute channels the excellent moral and economical lessons of the Authoress" (page viii). Even more backhanded references to the novel imply the extent to which, by mid-century, it had become absorbed into the discourse of social improvement at the cost of its place in the literary canon; a report on the sanitary conditions in

Scottish towns published in 1842 comments sardonically on "well meaning ladies" who apparently think that "distributing [...] cheap copies of the Cottagers of Glenburnie" is all that is needed to improve the condition of the poor.[14]

The decline in the critical fortunes of Hamilton's novel might be connected to the larger question of the reception of Romantic-era women writers in general, relatively few of whom – Jane Austen is the major exception – maintained their literary reputations in the later nineteenth and earlier twentieth centuries. In the case of *The Cottagers of Glenburnie*, however, the apparently growing consensus that the novel was of interest mainly to unsophisticated readers would have been an extra strike against it. Given that perception, it is all the more important, in any twenty-first century re-evaluation of it, to recognize the central place that it occupies in Hamilton's career as a whole. Far from being a simplistic diversion from the more ambitious concerns of her other fiction and her educational theory, *Glenburnie* exemplifies many of the complex and far-reaching ideas that Hamilton explored throughout her literary life.

Elizabeth Hamilton's Life and Writing

Elizabeth Hamilton was born in Belfast, probably in 1756. (The date is usually given as 1758, most notably by Elizabeth Benger, Hamilton's first and so far only biographer, but Benger also quotes Hamilton as saying, in a journal entry written on her last birthday, in July 1815, that in only "one year more [...] the period of six tens of years will be completed.'[15]) Her father was a Scottish merchant who died of typhus in 1759, leaving his widow with three young children to support. In 1762, also according to Benger, Hamilton's mother Katherine reluctantly "surrendered" Elizabeth, the youngest child, to the care of her paternal aunt and uncle, a Mr and Mrs Marshall, who lived just outside Stirling.[16] By Hamilton's own account, her childhood there was idyllic, and in the fragmentary memoir published by Benger, she is warm in her comments on her aunt and deeply affectionate in her reminiscences of her uncle. He was a farmer and had apparently been seen as a very poor match for her genteel but impoverished aunt, a situation that might remind readers of *Glenburnie's* Mr Stewart and Miss Osburne. Hamilton, at any rate, is as vigorous in her memoir as in her fiction in her denunciation of the attitudes that would assume such a marriage involved a catastrophic step downwards for the woman in question. "To Mr Marshall," she writes, "might well be applied what the poet Burns has said of an Ayrshire friend, that 'he held his patent of nobility direct from Almighty God.'"[7]

Hamilton's education was more or less typical for a Scottish girl of her class and era: she attended a day school in Stirling for a few years (Benger says that she started school "when she completed her eighth year" and completed her formal education "in her thirteenth year,"[8] during which time, she boarded in Stirling during the week, attending class three hours a day. While Benger does not itemize what was taught there, she does mention both that Hamilton excelled in geography and that she later regretted that she had not had the opportunity to study classics with her schoolmaster. Other scraps of information that survive suggest a relatively conventional form of schooling, perhaps resembling that outlined at the end of *Glenburnie*, in which village boys and girls attend class together but learn very different things. Yet if Benger was unsure about most of the details of Hamilton's education, she was adamant on one point: it was not mixed. Even though the school was run by a man, she insists that it either enrolled only girls or, at worst, that boys and girls attended on different days. Benger's firmness on this issue is something of a measure of the degree to which English ideas of sexual decorum were affecting Scottish educational practice, as her attitude implies that, by 1818, views had hardened against the sort of mixed education that she reluctantly admits was common in Scotland a generation earlier. Whether or not the school was in fact segregated by sex, it does not seem to have been divided by class. Hamilton herself, in one of her few direct comments on her schooldays, recalled being taught needlework in company with a group of girls from all classes, superintended by a "respectable matron" who made one girl read aloud while the others worked.[19] Out of school hours, she took lessons in music and drawing; at home on the weekends, she was drilled in religious subjects, required to learn Biblical passages by heart without any attempt to ensure that she understood them, an experience to which Benger traces the adult Hamilton's strong hostility to rote memorization as an educational tool.

Once her formal education ended, Hamilton continued to practice music and art at home, something that she later regretted as time wasted, as she had no particular talent for either, and she attended occasional lectures on more academic subjects during visits to Glasgow and Edinburgh. According to Benger, Hamilton's interest in philosophy was sparked by hearing and then corresponding with Henry Moyes (Benger spells the name "Moyse"[20]), a blind scientist who was one of several lecturers on philosophical and scientific subjects who, in the last years of the eighteenth century, reached out to audiences outside the universities, including women.[21] Much more importantly, however, she read widely in moral and educational philosophy. By Hamilton's own account, she initially did so with some trepidation: she relates an anecdote – that has been much quoted in twentieth and twenty-first century writing about her – about "hiding *Kaims's* [sic] *Elements of Criticism*, under the cover of an easy chair, whenever I heard the approach of a footstep, well knowing the ridicule to which I should have been exposed, had I been detected in the act of looking into such a book."[22] Such youthful worries notwithstanding, in her later life she was never hesitant about displaying in her own writing the sort of reading that she had done. Her girlhood interest in the work of Lord Kames was reinforced by what her published writing makes clear was a careful and detailed study of a range of philosophers, including John Locke, Thomas Reid, David Hartley, and, above all, Dugald Stewart. If Stewart lacks the reputation of the others today, he was nonetheless one of the most influential moral philosophers of the day (the monument to him on Calton Hill in Edinburgh is a tangible indication of the esteem in which he was held at the time of his death), and the pervasiveness of his influence on Hamilton's educational writing is a mark not just of her intellectual interests but also of the extent to which that work participates in the intellectual world of the late Scottish enlightenment.

Despite this fascination with moral philosophy, Hamilton's writing career might have initially looked set to follow

the pattern of that of a number of late eighteenth-century
women who hovered on the margins between social authorship[23] and publication, dipping into print in minor venues
and in more or less uncontroversially feminine modes. She
wrote a few poems but never assembled them into a collection; she also wrote an unpublished historical novel about
Lady Arabella Stuart, which apparently celebrated female
friendship and the quieter domestic virtues. Her first works
to go into print were a Highland travel journal, which Benger says was published anonymously and without Hamilton's consent in "a provincial magazine",[24] and a lightly
satirical moral essay for Henry Mackenzie's periodical *The
Lounger*. The books that Hamilton chose to publish between
1796 and her death in 1816, however, are much less conventional and predictable: varied in both genre and content,
they are all intellectually ambitious, with *The Cottagers of
Glenburnie* no less innovative than the work that precedes
and follows it. If Hamilton had, like so many other women
of the day, been both writing and reading for her own pleasure from young womanhood, by the time that she started
publishing, she seems to have been convinced that her writing had a purpose beyond private amusement and could
contribute in important ways to contemporary public
debates.

Hamilton was nearly forty, unmarried, and without any
surviving close relatives except an older widowed sister
when she finally began her publishing career in earnest in
1796. She had been caring for her uncle Mr Marshall until
his death in 1788 and then took up residence with her brother
Charles, who was on leave from his post with the East India
Company to translate the *Hedaya*, the Islamic code of laws.
Hamilton, who had become devoted to her brother during
his brief visits to Scotland and who had corresponded with
him during his time in India, moved to London to be with
him, a move that she clearly found intellectually stimu-
lating. As she later explained to Hector Macneill, it was
while in London with Charles that, for the first time,

Men of learning addressed themselves to me, as to a
being who was actually capable of thinking. Men of
wit seemed to imagine that I could understand them;
and both men and women, very superior both in point

of situation and abilities, to those with whom I had
been accustomed to associate, conversed with me so
much upon a footing of equality, that sometimes I was
inclined to exclaim with the *wee wife,* "Surely, *this is
no me!*"[25]

Her shock and grief when, in 1792, Charles died suddenly
of tuberculosis were no less intense than her pleasure in
London society and perhaps changed the direction of her
life even more dramatically, as her first published book,
Translations of the Letters of a Hindoo Rajah (1796) is in part a
tribute to Charles, and its account of Indian culture and
society is indebted to an interest in Asian subjects sparked
by her interaction with him. Her next book, *Memoirs of
Modern Philosophers* (1800) also grows in part out of her
time in London, but is less directly connected to her
brother, featuring as it does a satire of the ideas of members
of the circle around the radical philosopher William God-
win, some of whom Hamilton had met while living in
England. In particular, she had at one time been an acquaintance of the novelist Mary Hays, although the relationship
unsurprisingly failed to survive Hamilton's rather cruelly
satiric picture, in *Modern Philosophers,* of the would-be intellectual and woman of feeling Brigitina Botherem, generally
taken by readers then and since to be a caricature of Hays.

In the years immediately after launching her publishing
career, Hamilton led an increasingly restless life. In pursuit
of better health – she suffered from gout and from problems with her eyes for much of the last two decades of her
life – she travelled with her sister Katherine to various
places around the south of England, including Suffolk,
Gloucestershire, and Bath. Despite her chronic illness, she
produced some of the most ambitious work of her career in
the years following *Modern Philosophers. Letters on the Elementary Principles of Education* is an attempt to use the philosophy of Locke, Stewart, and others to demonstrate that an
understanding of how the mind works is vital if one is to
be successful in providing any type of education. This is an
idea that Hamilton developed in considerably more depth
in a later book, *A Series of Popular Essays* (1813) and that
also underpins *Hints Directed to the Patrons and Directors of
Schools* (1815), her last publication. The decade between the

appearance of *Elementary Principles* and *Popular Essays* saw
something of a hiatus in Hamilton's direct work on theories
of education, but she continued to explore her ideas on
the subject in other genres. *Memoirs of the Life of Agrippina*,
a speculative biography grounded in a reading of both the
major classical historians (in translation) and contemporary
historians such as Edward Gibbon, is shaped as much by
her work on educational theory as it is by the classics. Perhaps in part because Hamilton was worried that the classical
subject matter would be more of a stretch for her and more
controversial than her work on the philosophy of mind,
she makes a point of explaining in her preface that the book
is not designed to make an original contribution to classical
studies but is rather an attempt to use history to illustrate
her theories of how the mind and character develop. What
she is hoping to achieve, she explains, is to reach an audience of young women who would normally read nothing
but novels and to convey her ideas to them in a slightly
more palatable form than that of a moral essay. While both
Hamilton and Benger are insistent that *Agrippina* is not in
any way an historical novel, the book draws on some of the
narrative tactics of that genre, sweetening its philosophical
and moral arguments with the attractions of a compelling,
suffering heroine and – in its accounts of the events of the
reigns of Augustus and Tiberius – large doses of action and
intrigue. Like *Letters Addressed to the Daughter of a Nobleman*,
which is directed to children, and *The Cottagers of Glenburnie*, which addresses the poor, this book attempts to
convey theoretical concepts to an audience of less skilled
readers. In this case, however, Hamilton is aiming for perhaps the most challenging possible readership – easily bored
adolescents with short attention spans.

Hamilton spent this productive decade, and indeed, most
of the rest of her life, more or less settled in Edinburgh.
She had moved there in 1804 and, aside from six months in
the household of Lord Lucan, supervising the education of
his children (the eldest of whom was the nobleman's daughter addressed in her 1806 volume), she maintained herself
independently on the income from her writing and from a
pension granted by the king. Despite her relatively limited
means, she quickly became an active participant in the lively
intellectual society for which Edinburgh became famous in

the first years of the nineteenth century. She lived on sociable terms with the famous men of the city, including Sir Walter Scott and Francis Jeffrey, as well as with literary women, both residents and visitors, such as the poet and essayist Anne Grant, the playwright Joanna Baillie, and the Irish novelist Maria Edgeworth, to whom she paid a return visit during travels in Ireland in 1813. Scott thought well enough of her work to pay a polite compliment to *The Cottagers of Glenburnie* at the end of *Waverley* (1814), and they were on sufficiently friendly terms socially for Hamilton to send him a playful verse lament about the difficulty of getting access to such a famous man. He has received so much praise, she complains, that nobody who merely flatters his writing can get his attention any longer: "Tis no then at the Poet's Yet / That I sal tak my stand," she concludes, "But Freinship's wicket I'll beset."[26]

The other side of Hamilton's life in Edinburgh was her charitable work. She helped to found a House of Industry for indigent women, and published a pamphlet, *Exercises in Religious Knowledge* (1809), as a form of catechism for the inmates; the volume includes an account of the House (dated 1808) that suggests that Hamilton saw the theories of working-class education outlined in her other books as blueprints for practical charity. According to the pamphlet, the House has three divisions: a spinning-room, where the aged and infirm can earn some money while having a warm room in which to work; a lace manufactory, where younger girls are trained in the trade and get some training in needle work and in reading as well; and a school for servants, which at that point was still undeveloped because of the extra costs involved. The purpose of the latter, as the pamphlet explains, is not "so much [...] to make accomplished readers and needleworkers, as to make active, diligent, and sober-minded servants, well-instructed in their duty to God and man, and who have acquired habits which may accord with and support their principles."[27] Written as this was in the same year as the publication of *The Cottagers of Glenburnie*, it emphasizes the narrowness of the line between what the reforming characters say and do in the novel and what Hamilton saw as the sorts of activities that she herself should undertake.

Despite Hamilton's active life in society, as a writer and

as a charity worker, she was suffering from an increasing number of physical ailments in the years following her move to Edinburgh. During that time, she continued to travel in pursuit of health, spending time in the Lake District and elsewhere in England. Nothing worked. According to Benger, she was too ill to write during the winter of 1813-1814, following her return from Ireland; she suffered badly from illness and depression in the spring of 1816 as well. What was intended to be a permanent move back to England was delayed by her health, and when she did leave Edinburgh for the last time, in May 1816, she made it only as far as Harrogate in Yorkshire. She died there on July 23, leaving, in the words of Anne Grant, "a blank not easily filled" in Edinburgh society.[28]

Educational Theory and the Roles of Women in Hamilton's Writing

Hamilton's charitable activities in Edinburgh are a practical manifestation of her interest in women's social responsibilities, but her books provide her with a wider field for addressing the question of what women could and should do to improve the world around them. This is an issue that she raises very clearly and directly right from the start: in her first novel, *Translations of the Letters of a Hindoo Rajah*, Hamilton includes a somewhat satiric self-portrait in the form a young woman named Charlotte Percy (the echo of her brother's name is probably not accidental). Bereft of her only brother and the uncle who raised her, Charlotte becomes a drooping martyr to grief, wallowing in her own misery until an older, wiser male friend tells her sharply to pull herself together. When she laments that her bereavements have left her no duties or purpose in the world, he responds even more forcefully:

> And is the gift of reason then nothing? [...] And are the powers of the mind to lie dormant, because, forsooth, you have not now the management of a family: or the exercise of the benevolent affections to be given up, because you have not a fortune to build almshouses? These are the meer subterfuges of indolence [...] Why, (let me ask you farther) should your mind,

cultivated as it has been by education, and improved
by listening to the conversation of the enlightened and
judicious; why should it not exert its powers, not only
for your own entertainment, but for the instruction,
or innocent amusement of others?[29]

Concluding by roundly dismissing Charlotte's timid protest
that women writers are held in disdain – he considers such
prejudices the result of ignorant folly, and, as such, not
worth a moment's anxiety – he insists that Charlotte should
put her talents to public use, instructing others in the
lessons that she has learned through her own experience
and study. Launching her own literary career with a polemical blast, Hamilton here makes clear her conviction that
women both should and do have a direct influence on the
public life of the nation.

This is not to say that Hamilton sought a direct political
role for women or that she believed that the roles played in
society by men and women should be identical. On the contrary, in *Letters on the Elementary Principles of Education* she
explicitly rejects the idea that women should seek "an
equality of employments and avocations" with men.[30] Even
so, Hamilton's idea of the roles that women should play in
society is not a conservative one: she was almost as harshly
critical of the status quo as were more overtly radical contemporaries such as Mary Wollstonecraft and Mary Hays
and, like them, she saw a changed education for women as
the basic precondition for social reform. The main difference is that Hamilton grounds her ideas for reform in her
strong Christian faith, a fact that, along with her scepticism
about the benefit to women of aiming for the same goals
as men, has perhaps led later critics to underplay her radic-
alism.[31] Hamilton herself, however, saw her ideas as being
radical in the most basic sense of the term: she wanted to
go back to the roots of her society's ideas of virtue and
morality and, in doing so, to alter basic social values.
Women like Charlotte Percy are failing to understand or
fulfill their full potential, she suggests, because of the miseducation of both men and women. In particular, she
argues that through the typical upper-class male education
in classical literature and history, the most basic concepts
of virtue and worth have been skewed in a way that has a

particularly damaging effect on women. Such education, she argues, reinforces what she sees as a "primitive" link between physical strength and moral worth:

> [w]ith a contempt for the female sex, on account of this fancied inferiority [of physical strength], has been associated a contempt for those moral qualities which are allowed to constitute the perfection of the female character. Meekness, gentleness, temperance, and chastity; that command over the passions which is obtained by frequent self-denial; and that willingness to sacrifice every selfish wish, and every selfish feeling, to the happiness of others, which is the consequence of subdued self-will, and the cultivation of the social and benevolent affections; are considered as feminine virtues, derogatory to the dignity of the manly character.[32]

The argument here is explicitly Christian, but elsewhere, Hamilton develops a similar argument in more secular terms. In her *Popular Essays*, for example, she draws on the work of the Scottish historian William Robertson to reiterate her ideas about the ways in which "primitive" societies' emphasis on physical strength leads to the oppression of women, then goes on to argue that

> As the operations of intellect come, in the progress of civilisation, to be appreciated beyond the mere exertions of physical strength, it is according to the degree in which he enjoys the power of subjecting the minds and the wills of numbers, that the idea of self expands in the mind of man. Women are then no longer subjected to the cruel hardships of incessant labour and fatigue; for it is not now by his exemption from labour, that man's superiority is to be asserted. It is on the exertions of intellect that he rests his claim: and thenceforth a complete dominion over the minds, a complete subjugation of the intellectual powers of the feebler sex, becomes essential to the gratification of the selfish principle in his heart.[33]

Even in contemporary society, she argues, it is only "very superiorly enlightened minds" who are able to overcome the temptations to self-gratification implicit in seeing themselves part of an inherently superior class of human being and, then, acting in the "general interests of society," to encourage all people to develop their abilities to the highest degree possible.[34] In encouraging Charlotte to write, in other words, Mr Denbigh is not just sympathizing with a friend in a difficult situation, but, more importantly, placing himself in the vanguard of a revolution in social values.

The practical impact that Hamilton sees as arising from such a feminization of social values is best illustrated, perhaps, by turning briefly from her published work to her private praise of the abolitionist Thomas Clarkson. She presents Clarkson as offering a model of the sort of vitally important work that could be done by somebody who – like women – had no direct access to political power, and in one of her letters to Dr S–, she compares Clarkson's historical significance to that of Napoleon in terms that make clear her belief in the far-reaching impact that an individual can have simply by exercising his or her "powers of the mind" and "benevolent affections":

> That the son of a Corsican attorney should have prostrated the Kingdoms of Europe at his feet, and while yet but in youth tyrannise over the greater part of the civilised world, is perhaps no more extraordinary than that an obscure and unconnected individual should, by his unwearied exertions, have ameliorated the present condition of thousands, and removed the grand obstacle of civilisation and improvement of a continent more populous than Europe [ ] This surely ought to afford great encouragement to every friend of truth; as no one knows how far his single efforts may be productive of great and lasting good.[35]

Clarkson's triumph, in this view, arises from the fact that he is able to achieve on a major scale exactly what Mr Denbigh wants Charlotte Percy to do in a more minor way: having educated himself about the horrors of the slave trade, he has done his best to educate others, resulting in a changed and improved world. More generally, what this passage implies is that a society that educates its children in a manner that gives a proper weight to the "feminine" virtues will be one that is capable of recognizing Clarkson's writing on behalf of the slaves as more glorious and honourable than the military achievements of Napoleon and of rating the two figures accordingly. No less importantly, a society that values such humanitarian activity will also recognize that barring half its members from making any such contribution, by barring them from the cultivation of their reason, is wilfully and irrationally damaging itself.

In some ways, Hamilton's ideas on education could thus be considered even more radical than those of her contemporaries whose response to the obvious flaws in an educational system that drilled upper-class boys in the classics, taught upper-class girls to be decorative and refined, and that was more or less indifferent to the educations of everybody else, was to call for upper- and middle-class girls to have access to the same sort of education as their brothers. Hamilton herself didn't hesitate to claim that that was the case; provocatively enough, she argues that "champions for sexual equality" (whom she doesn't name, but who presumably include Hays and Wollstonecraft) are merely "acquiesc[ing] in the idea of man's superiority in all wisdom and perfection."[36] Such provocation notwithstanding, Hamilton is no enemy of intellectual training for girls, and she is also a firm supporter of "equality of employments" among children, if not adults, something that, for her, means that boys should be taught the "culture of the heart" with at least as much rigour as girls are taught to cultivate their minds.[37] Generally, she is sceptical of claims that, from earliest childhood, boys and girls are entirely different from one another and ought to be treated differently. Like Wollstonecraft, for example, she is dismissive of Rousseau's assumption that girls like only dolls and sedentary play, writing that "any little girl in high health and good spirits would [...] prefer beating the drum or whipping the top with her brother, to dressing and undressing the finest doll in her possession."[38] Yet the sorts of games that children play and the specifics of the lessons that they are given is of less interest to her than is making sure that the adults who are providing that education understand exactly what it is that they are doing. Grounding herself in the work of moral philosophers and educational theorists, Hamilton insists that it is only by a careful study of theories of the mind that anybody interested in educating children –

including mothers supervising infants in the nursery – can ensure that they are doing good rather than harm in their efforts.

This is a point that underlies all of Hamilton's arguments in *Letters on the Elementary Principles of Education*, her first work on the subject and the one in which she presents her ideas most fully and directly. Her intended audience for the book is primarily women of the middle and upper classes who are – or soon will be – educating their own children,[39] and she has two main goals in addressing them. The first, and perhaps more straightforward, is to convince her readers that the ideas absorbed in earliest childhood, particularly those relating to character and behaviour, or what she calls the education of the heart, have potentially huge political and social ramifications. She makes this point, at least in part, through references to the contemporary political situation and to the work of other women who have written on education and politics. In a respectful but firm disagreement with Hannah More, for example, Hamilton rebuts More's contention that the debate around the concepts of rights produces social insubordination, implying that what she sees as More's misdiagnosis of a social ill arises from her failure to consider the ramifications of moral philosophy. If there is indeed an increasing "disdain of control" in the closing years of the eighteenth century, Hamilton argues that it arises from "a more natural and more obvious source" than a new appetite among the working classes for the work of political pamphleteers. Rather, children of doting parents are learning from early infancy that their demands will be satisfied, whether that demand is reasonable or not. "In the passions and habits influenced by such circumstances," Hamilton concludes, "they will have more powerful incentive to the spirit of insubordination, than a respect for the rights of their fellow creatures could possibly produce."[40] If society is being turned upside down, in other words, it isn't the fault of Thomas Paine or Mary Wollstonecraft, but rather of mothers who are too fondly indulgent of their children.

The implications that Hamilton draws from this assumption are far-reaching indeed, as in her eyes, the study of educational theory becomes a form of political engagement that blurs the boundaries between public life and the

domestic responsibilities of women. Her argument here is
not just that adult women can and should take part in
debates on matters of public interest – although that was a
significant element of her work – but also that women were
responsible in a real and immediate way for the present
state of society, given the vital importance of the first few
years of a child's life to its future character and abilities.
According to Hamilton, women are not just capable of
studying theories of moral development; they in fact have a
responsibility to do so, as they provide the early education
of children, and, debating with or drawing upon the work
of a number of contemporary moral philosophers, she
insists that it is in earliest childhood that the foundations of
character are laid. Unless women understand theories of
mind sufficiently well to grasp what and how their children
need to learn, they are, Hamilton warns, laying the ground-
work for a society built on dangerously misguided values
and risking catastrophic problems in the political life of the
nation. One of the central points of *Memoirs of the Life of
Agrippina* is that a culture that assumes that "feminine"
virtues are irrelevant to the management of the state risks
a rapid decline from individual moral disorder into political anarchy. "In enumerating the causes which contributed to the vigour and elevation of the Roman character,"
Hamilton writes in her sketch of the social history of the
Republican era,

> we must not omit to mention the influence of female
> manners as one of the most important. Had the minds
> of the Roman youth received their first impressions
> from ignorance and folly, we may with some confi-
> dence pronounce, that the republic would not have
> produced many examples of manly virtue.[41]

Rather than angelically providing refuges from the struggles
of public life, women are thus the foundation of all social
order.

At first glance, this might sound a merely glib or trivial
claim – at best, perhaps a slightly more complex version of
the old saw about the hand that rocks the cradle. Hamilton's point, however, is both more precise and more far-
reaching. Her argument is not a sentimental claim that a
mother's influence lingers into adulthood; rather, she notes

that "the desires and aversions which are the springs of human conduct [...] commence [...] with our existence," and then, grounding herself in Locke, argues as a concomitant that it is "by means of early and powerful associations, that the desires and aversions of the soul are principally excited," making it "a duty of the first importance" to regulate "the associations which are formed by the tender mind."[42] One might be able to teach a child who has absorbed faulty or inappropriate associations to read Greek and Latin or to do mathematics – although Hamilton sees problems even for the intellectual training of such a child – but he or she will inevitably be at risk of growing into an adult who is driven by irrationality and prejudice and who is incapable of making a positive contribution to the wider society. As she proclaims,

> To qualify a human being for the true enjoyment of existence, the highest cultivation of the intellectual powers will not be sufficient, unless these powers be properly directed; this direction they must receive from the bias that has been given to the desires and affections of the heart. If these desires and affections have been corrupted by improper indulgence, or perverted and depraved by means of powerful impressions made upon the tender mind; we may give our children knowledge, we may give them learning, we may give them accomplishments, but we shall never be able to teach them to apply these acquirements to just or noble purposes.[43]

Potential Clarksons, in other words, are being lost to society not just because of the wilful disregard of women's direct contributions to public debate, but, even more fundamentally, because even those women who never step out of their private, domestic world affect the public sphere through the miseducation of their children in the nursery. Moral education begins at birth, Hamilton argues, and the strength of early associations and prejudices is so powerful that both character and intellect will suffer in later life, no matter how good the intellectual training, if this early education has been botched.

Of course, this latter point was not an idea unique to Hamilton. Jean-Jacques Rousseau, perhaps the single most influential educational theorist of the day, also believed that proper education started at birth and that the moral values absorbed through early experiences determined the child's future potential as a man and a citizen. (For Rousseau, unlike Hamilton, the public-spirited citizen is invariably male.) He, however, used this belief to argue that, ideally, women should have as little possible to do with male children, even as infants. His exemplary child Emile is taken from both mother and wet nurse as quickly as biologically possible, then raised in an intense, one-on-one relationship with a male tutor. The Scottish moral philosophers who influenced Hamilton were also interested in the question of how moral values were inculcated or reinforced during the early years when, more or less inevitably, children of both sexes were being educated by, or under the supervision of, their mothers. For example, Lord Kames, whom Hamilton credits with sparking her own work on educational theory, insists, with Rousseau, on the vital impact of these early years. Rather more practically, however, he accepts that mothers are going to interact with their infants and so assumes, unlike Rousseau, that that fact means that providence must have ensured that mothers can't get things too badly wrong. "Hard indeed," he proclaims, "were the lot of the generality of the human race" if mothers didn't instinctively do what was best for their children, without needing to understand the implications or results of their actions.[44] In making this argument, Kames was in philosophic dialogue not just with Rousseau, but also and more importantly with a tradition of moral philosophy that asserted that ideas of morality were distinct from and possibly antecedent to any sort of intellectual development. This idea, originally formulated by Kames' older contemporary Francis Hutcheson, was built around the hypothesis that there is a sort of moral sixth sense, by which uncorrupted humanity is led instinctively to prefer the good to the bad, independently of any sort of reasoned argument for the former over the later. The implications of this idea were wide-ranging and much debated by Scottish philosophers working later in the century, but in the context of Hamilton's writing, the most important point is the one that Kames makes, that by separating reason and morality, for whatever cause, one might also sidestep the apparent problem of asserting that moral education begins at birth at the same time as one assumes that theories of morality and the mind are too abstruse and complex for most women to compre- hend. To oversimplify somewhat, if there is a moral sense, moral education is more or less irrelevant, just as an educa- tion in seeing or smelling would be.

Hamilton was uninterested in entering into the tangled debate about moral sense in any detailed way and is dismis- sive in *Elementary Principles of Education* about the more abstruse reaches of metaphysical thought. She did, how- ever, confront directly the Kamesian argument that early education does not require any specialist knowledge, arguing that even if morality is instinctive, it can still be trained and refined by instructors who know what they are doing. Most basically, she points out that as the physical senses can in fact be trained and honed, there is no way to argue by analogy that it is pointless to attempt to refine by education any moral sense we might possess. On a rather more sophisticated level, she turns to the work of Dugald Stewart – "an authority to which I am always proud to refer" as she notes[45] – to buttress her own ideas about the importance of training women in philosophy. Stewart agrees in principle with Hutcheson that there is something that might be called a moral sense and that is beyond or above reason, but like Kames, he expresses that agreement in a manner that might initially seem to offer little support for Hamilton's views. In one of his more direct statements on the subject, he compares the way we make moral and aesthetic judgments – a link also made by Hutcheson and others – arguing that

> Education may vary, in particular cases, the opinions
> of individuals with respect to the beautiful and the
> sublime. But education could not create our notions
> of Beauty or Deformity, of Grandeur or Meanness.
> In like manner, education may vary our sentiments,
> with respect to particular actions; but could not create
> our notions of Right and Wrong, of Merit and
> Demerit.[46]

What Hamilton does is to reverse Stewart's emphasis, so that the key point becomes not the main, Hutchesonian argument that morality is innate, rather than shaped by

social context (Stewart was disputing David Hume's views
on the subject), but rather the minor concession that education can influence the way we perceive or respond to questions of right or wrong. While at least as hostile to Hume's
scepticism as Stewart could be, Hamilton builds upon this
point to insist that those who have been taught to exercise
reason and judgment on questions of morality, rather than
simply letting instinct guide them, will be much better prepared not merely to act correctly in their own day-to-day
lives but also to train others in the proper development of
their moral character. Nor was Hamilton distorting Stewart's ideas too seriously in doing so; he made clear elsewhere that he believed there was an intellectual component
to moral sentiment. Even as he concedes that "[t]he decisions of the understanding [...] with respect to moral truth,
differ from those which relate to a mathematical theorem,
or to the result of a chemical experiment, inasmuch as they
are always accompanied with some feeling or emotion of
the heart," he insists nonetheless "that it is the intellectual
judgment which is the ground-work of the feeling, and not
the feeling of the judgment."[47] This is a point that Hamilton uses as the foundation of her arguments about education, as she sees the lack of "intellectual judgment" applied
not just to one's own moral feelings but, more importantly,
to the attempt to inculcate those feelings in others, as a fatal
failing in contemporary educational systems. In support of
this point, she turns yet again to Stewart, who, far more
than Kames and hardly less than Rousseau, was prepared to
admit the difficulty of early education. He notes gloomily,
in a passage that Hamilton quotes:

> To watch over the associations which they [children]
> form in their tender years; to give them early habits of
> mental activity; to rouse their curiosity, and to direct
> it to proper objects; to exercise their ingenuity and
> invention; to cultivate in their minds a turn for specu-
> lation, and, at the same time preserve their attention
> alive to objects around them; to awaken their attention
> to the beauties of nature, and to inspire them with a
> relish for intellectual enjoyment; these form *but a part*
> of the business of education, and yet the execution
> of even this part requires an acquaintance with the

general principles of our nature, which seldom falls to
the share of those to whom the instruction of youth
is commonly entrusted.[48]

What is essential in these arguments for Hamilton's work
is, first of all, the idea that even if morality and reason are
separated from one another at the most basic level, it is still
possible to make reasoned judgments about morality, and
second, in an argument diametrically opposed to Kames',
that morality is best taught by those who have reasoned
upon it. Even if Stewart is pessimistic about the likelihood
of qualifying those who provide such education to do so
effectively, his insistence upon the importance and difficulty
of the task gives Hamilton a firm rationale for her own
attempts to reform educational practice.

This attempt to convince women of the importance of
early education is merely the first, and perhaps the less
important, of the two main goals of Hamilton's educational
writing. The second is that of educating the adult women
who are reading it. "[T]he woman who would educate her
children with success," Hamilton writes, "must begin by
educating herself,"[49] and the most basic lesson she has to
learn is that of how the human mind works. This is the
point at which Hamilton departs from her predecessors and
makes what is probably her most original and important
assertion: she insists that not only is a basic grasp of the
philosophy of the mind within the reach of most women,
but also that cultivating such an understanding is a basic
female duty. To those who object that such a course
requires a degree of study and attention to which women
are unaccustomed and of which they are probably incapable, she responds, with a characteristically satiric edge,
that if card-playing fashionable women wouldn't dream of
taking up whist without a basic understanding of the principles of the game, women who want to educate their
children should be willing to expend at least as much intellectual energy in that pursuit.[50] She is similarly brisk in
her dismissal of any fears women themselves might have
about their capacities for such study, noting that she was,
regrettably and foolishly, slowed in her own intellectual
development because Locke's and Hartley's reputations for
being difficult inhibited her in the pursuit of her own philo-

sophical interests. Yet in her study of Kames and others she found both the conceptual groundwork and philo-sophical vocabulary to explore and communicate her ideas in a more effective manner than she had previously been able to do. As both an educator and as a self-educated woman, Hamilton challenges her women readers by instruc-tion and example to reform themselves as an essential step in the reform of not just their own children but also of society as a whole.

Mrs Mason and Education in The Cottagers of Glenburnie

It might seem a long way from Stewart's and Kames' fine-spun arguments about moral sense to Hamilton's depiction of working-class fecklessness, but *The Cottagers of Glenburnie* depicts a range of educational practice and illustrates in a series of vignettes a number of the arguments about educa-tion that Hamilton had made elsewhere. The two main plots both focus on working-class education, with Mrs Mason's narrative of her own childhood serving as a model of what should be done, while the chaotic MacClarty household embodies everything that can go wrong. Of course, Hamil-ton doesn't limit herself just to the working classes: she also opposes good and bad methods of instruction for the aris-tocracy in her account of the differing lessons absorbed by the children of the first and the second marriages of the Earl of Longlands, while the sisters Bell and Mary Stewart exem-plify failed and successful middle-class education. Yet the novel was praised at the time and has been remembered since mainly for its portrayal of working-class life. While Hamilton uses the episodic structure of the novel to suggest the interconnection of the classes in her society and to imply that failures to properly educate the poor will cause problems for people of all classes, she makes the stories of the Longlands and the Stewarts subordinate to those of the MacClartys and the Morisons. Just as in *Elementary Prin-ciples of Education* she ties public disorder to society's failure to recognize the importance of the intellectual training of middle-class domestic women and the moral education of young children, in *Glenburnie*, she dramatizes the ways in which failed working-class education will cause wider social disruption.

Mrs Mason is not only the main instructor of the working classes in the novel; she also provides an example of
what one can expect from an education that has gone
well.[51] Although orphaned, impoverished, and worked so
hard while still a child that she has little time for anything
but work and sleep, she seizes the chances that she does
have for self-improvement. Despite her own lower class origins and apparently haphazard education, Mrs Mason
becomes something of a case study in the process of mental
and intellectual development that Hamilton sketched in
both *Elementary Principles of Education* and *Popular Essays*.
What she learns differs dramatically from the sort of lessons envisioned for middle- and upper-class children in
Hamilton's other books, but the progress of her mental
development exemplifies the processes of training sketched
out there. Beginning with the cultivation of her heart,
through the efforts of a careful and loving if sickly mother,
then moving on through a series of varied and increasingly
complex household tasks, carried out under the eye of well-
trained older servants who make demands on both her
attention and judgement, the young Betty Mason is both
eager and well-prepared for the intellectual training that she
eventually receives from Miss Osburne and Miss Malden.
In effect, the opening account of Mrs Mason's life provides
the remedy for what Hamilton claims, near the end of the
novel is the tendency of working-class life to deaden the
intellectual abilities of girls (an idea later echoed and
expanded upon in *Popular Essays*). One might quibble about
the realism of Hamilton's novel – Miss Malden's willingness
to instruct Mrs Mason in the finer points of ancient history
as Mason reads aloud to her seems a particularly egregious
stroke of luck – but the polemical point is clear enough.
Mrs Mason turns out to be a model servant, who demonstrates both moral and physical courage in her employers'
service, but her character is shaped in part by her employers' willingness to take some responsibility for educating
her.
The dangers of miseducation of the working class are
illustrated even more vividly than are the benefits of a
proper education. Hamilton makes this point in the first
part of the novel through her gallery of bad servants, whose
impact is catastrophic. Ambitious, amoral Jenny alternately

terrorizes and bribes the young Lord Lintop, who grows up into a selfish, bad-tempered, superstitious man, while the drunken Mrs Dickens and the nursery maid Sally, a good-time girl far more interested in footmen than the children in her charge, cause the fire that destroys the Longlands' townhouse, leaves Mrs Mason permanently lamed, and kills Mrs Dickens herself. The implication that it is in the interests of the upper classes to ensure proper education for those they employ is clear enough, but the novel does not suggest merely that the education of the poor is a matter of selfish concern to the rich. The central and most famous part of the novel focuses on Mrs Mason's attempt to reform her poorly-educated working-class cousins and, in doing so, it reiterates the message that the education of the lower classes is a matter of broad social concern, and not just because of the risks of bad servants. The chaos caused by faulty education among the poor destroys the poor themselves and leaves them adrift in a society that can offer neither hope nor cure because the interconnection of classes means that social failure on one level disrupts the entire system.

By the time Mrs Mason leaves the MacClarty household, the family has shattered: the husband is dead, the elder son is being sent to India as an unwilling soldier, and the younger is already displaying the sullen selfishness that leads to his eventual break with his mother. Yet as Hamilton makes clear, the MacClartys begin with everything that her culture assumed would produce contented family life: they have a good farmhouse and a comfortable living from their land; Mr MacClarty is a hard worker, a responsible father, and a devout man; Mrs MacClarty has both the will and industry necessary to run a household, and she is a loving mother, devoted to her children. The trouble is that the parents' education has left them with what Hamilton presents as all the proper values, but with no idea of how to use them to direct their actions. At its most basic, *The Cottagers of Glenburnie* is a book in which Hamilton links physical and intellectual slovenliness. She insists that the "coud'na be fashed" attitude of the MacClartys arises not from bad hearts or inherent vice but is rather the result of the characters' intellectual laziness, as they fail to reason about the long-term effects of their actions, practical or moral. Mrs MacClarty's inability to see it might be better to take the trouble to clean her dairy rather than to put up with the ongoing inconvenience of butter stiff with cows' hair is, in Hamilton's view, exactly the same sort of intellectual failure as is her blind indulgence of her children's demands for immediate pleasure, an indulgence that – inevitably, in Hamilton's world – leads to death and misery. In *Elementary Principles of Education*, Hamilton compares the ineffectual mistress of a family to a novice chess player who damages her own interests by her failure to see more than a single move ahead;[52] the metaphor suggests that for Hamilton, like Dugald Stewart, moral reasoning is, if not quite the same as, at least analogous to inductive logic. Those who, like the MacClartys, have good intentions but fail to think through the probable results of their tolerance of dirty houses and hairy butter, or of their taste for public amusements, manifest the results of a failure to train the moral sense in the same way that one trains the intellect.

In effect, Mrs Mason's effort to reform her cousin is grounded in an attempt to instruct her in the sorts of information that Hamilton provides for her middle-class audience in *Letters on the Elementary Principles of Education*. Mrs Mason's failure is not a result of any presumed inability of the working classes to grasp such lessons – after all, the Morisons prove to be remarkably docile and capable learners – but rather of what the book presents as Mrs MacClarty's stubborn refusal to admit that what she considers Mrs Mason's "conceity" middle-class notions are relevant to her. Mrs MacClarty assumes that class determines what it is appropriate for her to do, but what Hamilton attempts to dramatize in this novel is the idea that even if individual duties and responsibilities do vary according to class, the principles that lead one to the successful fulfilment of those duties are the same for all. The ability of Mrs Mason both to instruct and win the affections of the sensible characters of all classes – the Longlands children, Mr Stewart and Mary, and the Morisons – is an implicit demonstration of Hamilton's contention that the foundations of education don't vary with class or gender. When Mrs MacClarty assumes that a preference for clean butter and bug-free beds is a bothersome middle-class affectation, or when Mr MacClarty piously trusts to God to ensure his children have good hearts because he believes himself incapable of providing a sophisticated education, Hamilton implies that they are limiting themselves by assuming that they are bound by a divinely ordained social system that they can do nothing to alter. In contrast, she suggests that what Mrs Mason attempts is to show them their full human potential as reasoning beings, a potential that they have both the right and duty to develop.

The problem here is that it can be difficult not to feel at least some sympathy for Mrs MacClarty as she bristles at Mrs Mason's comments about the dirt in her house or as she snaps back, following some well-intentioned advice on the management of her children, that "maidens' bairns are aye weel-bred". Hamilton's story is at its liveliest and her writing at its sharpest in her depiction of the slovenly MacClartys, and even if Mrs Mason resembles Hamilton in some ways, the character differs sharply from her creator in one vital respect: Mrs Mason appears to lack any sense of humour. Her righteous horror when she bustles out to let Mrs MacClarty know that the children have thrown mud at her newly washed windows – she reflects that never in twenty years of working with the young had she seen such "unprovoked malignity" – might seem almost as disproportionate to us as it does to Mrs MacClarty herself. The MacClarty children might indeed be dismayingly lazy, sullen, and rude, but Mrs Mason, perhaps inevitably, comes across as self-righteous and, despite the novel's insistence on her kindness and humility, rather self-satisfied and condescending in her attitude towards her cousins. There is at least some evidence that readers in or near Hamilton's time saw her in this way. The American writer Caroline Matilda Kirkland, for one, noted of a character in her book about life on the American frontier that she is able to help her employers to transform their household "[w]ithout dictating, like good Mrs Mason, in the Cottagers of Glenburnie, (whose benefits I have sometimes thought, must have been harder to bear than other people's injuries)."[53] Even if the theory behind Mrs Mason's attempts to educate her working-class cousins is the same as that anchoring Hamilton's educational writing for middle-class women and aristocratic children, the content and style of her lessons risks sounding patronizing, in part because

Hamilton tends to shift from instructing by satiric narrative to a reliance on something closer to lecture and homily when she focuses on Mrs Mason's reforming efforts. Readers at the time recognized the value of Hamilton's comic narrative as an educational device; Francis Jeffrey, for one, argued that the peasant readership who picked up *Glenburnie* would learn more from its amusing incidents than from lectures. Likewise, a self-described "Plain-Spoken Englishwoman" thought that *The Cottagers of Glenburnie* had "done more towards impressing moral and religious truths on the minds of the lower classes, than many a homily delivered for that purpose."[54] That there are limitations to educating by homily is also precisely the point that Hamilton makes in the preface of *Agrippina* as she discusses the value of narrative in instructing middle-class girls, but in *Glenburnie*, she attempts to make her readers learn not just from comic anecdote, as she portrays the chaotic disorder of the MacClarty household, but also from the well-meaning lectures provided by Mrs Mason. Given Hamilton's own theories of art and education, it is hardly surprising that exemplary Mrs Mason remains less compelling in narrative terms than is her slatternly cousin.

Yet even while recognizing that point, it is also important to note that in making Mrs Mason the voice of rationality and order, Hamilton does not limit her role to the conventionally feminine one of middle-class monitor of working-class household practice. On the contrary, Mrs Mason is more than happy to instruct anybody she sees going astray, undeterred by considerations of class or gender. She delivers an impromptu sermon on faith versus works to a Glenburnie church elder; she demonstrates a clear grasp of practical politics when she uses her Longlands connections to save Sandie MacClarty from execution for desertion; she debates church and educational policy with Mr Gourlay; and she manages social catastrophe with tact and discretion when she helps Bell Stewart reconcile herself to a potentially disastrous marriage. It is hardly surprising that the unfortunate Mr Mollins nearly collapses with shock when he sees Mrs Mason; he might have assurance enough to use a military commission and a few fashionable acquaintances to transform himself from a shoemaker's son into a fortune-hunting man of fashion, but by that point in the novel, she has established herself as a figure who is willing and able to stand up to anybody who causes disorder, not just at the level of the household, but in society as a whole. Hamilton's reliance on coincidence in resolving Bell's marriage – as she reveals that the supposedly dangerous man of the world bent on seducing Bell is in fact a basically good-hearted, love-struck youth of lower middle-class origins whom Mrs Mason has known from his childhood – seems at least partially justified by the ways in which this plot twist reaffirms our sense of Mrs Mason as the embodiment of domestic, social, and moral order. One of Hamilton's most striking innovations in this book might in fact be her decision to make the figure who brings order out of the chaos in the village of Glenburnie, as well as in the Stewarts' unhappy family, and who instructs men and women of all classes in their religious and social duties, a woman who might seem to be marginalized in almost every possible way: she is poor, lame, elderly, unmarried and childless (that is, even more of a social outsider than her fiftyish, invalid creator). Even so, and without any access to the conventional sources of social power, she becomes by force of reason and character the sole source of change and reform in the world of the novel, not just for the working classes, but for everybody she encounters. Like a more determined version of the middle-class Charlotte Percy in the *Hindoo Rajah* (or like Mrs Fielding, a wealthier and less timid version of Charlotte who appears in *Memoirs of Modern Philosophers*), Mrs Mason makes herself into a force for social change, even though she is living in a world that refuses to recognize that she can be of any particular use. This point might not make Mrs Mason's lectures any more appealing, but it does suggest that Hamilton was attempting rather more in this book than simply providing condescending advice on domestic management for working-class housewives.

Glenburnie, Scotland, and Romanticism

The Cottagers of Glenburnie is not, of course, about working-class life in general but very specifically about life in Scotland, and as such, it has an important place among Romantic-era literature on national cultures. Anticipating

Waverley by half a dozen years, it was one of the first
novels of Scottish regional life to achieve major popular
success, and despite its resolutely unromanticized plot, it
also fits in with the genre of the national tale.[55] Neither
Mrs Mason nor Mrs MacClarty makes quite such a swoon-
ingly romantic embodiment of the Scottish nation as (for
example), Lady Morgan's Glorvina (in *The Wild Irish Girl*
[1806]) does for Ireland or Mme de Staël's Corinne does
for Italy, but one would hardly expect them to do so.
Hamilton's aim, after all, is didactic and satiric, and she
intends to reform rather than to celebrate or memorialize.
Yet the fictional village of Glenburnie became emblematic
of a certain type of Scottishness for readers in the opening
years of the nineteenth century as Hamilton's contemporaries, including Anne Grant, Mary Brunton, and Scott himself acknowledged. Even if the book might seem less than
entirely calculated to appeal to Scottish national pride, it
was rapidly assimilated into what many readers and com-
mentators at the time saw as an emergent literary fashion
for all things Scottish.[56]

Like her younger contemporary Francis Jeffrey, Hamilton
is a writer who blurs the boundaries between Enlightenment and Romantic values,[57] and while in the educational
theories that anchor her work she looks back to the world
of eighteenth-century philosophers, her interest in a peculiarly Scottish national culture is grounded firmly in the
Romantic age. Yet especially when read against other
regional novels of the period, Hamilton's version of Scottish culture might begin to look oddly stylized. For one
thing, as critics such as Gary Kelly have noted, working-
class and national identities are more or less merged in
Glenburnie: the only Scots speakers are peasants, and part of
the way that Hamilton marks Mrs Mason as having trans-
cended the limitations of her class origins is by having her
speak standard English, as do the middle-class Stewarts.
(The aristocracy is almost totally deracinated: the young
man who inherits the Scottish Longlands estate at the end
of the novel is English born and bred.) Yet even more interestingly, given the intense interest in Scottish regional cultures at the time – and particularly that of the Highlands –
Hamilton's version of Scottish life is remarkably vague geo-
graphically. Granted, most readers seemed to assume that

Glenburnie was a Highland village, and the initial description of its setting, nestled as it is among mountains and
rivers, evokes the version of the Highlands presented in the
literature of the picturesque around that time. The culture
that Hamilton describes, however, did not necessarily seem
to her contemporaries to be characteristically "Highland."
One John MacCulloch made that point explicitly in his
book of Highland travels, writing that "we can find a Glenburnie every where, and, assuredly, as easily in the Low-
lands as the Highlands."[58] Even more interestingly, Mary
Brunton, justifying what she feared was her belated foray
into romantic fiction about Highlanders, explained in the
preface of *Discipline* (1815) that Hamilton had been writing
a very different type of book than she was: "the Manners
so admirably described in 'The Cottagers of Glenburnie,'"
she noted, "are those of a district where Highland peculiarities have yielded to constant intercourse with strangers."[59]
In Brunton's view, in other words, the society that Hamilton described was not one that was more or less pristinely
distinct from the modern world, as is more typical in the
genre of the national tale, but is rather one that exemplifies
contemporary degeneracy. Hamilton's peasants have almost
nothing in common with the exotically noble-minded
figures who make up all classes of Highland society in the
work of Brunton or, for that matter, of Anne Grant or Sir
Walter Scott. Nor, clearly enough, was Hamilton interested
in participating in the formation of what Peter Womack
has called the "myth" of the Highlands as a "romantic
country."[60]

    That the MacClartys' culture is more generically rural,
working-class, and non-English than it is specifically Highland is further emphasized by the point that it has much in
common with contemporary representations of Irish peasant life. One might compare, for example, Maria Edgeworth's 1809 novel *Ennui*, which features a description of
the dirty, dilapidated cottage of the narrator's loving but
slatternly nurse Elinor, or Mary Ann Hanway's *Ellinor*
(1798), in which the disgusted heroine, on a journey
through Ireland, contrasts the "neat straw-thatched cottage[s]" of England with the "mud-reared cabin[s]" of the
"half-famished" Irish peasants.[61] Even if rural deprivation
is not stressed as much in *Glenburnie* as it is in the works on

Ireland, the generic similarities in these representations of cottage life on the British peripheries remain striking and again suggest Hamilton's relative lack of interest in the sort of historical and cultural specificity on which Scott prided himself and which he emphasized by the lavishly detailed footnotes that he added to later editions of his novels. (Or, for that matter, that Hamilton provided in her representation of Indian society in *Translations of the Letters of a Hindoo Rajah*.) Yet for all the lack of specific local detail, *Glenburnie* remains distinct from representations of Irish or even English working-class life in one vital and obvious respect: the language that the characters use.

At first glance, admittedly, the use of Scots might seem more a matter of style than substance. Language notwithstanding, Hamilton has been criticized (by Kelly, among others, as already noted) for the implicitly anglicizing impact of the proposed reforms in this novel. Even Francis Jeffrey, in his main reservation about the book, worried that it approached a bit too closely at times to the firmly English church-and-state hierarchical vision of Hannah More's *Cheap Repository Tracts*. After all, the reformer's perspective is explicitly English: Mrs Mason is born in Scotland, but she spends much of her adult life in England, she speaks standard English, and she has English cottage life in mind as a measure of what Glenburnie could be. That said, this is still a novel that presents Scottish peasant life as part of a vibrant, if not always admirable, living world, a marked contrast with the deliberately backward-looking visions of Ireland in the work of Edgeworth or Morgan. Scots might be the language of peasants in this book, but it is not the language of the past: the Morisons, who exemplify the way forward for the working classes, are Scots speakers themselves, even if Hamilton does not mark their use of the language quite as strongly as she does that of the Mac-Clartys. More to the point, perhaps, by its use of Scots, the book addresses itself to Scottish readers in a way that, at that time, relatively few other novels had. By way of contrast, the books that are arguably the two most important examples of the Irish national tale published around that time, *Castle Rackrent* (1800) and *The Wild Irish Girl*, are both written in a manner that explicitly takes into account an English reader. Edgeworth's Thady Quirk speaks English that is inflected by Irish intonation and phraseology, but Edgeworth also provides a standard English speaking Editor to frame his account and explain any oddities. Morgan's novel is even more clearly calculated for an English audience, as her account of traditional Irish culture is related in the voice of an educated Englishman writing explanatory letters to his equally well-educated English friend. Morgan's and Edgeworth's versions of "autoethnographic" fiction are thus directed to and approach the "exotic" culture from the perspective of dominant English society,[62] yet as reviewers of *Glenburnie* were quick to point out, the accounts of the MacClartys are written in a manner that makes few concessions to the English reader. Francis Jeffrey, for one, noted with "a sort of malicious pleasure" that Hamilton's use of Scots made the novel "a sealed book" to the English reader, at least "until they take the trouble thoroughly to familiarize themselves with our antient and venerable dialect."[63] In a rather more disgruntled manner, *The British Critic* complained about the difficulty of choosing a satisfying excerpt from the book, as the passages "which are perhaps the best, abound with Scottish words and Scottish phrases, which [...] would hardly be intelligible to the natives of England, in a detached passage of such a moderate length as our limits will admit."[64] As late as the 1850s, long after one might have presumed that the Waverley novels had familiarized audiences with written representations of Scots, William Ross was regretting that the book's use of "dialect" might interfere with its usefulness as a teaching resource for his English readers.[65]

In making the MacClartys speak in broad Scots, Hamilton was, of course, linking the language with the poor and the less educated, but in recognizing that point, it is important not to overlook the fact that she was also assuming an educated readership that would be as comfortable with Scots as it was with Mrs Mason's reasoned arguments about educational practice. Mrs Mason might on one level embody English values, but Hamilton's language makes clear that she was not trying simply to anglicize the lower orders: she was speaking as a Scot to other Scots. Language was, of course, a vexed issue in later eighteenth- and early nineteenth-century Scottish literary circles, especially as writing "pure" English became something of a marker of literary sophistication. Francis Jeffrey might have been proud of the "antient" Scots language, but as a young man he had worried anxiously about mastering standard English. Likewise, Elizabeth Benger felt obliged to apologize for the "Scotticisms" that she noticed in the excerpts she printed from Hamilton's lost novel about Arabella Stuart. Yet if inadvertent "Scotticisms" were something that worried educated Scottish writers, Scots was another matter entirely, as writing it involved a deliberate linguistic and artistic choice. The written language in which Scots were educated was, after all, English, and even the working-class readers whom Hamilton was ostensibly addressing would have been drilled in the Bible as their basic text, and would hence have been at least as, if not more, familiar with written English than with Scots, whatever their spoken language. Perhaps in part as a consequence, at least some readers of the time, Scottish as well as English, took for granted that Scots was of limited value as a literary language. Hamilton's older contemporary John Moore, for example, a Scot of cosmopolitan, educated taste, was dubious about Robert Burns' use of Scots in his poems and urged him to write in standard English so that his poetry would not be marginalized by and inaccessible to mainstream English-speaking audiences – and possibly even future generations of Scottish readers.

Of course, what in fact happened with Scots in the early years of the nineteenth century was far more complicated than Moore expected. If it became a way of representing the poor, the rural or the uneducated – as Hamilton uses it in *Glenburnie* – it also became a mark of allegiance to a particular version of national culture. It is worth noting that Hamilton used Scots not only in *Glenburnie* but also in much of her verse, including the verse letter to Scott quoted above and "My Ain Fireside," a standard anthology piece throughout the century. In those cases, Hamilton is deliberately assuming a voice that is not quite her own, but in the poetry, she conveys a domestic life of neighbourliness and fireside comfort through her use of the same literary markers that she uses in *Glenburnie* to evoke Scottish rural life. In effect, domesticity and the domestic politics of the national tale slide together. Moreover, in all of this writing Hamilton asserts, even if only by implication,

the continued living importance of Scots as a literary language. At the very least, Scots gives her a flexibility of voice
that enables her to communicate in a wider range of regis-
ters than would be available to her as a unilingual writer of
English. Mrs Mason might be all but indistinguishable from
the English, but by choosing to write in Scots, both in *Glenburnie* and elsewhere, Hamilton makes clear that she is not.
Perhaps even more importantly, she also implies that she is
able to assume an audience of Scots *readers*, a point that
might explain in part the great success the novel had in
Scotland despite its unflattering depiction of the rural life
of the country. However unattractive the village of Glenburnie might be, at least initially, the book in fact has a
doubly flattering message for its middle-class Scottish
readers: on the one hand, they can identify with the more
or less gentrified and anglicized Mrs Mason as she attempts
to reform her backwards cousins, but on the other, they
can mark themselves off from the general English reader by
the greater literary flexibility that enables them to read with
ease a book that flaunts its non-English origins. Hamilton's
version of the national tale is, importantly and originally,
one that very consciously and explicitly speaks to the culture being observed, rather than providing an amused or
reverential representation of it geared more or less entirely
to outsiders.

   That is an argument, that may, of course, seem to take
one back to the perspective offered by those contemporary
readers, such as Spence, who saw this as a book directed
primarily to real-life versions of the MacClartys and
intended mainly for their reformation. Yet *The Cottagers of
Glenburnie* is of continuing interest in the twenty-first century, and not just as an example of the Romantic-era vogue
for improving the working classes. Hamilton's vision of
reform is one that assumes the intellectual training of the
poor is as important as it is for members of any other class
of society, and even if Mrs Mason might at times be a little
hard to take, the philosophy underlying her reforms is the
same as that which Hamilton insists should be applied in
the training of all young people, no matter what their class
background. No less importantly, Hamilton is writing a version of educational fiction that does not assume that one
has to be educated out of regionalism or into a uniformly

English cultural life. If her version of Scottish culture isn't at all times celebratory – and especially not of the rural working-class characters who are her main subjects – it still takes for granted that it is possible to reform what she sees as the problems in that society without sacrificing national identity in the process.

Endnotes

[1] Elizabeth Isabella Spence, *Sketches of the Present Manners, Customs and Scenery of Scotland*, 2 vols. in 1 (London: Longman, Hurst, Rees, Orme, and Brown, 1811), pp. 148-49, 150-51.

[2] Elizabeth Isabella Spence, *Letters from the North Highlands during Summer 1816* (London: Longman, Hurst, Rees, Orme, and Brown, 1817), pp. 49-50.

[3] Augustus J. C. Hare, ed., *The Life and Letters of Maria Edgeworth*, 2 vols. (Boston: Houghton, Mifflin & Co., 1895), vol. 1, pp. 169-70.

[4] Anna Laetitia Aiken LeBreton, ed., *Memoir of Mrs Barbauld, including Letters and Notices of her Family and Friends* (London; G. Bell & Son, 1874), p. 150.

[5] Sarah Tytler and J. L. Watson, *The Songstresses of Scotland*, 2 vols. (London: Strahan & Co., 1871), vol. 1, pp. 315-16.

[6] Elizabeth Benger, *Memoirs of the Late Mrs Elizabeth Hamilton*, 2 vols. (London: Longman, Hurst, Rees, Orme, and Brown, 1818), vol. 2, p. 73. Benger habitually uses initials rather than full names when printing Hamilton's correspondence. Usually, the names are easily identifiable by context: the D.S. whose *Philosophical Essays* she recommends to Dr S is obviously Dugald Stewart; a famous Scottish woman writer, initials J. B., is no less obviously Joanna Baillie. I have not, however, been able to identify Dr S., although he was apparently a figure of some intellectual repute who struck up an epistolary acquaintance with Hamilton after reading her 1801 *Letters on Education*.

[7] See Gary Kelly, *English Fiction of the Romantic Period* (London: Longman, 1989), pp. 90-92.

[8] See in particular Mellor's *Mothers of the Nation: Women's Political Writing in England, 1780-1830* (Bloomington: Indiana UP, 2000).

[9] "Biographical Notice of Mrs Elizabeth Hamilton," *The Scots Magazine and Edinburgh Literary Miscellany*, 78 (1816), p. 565.

[10] For examples of such travels, see Charles Lyell, *A Second Visit to the United States of North America*, 2 vols. (London: John Murray, 1849), vol. 2, pp. 221-2; C.J.C. Davidson, *Diary of Travels and Adventures in Upper India*, 2 vols. (London: Henry Colburn, 1843), vol. 1, p. 302; Matilda Betham Edwards, *Scenes and Stories of the Rhine* (London: Griffith and Farran, 1863), p. 179; and John Russell, *A Tour in Germany ... in the Years 1820, 1821, and 1822*, 2 vols. (Edinburgh: Constable and Co., 1825), vol. 2, p. 211. For an example of a reviewer using *Glenburnie* in the early part of the century, see *Blackwood's* review of *Annals of the Parish*, 9 (1821), pp. 203-09; for an example from mid-century,

see "The Health of Towns" in Hogg's *Weekly Instructor*, 4 (1846), pp. 267-70.

[11] "The Rev. Mr Hamilton's *New Tracts*." *Macphail's Edinburgh Ecclesiastical Journal and Literary Review*, 6 (1848), p. 264.

[12] Henry Cockburn, *Memorials of his Time*, 1856 (Edinburgh: T. Foulis, 1900), p. 260.

[13] The list appears in *The Cottagers of Glenburnie: A Scottish Tale*, published in London and Edinburgh in 1887 by Nimmo, Hay and Mitchell. The gender divide in the list of recommended prize books is also notable. Titles other than *Glenburnie* on the girls' list include *Life's Crosses and How to Meet Them*, and *A Needle and Thread: A Tale for Girls*, while the boys' list features works such as *The Far North: Explorations in the Arctic Regions*, *Great Men of European History*, and *Monarchs of the Ocean: Columbus and Cook*. The National Library of Scotland copy of the 1828 [eighth] Edition was given as a school prize, though interestingly, given the clear sense later in the century of the gulf between appropriate prize material for boys and girls, the 1828 recipient was a boy.

[14] *Reports on the Sanitary Condition of the Labouring Population of Scotland* (London: W. Clowes and Sons, 1842), p. 237.

[15] Benger, vol. 1, p. 272.

[16] Benger, vol. 1, p. 27. In another inconsistency, Benger says that Hamilton was six when, in 1762, she went to Scotland, but on the same page gives her birthdate as 25 July 1758. There was a query about Hamilton's birth date in *Notes and Queries* in 1873 (s4, no. 11 [1873], 523), in which the writer pointed out Benger's inconsistencies and wondered if the date had ever been verified in Belfast records; the sole response, published later in the same volume, refers only to other printed sources that, following Benger, give the 1758 birthdate.

[17] Benger, vol. 1, p. 20.

[18] Benger, vol. 1, pp. 35, 43.

[19] Elizabeth Hamilton, *Letters on the Elementary Principles of Education*, 2 vols. (Bath: G. G. and J. Robinson, 1803), vol. 1, p. 206.

[20] Although Benger gives no further details about her "Dr Moyse", the reference is clearly to Henry Moyes, whose lectures in Scotland, London, and the U.S. attracted a fair amount of attention in the 1780s and 90s. Benger is not the only writer to spell the name "Moyse": Benjamin Rush uses that spelling in his account of Moyes' supposed ability to distinguish colour by touch; this is also the spelling used in an anonymous verse addressed to Moyes, supposedly by Edinburgh ladies attending his lectures, and in the account of his influence on Thomas Garnett in *Public Characters* (see note 21).

[21] A prospectus for Moyes' London lectures was published around 1785 and gives an idea of what Hamilton might have learned from him. For a more detailed description of another course of such lectures, see Thomas Garnett, *Observations on a Tour through the Highlands*. 2 vols. London, 1800, 2: 196-205. In this book, Garnett, who was apparently inspired by Moyes' example (see *Public Characters 1799-1800* [London: Richard Phillips, 1799], p. 419) describes the lectures that he gave in Glasgow over the previous few years. Not all women of the era were convinced of the value of such lectures; see Anne Grant's dismissive

comments on a chemistry lecturer (presumably Garnett) who had been
attracting fashionable interest among the Glasgow ladies in 1797 (*Letters
on the Mountains*, 3 vols. London: Longman, Hurst, Rees, Orme and
Brown, 1807), vol. 3, pp. 64-66.

[22] Benger, vol. 2, p. 31.

[23] I am borrowing this term from Margaret J.M. Ezell; she applies it
in the context of late seventeenth-century manuscript exchange in *Social
Authorship and the Advent of Print* (Baltimore: Johns Hopkins UP,
1999).

[24] Benger, vol. 1, p. 52.

[25] Benger, vol. 2, p. 35.

[26] Untitled verses addressed by Elizabeth Hamilton to Sir Walter
Scott, NLS, MS 3886, folio 86. The verses are dated on the back, in a
different hand, 8 March 1815. "Yet" here means "gate".

[27] "An Account of the Edinburgh House of Industry," in Elizabeth
Hamilton, *Exercises in Religious Knowledge: for the Instruction of Young
People* (Edinburgh: Manners and Miller, 1809), p. 4 [separately pagi-
nated from the main text].

[28] J. P. Grant, ed. *Memoir and Correspondence of Mrs Grant of Laggan*,
2 vols. (London: Longman, Brown, Green, and Longmans, 1845), vol.
2, p. 129.

[29] Elizabeth Hamilton, *Translations of the Letters of a Hindoo Rajah*,
1796 (Peterborough, Ont.: Broadview Press, 1999), pp. 302-303.

[30] Hamilton, *Elementary Principles*, vol. 1, p. 252; see p. 126 of this
edition.

[31] Anne Mellor has recently made a vigorous case for seeing the
Hindoo Rajah as a more strongly feminist work than has traditionally
been recognized; see "Romantic Orientalism Begins at Home: Elizabeth
Hamilton's *Translations of the Letters of a Hindoo Rajah*", *Studies in Romanticism* 44 (2005), 151-164.

[32] Hamilton, *Elementary Principles*, vol. 1, pp. 249-50; see p. 125 of
this edition.

[33] Elizabeth Hamilton, *A Series of Popular Essays, Illustrative of Principles
Essentially Connected with the Improvement of the Understanding, the Imagination, and the Heart*, 2 vols. (Edinburgh: Manners and Miller, 1813),
vol. 2, pp. 83-84.

[34] Hamilton, *Popular Essays*, vol. 2, p. 86.

[35] Benger, vol. 2, pp. 71-72.

[36] Hamilton, *Elementary Principles*, vol. 1, p. 255; see p. 127 of this
edition.

[37] Hamilton, *Elementary Principles*, vol. 1, pp. 252, 256; see pp.
126-27 of this edition.

[38] Hamilton, *Elementary Principles*, vol. 1, p. 381.

[39] Hamilton vehemently attacked "writers on education" who interested themselves only in "people of rank and fortune," and insisted that
her *Letters* were aimed at "the cultivation of the faculties that are common to the whole human race" (vol. 1, p. 11). However, the inscribed
reader and nominal addressee of the letters is a friend, a woman who is
implied to be more or less of Hamilton's educated middle-class background.

[40] Hamilton, *Elementary Principles*, vol. 1, p. 222.

[41] Elizabeth Hamilton, *Memoirs of the Life of Agrippina, the Wife of Germanicus*, 3 vols. (Bath: G. G. and J. Robinson, 1804), vol. 1, p. 18.

[42] Hamilton, *Elementary Principles*, vol. 1, pp. 11-13.

[43] Hamilton, *Elementary Principles*, vol. 2, pp. 9-10; see p. 133 of this edition.

[44] Quoted in Lord Woodhouselee [Alexander Fraser Tytler], Memoirs of the Life and Writings of the Honourable Henry Home of Kames, 2 vols. (Edinburgh: W. Creech, 1807), vol. 1, p. 207.

[45] Hamilton, *Elementary Principles*, vol. 2, p. 7.

[46] Dugald Stewart, Outlines of Moral Philosophy. For the use of Students in the University of Edinburgh (Edinburgh: Constable and Co., 1793), p. 116.

[47] Dugald Stewart, *Philosophical Essays*, 3rd ed. (Edinburgh: Constable and Co., 1818), p. 111. The first edition of this work was published in 1810; Hamilton read it while she was working on her own *Popular Essays*. Obviously, it was not a direct influence on Hamilton's earlier educational writing, but it is still worth quoting in this context as the ideas are continuous with Stewart's earlier work. Indeed, Hamilton's ideas chimed so closely with Stewart's that after reading it, she wrote her friend Dr S– in some dismay that she found in several passages "the same thought [...] expressed in very nearly the same word" as hers, obliging her to revise to avoid the appearance of plagiarism (Benger, vol. 2, pp. 113-114; the letter is dated 1809, presumably an error on Benger's part, as context makes it clear that the essays were in print and that Hamilton was not reading a manuscript copy). On the other hand, Hamilton adds, she is proud of the fact that she is following the same intellectual track as Stewart, even if "at an immeasurable distance" (vol. 1, p. 114).

[48] Dugald Stewart, *Elements of the Philosophy of the Human Mind* (Edinburgh: W. Creech, 1792), p. 24 (subsequent volumes appeared in 1814 and 1827). Hamilton quotes this passage, at greater length than I do here, in the selection from the second volume of *Letters on the Elementary Principles of Education* included in this edition.

[49] Hamilton, *Elementary Principles*, vol. 1, p. 21.

[50] Hamilton, *Elementary Principles*, vol. 1, p. 22.

[51] Gary Kelly noted in *English Fiction of the Romantic Period* that "Mason" is an appropriate name for someone who is attempting to reconstruct society. Hamilton is echoing, perhaps borrowing, the name of Mary Wollstonecraft's middle-class governess in *Original Stories from Real Life* (1791).

[52] Hamilton, *Elementary Principles*, vol. 1, pp. 22-23.

[53] Caroline Matilda Kirkland, *Western Clearings* (New York: Wiley and Putnam, 1845), p. 183.

[54] "A Plain-Spoken Englishwoman," *Hints towards the Formation of Character* (London: Simpkin, Marshall, and Co., 1843), p. 300. Somewhat curiously, while Jeffrey contrasts Hamilton's entertaining narrative with what he finds the more offensively didactic *Cheap Repository Tracts*, the "Englishwoman" explicitly links the two works as exemplars of successful narratives for the working classes. The change might reflect the

mid-century tendency to relegate *Glenburnie* to a working-class audience. A mid-century manual on teaching methods also implies that *Glenburnie* is preferable to more theoretical works on the subject, though suggesting that it succeeds despite rather than because of narrative: in a list of recommended books on education, it rates *Cottagers of Glenburnie* more highly than *Letters on the Elementary Principles of Education*, noting that "though in the form of a tale" it is "we think, as a work on education, more *effective*" than the earlier book. (William Ross, *The Teacher's Manual of Method; or the General Principles of Teaching and School-Keeping* [London: Longman, Brown, Green Longmans, & Roberts, 1858], p. 189).

[55] For a full discussion of the genre of the national tale, see Katie Trumpener, *Bardic Nationalism: The Romantic Novel and the British Empire* (Princeton: Princeton UP, 1997). Liz Bellamy provides an excellent overview of the subject in a Scottish and Irish context in her "Regionalism and Nationalism: Maria Edgeworth, Walter Scott, and the Definition of Britishness" in *The Regional Novel in Britain and Ireland*, ed. K.D.M. Snell (Cambridge: Cambridge UP, 1998), pp. 54-77. Joep Leerssen provides a study of the Irish context for the national tale, focusing on Morgan, in "The Burden of the Past" in *Remembrance and Imagination* (Notre Dame, Indiana: U of Notre Dame P, 1997), pp. 33-67, while Ina Ferris looks at Christian Johnstone and the national tale in "Translation from the Borders," in *Eighteenth-Century Fiction* 9 (1997), pp. 203-22.

[56] For an amusing contemporary reaction to the fad for Scottish literature, see Sarah Green's 1824 novel *Scotch Novel Reading*. Recent criticism of the Romantic era has also begun to emphasize the importance of Scottish literature to the period. See, for example, the essays collected in Robert Crawford's *The Scottish Invention of English Literature* (Cambridge: Cambridge UP, 1998) for an analysis of the Scottish contribution to shaping the discipline of English literature in the later eighteenth century, and Leith Davis', Ian Duncan's, and Janet Sorenson's *Scotland and the Borders of Romanticism* (Cambridge: Cambridge UP, 2004) for essays exploring the contribution of Scottish literature to Romanticism. Gerard Carruthers' and Alan Rawes' *English Romanticism and the Celtic World* (Cambridge: Cambridge UP, 2003), while not focused only on Scotland, also features important work on Scottish romanticism.

[57] Jeffrey is, of course, usually seen as a strongly anti-Romantic voice, but despite his notoriously hostile reviews of Wordsworth and Coleridge, he was a sympathetic reviewer of many of his contemporaries, including Keats and Byron. On Jeffrey's often uneasy critical balance between aesthetic schools, see Demata and Wu's introduction to *British Romanticism and the Edinburgh Review*. They argue that Jeffrey "frequently found himself attempting to resolve the tensions between Romanticism and the eighteenth-century culture of which he was a product" (Massimiliano Demata and Duncan Wu, eds. *British Romanticism and the Edinburgh Review: Bicentenary Essays* [Basingstoke: Palgrave Press, 2002], p. 7).

[58] John MacCulloch, *The Highlands and Western Isles of Scotland in*

... *Letters to Sir Walter Scott*, 4 vols. (London: Longman, Hurst, Rees, Orme, Brown, and Green, 1824), vol. 1, p. 127. A later writer, John MacElheran, assumed that Glenburnie was in fact a Lowland village, writing in a polemical defence of Celtic culture that Highlanders are more a "more cleanly race" than Lowlanders and citing *The Cottagers of Glenburnie* as his evidence that, at the beginning of the century, "the Lowland Scotch housewife was a *dirty trollop*" (*The Condition of Women and Children among the Celtic, Gothic, and other Nations* [Boston: Patrick Donahoe, 1858], p. 317).

[59] Mary Brunton, *Discipline*, 1815 (London: Colburn and Bentley, 1832) p. 60.

[60] Peter Womack, *Improvement and Romance: Constructing the Myth of the Highlands* (London: Macmillan, 1989), p. 2. For a more recent work on the Romantic-era construction of the Highlands, which pays detailed attention to the work of Scott and Grant among others, see Kenneth McNeil, *Scotland, Britain, Empire: Writing the Highlands 1760-1860* (Columbus, Ohio: Ohio State UP, 2007).

[61] Mary Ann Hanway, *Ellinor; or the World as it is*, 4 vols. (London: Minerva Press, 1798), vol. 4, pp. 107-108.

[62] Autoethnography is a term coined by Mary Louise Pratt (in *Imperial Eyes: Travel Writing and Transculturation* [London: Routledge, 1992]); it has been used in studies of Romantic-era writing about Scotland by James Buzard (*Disorienting Fiction: The Autoethnographic Work of Nineteenth-Century British Fiction* [Princeton: Princeton UP, 2005]) and in the context of Irish writing by Joep Leerssen in "The Burden of the Past" (see note 55).

[63] Francis Jeffrey, "*The Cottagers of Glenburnie: A Tale &c.* by Elizabeth Hamilton," *The Edinburgh Review* 12 (1808), p. 402.

[64] "Mrs Hamilton's *Cottagers of Glenburnie*," *The British Critic* 32 (1808), p. 117.

[65] Ross, *The Teacher's Manual*, p. 189.

THE COTTAGERS OF
GLENBURNIE

To

HECTOR MACNEIL, Esq

Dear Sir,

Independently of all considerations of esteem or friendship, I know not to whom the COTTAGERS OF GLENBURNIE could be with such propriety inscribed, as to the Author of the SKAITH OF SCOTLAND.

To the genius displayed in that admired production of the Scottish Muse, this humbler composition of dull prose has indeed no pretensions; but if it shall be admitted, that the writers have been influenced by similar motives, I shall be satisfied with the share of approbation that must inevitably follow. Had I adhered to the plan on which those sketches were originally formed, and published them as separate pieces, in form and size resembling the tracts in the "Cheap Repository", I should have had no apprehensions concerning the justice of the sentence to be passed upon them; for then they would have had little chance of falling into other hands than those of the class of persons for whose use they were intended. This exclusive perusal is, however, a happiness which no author has a right to expect and which, to confess the truth, no author would very highly relish. For though we were to be assured, that of the number of readers in this reading age, one half read only with the intention of gratifying their vanity, by shewing their skill in picking out the faults, yet who would not prefer going through the ordeal of this *soi-disant* criticism, to the mortification of not being read at all?

Of the mode of criticism now in vogue, I believe your opinion coincides exactly with my own. We do not consider it as originating in the pride, or spleen, or malignity of the persons by whom it has been most freely exercised, but in a mistaken notion of the species of vigour and energy attached to the censorial character, and essential to the dignity of the critic's office. It is under this misconception that persons of highly cultivated talents sometimes condescend to make use of the contemptuous sneer, the petty cavil, the burlesque representation, – though modes of criticism in

47

which they may easily be outdone by the vulgar and illiter-
ate. But surely when men of genius and learning seem thus
to admit, that the decisions they pronounce stand in need
of other support than the justice and good sense in which
they are founded, they forget the consequences that may
follow. They forget, that the tone of ill nature can never be
in unison with the emotions that arise from the admiration
of what is beautiful, and that as far as they, by the influence
of their example, contribute to give this tone to the public
mind, they corrupt the public taste, and give a bias that is
inimical to its progress in refinement. But however the prevalence of this style of animadversion may in a general view
be lamented, it is not by authors of such trifling productions as the present, that it ought to be condemned: for is it
not some consolation to reflect, that let the meanest performance be judged with what asperity, or spoken of with
what contempt it may, it cannot be more severely judged,
or more contemptuously treated, than works acknowledged
to possess merit of the highest order? Let then the critics
do their worst; I have found a cure for every wound they
can inflict on my vanity. But there are others besides pro-
fessed critics, concerning whose opinion of the propriety or
tendency of this little work I confess myself to be more
anxious, and those are the well-wishers to the improvement
of their country.

A warm attachment to the country of our ancestors naturally produces a lively interest in all that concerns its
happiness and prosperity; but though in this attachment
few of the children of Caledonia are deficient, widely different are the views taken of the manner in which it ought to
be displayed.

In the opinion of vulgar minds, it ought to produce a
blind and indiscriminating partiality, for national modes,
manners, and customs; and a zeal that kindles into rage at
whoever dares to suppose that our country has not in every
instance reached perfection. Every hint at the necessity of
further improvement is, by such persons, deemed a libel on
all that has been already done; and the exposition of what
is faulty, though with a view to its amendment, an un-
pardonable offence. From readers of this description, you
will soon perceive, I cannot hope for quarter. Nor is it to
readers of this description alone that the intention with

which my Cottage Tale is written, will appear erroneous or absurd.

The politician, who measures the interests of his country by her preponderance in the scale of empire, regards all consideration for individual happiness as a weakness; and by the man who thinks riches and happiness synonymous, all that does not directly tend to increase the influx of wealth, is held in contempt. Each of these dictates to the opinion of numbers. In the school of the former, the political value of the various classes in society is judged of by their political influence; and in that of the latter, their importance is appreciated by their power of creating wealth. It is the few by whom the privileges are possessed, that are the objects of consideration in the eyes of both. The great mass of the people are, in their estimation, so many teeth in the wheels of a piece of machinery, of no farther value than as they serve to facilitate its movements. No wonder if, in their eyes, a regard to the moral capacities and feelings of such implements should appear visionary and romantic. Not less so, perhaps, than to the war-contriving sage, at the time he coolly calculates how many of his country-men may, without national inconvenience, be spared for slaughter!

Happily, there are others, to whom the prosperity of their country is no less dear, though its interests are viewed by them through a very different medium. National happi-ness they consider as the aggregate of the sum of individual happiness, and individual virtue. The fraternal tie, of which they feel the influence, binds them, not exclusively to the poor or to the affluent – it embraces the interests of all. Every improvement in the arts, which tends to give addi-tional grace to the elegant enjoyments of the wealthy; every discovery made by their countrymen in science; every step attained in the progress of literature, or philosophy – is to them a subject of heartfelt gratulation. But while they delight in observing the effects of increasing prosperity with which they are surrounded, they forget not the claims of a class more numerous than that of the prosperous. They forget not that the pleasures of the heart, and of the under-standing, as well as those of the senses, were intended by Providence to be in some degree enjoyed by all; and there-fore, that in the pleasures of the heart and the understanding, all are entitled to participate. Persons of this mode of thinking do not fancy the whole duties of charity to be comprised in some efforts towards prolonging the sensitive existence of those who, without such relief, must perish; nor do they consider extreme indigence was the only object on which their benevolence ought to be exerted, nor the physical wants of the lower orders, as the only wants that ought to be supplied. Nothing by which the moral habits, or domestic comforts of their brethren of any rank, can be materially injured or promoted, can to such minds be in- different. Precious in their eyes are the gleams of joy that illumine the poor man's cottage; sacred the peace that reigns in it; doubly sacred the virtues by which alone that peace can be established or secured. By minds such as these, my motives will not be misinterpreted. By one such mind, at least, I assure myself they will be judged of, with the indul- gence due to so many years of friendship.

May this be accepted as a testimony of the sincerity with which that friendship has ever been returned by,

Dear Sir,
Your obedient and faithful
humble servant,

THE AUTHOR

George-Street,
May 3 1808

Chapter I

An Arrival

In the fine summer of the year 1788, as Mr Stewart of
Gowan-brae, and his two daughters, were one morning
sitting down to breakfast, they were told by the servant,
that a gentlewoman was at the door, who desired to speak
with Mr Stewart on business. "She comes in good time,"
said Mr Stewart; "but do you not know who she is?" "No,
Sir," returned the servant, "she is quite a stranger, and
speaks Englished, and is very lame, but has a wonderous
pleasant countenance." Mr Stewart, without further
inquiry, hastened to the door, while the young ladies continued the interrogations.

"Did she come in her own carriage, or in a hack?" asked
Miss Stewart. "She came riding on a double horse," replied
the lad. "Riding double!" cried Miss Stewart, resuming
her seat, "I thought she had been a lady. – Come Mary, let
us have our breakfast – My goodness! I hope papa is not
bringing the woman here."

As she spoke, the door opened, and Mr Stewart entered
with the stranger leaning on his arm. Her respectful salute
was returned by Miss Stewart with that sort of reserve
which young ladies, who are anywise doubtful of being
entitled to all that they assume, are apt to put on when
addressing themselves to strangers, of whose rank they are
uncertain; but, by her sister Mary, it was returned with a
frankness natural to those who do not fear being demeaned
by an act of courtesy.

"Indeed you must breakfast with us, my good Mrs
Mason," said Mr Stewart, placing a chair; "my daughters
have often heard of you from their mother. They are no
strangers either to your name or character; and therefore
must be prepared to shew you esteem and respect."

Miss Stewart coloured, and drew up her head very scorn-
fully; of which Mrs Mason took no notice, but humbly
thanking the good gentleman for his kindness, added, "that
he could scarcely imagine how much pleasure it gave her,
to see the children of one whom she had so loved and honoured; and she was loved and honoured by all who knew

her," continued she. "Both the young ladies resemble her: may they be as like her in their minds as in their persons!"

"God grant they may," said the father, sighing, "and I hope her friends will be theirs through life."

Miss Stewart, who had been all this time looking out of the window, began her breakfast, without taking any notice of what was said; but Mary, who never heard her mother spoken of without sensible emotion, bowed to Mrs Mason, with a look expressive of her gratitude; and observing, with compassion, how much she appeared exhausted by the fatigue of travelling, urged the necessity of her taking refreshment and repose. Mr Stewart warmly seconded his daughter's invitation, who, having learned that Mrs Mason had travelled night and day in the stage coach, and only stopped at ———, until a horse could be prepared to bring her forward to Gowan-brae, was anxious that she should devote the remainder of the day to rest. The weary stranger thankfully acceded to the kind proposal; and Mary, per-ceiving how lame she was, offered her assistance to support her to her room, and conducted her to it with all that respectful kindness, which age or indisposition so naturally excite in an artless mind.

When Mary returned to the parlour, she found her father at the door, going out; he gave her a smile of appro-bation as he passed, and kindly tapping her on the neck, said, "she was a dear good lassie, and a comfort to his heart."

Miss Bell, who thought that every praise bestowed on her sister, conveyed a reproach to her, now broke silence, in evident displeasure with all the party.

"She was sure, for her part, she did not know what people meant by paying such people so much attention. But she knew well enough it was all to get their good words; but for her part, she scorned such meanness. She scorned to get the good word of any one, by doing what was so improper."

"And what, my dear Bell, is improper in what I have now done?" said Mary, in a mild tone of expostulation.

"Improper!" returned her sister, "I don't know what you call improper, if you think it proper to keep company with a servant, and to make as much fuss about her too as if she were a lady. Improper, indeed! And when you know too, that Captain Mollins was to come here to-day; and that I had hoped my father would ask him to dinner: – but my friends are never to be minded – they are to be turned out to make room for every trumpery person you chuse to pick up!"

"Indeed, sister, you do me injustice," said Mary; "you know I did not bring Mrs Mason here; but when I heard her name, I recollected all that our dear mother had often told us of her extraordinary worth: and I thought if it had pleased God to have spared her, how glad she would have been to have seen one she so much esteemed; for, though my mother was born in a higher station, and bred to higher views, than we have any right to, she had no pride, and treated all who were worthy of her notice with kindness."

"Yes," replied Miss Bell, "it was her only fault. She was a woman of family; and, with her connexions, if she had held her head a little higher, and never taken notice of people because of their being good, and such stuff, she might have lived in a genteeler stile. I am sure she gave as much to poor people every year, as might have given hand-some dinners to half the gentry in the country; and, to curry favour with my father, you encourage him in the same mean ways. But I see through your mean arts, Miss, and I despise them."

"Indeed sister, I have no arts," said Mary. "I wish to follow the example that was set us by the best of mothers, and I am sure we cannot have a better model for our conduct."

"Do as you please, Miss!" cried her sister, choking with rage; and leaving the room, slapped the door after her with a violence which awaked their guest, and brought their father up from his study to see what was the matter. He found Mary in tears, and instantly conjectured the cause of the uproar. "I see how it is," said he: – "Bell has been giving vent to the passion which I saw brewing in her breast, from the moment that I brought this worthy woman into the room. The ridiculous notions that she has got about gen-tility, seem to have stifled every good feeling in her mind. But it is my own fault. This is the effect of sending her, on account of these accomplishments, to that nursery of folly and impertinence, where she learned nothing but vanity and idleness."

"Indeed, Sir," said Mary, "my sister is very accom-plished, and very genteel; and it is natural that she should wish to get into genteel company, to which she thinks our taking notice of people in an inferior station presents an obstacle."

"Then she thinks very foolishly, and very absurdly," replied Mr Stewart. "My father was an honest man, and therefore I am not ashamed of my origin; but, were I ashamed of it, could I by that make any one forget it? Does not all the country know, that I am but a farmer's son? and though, by being factor on the estate of Longlands, I have been brought into the company of higher people, it is by my character, and not by my situation, that I have gained a title to their respect. Depend upon it, Mary, that as long as people in our private station rest their claim to respect upon the grounds of upright conduct, and unblem-ished virtue, they will not fail to meet with the attention they deserve; and, that the vain ambition of being esteemed richer or greater than we really are, is a contemptible mean-ness, and will not fail to expose us to many mortifications. What in reality can be more mean, than to be ashamed of noticing a deserving person, because they are poor? – unless, indeed, it be the meanness of courting the favour of one who is rich, and wicked."

Mary expressed her assent; and Mr Stewart proceeded. "As to Mrs Mason," said he, "she was, it is true, but a servant in the house of Lord Longlands; and was brought up by the old lady from a child to be a servant. Your mother was then in the house, in a state of dependence, as a poor relation; and would have found her situation miser-able, had it not been alleviated by the kind attentions of this good girl Betty Mason, who performed for her many friendly offices essential to her comfort; and was, in sick-ness, her sole support and consolation, for the old lady, though pride made her treat my wife as a relation, so far as to give her a seat at her table, was a woman of a coarse and selfish mind, and gave herself little trouble about the feelings or comforts of any one. What my poor dear angel suffered while she was in that great house, was well known to me, and went to my heart. When seized with a fever at a time the house was full of company, she was so neglected, that she would inevitably have lost her life, but for the care of Mason, who watched her night and day. She always called her her preserver: – and can we, my dear Mary, forget the obligation? No, no. Never shall one who shewed kindness to her, find aught but kindness at Gowan-brae. Tell your sister that I say so; and that if she does not chuse to treat Mrs Mason as my guest ought to be treated, she had better keep her room – But who comes here? A fine gentleman, I think. Do you know who he is?" "I never saw him, sir," returned Mary; "but I suppose it is a Captain Mollins, whom my sister met with when she went to the ball with Mrs Flinders."

"Mrs Flinders is a vain giddy woman," said Mr Stewart, "and I do not like any one the better for being of her acquaintance; but I will not prejudge the merits of the gentleman." Captain Mollins was then shewn in, and received by Mr Stewart with a grave civility, which might have embarrassed some people – but the captain was not so easily abashed; saying, that he had the honour of bringing a message for Miss Stewart, from Mrs Flinders. He took his seat, and began talking of the weather with all the ease of an old acquaintance.

Miss Stewart, who, in expectation of the captain's visit, had changed her dress, sailed into the room, with a smile, or rather simper, on her countenance; through which, an acute observer would however, have seen the remains of the recent storm. Her eyes sparkled, but her eyebrows were not yet unbent to the openness of good humour: her voice was, however, changed to the tone of pleasure; and so much wit did she find in the captain's conversation, that every sentence he uttered produced a laugh. They had, indeed, all the laugh to themselves; for, as they only spoke about the ball, and as neither Mr Stewart nor Mary had been there, they could have no clue to the meaning of the many brilliant things that were said. But when the old gentleman heard the captain ask his daughter, whether she was not acquainted with some of the quizzes whom he had seen speak to her, and saw his daughter blush indignant at the charge, he thought it time to ask for an explanation; and begged the captain to inform him of whom he spoke.

The captain turned off the question with a laugh – saying, "he was only rallying Miss Stewart about a gentleman in a green coat, who had the assurance to ask her to dance – one of the town's-people – and you know, Sir, what a vulgar set they are, he, he, he!"

"O shockingly vulgar indeed," said Miss Stewart; "but we have no acquaintance with them, I assure you – *we* visit none but the families in the country."

"Then you have no remorse for your cruelty to that poor Mr Fraser," cried the captain. "He looked so mortified when you refused him – I shall never forget it, he, he, he!"

"Ha, ha, ha – Well you are so comical," said Miss Stewart, endeavouring to prevent her father, who was about to speak; but the old gentleman would be heard. "Was it Mr Fraser, did you say, Sir, that asked my daughter?"

"Yes, Fraser, Fraser, that was his name, I think – a little squat vulgar fellow – one you probably don't know."

"But I do know him, Sir," returned Mr Stewart; "that little fat vulgar fellow is my nephew, Sir – my daughter's cousin-german! A man of whose notice she ought to be proud, for he is respected as a benefactor to the whole neighbourhood. Were she to be ashamed to acknowledge her relationship to such a man, because he wears plain manners, and a plain coat, I should be ashamed of her. Had my nephew been less successful in business than he has been, he would have still merited esteem; for though of no high birth, he possesses the heart, and soul, and spirit, of a gentleman."

"Very true, Sir – very true, indeed," said the captain, with undaunted assurance. "Mr Fraser is a very worthy man; he gives excellent dinners; I have the honour of knowing him intimately; have dined with him twice a week ever since I have been at –; a very worthy man indeed. I believe he dines with Mrs Flinders to-day, and will probably see Miss Stewart home; for I hope she won't mortify her friend, by refusing her invitation."

Miss Stewart looked at her father, who was exceedingly averse from the proposal. At length, however, she carried her point, as she generally did; for Mr Stewart, though he saw, and hourly felt, the consequence of his indulgence, wanted the firmness that was necessary to enforce obedience, and to guide the conduct of this froward and self-willed child.

Chapter II

Dissertation on Dress – Antiquated Precepts – History of Mrs Mason's Childhood

Mr Stewart being called away on business, left it in charge with his daughter Mary, to prevent the departure of their guest during his absence; a commission which she gladly undertook to execute, saying, that she should watch for the moment of her awaking, in the adjoining room. In going to it, she passed the door of her sister's apartment, which stood ajar, as was indeed its usual state; for she had, among her other accomplishments, acquired such a habit of slapping it after her, that the spring of the lock was always broken.

Mary, hearing herself called on, entered, and asked if she could render her any assistance in dressing "O yes," cried Bell, "if you will only come and help me to find my things; I don't know, I am sure, where they are all gone to. I have looked all these drawers through, and I cannot find a single pair of stockings fit to put on. What shall I do? I have nothing fit to wear. O me! what shall I do?"

"What! nothing fit to wear, among all these heaps of clothes?" said Mary, "I believe, few girls in the country have such a well-stored wardrobe. We, at any rate, have no reason to complain, as we always find my father" –

"My father!" interrupted Bell, "I am sure my father would never let us wear any thing in the fashion, if he could. But what should he know about dress, at Gowanbrae? – I wonder you have not more spirit than to fall in with his old-fashioned notions."

"My father wishes us always to be dressed according to our station, and our fortune," returned Mary; "and I think it a pity such notions should ever be out of fashion."

"But they are," said Bell, "and that's enough. Who thinks of being so mean as to confess, that they cannot afford any thing expensive? I wish you saw how the young ladies in Edinburgh dress! I don't mean those who have fortunes, for there is nothing in that; but those who have not a shilling to depend on. Yet they are all so fine, that one is ashamed to be seen beside them! Look there, and see whether I have one decent thing to put on."

"Indeed, your things are very good," returned Mary, "if you would be persuaded to keep them properly. I wonder, you would not do it for the sake of having a comfortable room; for it is always so strewed with litter, that one never can find a chair to sit down on, and think how your things must be spoiled by the dust."

"But who can be at the trouble of fold-folding their things as you do," cried Bell; "and besides, it is so like an old maid. Well, now that you have put that gown in order, I think it will do; and now, if you would let me have your new cap, I should be quite smart."

"And why not wear your own? It is surely the same, if not better than mine is."

"O no," returned Miss Bell, "it is all torn to pieces."

"How?"

"Why, I forgot to put it in the box; and so it met with a misfortune. How could I help it? I am sure I never saw such a thing in my life, nor any one else. These vile little terrier puppies! I never knew the like of them; but they are just kept about the house to plague me. I had only lain down upon my bed to read a novel I got from Mrs Flinders, when I heard the nasty things come into the room; but I could not be at the trouble to put them out, I was so interested in the book. Little did I think it was my cap they were tearing to pieces, all the while they went bouncing and jumping about the room. Whurt, whurt! cried one; Wouf, wouf! cried the other; but I still read on, till I was so much affected by the story, that I was obliged to get up to look for my pocket-handkerchief – when, lo! the first thing I beheld, was the fragments of my poor cap! not one morsel of it together. The lace torn into perfect scraps, and the ribbon quite useless! Do now let me have your cap like a good creature, and I promise to take care of it."

Mary, who was indeed a good creature, could refuse her sister nothing, when she spoke to her with temper. She brought her the cap, and assisted her in dressing her hair for it; but could not avoid taking the opportunity of giving her a few cautionary hints, with regard to forming hasty intimacies with the strangers she met at Mount Flinders. Bell was instantly in arms in defence of her friend's associates, who were all *excessively genteel*; but happily the carriage was at the door, and the coachman so impatient, that she had no time for a further discussion. She was no sooner gone than Mary went to inquire for her guest; and as the cordial invitation she carried her, was given with evident good will, it was accepted of in the spirit of gratitude.

Mr Stewart did not return till the evening of the following day; but in the interim the time past cheerfully. The conversation often turned upon a topic that was ever interesting to the heart of Mary – the virtues of her mother, on which she delighted to expatiate; she likewise spoke of her brothers, who had been recommended by her mother to her particular care. "I deeply feel," said Mary, "the importance of the trust; and I daily pray to God for strength to execute it: but what, alas! can I do for my brothers, but give them the best advice I can, when they are at home with me, and write to them when they are at school? They are indeed very good boys, and never refuse to attend to what I say, unless in regard to the respect I wish them to pay my sister. But she is constantly finding fault with some of them; and is, I fear, so jealous of their attachment to me, that she will never love them as she ought, which makes me very unhappy; for I have been used to hear my mother say, that young men generally turned out well, who had a peaceful happy home: and besides, what can be so delightful as a family of love!"

"True," replied Mrs Mason, "it is one of the characteristics of heaven. But in this life, my dear Miss Mary, every one must have their trials; and were it not for the contrariety of dispositions and tempers, how few trials should we have to encounter in domestic life! To yield to those who, in their turn, yield to us, is an easy task, and would neither exercise our patience, nor forbearance, nor fortitude; and are not these most precious virtues?"

"How like that is to my good mother!" cried Mary. "O, Mrs Mason, if I had always such a friend as you beside me, to put me in mind of my duty, and to support me in performing it, I think I should never sink under it, as I sometimes do."

"And have you not a friend, a guide, and a supporter,

in Him who called you to these trials of your virtue? Consider, my dear young lady, it is your Heavenly Father who has set the task, – perform it as unto Him, and when you have to encounter opposition, or injustice, you will no longer find them intolerable."

"Thank you, thank you," replied Mary; "I fear I do not always reflect so much on this as I ought. I shall, however, endeavour to keep it more in mind for the future. But tell me, Mrs Mason, how it is that you come to think so justly – so like my dear mother? You must, like her, have had the advantage of an excellent education. And yet, pardon me, for I suppose I have been misinformed, but I understood that you were not, when young, in a situation in which you could be supposed to receive the benefit of much instruction. I now see you have had greater advantages than I imagined."

"Yes," replied Mrs Mason, smiling, "my advantages indeed were great. I had a good mother, who, when I was a little child, taught me to subdue my own proud spirit, and to be tractable and obedient. Many poor people think, that their children will learn this time enough, when they go into the world; and that as they will meet with hardships when they grow up, it would be a pity to make them suffer by contradicting them when they are little. But what does a child suffer from the correction of a judicious parent, in comparison of what grown people suffer from their passions? My mother taught me the only true road to obedience, in the love and fear of God. I learned from her to read, but she read ill herself, and could not instruct me in a proper method; nor could she afford to send me to school, for she was reduced to extreme poverty. She died when I was ten years old, and I thank God for enabling me to add to the comforts of the last year of her life by my industry."

"Why, what could you do for her at that tender age?" said Mary, "you were but a little child."

"I was so, Miss," replied Mrs Mason, "but I could knit stockings though I wore none; and having knit a pair for the gardener's wife at Hill Castle, I was recommended by her to the housekeeper, who had the gout in her feet, and wanted a pair knit of lamb's wool, to wear in the winter. I happened to please her; and when she paid me, she not only

gave me twopence over and above the price, but a bit of
sweet-cake, which I immediately put in my pocket, saying, I
would take it to my mother. This brought on some questions, the result of which was an order to come to the castle
daily for my mother's dinner. Never, never, shall I forget
the joy of heart with which I went home with these glad
tidings; nor the pious gratitude with which my mother
returned her thanks to God for this unlooked-for mercy!
She hoped that I would gain the favour of my benefactors
by my diligence and industry, and she was not disappointed. The housekeeper spoke of me to her lady, who
desired that when I next came I might be taken up to her
room, that she might see me. Her orders were obeyed next
day, and with trembling limbs and a beating heart did I
approach her. She asked me several questions, and was so
well satisfied with my answers, that she said she was sure I
was a good girl, and that she would give me education to
make me a good servant, and that I should live at the castle
under the care of Jackson. Seeing me hesitate, she looked
angry, and asked me if I was too proud to be a servant
under Jackson. 'O no,' I cried, 'I would be happy to do anything for Mrs Jackson, but I cannot leave my mother. She
is not able to leave her bed, and I do every thing for her;
she has no one but me to help her.'
    " 'It is very true, my lady,' said the housekeeper; and
she then gave such an account of all I did for my mother, as
seemed to astonish the old lady, who in a gentler tone said,
that I was a good girl, a very good girl; and should come
to live with her when my mother died, which could be at
no great distance The possibility of my mother's death had
never before occurred to me; and when my lady put half-
a-crown into my hand, which she said was to serve for earnest, I looked at it with horror, considering it as making a
sort of bargain for my mother's life. With tears running
down my cheeks, begged her to take back the money, for
that I should be ready to serve her by night or day, for what
she pleased to give me; but she refused, and telling me I
was a little fool, bade me take the silver to my mother, and
say that she should have as much every week.
    " 'Your ladyship will not be long troubled with the pen-
sioner,' said the housekeeper; 'for I am much mistaken, if
she has many weeks to live.' I was so struck at hearing this

sad sentence, that I went home with a heavy heart, and
complained to my mother of her having concealed from me
that she was so very ill. She said she knew how much I
had to do, that my exertions were beyond my strength; and
therefore she had not had the heart to afflict me, with speaking of her situation. But she saw that her trust in Providence had not been in vain. The Lord, who had through life
so graciously supplied her wants, had heard her prayers in
behalf of her child. 'Yes,' repeated she, 'my prayers have
been answered in peace. I know that my Redeemer liveth:
continue to serve him, my dear bairn; and though we now
part, we shall hereafter meet in joy.' She continued some
time apparently engaged in fervent prayer. At length her
lips ceased to move, and I thought she had fallen asleep. I
made up our little fire; and, having said my prayers, gently
crept to bed. She was then gone, but I did not know that
her soul had fled. Cold as she was, I did not think it was the
coldness of death! But when I awoke in the morning, and
found that she no longer breathed, and saw that her face
was altered, though it still looked mild and pleasing, I was
seized with inexpressible terror: this did not, however, last.
I recollected God was still present with me; and casting
myself on my knees before HIM, I held up my little hands
to implore his protection engaging, in the language of simplicity, that I would be evermore His obedient child.

"This action inspired me with courage. I deliberately
dressed myself, and went over to the farmer's to tell of my
sad loss, which was indeed proclaimed by my tears rather
than my words. Nothing could exceed the kindness of all
our neighbours upon this occasion. They clubbed among
them the expences of my mother's funeral and resolved that
all she had should be kept for me. They made a sort of rude
inventory of her little effects; and on searching her pockets,
discovered the half-crown piece which had been the prelude
to all my sorrows. At sight of it, my tears flowed afresh,
and I cried out that I would not have that big shilling – I
would never touch it, for it was it that had brought on my
mother's death. I then, as well as I could, told all that my
lady had said to me, when she gave it, and was greatly surprised to find, that, instead of joining in my aversion to the
half crown, my good neighbour considered it as an aus-
picious omen of my future fortune. Nor have I had any

reason to view it in a contrary light; for though my life, (the rest of which has been spent in Lord Longland's family,) has not been free from troubles, it has been swee-tened by many mercies. But I must have tired you with talk-ing of myself," continued Mrs Mason; "for what interest can you take in the story of my childhood?"

"But I do indeed, Mrs Mason, I take a great interest in it," cried Mary; "and I have learned from it more of the conse-quences of early education, than from many of the books I have read upon the subject. Pray tell me how you went on at Hill Castle? and tell me how soon it was that you saw my mother, and what she was then like?"

"She was then exactly what you are now, my dear young lady. The same height, the same soft voice, the same fair complexion, and the same mild expression in her eyes I could almost think it her, that now stood before me."

"Well, but you must go on from the time you went home. Did the old lady receive you kindly?"

"She meant to do so," returned Mrs Mason; "but she had a stern manner, and exacted such minute and punctual obedience, as rendered it difficult to please her. Indeed she was never pleased except by those who flattered her grossly; such it was, as I soon saw, by flattery, that her own woman, Mrs Jackson, had made herself such a favourite. But though I could not approve the means, I must say this for Mrs Jack-son, that she did not make a bad use of her favour, at least with regard to me, or to those she thought she had in her power; but she was so jealous of any one obtaining my lady's ear except herself, that it made her often guilty of endeavouring to create a prejudice against those whose influence she had any dread of, I was warned of this by my first friend, the old housekeeper, who, on the day after I went home, called me into her little parlour, and said, that as she had been the means of bringing me to the house, she would always be my friend as long as I was good, and obedi-ent; but that, as she wished me well, she would not have me speak of her kindness: 'for that,' said she, 'would not please Mrs Jackson, for she likes to think that people owe everything to her, and you must make it your first business to please Mrs Jackson – aye, even before my lady herself. For though my lady may be angry, she will forget and for-give; but if you once shew Jackson that you wish to please any body before her, she will neither forget nor forgive it to you as long as you live: and while you look to her as all in all she will be very kind to you, and make my lady kind to you too; for she does with my lady what she pleases.'

"I dropped my little curtsey, and, 'thank you, ma'am,' at the end of her discourse, but suppose I did not seem satisfied, for she asked me if I was thinking of what she had been saying to me? 'Yes, ma'am,' said I, 'but' – 'But what?' said she. It was in vain she asked; I could not express myself – for I could not point out where the error lay, though I felt that the conduct she recommended, was somewhat opposite to that uprightness and sincerity which my mother had so strictly enforced. I resolved, however, to exert myself to gain Mrs Jackson's good will, by diligence and attention; and thought, in spite of all the housekeeper said, that she must love me the better for being grateful to whoever was kind to me.

"As our progress in every thing depends upon our diligence, and as even in childhood we soon learn what we resolve to learn, Mrs Jackson had little trouble in the task of teaching me. I soon worked at my needle as well as was possible for a child my age; and she did not spare me, for she was to boast to my lady at night of what I had performed in the day. I never had a minute's time to play; but though such close confinement was not good for my health, it was good for giving me a habit of application; the most essential of all habits for those who are to earn their bread.

"By the time I was twelve years old, Mrs Jackson found me so useful an assistant, that I should probably have been fit for nothing but needle-work all my life long had not my lady been so pleased with my performance, as to resolve to employ me in assisting her in the embroidering of a set of chair-covers, which were to be done in a fancy way of her own contrivance. I now sat all the day in her dressing-room, and had nothing to complain of except hunger; but of my being hungry my lady never thought, though she must have known that I often fasted nine, and sometimes ten hours at a time; for I never durst rise from my work until she went down to dinner; but though thoughtless of my wants, she was in other respects very kind to me, and gave me every encouragement by praising my work. The more satisfaction she expressed in me, the less gracious did Mrs Jackson become. She would on some days scarcely speak to me; and though I begged to know if I had offended her, would make me no other answer than that I was now too fine a lady to mind anything she could say. This made me very unhappy so that I often cried sadly when I was sitting at my work alone; and was one day observed by my lady, who, though my back was towards her, had seen my face in the glass as she entered the room. She asked what was the matter with me, in a tone so peremptory that I dared not refuse to answer; and with many tears I confessed, that Mrs Jackson was displeased with me, and I knew not for what.

" 'But I shall know,' said my lady pulling the bell with violence. 'Jackson cannot be angry without a cause.' Jackson appeared; and without hesitation denied the charge. 'Me angry with the poor child!' said she; 'how could she think me angry with her? Am not I her best friend? But it is evident what the matter is, my lady; the poor young creature is broken-hearted from confinement; and besides, she is getting uppish notions, from sitting up like a lady from morning to night. But your ladyship pleases to have her beside you, to be sure, or you would not have her, and so I said nothing; but if I were to presume to speak, I should say, that it would do the poor thing more good to let her do a little stirring work under the housemaid now and then; for I don't like to see young creatures spoiled till they are good for nothing; but if your ladyship thinks that she can work the chair-covers better than I can, your ladyship knows best.'

"Whether my lady saw through the motives of this advice or no, I cannot tell, but she complied with it; and I was immediately consigned to Molly the housemaid, who was one of the most active and clever servants I have ever known.

"I had been so cramped by constant sitting that I found it very difficult to go about my new occupation with the activity which Molly required and of which she set me the example. But I soon acquired it; and Molly confessed that she never had to tell me the same thing twice. This made her take pains with me; and I have often since found the advantage of having learned from her the best way of doing all sorts of household work. She was of a hasty temper, but very good-natured upon the whole; and if she scolded me heartily for any little error in the way of doing my work, she praised me as cordially for taking pains to rectify it. As there were many polished grates to scour, and a vast number of rooms to keep clean, we had a great deal to do, but it was made easy by regularity and method; so that in winter we had time to sit down to our needles in the evening, and in summer generally contrived to get a walk as far as the dairy.

I was a year and a half under Molly, and thought it a happy time; for though I worked hard, I got health and spirits, and was as gay as a lark. When Molly was going to be married, she desired the housekeeper to ask my lady to permit me to be her bridemaid. We were both called into my lady's room, when she repeated the request; and taking me by the hand, 'It is but justice,' says she, 'to tell your ladyship, how this lassie has behaved. I thought when she began, she never would have made a servant, because she never had been used to it; but I soon found she had a willing mind, and that was every thing. She has been greater help to me, than some that were twice her age; and in the eighteen months she has been with me, she has never disappointed me by any neglect, nor ever told me an untruth, or given me a saucy answer. And as she has been civil and discreet, I wish to put what respect on her is in my power; and if your ladyship pleases to let her be my bridemaid, I shall take it as a great favour to myself.' My lady looked at Jackson, who was dressing out her toilet, and had stopped to listen to Molly's speech. 'Do you think she can be spared, Jackson?' said my lady. 'Indeed,' replied Jackson, 'if you ask me, my lady, I certainly do not think she can.'

" 'If you please, my lady,' said Molly, 'the new housemaid says she will think nothing of doing all the work to give a play to poor Betty: the dairy-maid too will help her; there is not a servant in the house that would not, she is so obliging and so good-natured a lassie.'

" 'O if you are to dictate to my lady, that's another thing,' cried Jackson; 'I supposed my lady was to do as she pleased.'

" 'And so I will,' said my lady, peevishly; 'go down stairs now (to me,) and I will think of it.' In a short time, Jackson came down exultingly, and bid me go to my work, for that my lady did not chuse that I should have my head turned, and be made good for nothing by going about to weddings.

"I made no answer, but I could not help being much vexed; for it was the first time I had had the prospect of any pleasure; and the idea of seeing a dance, and enjoying all the merriment of such a happy day, had quite elated my spirits, which were now as suddenly depressed. I endeavoured to hide my tears, but Jackson, who was put out of temper by the consciousness of having treated me harshly, was glad to throw the blame from herself, and therefore accused Molly of having spoiled and misled me, by filling my head with folly.

"I had learned to submit to the injustice of passion, when I myself was alone concerned, but I could not hear Molly accused, without expressly denying the charge that was made against her. I said she had not filled my head with folly, but that she had filled my heart with her kindness, and that I should wish her well as long as she lived. I spoke this in a resentful accent, and immediately went out in great perturbation. No sooner was I alone, than I began to reflect with great horror on the impropriety of which I had been guilty, in speaking to Jackson in such a tone of resentment; and, recalling all her kindness to me when I first came to the castle, I felt that I had been wrong treating her for a moment as an enemy when she was perhaps my best friend. She no doubt (said I to myself) saw, that a scene of mirth was no proper place for me. I ought then to have been thankful to her for her care; and I have, on the contrary, been pert – O how ungrateful! May God forgive me! But will Mrs Jackson forgive me? This was not so easy to answer; however, I resolved to try; and when I met her in the evening, I spoke to her, though she would not speak to me; and in a beseeching manner, begged she would forgive me, for that I knew she had ever been my best friend; and that I could not bear the thoughts of her displeasure. She was soothed by my humility; and after a little while spent in vindicating her own motives, she promised to be reconciled to me and that she should be as much my friend as ever."

Chapter III

History of Mrs Mason continued

After dinner, Mrs Mason, at Miss Mary's request, resumed the account of her life, which we shall give as nearly as possible in her own words, without taking notice of the observations that were made by her young friend; or of the interruptions that occurred to break the thread of her story.

Jackson, who had now got over her fears of my lady's taking a fancy to me, began to wish for my assistance in the work she was about; and got my lady prevailed upon to put me once more under her direction. She took care that I had full employment, and I thank her for it, though it was not to shew her good will that she did it, but the contrary; for she still retained a grudge at me, for the affection I had expressed for Molly; and it was in this spirit that she laid out my work. As you have been at Hill Castle, you must remember the old tower, and that there are four rooms in it, one over the other to the top. The lowest of these rooms, that on the ground floor, with the iron-barred windows, was Jackson's own apartment, and where I likewise slept in a little press-bed. There could not, to be sure, be a more dismal-looking place; and indeed they said it had back in the old times been used as a prison, and was said by all the servants to be haunted. But I had no leisure for thinking of such things; for besides the quantity of needlework which Mrs Jackson exacted from me I had all the apartments of the tower from top to bottom committed to my care, and had to sweep and dust them, and to rub the furniture every day; so that in the day I was too busy, and by the time I went to bed, too sleepy, to think about the ghost.

Ever since I had been at the castle, the tower rooms had only been occasionally in use, when the house was full of company; but now the upper one was, we heard, to be occupied by a cousin of my lady's, who was spoken of by Jackson with the contempt which servants are too apt to feel towards the humble friends or poor relations of the families they live with. I thought, I confess it, with some vexation of the additional trouble which this new guest was to occasion me; and on the evening of her arrival, went to make up her room with no great cheerfulness. On opening the door, I saw the young lady sitting at the window, and would have gone back, but she desired me to come in, in a voice so sweet, and yet so sorrowful, that it seemed to go to my very heart. I saw she had been weeping, but she dried her tears, and condescended to enter into conversation with me, asking me how long I had been at service, and other kindly questions.

"Four years at service, and not yet fifteen!" said she; "poor girl! your parents must have been in great distress to part with you so soon." "I had no parents, Ma'am," said I; "my father was carried off in a fever before I was born, and my mother died ten years after; and then my lady was so good as let me come here to learn to be a servant."

"And you were thankful for getting leave to come to learn to be a servant," said Miss Osburne; "what a lesson for me!" She seemed for some moments busied in thought, and then speaking to me again: "You are right to be thankful, Betty; God Almighty, who is the father of the fatherless, will never forsake us while we trust in Him; and we ought to submit ourselves to all His dispensations, and even to be thankful for those that appear the darkest."

While I looked at her lovely face, as it was again bathed in tears, which fell fast as she spoke to me, I thought her an angel! So superior did she seem to any human being that I had ever seen. The meekness with which she bore her afflictions, increased my respect; but that one, in the rank of a lady, could have her heart thus touched by grief, appeared to me incomprehensible; for I was then so ignorant as to think, that the sorrows of life were only tasted in their bitterness by those of lowly station.

You, my dear Miss Mary, have doubtless heard enough of the history of your mother's family, to know the sad change of circumstances which she experienced on the death of her parents, an event that had then lately taken place. I was unable to form in my mind any notion of how this change affected her; for to me she appeared to be still placed in a situation so high above all want, as to be most enviable. She had no hard work to do, no task to perform, and which, sick or well, must be accomplished; but servants to attend her, and fine rooms to sit in and plenty

of fine clothes to wear, and the niceties of a plentiful table
to eat. Alas! I soon learned, from closer observation how
little these things tend to happiness; and that peace of mind,
the *only* happiness to be had on earth, is distributed by
Providence with an equal hand among all the various classes
in society.

The kind manner in which Miss Osburne spoke to me,
made me take such pleasure in serving her, as made all my
work seem light. My attention did not escape her notice,
and O how richly did she repay it! Finding that I read indif-
ferently, and not so as to understand what I read, she proposed giving me a daily lesson, which I thankfully accepted,
and, that it might not interfere with my work, I got up an
hour earlier every morning which I employed so diligently
that even Mrs Jackson was fully satisfied. I had now
acquired sense enough to know what an inestimable benefit
was conferred upon me by my dear Miss Osburne's kind
instructions. To her goodness I am indeed indebted for all I
know. From her I not only learned to read with propriety,
to write a tolerable hand, and to cast accounts; but, what
was more valuable than all these, from her I learned to
think. She opened to me the book of Providence, and
taught me to adore the wisdom, the justice, and the mercy
of my God, in all his dealings with the human race. She
taught me to explore my own heart; to be sensible of its
errors and its weaknesses and to be tender of the faults of
others, in proportion as I was severe upon my own. My
mother had endeavoured to lay in me the foundation of
Christian principles when I was a child; but it was not until
I had learned from this dear young lady to search the scrip-
tures for instruction, instead of running them over as a
task, that Christian principles were rooted in my heart.

What could I do for her in return? If I could have laid
down my life, it would have been too little; and if, in any
instance, I proved of service, or of comfort to her, I consider it a happiness for which I am most truly thankful.

Her situation at Hill Castle was indeed a thorny one.
She was there encompassed with many evils; and, in one
instance, beset with snares, which it required no common
prudence to escape. But her prudence was never put to
sleep, as in other young people it often is, by vanity; and
with all the meekness and gentleness of a saint, she had all

the wisdom and the firmness of a noble and enlightened mind. My lady and Jackson were the only persons that ever saw Miss Osburne without loving her. But my lady, though she sometimes took fancies to particular people, which lasted for a little while, never loved any one for their good qualities; and had a spite at Miss Osburne for being so much better informed, and so much wiser than she was herself; and it was enough to prevent Jackson from loving her, that she was so much loved by me.

But notwithstanding all my lady's crossness to her, Miss Osburne endeavoured to make her happy, by labouring to bring about a reconciliation between her and her son; and she so far succeeded, as to prevail upon him to come to the castle on the death of his lady, and to leave his little boy, (the present lord) under his mother's care. I never thought my lady loved the child; but, as the heir of the family, she was proud of him, and indulged his humour in every thing, so that his temper was quite spoiled. He took a fancy to play in Jackson's room, in preference to the nursery, and was attended by his maid, a very artful woman, who had contrived to make the child fond of her, by giving him in secret quantities of sweet-cake, which on account of his stomach he was forbid to eat.

When he could not be bribed into doing what she pleased, she had nothing for it but to frighten him; and in order to do so effectually, used to tell him stories of hob-goblins, and to make a noise as of some spirit coming to take him away, on hearing which, the little creature would run panting and terrified, to hid his head in her lap. You can have no notion how his nerves were shook by this. I believe he feels it to the present day, and am sure that much of his oddity, and of his bad temper, of which the world talks so much, might all be traced to the bad management of Jenny Thomson.

It one day happened, that while I was busied in getting up a suit of lace for my lady, the little lord came into our room as usual, to play. Two pieces of the lace which I had ironed were hung on the screen by the fire, and while I was smoothing out another for the iron, he snatched one of the pieces from the screen, and twisted it round his neck. I flew to rescue it, and called to Jenny to desire him to give it up, which she did in a wheedling tone, promising at the same time that she would give him a piece of plumb-cake.

"I know that you have none to give me," cried he; "I have eat it all up, so I don't mind you." "And don't you mind me?" cried I, "what mischief are you doing me! Your grandmamma will be so angry with me, that I must tell her the truth, and then she will be angry with you too. "I don't care," cried Lord Lintop, twisting the lace the firmer round his neck. Seeing that no other means would do, I took hold of him to take it from him by force. He immediately set up a scream of passion, but I persisted, and disengaged the lace as gently as I could from his grasp; but no sooner had I succeeded, than be snatched up the other piece, and, in a transport of rage, threw it on the fire, throwing the screen down at the same time with great violence.

The fire was strong, and the lace dry, so that its destruction was the work of a moment. At the expence of burning my hand and arm, I saved a fragment, but it could be of no use, and I really became sick with terror and vexation.

Jenny desired me not to vex, for that it was easy to say that the screen only fell by accident, and that my lord would be a good boy, and say that he saw it fall, and that the lace which hung on it fell into the fire; "and then what can my lady say, you know?" cried she, perfectly satisfied with the arrangement.

Her story might do very well, I said, provided there was none to witness against us.

"And who can witness against us?" said she, "has not the door been shut all the time? Who then can witness against us?"

"O Jenny," returned I, "there are witnesses, whom no door can shut out, – God and our own consciences. If these witness against us, what does it signify whether my lady be pleased or no? I hope I shall never be so wicked as to tell a wilful falsehood."

"Wicked, indeed!" repeated Jenny angrily "Where have you lived all your days I wonder, that you can talk such nonsense! as if servants must not always do such things if they would keep their place? I know more of the world than you do, Mrs Wisdom, and can tell you, that you will not find many masters or mistresses that do not like better to be imposed upon than to know the truth, when it does not happen to be agreeable. How long think you I should keep my place, were I to tell all the truths about every thing that Lord Lintop does? but I know better; I always think with myself, before I go up, of what they would like to hear; and in all the places I have been in, I have found it turn to my advantage. Take my advice, and tell the story as I have made it out, or depend upon it, you will get yourself brought into a pretty scrape."

She was called to go up to my lady with her little charge, and I was left alone in a very disconsolate state. The temptation to follow her advice was strong; but, thank God, my principles were stronger; and the consequences of beginning a course of sin by departing from truth, were so deeply imprinted on my mind, that I was preserved from the snare.

On telling Jackson what had happened, she was at first thrown into a mighty passion, and would have cast the blame on me if it had been possible; but though always unreasonable while her anger lasted, she was too good a woman not to be shocked at the thoughts of making up a deliberate and wicked lie, in order to deceive her mistress. We were still in consultation, when my lady rung her bell for Jackson, who returned in a moment, to tell me that I must immediately go up and answer for myself; but that as *my friend* Miss Osburne was there, I need not be afraid, for she would certainly take my part.

I went up, as you may believe, with a beating heart. As soon as I opened the door, my Lady, in a sharp voice, asked me what I had done with her fine lace? adding that I had better tell the truth at once, than make any evasion. "I will indeed tell the truth, my Lady," said I; "and though I am very sorry for the loss, your ladyship will be convinced that I could not help it, and am not to blame." I then told the story simply as it had happened; but while telling it, plainly saw that what I said made no impression. When I had finished, my lady looked me full in the face, her eyes quite wild with rage and indignation, and bursting into a sort of scornful laugh, "A pretty story truly you have made out indeed!" cried she. "This is all the good of your reading the Bible forsooth. First to destroy my lace through carelessness, and then to lay the blame upon the poor child! the heir of the family! one whom such a creature as you ought to have thought yourself honoured in being permitted to wipe the dirt from his shoes! And yet you dare to lay your faults to his door; to complain of him, and to complain of him to me? What assurance! But I am happy to have detected you; you are a vile hypocrite, and shall no longer be harboured in this house. I give you warning to provide yourself to another place."

"I am sorry to have offended your ladyship," said I, very humbly; "but indeed I have told the truth, and I am sure Jenny cannot be so wicked as not to confirm every word I have said."

"Pardon me for interfering," said Miss Osburne, "but I have such good reason for having a high opinion of Betty's principles, that I am convinced she is incapable of being guilty of what you attribute to her. I could stake my life on her sincerity. Do, my dear madam, take a little time for enquiry before you condemn."

This reasonable advice seemed like throwing oil on the fire of my lady's pride, and she became more angry than ever. She, however, desired Jenny to be immediately called. As soon as she entered, she was desired to tell without fear, in what manner the accident had happened. "I am sure, my lady," said the artful girl, "it was, as your ladyship says, an accident; for I am sure Mrs Mason had no intention whatever to drive down the screen, nor do I believe she saw when she did it, for it was in turning round that she pushed it over, and the lace just fell into the fire, and was burned in a moment."

"And where was Lord Lintop at the time?" asked Miss Osburne.

"I believe he was standing at the table," returned Jenny hesitatingly. "O now I recollect, he was playing with his little coach, the coach which her ladyship gave him, and which he is so fond of, that he would never let it be out of his hand; but indeed he loves everything that his grand-mamma gives him; I never saw so dear a tractable creature in all my life."

"Are you sure that he was then playing with the coach?" asked Miss Osburne. "O very sure and certain," returned Jenny; "I remember it particularly, because I had just put a string to it, as we went into Mrs Jackson's room."

"I shall refresh your memory, however," said Miss Osburne,

rising, and opening the door of a closet, from whence she returned with the coach in her hand. "This toy has been in that closet since yesterday evening, when I took it from the child, when he was going to bed. In this instance, therefore, you have not been correct."

"That is of no consequence," said my lady; "the child might have been playing with some other toy: all I ask is, did he touch the lace?"

"He! poor innocent darling!" cried Jenny; "no, as I hope to be saved, he was not even near it."

"O Jenny, what a sin are you committing!" I exclaimed. But her ladyship commanded me to be silent, and to leave the room.

I went grieved and astonished at her injustice, but rejoicing in my innocence; Jackson was very kind to me, and assured me that my Lady would, when left to herself, come round, but that there would be no good in speaking to her at present. There was indeed no good in it; for all that Miss Osburne said in my defence, only made her more positive in asserting the truth of Jenny's story; and, when my amiable friend would have questioned the child, she helped him to all his answers; and it is surprising how soon children can observe who is on their side, and how soon they can learn to practise the little arts of cunning and deceit.

My leaving the castle was now a thing fixed and certain; and the only consolation I could receive in the view of it was from a knowledge of carrying with me the good-will of all that knew me. I was shocked at the thoughts of being thrown into the world without a friend but I was reminded by dear Miss Osburne that the friendship of man is but a bending reed, in comparison with the protection of Him, who is to all that put their trust in Him, a tower of strength.

I was now to go in three days, and was not yet provided in a place; but Miss Osburne had written about me to a friend of hers, and I hoped her application would be successful. In the mean time, Lord Longlands arrived at the castle to prepare his mother for the reception of his intended bride, the heiress of Merriton, whose great fortune made her a more acceptable daughter-in-law to the old lady, than my Lord's first wife had been, and Jackson seeing my Lady in such high good humour, thought it a favourable

time to soften her in my behalf. She began by telling her
how sorry I was to leave the castle, and then ventured to
say many things in my praise; taking care at the same time
to contrast all she said in my favour, with the idleness and
self-conceit of Jenny, whose word, she said, would never be
taken before mine by any one who knew us both, as she
did. Poor Jackson, had reason to repent her zeal; for she
found my lady so prepossessed in favour my adversary, that
all she said against her was attributed to spite. And she
now saw, that by having accustomed her Lady to flattery,
she had exposed her to the arts of a more cunning flatterer
than herself. In fact, Jenny looked to Jackson's place, and
would have succeeded in her designs, had it not been for a
very extraordinary accident, which brought all her character to light.

On the morning that I was to leave the castle, Miss
Osburne told Lord Longlands, that his mother was that day
to part with the most attached and faithful creature in the
world, on account of her having thrown the blame of burning a piece of lace on little Charles. My Lord enquired into
the particulars, and resolved to have the matter investigated
fairly before I went; and on my lady's coming in, told her
his design. Both Jenny and I were summoned to appear; and
my Lord having first requested that no one should speak
but the person he called on for an answer, first desired me
to tell my story; and when I had finished, called on Jenny
for hers. She began much in the same way she had done
before; but, in concluding, added what she had not then
said, that I had immediately entreated her not to tell how it
happened, but to join me in saying it was Lord Lintop
who threw down the skreen; for that my lady would not be
angry if she thought he did it. She was then beginning a long
harangue upon her good will to me, and the hardships she
lay under in being looked down upon by all the servants in
the house, because she would not join me in making up a
story against her dear innocent child, to save me from my
Lady's anger. Lord Longlands desired her to stop: and then
asked me what I had done with the lace, which the child
had twisted up, and which I said was torn. I had, I said,
given it to Mrs Jackson. She was called on, and the lace was
produced in the state I had described it. On examining it,
my Lord called for his son, and, taking him on his knee,

asked him if he remembered the story he had told him of the little boy who always spoke the truth. "Yes, papa," said the child. "Then," said my Lord, "will you be a good boy like him, that I may love you?" "Yes, papa," said the child. "Well, then, tell me truly what you did with the piece of lace you tore from this?" holding up the fragment. The child coloured as red as scarlet: and my Lord kissing him, very mildly, and, in a cheerful encouraging voice, repeated the question "I – I believe – I hid it, papa," said he.

"Where did you hide it, my dear? tell me truly, and you shall have a ride upon the little horse this very evening." The boy looked round for Jenny, as fearing to displease her: but her face was hid from him by the back of the chair; and his papa seeing how it was, asked if Jenny had helped him to hide it? "No, no." "Where then had he put it?" "He had put it," he said; "in the back of his coat." This seemed very unintelligible; but, as he persisted in it, my Lord begged of Miss Osburne to desire one of the maids to bring all the child's clothes into the room. Jenny would have gone for them, but was not permitted to leave the room. As soon as they were brought in, Lord Lintop pointed to the little green coat, which I well remembered him to have worn, and, turning it over, shewed a rip in the seam, just by the pocket hole, which Miss Osburne enlarged with her scissors, and in a moment produced the lace. "You are a good boy, indeed," exclaimed my Lord, again caressing the child. "Now tell me, Charles, whether the piece of lace that you threw into the fire was completely burned or not?" "I don't know indeed, papa: for I was very naughty; but I won't be naughty again, if you will forgive me. I did not intend to tear the lace, but was only just making a rope of it about my neck; and so Mrs Mason flew to take it from me, and I did not like to have it taken; and held it, and we struggled a great while – and – and –"

"And you were angry, and threw the other piece into the fire, to vex Mrs Mason: did you not?"

"Yes, papa."

"You are an excellent evidence," cried my Lord, "and shall have the ride I promised you; but now, mark the consequences of being naughty. Look at that woman there (turning to Jenny); see how she is overwhelmed by shame and disgrace, for having wickedly persevered in telling a wicked lie, which she probably thought would never be detected. But liars never escape detection; sooner or later they fall into their own snares." Jenny loudly sobbing, now fell down upon her knees to ask forgiveness; but my Lord, waving his hand, bade her instantly leave the room, and deliver up to his mother's maid all that she had in her charge. "Nor dare, upon your life," cried he, "to approach this boy, or to speak one single word to him while you live. Go, vile woman, – had I known your character, I should sooner have seen him in his grave, than placed him under your care!"

I was really sorry for the poor girl, and was bold enough to intercede for her, but to no purpose. My Lord was inflexible: "for a liar," he said, "could have no good principle." "His Lordship acts wisely, and nobly," cried Miss Osburne; "and now that no doubt can rest upon the integrity of poor Mason, I hope, Madam, you will not part with her?"

"I have no wish to part with her," said my Lady. "That is not sufficient," rejoined Lord Longlands; "she has been injured, and the injury must be repaired." Then ringing the bell, he desired the housekeeper and Jackson, with all the other servants who were at hand, to attend. They quickly obeyed the summons; very anxious to know what was going forward.

As soon as they were all assembled, my Lord addressed them in a speech which I shall never forget. "I sent for you," said he, "in order to inform you, that the woman who has left the room, is discarded from my service, on account of her having been guilty of telling a wicked and malicious lie, in order to throw the blame of a trifling accident upon an innocent person. It likewise has been proved to our satisfaction, that the conduct of this young woman, whom she would have injured, has not only been blameless, but highly meritorious; for she has shewn that she feared God, by speaking the truth before him with an upright heart. For what you have suffered, Mrs Mason," added he, "both my mother and I are heartily sorry; and my son, who was the first occasion of it, is ready to make you all the reparation in his power, by asking your pardon. – Go, child, and ask Mrs Mason to forgive you."

I would have prevented his having the mortification, but

my lord insisted that he should; and then taking from his purse this large gold piece, he presented it to me, desiring me to keep it as a memorial of the happy consequences that result from a faithful adherence to truth and sincerity.

Here Mrs Mason shewed the gold coin to Miss Mary Stewart. And as speaking of its history led to a digression, which it is unnecessary to follow, we shall close the Chapter.

Chapter IV

History of Mrs Mason continued

As soon as an opportunity offered for resuming her story, Mrs Mason, at Mary's request, proceeded as follows: –

"My Lord Longlands left the castle in a day or two for Merriton Hall; and on the day after his arrival there, he wrote to Miss Osburne, to inform her, that he had prevailed on his intended bride to take me into her service as her waiting maid; and hoped Miss Osburne would prevail on his mother to part with me, to which the old dowager did not very readily consent. But though she made a great favour of it, it was at length happily settled; and on the night that Lord and Lady Longlands arrived at the castle, after their marriage, I entered on my place. I found my young mistress so amiable, so reasonable, and sweet tempered, that pleasing her would have been an easy task, even to one less disposed to please her than I was. I was congratulated by all the servants on my promotion, and indeed thought myself the happiest creature in the world. But my happiness was soon overcast; for in the midst of all the bustle of this first and only gay season at the castle, your dear mother, my kind benefactress, was seized with a fever of a very malignant and dangerous nature. She was three days ill before the dowager lady could be persuaded that any thing ailed her but a cold; but when the doctor was at last sent for, and explained the nature of her complaint, all communication was cut between the tower and the other part of the house; and, as I had already exposed myself to the infection, I was, at my earnest entreaty, permitted to remain with the dear sufferer, whom I nursed night and day for several weeks. Nor did I ever catch the infection; from which I was preserved, under Providence, by the attention I paid to the doctor's advice; for, though the weather was then cold, I followed his directions in keeping the windows constantly up, so that a current of fresh air passed continually through the room, which was a great comfort to the patient, and I believe tended more to her recovery than all the medicines she swallowed.

At length, thank God, she did recover; and, O, how

much did she then overrate the little service I had had it in my power to perform! For what did I more than was my bounden duty? Never shall I forget the day she first was permitted to go down stairs. With what unfeigned piety did she return thanks to the Almighty for her preservation! How earnestly did she pray, that the life He had preserved might be spent in his service, and in the service of her fellow creatures! And it was so spent; I am certain that it was, though I, alas! had no longer the benefit of beholding her example: for, before she recovered, my lord and lady had set off for England, and had reached their seat in Yorkshire, to which I was ordered to follow them by the stagecoach.

I was much agitated at the thoughts of leaving the castle, though I expected to return to it with my lady in the following summer. But it had been my little world, and I was a stranger to all without its walls: and, where I was going, I should have no kind Miss Osburne to direct and counsel me; no one who cared for me as Jackson did; or the old house-keeper, for whom I regularly knit a pair or two of lamb's wool stockings every year as long as she lived. I went away loaded with keepsakes from her, and from Jackson, and indeed from all the servants in the family, who vied with each other in shewing their good will. I did not see the dowager countess; but Jackson told me, she was in such bad humour at my lord taking his son away to send to school, that she could not see any one with pleasure who was going to his house. Your poor mamma suffered more from this bad temper of the old lady, than the servants did; but she neither complained of it herself, nor would suffer a complaint of it to be made before her. I durst not even drop a hint of it when we parted, which we did with many tears on both sides.

I was received very graciously by my amiable mistress, and had the comfort of finding a very well regulated family, where, though there was a number of servants, there was no confusion, every one's business being so well ordered, and so distinctly defined. My lady in arranging her household was much indebted to the advice of an old aunt, a maiden lady who lived with her, and who had a great deal of good sense, and, with a sober and religious turn of mind, was at the same time so lively and chearful, that her company was liked by young and old.

The family soon went to London, where my lord and
lady were obliged to go to great assemblies, and to places of
public amusement, as other great people do; but Miss
Malden never went to any of these places, and when they
were out, spent all her time in reading. As her eyes were
weak, she was obliged to employ her maid to read for her,
which the poor girl thought a grievous task. Upon her complaining of it to me, I told her how willingly I should relieve
her, if she could prevail on her lady to accept my services.
On the first evening that she happened to be alone, I was
accordingly sent for. The book that she was then engaged
in, was a history of the Old World, before the coming of
our Saviour. The subject was new to me, and the names
were many of them very hard; but as I took pains, I soon
got into the way of pronouncing them. And Miss Malden
observing that I took pleasure in understanding what I read,
was so kind as to take the trouble of explaining to me all
the difficult passages. She said she was sensible, that to one
like me, it could be of little consequence to know what
had been done so many ages ago by great kings and warriors, but that there was no sort of knowledge without its
use. That the observations I made upon the consequences
of the pride, vain glory, and ambition of those conspicuous
characters of whom we read, would improve the powers of
my understanding, and open my mind to perceive the value
of those Christian principles, which led to peace here, and
happiness hereafter: and to prove that it was not in the
power of all the riches, or all the glory of the world, to give
content; for that to fear God, and keep his commandments,
was the end of life. I learned a great deal from the comments of this good lady, upon what I read to her; and as all
her instructions were given with a view to strengthen me
in the performance of duty, I have reason to be thankful
for such an opportunity of improvement. During the five
years that she lived, I continued to be her reader every
winter; for it was only in winter that she was ever left alone
by my lady who, when in the country, lived a very domestic
life. She had all this time but one drawback on her happiness, – the want of children; but at length this blessing was
also granted; and in the sixth year of her marriage, she produced a daughter. The joy of this event was clouded by
the death of her good aunt, who expired after a short ill-

ness, before Lady Harriot was six weeks old. Her death
was the death of the righteous, full of faith, and hope, and
joy. She saw that it would be a loss to my lady, whose only
fault was an extreme indolence of temper; but she did what
she could to counsel her against the consequences. And
among other pieces of advice, recommended it to her, to
place the whole management of her nursery under my care.
My lady told me this, when she proposed it to me, and told
me also the reasons she had given, which were too honourable for me to repeat. I knew nothing of the management
of children, but resolved to fulfil the trust to the best of my
abilities, and to spare no pains to learn the best modes of
treating them, in sickness and in health. As the family
increased, my duties enlarged; but the only, and the perpetual difficulty with which I had to struggle, arose from the
obstinacy and self sufficiency of the nurses. Knowing, however, that I had the authority of my lord and lady on my
side, I generally prevailed; and after two or three months,
brought them into my ways: but I saw enough to convince
me, how sadly off the children of great families must be,
when they are left altogether to the management of such
sort of people.

Finding it to be the great object with the nurses to save
themselves trouble, I laboured to convince them, that, by
firmly adhering to my plan, they would most certainly
attain their end: for, that nothing could be so troublesome
as children, whose tempers were spoiled by mismanagement. Very little trouble, indeed, did these little darlings
cost to any of them; and as to myself, the constant vigilance
with which I watched over them, was a source of pleasure
and delight. From being always kindly treated, and having
their little humours checked in the bud, from a certainty,
that they would never obtain their object by crying, or by
peevishness, they were the most docile and tractable little
creatures in the world. They learned to be thankful for all
that was done for them, and to treat others with respect, as
they themselves were treated. As they were never out of
my sight, I could answer for it, that they never saw or heard
a thing that was improper, nor witnessed a single instance
of falsehood or deceit. You may imagine how much I
became attached to them, and yet it is impossible that you
should: for none but a mother, and a fond mother, can

know what my heart felt, and still feels towards them. My love for them made every thing a pleasure; and while a sense of being accountable to God for the manner in which I discharged my trust encreased my diligence, I was full of gratitude for being appointed to the delightful task.

Some months after the birth of Master Edward, the fourth and last of her children, my lady went with my lord to Scotland, to pay a visit to the countess dowager, whom they had never seen since the year they were married; owing to some quarrel about an estate, which the old lady would not give up to my lord, though he had a right to it, and she had no other child but himself. But her heart was set upon the world, and when that is the case, it signifies little whether people be poor or rich, for they still think they can never have enough: and though they have much more than they can use, they go on craving and craving for more, till they drop into the grave. So it was with the old lady, who got fonder of money every year she lived; and though she would not part with the estate, she was brought to forgive my lord for claiming it, and expressed a wish to see him, which his lady urged him to comply with.

I should much have liked to have gone with them, but they resolved on leaving all the children under my care in Yorkshire, except Master Meriton, the elder of the two young gentlemen, who was to accompany them, attended by the woman who had been his nurse.

The two young ladies, and the infant with his nurse were left entirely to my care; and, thank God, all that I undertook to do for them prospered. In order to be able to instruct them, I was at pains to instruct myself. Lady Charlotte, though little more than five years old, could read very prettily; and in reading, neither she nor any of the other children ever had another mistress, nor had I any trouble in teaching them; for though I gave them very short lessons, I had got the way of making them attend to their book while they were engaged with it, and took care that they should never find it wearisome. When my lord and lady returned, they expressed the highest satisfaction with the progress that their children had made; and, to shew their satisfaction, made me a handsome present, which was more precious to me, on account of its being a proof of approbation, than ten times its value. I was not, however, to get leave to enjoy it in peace; for I soon observed, that it had stirred up the envy of Mrs Dickens, who, during, the time they had been in Scotland, had insinuated herself into my lady's favour in an extraordinary manner, and conscious of her influence, she took every occasion of shewing that she would not be directed by me.

The girl who kept Master Edward had been in a manner brought up to the business under my immediate eye; she was a staid and sober person, of good principles, and very diligent in the discharge of her duty; but she soon became the object of dislike to Mrs Dickens, who, as I afterwards found, told my lady in secret a thousand lies of the poor girl. All now went wrong. Contention followed contention. I gave up many things, for the sake of peace; every thing indeed except where the interests of the children were at stake; but there I thought it my duty to be firm.

I shall not trouble you with an account of all the ways which this wicked woman employed to effect her purpose, and she did effect it; for she had contrived to make my lady think, that I set my judgment above hers, and boasted of having more authority in the nursery than her ladyship had, and that all the people in it were my servants. My lady was too indolent to make strict inquiry into the truth. Mrs Dickens had made herself agreeable by flattering her about the children, whom she praised as if they had not been human creatures: while I, wishing my lady to throw her praise and blame into the proper scales, was at pains to point out their faults, as well as their perfections. Still, however, my lady had too much regard for me to hurt my feelings.

In order to gratify Dickens, without appearing to blame me, she, on our going up to town, told me, that my lord and she had resolved to make an alteration in the establishment; to place the two young ladies under my care, and the children in the nursery under the care of Dickens.

I had nothing to do but to obey. An apartment was fitted up for the young ladies and me, immediately under the nursery, which was at the very top of the house. It consisted of a sitting room, in which was a settee bed for me to sleep on, and opened with folding doors into a small room, in which were two field beds for the young ladies. I had reason to rejoice in the change, for I once more lived in peace; but I was not without anxiety on account of the dear infants, as I by no means thought the woman, who had been taken on Mrs Dickens's recommendation to supply the place of Peggy, was at all equal to the charge. But as my opinion was not asked, I had no right to give it, nor indeed had I many opportunities of observation, as our establishments were quite distinct We came to town in November, and it was now the end of March; the 28th was Mr Meriton's birth-day, who was then three years old. It was kept with great pomp and splendour, all the first company in London were invited to the great ball that was given on the occasion; and as the housekeeper had a great deal to do, I, after the young ladies went to bed, gave her all the assistance in my power, which kept me up long beyond my usual time I was very much fatigued, and consequently very much inclined to sleep; but sleepy as I was, the habit of watchfulness was so strong in me, that I awaked at every little noise that stirred. I thought I heard a sort of crackling in the nursery over my head, and sat up to listen; but it ceased, and I again returned to rest. In about half an hour I was again awoke. The room was full of smoke, and the smell of fire so strong that I had but a moment for recollection; but, thank God, my presence of mind did not forsake me, I flew to the beds of my little charges; and taking up Lady Harriet in my arms, and dragging Lady Charlotte half asleep after me, I hastened to the stairs: the smoke came from above, so that as we went down, we breathed more freely, and reached my lady's room in an instant. The door was unbolted; it was no time for ceremony, I rushed in; but mindful of my lady's situation, I spoke as calmly as in such circumstances was possible. I intreated them instantly to rise, but did not wait to say more; for seeing the smoke increase, I hastened on with the children, crying out "fire!" to alarm the servants above and below. The housekeeper was the first to hear me: to her I left the children, and again flew up stairs. I met my lord, carrying my lady in his arms, and calling out for help; but I did not stop, for I knew they were in safety.

I was soon at the foot of the nursery stairs. But oh! what a smoke had I then to pass through! how I got through it, God only knows; for it was his Almighty arm that supported me. On opening the nursery door, the flames burst out upon me; but I had had a thought how it would be, and had wrapped myself in a blanket, which I knew the flames would not lay hold of, as they would upon my cotton night-gown. I could not speak for suffocation; but getting to the first of the two beds, I dragged off the clothes from Mrs Dickens, which was all I could do to awaken her. I then seized the child, who slept in a little bed beside her, and was making my way out, when the little infant set up a scream. He slept with his maid in a detached bed, to which the flames had not yet reached, but all between was in a blaze. I made a spring, and reached the place: but no maid was there, only the child alone. I snatched him up beneath my arm, and, again passing by her, made an effort to call out to poor Dickens. She started up, and I thought followed me; but this effort to save her had nearly cost me dear; for I thought I should have expired instantly. Providence restored my strength, and darting through the flames, I got to the top of the stairs, where, I believe, I fainted, for I fell down the whole flight altogether senseless; nor do I remember anything further, till I found myself in a strange bed, with strange faces round me.

I called out to ask if the children were safe? "They are; they are safe!" returned a voice which I knew to be my lord's. He advanced to my bed-side. "You are my preserver, Mason," said he; "thank God you are restored to life. We shall never forget that you have saved us and ours from destruction. Think in the mean time of nothing but of taking care of yourself."

Pain now reminded me of the escape I had made. The pain I suffered was indeed excessive; nor could it be other-wise, for I had broke my thigh bone in the fall, and dis-located the joint immediately above; so that I soon knew that lameness for life would be my portion. But the thoughts of having been instrumental in saving the lives of the family, was a cordial which kept up my heart. Still, how-ever, I was very anxious to learn all the particulars of the sad disaster. The nurse who took care of me, would tell me nothing. There was no use in asking the surgeons; for they only desired me to keep myself quiet, and to give myself no anxiety.

In a few days the housekeeper came to see me, and

though she resolved to be extremely cautious, she could not resist the temptation of being the first to tell me all.

"I was scarcely in my senses with fright," said she, "but flew, as you desired me, to awaken the servants. And men and women were all up in a minute, some flying one way, and some another, till my lord brought them all to order by his commanding voice. He sent one to alarm the neighbours; one for the fire engines; and one over all the way to the Colonel's, to ask shelter for the family; and placing my lady in a chair by the parlour door, he ran up stairs again in distraction, thinking his sons were lost. The smoke was so thick he did not see you, but he heard your fall, and received his children from your arms, though you knew nothing of it. Two of the men were at his back; and he made them lift you, and carry you over with the rest: for my lady was by this time carried over likewise, and all the children. In the midst of this bustle, some one called out for James, but no one had seen him. I went to his door, but it was locked. At last he answered. "Don't you know that the house is on fire," cried I? He first swore, and then blessed himself, but out he came sure enough, and who came with him do you think, but Sally, the saucy minx, crying and screaming, that she was ruined! she was ruined!

"Ruined!" cried I, "who cares for your being ruined? but what will you say to setting my lord's house on fire, and burning all the family in their beds!" No more time was there for speaking; the staircase was all in a blaze. The flames came with such speed, that little could be saved even out of my lord's room, except papers, and such like. We were all obliged to fly with what we had on, and all were safe except poor Mrs Dickens."

"And did she perish!" cried I, in great agony. "O yes, poor soul," returned the housekeeper, "she did indeed perish! Never was there anything so horrid, or so shocking! God in his mercy preserve us all from such a dreadful end!"

Here poor Mrs Nelson perceiving how much I was agitated, and recollecting that she had been warned against telling me the woeful tale, stopped short to comfort me, and entreated that I would deny having heard any thing of the matter from her.

"O no," said I, "Mrs Nelson; let us never allow ourselves

to depart from truth; it is the beginning of all iniquity. But O that unhappy woman! hurried into eternity with all her sins upon her head! without a moment, a single moment, to pray for mercy on her soul. And yet, perhaps, she might, perhaps" –

"No, no," cried Mrs Nelson, "she was in no state to pray; for she was in a state of intoxication, utterly deprived of her senses. Sally has confessed all. You never heard such plans of wickedness. Sally, it seems, had been her emissary and confidant, when they lived together at Sir William Blendon's. And it was with a view to get her to be under her, that she fell out with Peggy, and got her turned out, and got all the management of the nursery to herself. They then went on at full career, no one to coutroul them, going out, one or other of them, night after night, to the feasts and junkettings which in this wicked town go on among servants all the winter. And for the men servants, there may to be sure be some excuse, for you know, poor fellows, they never get leave to go to bed till morning, and it cannot be expected that they should sit and mope alone; but then when they carouse together, they entice the maids to meet them, by giving them balls, and treats, and such like, of which no good can come, nor, to be sure, would any woman, who regards her character, go to be seen at such places, though they were to be made, as Sally was, queen of the ball. For it seems she was greatly taken out, and had more lovers than any of them among the footmen. Mrs Dickens did not go to meet lovers, but to get drunk; and when she staid at home, Sally brought her enough to please her; but she never ventured on a great dose till near bed time, when she was pretty sure of being safe. One night indeed my lady came up to the nursery when she was conscious of being in no condition to speak to her, and what do you think the wicked woman did? It makes ones hair stand on end to think of it! Why she fell down on her knees, and pretended to be saying her prayers! and as my lady would not disturb her devotions by speaking, she thought she had a fine escape. O poor woman! little did she think how soon she should be called to answer for this hypocrisy, without a moment's time to pray for mercy on her soul!"

It seems that on the night of the fire, Sally, having an

assignation with James, pressed her to take even more than her usual quantity; and as she was very far gone, she was obliged to help her in taking off her clothes, and in getting into bed, that bed from which she was no more to rise! Sally, after having watched till all was quiet, put out her candle, as she thought; but she confessed she only turned it down, for she never would use an extinguisher, and as the candlesticks have wide sockets, a long piece of small candle can scarcely be put down in them, without the chance of turning over: but did not wait to see, whether it did or no; nor is she certain, whether she might not have let a spark fall into the linen-press, where she had just been with the candle; for she says she never had any fear of fire in all her life, and whenever she went into a press, always thrust the candle before her, without dread or care.

"It was," I said, "from the linen-press that the flames issued, when I entered the room."

"That might be," said Mrs Neilson; "but the chair with the candle was just beside it, so there is no saying which took fire first."

"And was there no attempt made to save Mrs Dickens?" cried I; "did she never awake?"

"Yes, yes," said Mrs Neilson, "she awoke, and got to the windows; the people of the street saw her, and heard her screams; for she screamed most terribly! and they got a ladder, and put it up, and thought to have brought her down on it, but before anyone could make the top, the floor fell in, and she disappeared!" Here Mrs Mason was obliged to pause, so much was she agitated with the recollection of this dreadful scene. When she had a little recovered, she proceeded, as will be found in the next Chapter.

Chapter V

Mrs Mason's Story concluded

As soon as the doctors thought it safe for me to speak to them, the children were brought to see me; and you may imagine what joy it gave me to embrace the little darlings, and to hear them tell me, that they knew I had saved their lives; and that God had permitted me to save them, because He loved me for being good. Pretty little creatures! I shall never forget how their fond expressions went to my heart. They were attended by Peggy, who was sent for by my lady, and taken back into her service as soon as she learned all the history of the impositions practised by Dickens to get her away.

I was, however, grieved by the bad accounts of my lady's health. She continued poorly, and my lord thinking she would be better in the country, took a furnished house at Richmond, about four miles from London, where she was shortly after delivered of a dead child. Her recovery was long doubtful; and by the doctor's advice, my lord went with her to spend the summer at Clifton, near the Bristol hot-wells; which seemed to me like a sentence of death, for it is there that people who have consumptions are, if able to afford it, sent to die. But it pleased God, that my lady should not be taken from her family so soon.

By the time that I was able to go to Clifton, which was about the middle of July, I found her restored almost to usual health. I could then only walk on crutches, but I was so wearied of doing nothing, that I was very anxious to resume my duty; and as I had one of my lord's carriages to travel in, I could suffer nothing from the journey.

I was extremely anxious before leaving London to see Sally, who had been represented to me as suffering under all the horrors of remorse, on account of the misfortunes she had occasioned; but it was not till after many messages, that I could prevail on her to come to me. She, however, came at length; and began, as soon as she saw me, to profess her sorrow for what I suffered, and to beg my forgiveness. She wept bitterly; and hoping that her heart was touched by penitence, I endeavoured to comfort her, by expatiating on

the mercies of God, and on the hopes that were held forth
in the Gospel to those who truly repented of their sins.

It was a language she did not understand, for she had
been brought up in deplorable ignorance; and told me she
had never heard any body speak of such things, but a neighbour, who was a Methodist, and that she thought it had
been all tabernacle talk. It was very melancholy to hear a
woman, in whom the greatest of all possible trusts had been
reposed, acknowledge herself thus ignorant of all the doctrines of Christianity. What wonder that her moral conduct
should have been so bad! for on what foundation can the
moral conduct of one in her station, or indeed in any
station, rest, when you take away the fear of God?

Hoping that I might by my instructions make some
impression upon her mind, I spared no pains with this
unfortunate creature; and might, I really believe, have succeeded in confirming her good resolutions, had she not
been laid hold of by some enthusiasts, who laboured at
what they called her conversion. Before any good habit had
been formed, and while her mind was yet in a state of profound ignorance, her imagination was so warmed by their
discourses, as to make her boast of being in a state of grace;
and before I left London, her divine raptures were quoted
by some of these pious visionaries, as a proof of saintship.
But, alas! the fire of zeal was soon exhausted; and the poor
creature being destitute of solid principle, and considering
herself in a state of reprobation, flew to the society of her
former associates, as a resource from thought. The consequences were dreadful: she was soon plunged into vice, and
died in misery; but this did not come to my knowledge for
several years.

On going to Clifton, I was received by my lord and lady
more like a friend than a servant. They indeed told me, that
I was to be as a servant no longer: for that I was henceforth
to be English governess to their children, with a salary of
thirty pounds a year. A Swiss governess for the young
ladies had been already some weeks with them; and though,
I confess, I had a sort of prejudice against her at first, on
account of her being a foreigner, I soon found that she was
a person of great integrity, and had a truly pious and amiable mind. She was as agreeably disappointed in me as I was
in her: for she thought it impossible that a person could

be so suddenly raised, without assuming some airs of arrogance and self-conceit. But I had seen enough of this to be upon my guard, lest my heart should be puffed up; and had always thought it a base thing in a person, who saw themselves regarded more than others, to take advantage of it for the indulgence of their own capricious humours. For twelve years, Mademoiselle and I went on hand in hand, labouring for the good of our pupils; and had the pleasure of seeing them grow up, under our eyes, promising to be blessings to the land, and the pleasure and glory of all their connexions.

My lord and lady doated on their children; and well they might, for never were any like them. The young ladies, so graceful, so sweet-tempered, and so accomplished! and the young gentlemen, so well behaved, and at the same time so clever, that all their masters said, they learned better and faster than any scholars they had. Lady Charlotte was very handsome; and had many admirers, before she was out eighteen; but she had no liking to any of them; and said, she should never marry any on whom she could not look up to as a friend and guide. She was just nineteen when young Sir William Bandon came to spend the Christmas holidays at the Park; and I soon perceived, by the way she spoke of him, that his attentions were agreeable to her. We went up to town, and Sir William soon after declared himself. My lord was highly pleased with his character; so that every thing was soon agreed on, and the marriage was to take place at Easter; but, alas! before Easter, my lord was carried off by a fever of less than a fortnight's duration.

By this event, all our joy was changed into mourning. I could not have felt more if I had lost a father. He was, indeed, as a father to all his dependants. A friend to the poor; and, in all his conduct, and example to poor and rich. He had great influence; and he made it his business to exert it for the glory of God, and the good of society. O what a change did his death occasion! succeeded as he was by one so little like himself!

Lord Lintop had indeed never been a comfortable son to him; but my lord left him no excuse, for he was the kindest and best of fathers. My lady too, had, from the time he was a boy, done all in her power to gain his affections; but he had an inveterate prejudice against her, on account of her being a stepmother – a prejudice which, I verily believe, was first sown in the nursery by his maid, Jenny Thomson, who used always to threaten him with a step-mother as with a monster – and he never got the better of the impression. He was indeed of a cold and reserved temper, and had a very narrow heart. Much inclined to avarice, except upon his own pleasures, and they were all of the selfish sort.

As my lord died without a will, he immediately entered upon possession of all. My lady having nothing at her disposal but her own fortune, and her jointure, which was to be sure very great; yet I thought it a sad thing to see her and her children turned out, as it were, of her own house, and obliged to go to seek a place to lay her head. But to her, alas! it was of no consequence where she went; the hand of death was on her, and in three months she followed my lord to the grave!

"I find I must pass over this," said Mrs Mason, wiping the tears from her eyes: "there is no need of distressing you with an account of all my sorrows. It was the least of them, that I found myself without a home! I had saved of my wages about one hundred and fifty pounds, which my lord's steward had placed out for me, at five per cent in the public funds. Lady Charlotte, upon her marriage, presented me with fifty more, and promised to give me twenty pounds a year, until her own brother, Mr Meriton, should come of age. I would have refused the annuity, but she insisted on it, saying she was ashamed it was so little; but that Lord Longland's taking advantage of a clause in her mother's settlement, had refused paying her fortune, till her brother Edward was of age: "and then," said she, "Mrs Mason," throwing her arms affectionately round my neck, "then we may all be happy." She had written to her brothers she said; for I forgot to mention, that they had the year before, been sent abroad, to their travels with their tutor, and are now, I believe, in Switzerland, where Lady Charlotte and Sir William are to see them in their way to Italy. They pressed me to accompany them; but my lameness was such an obstacle, that I could not think of going to be a burthen to them; and while I hoped that Lady Harriet would be left at home, I wished to stay, that I might be near her; but at length the guardians consented that she should go with her sister, so I was at once bereft of them all.

Thus have I been suddenly, in the course of a few months, deprived of all my earthly comforts, and thrown from a state of ease and luxury into a state of comparative indigence. But how ungrateful should I be to God, were I to repine! How rich would my poor mother have thought herself with thirty pounds a year! Nay, with the half of that sum. Ill would it then become me to murmur at the wise dispensations of Providence, which have doubtless been ordered not less in wisdom than in mercy. My first thoughts were to go into a lodging in London, and take in needlework, by which I should be able to earn a sufficiency for the supply of all my wants, but from being unable to take exercise, good air has become so essential to my health, that I dreaded the consequences of being pent up in the unwholesome atmosphere of that immense place; and had besides such a hankering after my native country, that I wished of all things to return to it. While I was still hesitating, a young man, who came up to London to seek a situation as a gardener, brought a letter to me from a niece of Jackson's, with whom I had continued to correspond; and by his conversation, concerning all the friends of my youth, increased my desire of revisiting scenes that were still dear to my recollection. He told me of a cottage near Hill Castle that was now empty; and advised me to ask it of the young earl, who could not surely refuse such a trifle to one who had been so long in the family, and to whom, as he said, the family owed such obligation. But he was mistaken. I petitioned for it, and was refused.

Perhaps to soften the refusal I was at the same time told that Lord Longlands had resolved against having any cottages on his estate, and was to have them all destroyed.

"True," said Miss Mary, "it is very true, indeed. My father was directed to give orders for that purpose, but took the liberty of remonstrating. All that he could do, however, was to prevent the poor cottars from being turned out for another term, but they are all to go at Martinmas; and as fast as their houses are empty, they are to be thrown down. The cottage you wish for is already demolished to the very ground, and has left the place so desolate! It goes to one's heart to see it. But after refusing it to you, the owner can have no heart. I hope you will never ask another favour from him while you live!"

"I hope I shall have no need," replied Mrs Mason. "But though I should have been thankful for his granting my request, I have no right to resent his refusing me."

"And I shall thank him for refusing you, if it brings you to live nearer us," said Miss Mary.

"Though I shall be at double the distance, still it won't be far," returned Mrs Mason. "I am to take up my residence at Glenburnie."

"At Glenburnie!" repeated Miss Mary; "what place can there be at Glenburnie fit for you to live in?"

"O I shall make it fit," said Mrs Mason; "and if I am so happy as to be useful to the good people there, I shall think myself fortunate in my choice. On being refused by Lord Longlands, I gave up all thoughts of settling on his territories, and made inquiries in the neighbourhood of Meriton. Through the friends of the young man I have already mentioned, I heard that the only relation I have in the world was married to one of the small farmers in Glenburnie, and to this couple I applied to take me as a lodger. I had great difficulty in bringing them to the point, as they feared I would not be pleased with the accommodation; but at length with them three months upon trial, and that at the end of that time we should each be at liberty to separate without offence. From all that I have heard, no situation could be more suitable to my purpose. In a place where money is scarce, my income, slender as it is, may be useful. After a life of full employment I could not be happy in idleness; and as these good people have a large family, I shall have among them constant employment, in the way that habit has rendered most delightful to me, that of training youth to usefulness and virtue."

Miss Mary began her fears of the trouble to which Mrs Mason was about to bring upon her own head, when her father entered; and from the way in which he spoke upon the subject, she soon saw that he had already discussed it, and knew Mrs Mason's determination to be unalterable. They, however, prevailed upon her to remain their guest for another night; and obtained her promise, that if her situation at Glenburnie proved uncomfortable, she would return to Gowan-brae.

Chapter VI

Domestic Sketches – Picture of Glenburnie – View of a Scotch Cottage in the last century

Early on the following morning, Mr Stewart and Miss Mary met to consult together, upon the means they should employ to render Mrs Mason's situation at the farmer's somewhat comfortable; and after some deliberation, resolved, that they would postpone, till they had visited the place, and seen what the house afforded.

In the course of their conversation, Miss Mary expressed her surprise, that so good a couple as the Earl and Countess of Longlands should not have thought it an incumbent duty, to make an ample provision for one who had rendered them such important services.

"You are mistaken," said Mr Stewart, "they were not deficient in gratitude, and to my certain knowledge, intended to settle on her a very liberal independency. But my lord was still in the prime of life, and thought he had many years to live. He therefore delayed to do, what he imagined might at any time be accomplished: and after his death, his lady, who was always indolent, gave herself up to the indulgence of grief, to the utter forgetfulness of every duty; but of this you will have no hint from Mrs Mason: for hers is truly a good mind, and one that sees every thing in the best light. She knows not what I have endeavoured to do for her with the present lord, and she shall never know it, for it would only hurt her to be assured of his total want of liberality and gratitude."

Mr Stewart was here interrupted by the unexpected entrance of his eldest daughter, and her friend Mrs Flinders, whose animated looks bespoke the near prospect of some new scheme of pleasure. After a few preliminary remarks on the fineness of the season, &c. &c. Mrs Flinders gradually disclosed the purpose of her visit, which was no other than to obtain Mr Stewart's consent to his daughter's accompanying her to the Edinburgh races. Mr Stewart

was on many accounts adverse to the proposal; nor did
Mrs Flinders's assurances of the great advantages to be
derived to a young lady, from being seen in public, and
introduced to all the people of fashion at the races, produce
the least alteration in his sentiments: But he had not firmness to resist the torrent of intreaty; and after having permitted a reluctant consent to be extorted from him, the
remaining articles were easily adjusted. His daughter had no
difficulty in obtaining from him the money she thought
requisite for the purchase of new dresses; and her sister,
ever willing to promote her gratification, promised to pack
up, and send her, with other things, some handsome ornaments that had been presented to her by a near relation, to
whom she had paid attention in a fit of illness.

Elated with her victory, Bell seemed to tread on air; and
after she got into the carriage, called out to her sister, that
she should write her a full account of the race week. She
bowed graciously to her father as the carriage drove off; but
he appeared not to notice the salute. Pensive and dissatis-
fied, he returned to the house, and found Mary with Mrs
Mason, giving her an account of all that had just passed.
"Well," said he, addressing himself to Mrs Mason, "you
have heard of the new trouble that has been prepared for
me by this giddy woman, to whom Bell has unfortunately
attached herself? These races! How unfit a scene for a young
woman in my daughter's station; and under how unfit a
conductor will she there appear! I wish I had been more
firm; but I could not. O that she were not too headstrong
to take advice, and too self-sufficient to think that she
stands in need of an adviser. I am troubled about her intimacy with these Flinders's more than I can express."

"But, Sir," said Mrs Mason, "have you not a right to dictate to your daughter what company she ought to keep? If
you really think Mrs Flinders an improper associate, why
do you permit her to go to her house?"

"Because," replied Mr Stewart, "I cannot bear to see my
child unhappy. I have not courage to encounter sour looks,
and all the murmurings of discontent. This girl, who is
when in good humour so lively and engaging, treats every
opposition to her will as an act of cruel tyranny; and I cannot bear being treated by the child I doat on as a tyrant."

"Still my dear Sir," said Mrs Mason, "as Miss Stewart

is not deficient in understanding, you might, I think, by a little firmness, teach her the propriety of submitting to your will."

"Alas!" returned Mr Stewart, "she always thinks herself in the right; and it is impossible, utterly impossible, to convince her, in any instance, that she is otherwise. Her mind got a wrong bias from the first, and I fear it is now too late to think of curing it. But I have myself to blame. Had she been brought up with the rest of my family, under the watchful eye of their dear mother, she would never have been thus froward and intractable, yet I know not how our other children escaped spoiling, for my wife was all tenderness and indulgence."

"True," replied Mrs Mason, "but her indulgence would be of a nature tending to foster the best affections of the heart, not the indulgence of the passions, which engenders pride and selfishness."

"Your distinction is a just one," said Mr Stewart, "but unhappily her grandmother could not discriminate; and after the death of my parents, Bell came home to us, when I saw that she was too unmanageable for her mother's gentle spirit to controul; and I therefore urged sending her to a school, where a daughter of a friend was going; but there, alas! instead of getting quit of her bad habits, she lost the good that counterbalanced them, and acquired such a love of dress, and so many foolish notions about gentility, as have utterly destroyed all relish for domestic happiness. Think of her flying off as she has done, the very day that we expect her brothers home from school! Is it not heartless?"

"So she will admit when she is herself a mother," replied Mrs Mason. – The rest of her speech was lost; for from the bark of joy which the dogs began to send forth, Mr Stewart perceived that his sons were near at hand, and eagerly flew out to meet them. They were already folded in Mary's arms, and sprung to their father with all the alacrity of confiding love. Every care was now forgotten, without doors and within, above stairs and below, all was holiday at Gowan-brae. Mrs Mason, to whom the sight of a happy family afforded one of the highest gratifications, was no unmoved spectator of the joyful scene. She readily consented to postpone her departure till the following day, and

promoted, by her cheerfulness, all the amusements of the
evening.

In order to gratify the boys, it was proposed, that the
whole party should accompany Mrs Mason to Glenburnie,
on an Irish car, a vehicle well adapted to such excursions,
and which was consequently a great favourite with the
younger part of the family. Just as they finished an early
dinner, the car was brought to the door. Robert, the eldest
boy, begged leave to drive, to which, as the roads were
good, and the horse steady, Mr Stewart made no objection.
They were all seated in a moment; Mrs Mason and Mr
Stewart on one side, and Mary and her two younger
brothers on the other. Robert vaulting into his proper
station, seized the reins, and, after two gentle strokes with
the whip, prevailed on old gray to move forward, which he
did very sagaciously, with less speed than caution, until
they reached the turnpike road, where he mended his pace
into a sober trot, which in less than two hours brought
them to the road that turns in to the Glen, or valley of
Glenburnie.

They had not proceeded many paces, until they were
struck with admiration at the uncommon wildness of the
scene, which now opened to their view. The rocks which
seemed to guard the entrance of the Glen, were abrupt and
savage, and approached so near each other, that one could
suppose them to have been riven asunder, to give a passage
to the clear stream which flowed between them. As they
advanced, the hills receded on either side, making room for
meadows, and corn fields, through which the rapid burn
pursued its way, in many a fantastic maze.

If the reader is a traveller, he must know, and if he is a
speculator in canals he must regret, that rivers have in
general a trick of running out of the straight line. But however they may in this resemble the moral conduct of man,
it is but doing justice to these favourite children of nature,
to observe, that in all their wanderings, each stream follows
the strict injunctions of its parent, and never for a moment
loses its original character. That our burn had a character
of its own, no one who saw its spirited career could possibly have denied. It did not, like the lazy and luxuriant
streams, which glide through the fertile valleys of the south,
turn and wind in listless apathy, as if it had no other object

than the gratification of ennui or caprice. Alert, and, im-
petuous, and persevering, it even from its infancy dashed
onward, proud and resolute; and no sooner met with a
rebuff from the rocks on one side of the Glen, than it flew
indignant to the other, frequently awaking the sleeping
echoes, by the noise of its wild career. Its complexion was
untinged by the fat of the soil; for in truth the soil had no
fat to throw away. But little as it owed to nature, and still
less as it was indebted to cultivation, it had clothed itself in
many shades of verdure. The hazel, the birch, and the
mountain-ash, were not only scattered in profusion through
the bottom, but in many places clomb to the very tops of
the hills. The meadows and cornfields, indeed, seemed very
evidently to have been encroachments made by stealth on
the sylvan reign: for none had their outlines marked with
the mathematical precision, in which the modern improver
so much delights. Not a straight line was to be seen in Glenburnie. The very ploughs moved in curves; and though
much cannot be said of the richness of the crops, the ridges
certainly waved with all the grace and pride of beauty.

The road which winded along the foot of the hills, on
the north side of the Glen, owed as little to art as any
country road in the kingdom. It was very narrow, and much
encumbered by loose stones, brought down from the hills
above, by the winter torrents.

Mrs Mason and Mary were so enchanted by the change
of scenery, which was incessantly unfolding to their view,
that they made no complaints of the slowness of their progress, nor did they much regret being obliged to stop a few
minutes at a time, where they found so much to amuse
and to delight them. But Mr Stewart had no patience at
meeting with obstructions, which with a little pains could
have been so easily obviated; and as he walked by the side
of the car, expatiated upon the indolence of the people of
the Glen, who, though they had no other road to the market, could contentedly go on from year to year, without
making an effort to repair it. "How little trouble would it
cost," said he, "to throw the smaller of these loose stones
into these holes and ruts, and to remove the larger ones to
the side, where they would form a fence between the road
and the hill. There are enough of idle boys in the Glen to
effect all this, by working at it for one hour a week during

the summer. But then their fathers must unite in setting them to work; and there is not one in the Glen who would not sooner have his horses lamed, and his carts torn to pieces, than have his son employed in a work that would benefit his neighbours as much as himself!"

As he was speaking, they passed the door of one of these small farmers; and immediately turning a sharp corner, began to descend a steep, which appeared so unsafe, that Mr Stewart made his boys alight, which they could do without inconvenience, and going to the head of the horse, took his guidance upon himself.

At the foot of this short precipice, the road again made a sudden turn and discovered to them a misfortune which threatened to put a stop to their proceeding any further for the present evening. It was no other than the overturn of a cart of hay, occasioned by the breaking down of the bridge, along which it had been passing. Happy for the poor horse that drew this ill-fated load, the harness by which he was attached to it was of so frail a nature, as to make little resistance; so that he and his rider escaped unhurt from the fall, notwithstanding its being one of considerable depth.

At first, indeed, neither boy nor horse were seen; but as Mr Stewart advanced to examine, whether by removing the hay, which partly covered the bridge, and partly hung suspended on the bushes, the road might still be passable, he heard a child's voice in the hollow exclaiming, "Come on, ye muckle brute! ye had as weel come on! I'll gar ye! I'll gar ye! That's a gude beast now; come awa! That's it! Ay, ye're a gude beast now."

As the last words were uttered, a little fellow of about ten years of age was seen issuing from the hollow, and pulling after him, with all his might, a great long-backed clumsy animal of the horse species, though apparently of a very mulish temper.

"You have met with a sad accident," said Mr Stewart; "how did all this happen!"

"You may see how it happened, plain enough," returned the boy, "the brig brak; and the cart couppet."

"And did you and the horse coup likewise?" said Mr Stewart.

"O aye, we a' couppet thegether, for I was riding on his back."

"And where is your father, and all the rest of the folk?"

"Whar sud they be but in the hayfield? Dinna ye ken that we're taking in our hay? John Tamson's and Jamie Forster's was in a wook syne, but we're ay ahint the lave."

All the party were greatly amused by the composure which the young peasant evinced under his misfortune, as well as by the shrewdness of his answers; and having learned from him, that the hayfield was at no great distance, gave him some halfpence to hasten his speed, and promised to take care of his horse till he should return with assistance.

He soon appeared, followed by his father, and two other men, who came on, stepping at their usual pace. "Why, farmer," said Mr Stewart, "you have trusted rather too long to this rotten plank, I think," (pointing to where it had given way,) "If you remember the last time I passed this road, which was several months since, I then told you that the bridge was in danger, and shewed you how easily it might be repaired?"

"It is aw true," said the farmer, moving his bonnet, "but I thought it would do weel enough. I spoke to Jamie Forster and John Tamson about it; but they said they wad na fash themselves to mend a brig that was to serve a' the folk in the Glen."

"But you must now mend it for your own sake," said Mr Stewart, "even *though a' the folk in the Glen* should be the better for it."

"Aye, sir," said one of the men, "that's spoken like yoursel'! would every body follow your example, there would be nothing in the world, but peace and good neighbourhood. Only tell us what we are to do, and I'll work at your bidding, till it be *pit mirk*."

"Well," said Mr Stewart, "bring down the planks that I saw lying in the barnyard, and which, though you have been obliged to step over them every day since the stack they propped was taken in, have never been lifted. You know what I mean."

"O yes, sir," said the farmer, grinning, "we ken what ye mean weel eneugh: and indeed I may ken, for I have fallen thrice ow're them since they lay there; and often said they sud be set by, but we *cou'dna be fashed*."

While the farmer, with one of the men, went up, taking

the horse with them, for the planks in question, all that
remained set to work, under Mr Stewart's direction, to
remove the hay, and clear away the rubbish; Mrs Mason
and Mary being the only idle spectators of the scene. In
little more than half an hour, the planks were laid, and covered with sod, cut from the bank, and the bridge now only
wanted a little gravel, to make it as good as new. This addition, however, was not essential towards rendering it passable for the car, which was conveyed over it in safety; but
Mr Stewart foreseeing the consequences of its remaining in
this unfinished state, urged the farmer to complete the job
on the present evening, and at the same time promised to
reimburse him for the expence. The only answer he could
obtain was, "ay, ay, we'ell do't in time, but Ise warrant *it'll
do weel eneugh.*"

Our party then drove off, and at every turning of the
road, expressed fresh admiration at the increasing beauty of
the scene. Towards the top of the Glen, the hills seemed
to meet, the rocks became more frequent, and more prominent, sometimes standing naked and exposed, and sometimes peeping over the tops of the rowan tree and weeping
birch, which grew in great abundance on all the steepy
banks. At length the village appeared in view. It consisted
of about twenty or thirty thatched cottages, which, but for
their chimneys, and the smoke that issued from them,
might have passed for so many stables or hog sties, so little
had they to distinguish them as the abodes of man.

That one horse, at least, was the inhabitant of every
dwelling, there was no room to doubt, as every door could
not only boast its dunghill, but had a small cart tilted up
on its end directly before it; which cart, though often
broken, and always dirty, seemed ostentatiously displayed
as a proof of wealth.

In the middle of the village stood the kirk, an humble
edifice, which meekly raised its head but a few degrees
above the neighbouring houses. It was, however, graced by
an ornament of peculiar beauty. Two fine old ash trees,
which grew at the east end, spread their protecting arms
over its lowly roof; and served all the uses of a steeple and a
belfry, for on one of the loftiest of these branches was the
bell suspended, which, on each returning Sabbath,
          "Rang the blest summons to the house of God."

On the other side of the churchyard stood the Manse, distinguished from the other houses in the village, by a sash window on each side of the door, and garret windows above; which shewed that two floors were, or might be, inhabited: for in truth the house had such a sombre air, that Mrs Mason, in passing, concluded it to be deserted.

As the houses stood separate from each other at the distance of many yards, she had time to contemplate the scene, and was particularly struck with the numbers of children, which, as the car advanced, poured forth from every little cot to look at the strangers, and their uncommon vehicle. On asking for John MacClarty's, three or four of them started forward to offer themselves as guides; and running before the car, turned down a lane towards the river, on a road so deep with ruts, that though they had not twenty yards to go, it was attended with some danger. Mrs Mason, who was shook to pieces by the jolting, was very glad to alight; but her limbs were in such a tremor, that Mr Stewart's arm was scarcely sufficient to support her to the door.

It must be confessed, that the aspect of the dwelling, where she was to fix her residence, was by no means inviting. The walls were substantial; built, like the houses in the village, of stone and lime; but they were blackened by the mud which the cartwheels had spattered from the ruts in winter; and on one side of the door completely covered from view by the contents of a great dunghill. On the other, and directly under the window, was a squashy pool, formed by the dirty water thrown from the house, and in it about twenty young ducks were at this time daubling.

At the threshold of the door, room had been left for a paving-stone, but it had never been laid, and consequently the place became hollow, to the great advantage of the younger ducklings, who always found in it a plentiful supply of water, in which they could swim without danger. Happily Mr Stewart was provided with boots, so that he could take a firm step in it, while he lifted Mrs Mason, and set her down in safety within the threshold. But there an unforeseen danger awaited her, for there the great whey pot had stood since morning, when the cheese had been made; and was at the present moment filled with chickens, who were busily picking at the bits of curd, which had hardened

on the sides, and vainly mocked their wishes. Over this
Mr Stewart and Mrs Mason unfortunately stumbled. The
pot was overturned, and the chickens cackling with hideous
din, flew about in all directions, some over their heads,
and others making their way by the pallin (or inner door)
into the house.

The accident was attended with no farther bad consequences, than a little hurt upon the shins; and all our party
were now assembled in the kitchen; but though they found
the doors of the house open, they saw no appearance of
any inhabitants. At length Mrs MacClarty came in, all out
of breath, followed by her daughters, two big girls of eleven
and thirteen years of age. She welcomed Mrs Mason and
her friends with great kindness, and made many apologies
for being in no better order to receive them; but said, that
both her gudeman and her thought that her cusine would
have staid at Gowan-brae till after the fair, as they were too
far off at Glenburnie to think of going to it; though it
would, to be sure, be only natural for Mrs Mason to like to
see all the grand sights that were to be seen there; for, to
be sure, she would gang many places before she saw the
like. Mrs Mason smiled, and assured her she would have
more pleasure in looking at the fine view from her door,
than in all the sights at the fair.

"Ay, it's a bonny piece of corn to be sure," returned
Mrs MacClarty, with great simplicity; "but then, what with
the trees, and rocks, and wimplings o' the burn, we have
nae room to make parks of ony size."

"But were your trees, and rocks, and wimplings of the
burn, all removed," said Mr Stewart, "then your prospect
would be worth the looking at, Mrs MacClarty! would it
not?"

Though Mr Stewart's irony was lost upon the good
woman, it produced a laugh among the young folks, which
she, however, did not resent, but immediately fell to busy-
ing herself in sweeping in the hearth, and adding turf to the
fire, in order to make the kettle boil for tea.

"I think," said Miss Mary, "you might make your daughters save you that trouble;" looking at the two girls, who
stood all this time leaning against the wall.

"O poor things," said their mother, "they have not been
used to it; they have eneugh of time for wark yet."

"Depend upon it," said Mrs Mason, "young people can never begin too soon; your eldest daughter there will soon be as tall as yourself."

"Indeed she's of a stately growth," said Mrs MacClarty, pleased with the observation, "and Jenny there is little ahint her; but what are they but bairns yet for a' that! In time, I warrant, they'll do weel eneugh. Meg can milk a cow as weel as I can do, when she likes."

"And does she not always like to do all she can?" said Mrs Mason.

"O, we manna complain," returned the mother, "she does weel eneugh."

The gawky girl now began to rub the wall up and down with her dirty fingers; but happily the wall was of too dusky a hue to be easily stained. And here let us remark the advantage which our cottages in general possess over those of our southern neighbours; theirs being so whitened up, that no one can have the comfort of laying a dirty hand upon them, without leaving the impression, an inconvenience which reduces people in that station, to the necessity of learning to stand upon their legs, without the assistance of their hands, whereas in our country, custom has rendered the hands in standing at a door, or in going up or down a stair, no less necessary than the feet, as may be plainly seen in the finger marks which meet one's eyes in all directions.

Some learned authors have indeed adduced this propensity, in support of the theory which teaches, that mankind originally walked upon all fours, and that standing erect is an outrage on the laws of nature; while others, wishing to trace it to a more honourable source, contend, that as the propensity evidently prevails chiefly among those, who are conscious of being able to transmit the colour of their hands to the objects on which they place, them, it is decidedly an impulse of genius, and in all probability derived from our Pictish ancestors, whose passion for painting is well known to have been great and universal.

Chapter VII

A peep behind the Curtain – Hints on Gardening

While Mrs MacClarty was preparing tea for her guests, Mrs Mason cast her exploring eye on the house and furniture. She soon saw, that the place they were in served in the triple capacity of kitchen, parlour, and bedroom. Its furniture was suitably abundant. It consisted, on one side, of a dresser, over which were shelves filled with plates and dishes, which she supposed to be of pewter, but they had been so bedimmed by the quantities of flies that sat upon them, that she could not pronounce with certainty as to the metal they were made of. On the shelf that projected immediately next the dresser, was a number of delf and wooden bowls, of different dimensions, with horn spoons, &c. These, though arranged with apparent care, did not entirely conceal from view, the dirty nightcaps, and other articles, that were stuffed in behind.

Opposite the fireplace were two beds, each inclosed in a sort of wooden closet, so firmly built as to exclude the entrance of a breath of air, except in front, where were small folding doors, which were now open, and exhibited a quantity of yarn hung up in bunches, affording proof of the goodwife's industry. The portable furniture, as chairs, tables, &c., were all, though clumsy, of good materials; so that Mrs Mason thought the place wanted nothing but a little attention to neatness, and some more light, to render it tolerably comfortable.

Miss Mary Stewart took upon herself the trouble of making tea, and began the operation by rincing all the cups and saucers through warm water, at which Mrs MacClarty was so far from being offended, that the moment she perceived her intention, she stepped to a huge Dutch press, and having, with some difficulty, opened the leaves, took from a store of nice linen, which it presented to their view, a fine damask napkin, of which she begged her to make use.

"You have a noble stock of linen, cousin," said Mrs

Mason. "Few farmers' houses in England could produce the like; but I think this is rather too fine for common use."

"For common use!" cried Mrs MacClarty, "na, na, we're no sic fools as put our napery to use! I have a dizen table-claiths in that press thirty years old, that were never laid upon a table. They are a' o' my mother's spinning. I have nine o' my ain makin' forby, that never saw the sun but at the bookin washing. Ye needna be telling us of England!"

"It is no doubt a good thing," said Mrs Mason, "to have a stock of goods of any kind, provided one has a prospect of turning them to account, but I confess I think the labour unprofitably employed, which during thirty years is to produce no advantage, and that linen of an inferior quality would be preferable, as it would certainly be more useful. A towel of nice clean huckaback would wipe a cup as well, and better, than a damask napkin."

"Towels!" cried Mrs MacClarty, "na, na, we manna pretend to towels; we just wipe up the things wi what comes in the gait."

On saying this, the good woman, to shew how exactly she practised what she spoke, pulled out from between the seed tub, and her husband's dirty shoes, (which stood beneath the bench by the fire side), a long blackened rag, and with it rubbed one of the pewter plates, with which she stepped into the closet for a roll of butter.

"There," says she, "I am sure ye'll say that ye never ate better butter in your life. There's no in a' Glenburnie better kye than our's. I hope ye'll eat heartily, and I'm sure ye're heartily welcome."

"Look, sister," cried little William, "see there the marks of a thumb an two fingers! do scrape it off, it is so nasty!"

"Dear me!" said Mrs MacClarty, "I did na mind that I had been stirring the fire, and my hands were a wee sooty; but it will soon scrape off, there's a dirty knife will take it off in a minute."

"Stop, stop," cried Miss Mary, "that knife will only make it worse! pray let me manage it myself!"

She did so manage it, that the boys, who were very hungry, contrived to eat it to their oatcakes, with great satisfaction; but though Mrs Mason made the attempt, the disgust with which she began, was so augmented by the sight of the numerous hairs which, as the butter was spread, bristled up upon the surface, that she found it impossible to proceed.

Here, thought she, is a home in which peace and plenty seems to reign, and yet these blessings, which I thought invaluable, will not be sufficient to afford me any comfort, from the mere want of attention to the article of cleanliness. But may I not remedy this? She looked at Mrs MacClarty, and in the mild features of a face, which, notwithstanding all the disadvantages of slovenly dress, and four days soil, (for this was Thursday) was still handsome, she thought she perceived a candour that might be convinced, and a good nature that would not refuse to act upon conviction. Of the countenances of the two girls she could not judge so favourably. The elder appeared morose and sullen, and the younger stupid and insensible. She was confirmed in her opinion by observing, that though their mother had several times, desired them to go to the field for their father, neither of them stirred a step.

"Do you not hear your mother speaking to you?" said Mr Stewart, in a tone of authority. The eldest coloured, and hung down her head; the younger girl looked in his face with a stupid stare, but neither of them made any answer.

"*Ye'll* gang, I ken, my dear," said Mrs MacClarty addressing herself to the younger; "O ay, I ken ye'll gang like a good bairn, Jean."

Jean looked at her sister; and Mrs MacClarty, ashamed of their disobedience, but still willing to palliate the faults which her own indulgence had created, said, "that indeed they never liked to leave her, poor things! they were sae bashful; but that in time they would do weel eneugh."

"They will never do well if they disobey their mother," said Mr Stewart; "you ought to teach your children to obey you, Mrs MacClarty, for their sakes, as well as for your own. Take my word for it, that if you don't, they, as well as you, will suffer from the consequences. But come, boys, we shall go to the field ourselves, and see how the farmer's work goes on."

Mrs MacClarty, glad of his proposal, went to the door to point the way. Having received her directions, Mr Stewart pointing to the pool at the threshold, asked her how she could bear to have such dirty doors. "Why does not your husband fetch a stone from the quarry?" said he. "People, who are far from stones and from gravel, may have some excuse; but you have the materials within your reach, and by half-a-day's labour could have your door made clean and comfortable. How then can you have gone on so long with it in this condition?"

"Indeed, I kenna, Sir," said Mrs MacClarty; "my gude-man just canna be fash'd."

"And cannot you be fash'd to go to the end of the house to throw out your dirty water? don't you see how to install a drain would from that carry it down to the river, instead of remaining here to stagnate, and to suffocate you with intolerable stench?"

"O, we're just used to it," said Mrs MacClarty, "and we never mind it. We cou'dna be fash'd to gang sae far wi' a the slaistery."

"But what," returned Mr Stewart, "will Mrs Mason think of all this dirt? She has been used to see things in a very different sort of order; and if you will be advised by her, she will put you upon such a method of doing every thing about your house, as will soon give it a very different appearance."

"Ay," said "Mrs MacClarty, "I ay feared she would be owre nice for us. She has been sae lang amang the Englishes, that she maun hae a hantel o' outlandish notions. But we are owre auld to learn, and we just do weel enough."

Mr Stewart shook his head; and following his sons, who had by this time disengaged the gate from the posts, to which it had been attached by an old cord of many knots.

While Mr Stewart had been engaging the farmer's wife in conversation at the door, his daughter had been earnestly exhorting Mrs Mason to return to Gowan-brae, and to give up all thoughts of remaining in a situation in which she could not probably enjoy any degree of comfort; but her arguments made no impression. Mrs Mason adhered inflex-ibly to her resolution of making a trial of the place; and on Mrs MacClarty's entrance, begged to see the room she was to occupy.

"That you sal," said Mrs MacClarty, "but, indeed, it's no in sic order as I could wish, for it's cram fou o' woo': it was put in there the day of the sheep shearing, and we have never ta'en the fash to put it by; for, as I said before, we

did not expect my cousin till after the fair." She then
opened the door, that was placed in the middle, exactly
between the two beds, the recesses of which formed the
entry of the dark passage through which they groped their
way to the spens, or inner apartment, which was nearly of
the same size as the kitchen. Mrs Mason was prepared for
seeing the fleeces, which were piled up in the middle of the
floor; but was struck with dismay at the fusty smell, which
denoted the place to be without any circulation of air. She
immediately advanced to the window, in the intention of
opening it for relief. But, alas! it was not made to open; and
she heard for her comfort, that it was the same with all the
other windows in the house. The bed which was opposite
to it, was shut up on three sides, like those in the kitchen.
At the foot was a dark closet, in which Mrs Mason's trunks
were already placed. Between the window and the fire-place
was a large chest of drawers of mahogany; and on the other
side the window an eight-day clock in a mahogany case.
The backs of the chairs were of the same foreign wood,
betokening no saving of expence; yet, upon the whole, all
had a squalid and gloomy aspect.

Mrs MacClarty tossed down the bed to shew the fineness
of the ticken, and the abundance of the blankets, which
she took care to tell were all of her own spinning. She
received the expected tribute of applause for her good
housewifery, though Mrs Mason could not help observing
to her, what a risk she ran of having it all lost for want of
air. "See the proof of what I say," said she, "in that quantity of moths! they will soon leave you little to boast of
your blankets."

"Moths!" repeated Mrs MacClarty, "there never was sic
a sight o' moths as in this room; we are just eaten up wi'
them, and I'm sure I kenna how they can win in. For no ae
breath o' wind ever blew here!"

"That is just the thing that induces them to breed in this
place," returned Mrs Mason. "Plenty of air would soon
rid you of the grievance; since the window is unfortunately
fast, I must beg to have a fire kindled here as soon as your
maid comes from the hay-field."

"A fire!" repeated Mrs MacClarty, "I thought you had
found it owre warm."

"It is not to increase the heat that I ask for a fire,"

returned Mrs Mason, "but to increase the circulation of air. If the doors are left open, the air will come sweeping in to feed the fire, and the room, will by that means be venti- lated, which it greatly stands in need of. I can at present breath in it no longer."

By the help of Miss Mary's arm, Mrs Mason got out into the open air, and gladly assented to her friend's proposal of taking a view of the garden, which lay at the back of the house. On going to the wicket by which it entered, they found it broken, so that they were obliged to wait, until the stake which propped it was removed: nor was this the only difficulty they had to encounter; the path, which was very narrow, was damp, by sippings from the dirty pool; and on each side of it, the ground immediately rose, and the docks and nettles which covered it, consequently grew so high, that they had no alternative but to walk sideways, or to separate.

"Ye'll see a bonny garden if ye gang on,' said Mrs Mac- Clarty. "My son's unco proud o't."

"I wonder your son can let these weeds grow here so rank," said Miss Mary; "I think, if he is proud of the gar- den, he should take some pains to make the entrance to it passable."

"O, it does weel eneugh for us,"returned the contented mother. "But saw ye ever sic fine suthern wood? or sic a bed o thyme? we have twa rose bushes down yonder too, but we canna get at them for the nettles. My son gets to them by speeling the wa', but he would do ony thing for flowers. His father's often angry at the time he spends on them."

"Your husband then has not much taste for the garden, I suppose," said Mrs Mason; "and indeed so it appears, for here is ground enough to supply a large family with fruit and vegetables all the year round, but I see scarcely any thing but cabbages and weeds."

"Na, na, we have some leeks too," said Mrs MacClarty, "and green kail in winter in plenty. We dinna pretend to kick-shaws; green kail's gude enough for us."

"But," said Miss Mary, "any one may pretend to what they can produce by their own labour. Were your children to dress and weed this garden; there, might be a pretty walk; there, you might have a plot of green pease, there, another of beans, and under your window you might have a nice border of flowers to regale you with their sweet smell. They might do this too at very little trouble."

"Ay, but they canna be fashed," said Mrs MacClarty; "and it does just weel eneugh."

Mr Stewart now appeared, and with him the farmer, who saluted Mrs Mason with a hearty welcome, and pressed all the party to go in and taste his whisky, to pre-vent, as he said, the tea from doing them any harm. As the car was now ready, Mr Stewart begged to be excused from accepting the invitation; and after laying a kind injunction on Mrs Mason to consider no place so much her home as Gowan-brae, he set off with his family on their return homewards.

Chapter VIII

Family Sketches

Mrs Mason, unwilling to give trouble, and anxious not to disgust her new acquaintances by the appearance of fastidiousness, gave no further directions concerning her apartment, than was barely necessary towards putting it in a habitable state. This being done, she entered cheerfully into conversation with the farmer, whom she found possessed of much plain good sense, and a greater stock of information than she could have supposed within his reach. She was struck with the force and rationality of his observations on various subjects, and almost sorry when their chat was interrupted by a call to supper, which was now upon the table. It consisted, besides the family dishes of sowens and milk, of a large trencher full of new potatoes, the first of the season, and intended as a treat for the stranger. The farmer and his three sons sat down on one side, the goodwife and her two daughters on the other, leaving the arm chair at the head for Mrs Mason, and a stool at the foot for Grizzy, who sat with her back to the table, only turning round occasionally to help herself.

When all were seated, the farmer, taking off a large blue bonnet, which, on account of his bald crown, he seldom parted with through the day, and looking round to see that all were attentive, invited them to join in the act of devotion which preceded every meal, by saying, "Let us ask a blessing."

Mrs Mason, who had been so long accustomed to consider the standing posture as expressive of greater reverence, immediately stood up but she was the only one that moved: all the rest of the party keeping their seats, while the farmer, with great solemnity, pronounced a short, but emphatic prayer. This being finished, Mrs Mason was desired to help herself, and such was the impression made by the pious thankfulness, which breathed in the devotional exercise in which she had just engaged, that viands less acceptable to her palate, would at that moment have been ate with relish. The sowans were excellent; the milk was sweet; and the fresh-raised potatoes, bursting from the coats in which they had been boiled, might have feasted a queen. It is indeed ten thousand to one that any queen ever tasted of the first of vegetables, in this its highest state of perfection. Mrs Mason was liberal of her praise; and both the farmer and his wife were highly gratified by her expressions of satisfaction.

The meal concluded as it had begun with prayer; and Mrs Mason retired to her room, under a full conviction, that in the society of people who so sincerely served and worshipped God, all the materials of happiness would be within her reach.

Her bed appeared so inviting from the delicate whiteness of the linen, that she hastened to enjoy in it the sweets of repose; but no sooner had her head reached the pillow, than she became sick, and was so overcome by a feeling of suffocation, that she was obliged to sit up for air. Upon examination she found, that the smell which annoyed her, proceeded from new feathers put into the pillow before they had been properly dried, and when they were consequently full of the animal oil, which, when it becomes rancid, sends forth an intolerable effluvia.

Having removed the annoyance, and made of her clothes a bundle to support her head, she again composed herself to sleep. But alas, in vain! for the enemy by whom she was now attacked, she found to be sworn against sleep. The assault was made by such numbers in all quarters, and carried on with such dexterity by the merciless and agile foe, that after a few ineffectual attempts at offensive and defensive warfare, she at length resigned herself to absolute despair. The disgusting idea of want of cleanliness, which their presence excited, was yet more insufferable than the piercing of their little fangs. But on recollecting how long the room had been filled with the fleeces, she gladly flattered herself, that they were only accidental guests, and that she might soon be able to effect their banishment.

As day advanced, the enemy retired and poor Mrs Mason, fatigued and wearied, at length sunk to rest. Happily she was undisturbed by the light; for though her window, which was exactly opposite to the bed, was not shaded by a curtain, the veil of dust which it had contracted in the eighteen years it had stood unwiped, was too thick to permit the rays of the sun to penetrate.

As the clock struck eight, she hastened out of bed, vexed at having lost so much of the day in sleep; and on perceiving, when about half dressed, that she had in her room neither water nor hand-bason to wash in, she threw on her dimity bed gown, and went out to the kitchen, to procure a supply of these necessary articles. She there found Meg and Jean; the former standing at the table, from which the porridge dishes seemed to have been just removed; the latter killing flies at the window. Mrs Mason addressed herself to Meg, and after a courteous good-morrow, asked her where she should find a hand-bason? "I dinna ken," said Meg, drawing her finger through the milk that had been spilled upon the table.

"Where is your mother?" asked Mrs Mason. "I dinna ken," returned Meg, continuing to dabble her hands through the remaining fragments of the feast.

"If you are going to clean that table," said Mrs Mason, "you will give yourself more work than you need, by daubing it all over with the porridge; bring your cloth, and I shall shew you how I learned to clean our tables when I was a girl like you."

Meg continued to make lines with her fore finger.

"Come," said Mrs Mason, "shall I teach you?"

"Na," said Meg, "I sal dight nane o't. I'm gain' to the schul."

"But that need not hinder you to wipe up the table before you go," said Mrs Mason. "You might have cleaned it up as bright as a looking-glass, in the time that you have spent in spattering it, and dirtying your fingers. Would it not be pleasanter for you to make it clean, than to leave it dirty?"

"I'll no be at the fash," returned Meg, making off to the door as she spoke. Before she got out, she was met by her mother, who, on seeing her, exclaimed: "Are ye no awa yet bairns! I never saw the like. Sic a fight to get you to the schul. Nae wonner ye learn little, whan you'r at it. Gae awa like good bairns, for there's nae schul in the morn ye ken, it's the fair day."

Meg set off after some farther parley; but Jean continued to catch the flies at the window, taking no notice of her mother's exhortations, though again repeated in pretty nearly the same terms.

"Dear me," said the mother, "what's the matter wi' the

bairn! what for winna ye gang, when Meg's gane? Rin, and
ye'll be after her or she wins to the end o' the loan."

"I'm no ga'an the day," says Jean, turning away her face.
"And wharfor are no ye ga'an, my dear?" says her mother.
"Cause I hinna gotten my questions," replied Jean.

"O, but ye may gang for a' that," said her mother; "the
maister will no be angry. Gang, like a gude bairn."

"Na," said Jean, "but he will be angry, for I did no get
it the last time either."

"And wharfor did na ye get it, my dear," said Mrs
MacClarty in a soothing tone. "Cause 'twas unco kittle, and
I cou'd no be fashed;" replied the hopeful girl, catching as
she spoke another handful of flies. Her mother, finding that
intreaties were of no avail, endeavoured to speak in a more
peremptory accent, and even laid her commands upon her
daughter to depart immediately: but she had too often permitted her commands to be disputed, to be surprised at
their being now treated with disrespect. Jean repeated her
determined purpose of not going to school that day; and
the firmer she became in opposition, the authoritative tone
of the mother gradually weakened, till at length by saying,
that "if she did na gang to the schul, she sudna stand
there," she acknowledged herself to be defeated, and the
point to be given up.

Mrs Mason, who had stood an unobserved spectator of
this scene, was truly shocked at such a dereliction of the
parental authority, as she believed must inevitably produce
consequences of the most deplorable nature. She came forward, and stopping the little girl, as she was slinking out at
the door, asked her "If she really meant to disobey her
mother, by staying from school?" Jean made no answer, but
the indulgent mother, unwilling that any one should open
her eyes to that to which she resolved to be blind, instantly
made her spoilt child's apology, by observing, that, "The
poor thing had na gotten her questions, and did na like to
gang, for fear o' the maister's anger."

"But ought she not to have got her questions, as her
master enjoined, instead of idling here all the morning?"
said Mrs Mason. "O ay,"returned Mrs MacClarty, "she
shu'd ha' gotten her questions nae doubt; but it was unco
fashious, and ye see she has na' a turn that gait poor
woman! but in time she'll do *weel enough*."

"Those who wait till evening for sunrise," said Mrs
Mason, "will find that they have lost the day. If you permit
your daughter, while a child, to disobey her parent and
her teacher, she will never learn, to obey her God. But perhaps I interfere too far. If I do, you must forgive me; for
with the strong impression which I have upon my mind of
the consequences of a right education, I am tempted to
forget that my advice may sometimes be unacceptable."

"Hoot," said Mrs MacClarty, who did not perfectly com-
prehend the speech, "maidens' bairns are aye weel-bred, ye
ken, cousin; but I fear ye hinna sleepit weel, that ye have
been sae lang o' rising. It's a lang time since the kettle has
been boiling for your breakfast."

"I shall be ready for it very soon," said Mrs Mason, "but
I came in search of a bason and water, which Grizzy has
forgot to put in my room, and until I wash, I can proceed
no farther in dressing myself."

"Dear me," replied Mrs MacClarty, "I'm sure you're
weel eneugh. Your hands ha' nae need of washing, I trow.
Ye ne'er do a turn to file them."

"You can't surely be in earnest," replied Mrs Mason.
"Do you think I could sit down to breakfast with unwashed
hands? I never heard of such a thing, and never saw it done
in my life."

"I see nae gude o' sic nicety," returned her friend, "but
it's easy to gie ye water eneugh, though I'm sure I dinna ken
what to put it in, unless ye tak ane o the porridge plates:
or may be the calf's luggie may do better, for it 'ill gie you
enough o room."

"Your own bason will do better than either," said Mrs
Mason. "Give me the loan of it for this morning, and I shall
return it immediately, as you must doubtless often want it
through the day." "Na, na," returned Mrs MacClarty, "I
dinna fash wi' sae mony fykes. There's ay water standing in
some thing or others for ane to ca their hands through
when they're blacket. The gudeman indeed is a wee conceity
like yourself, an' he coft a brown bason for his shaving in
on Saturdays, but it's in use a' the week haddin' milk, or
I'm sure ye'd be welcome to it. I sal see an' get it ready for
you the morn."

Poor Mrs Mason, on whose nerves the image presented
by this description of the alternate uses of the utensil in

question, produced a sensible effect, could scarce command voice to thank her cousin for the civil offer. Being, however, under the necessity of chusing for the present, she without hesitation, preferred the calf's bicker to the porridge plate: and indeed, considered the calf as being so much the cleanlier animal than his mistress, that she would in every way have preferred him for an associate.

Mrs Mason was not ill pleased to find that she was to breakfast by herself; the rest of the family having long ago finished their morning repast, were now engaged in the several occupations of the day.

The kail pot was already on the fire to make broth for dinner; and Mrs MacClarty busied in preparing the vegetables which were to be boiled in it. When her guest, on hearing her desire Grizzel to make haste, and sit down to her wheel, thought it time to remind her, that her bed was still to make, and her room to be put in order; and that Grizzy's assistance would be necessary for both.

It was not easy to persuade the good woman that it would not be time enough in the dusk of the evening; but as Mrs Mason declared it essential to her comfort, Grizzy was ordered to attend her, and to do whatever she desired. By her directions, the stout girl fell to work, and hoisted out the bed and bed-clothes, which she carried to the barn-yard; the only place about the house where there was a spot of green grass. The check curtains followed, and in their removal effected the sudden ruin of many a goodly cobweb, which had never before met with the smallest molestation. When the lower vallence was removed, it displayed a scene still more extraordinary; a hoard of the remains of all the old shoes that had ever been worn by any member of the family; staves of broken tubs, ends of decayed rope, and a long et cetera of useless articles, so covered with blue mould and dust, that it seemed surprising the very spiders did not quit the colony in disgust.

Mrs Mason sickened at the sight. Perceiving what an unpleasant task she should be obliged to impose on her assistant, she deemed herself in justice bound to recompense her for the trouble; and, holding up a half-crown piece, told her, that if she performed all she required of her on the present occasion, it should be her own. No sooner was Grizzy made certain of the reward, which had till now been promised in indefinite terms, than she began in such good earnest, that Mrs Mason was glad to get out of the room. After three large buckets full of dirt and trumpery had been carried out, she came to Mrs Mason for fresh instructions. Then proceeded to wash the bed-posts with soap and water. After which, the chairs, the tables, the clock-case, the very walls of the room, as well as every thing it contained, all underwent a complete cleaning.

The window, in which were nine tolerably large panes of glass, was no sooner rendered transparent, than Grizzy cried out in extacy, "that she cou'd na' have thought it would have made sic a change. Dear me! how heartsome it looks now to what it us't!" said the girl, her spirit rising in proportion to the exertion of her activity.

"And in how short a time has it been cleaned?" said Mrs Mason. "Yet, had it been regularly cleaned once a week, as it ought to have been, it would have cost far less trouble. By the labour of a minute or two, we may keep it constantly bright; and surely few days pass in which so much time may not be spared. Let us now go to the kitchen window, and make it likewise clean." Grizzy with alacrity obeyed. But before the window could be approached, it was found necessary to remove the heap of dusty articles piled up in the window sill, which served the purpose of family library, and repository of what is known by the term odds and ends.

Mrs MacClarty, who had sat down to spin, did not at first seem willing to take any notice of what was going forward; but on perceiving her maid beginning to meddle with the things in the window, she could no longer remain a neutral spectator of the scene. Stopping her wheel, she, in a voice indicating the reverse of satisfaction, asked what she was about? Mrs Mason took it upon her to reply. "We are going to make your window bright and clean for you, cousin," said she. "If you step into my room, and take a look of mine, you will see what a difference there is in it, and this, if these broken panes were mended, would look every bit as well." It does *weel eneugh*," returned Mrs MacClarty. "It wants nae cleanin'. It does just *weel enough*. What's the gude o' takin up the lass's time wi' nonsense? she'll break the window too, and the bairns hae broken eneugh o' it already,"

"But if these panes were mended, and the window cleaned, without and within," said Mrs Mason, "you cannot think how much more chearful the kitchen would appear."

"And how long would it bide clean if it were?" said Mrs MacClarty. "It would be as ill as ever or a month, and wha cou'd be at the fash o' ay cleanin at it?"

"Even once a month would keep it tolerable, but once a week would keep it very nice; your little girls might rub it bright of a morning, without the least trouble in the world. They might learn too, to whiten the windowsill, and to keep it free from rubbish, by laying the books, and all these articles, in their proper places, instead of letting them remain here covered with dust. You cannot imagine what good it would do your young people, did they learn by times to attend to such matters; for believe me, cousin, habits of neatness, and of activity, and of attention, have a greater effect upon the temper and disposition than most people are aware of."

"If my bairns do as weel as I hae done, they'll do weel enough," said Mrs MacClarty, turning her wheel with great speed. Mr MacClarty's voice was just at that moment heard calling on Grizzy to drive the fowls out of the cornfield, which necessarily put a stop to all further proceedings against the window. Mrs Mason therefore returned to her own apartment; and greatly pleased with the appearance which it now assumed, chearfully sat down to her accustomed labours of the needle, of which she was such complete mistress, that it gave no interruption to the train of her reflections. On taking a view of her present situation, and comparing it with the past, she carefully suppressed every feeling that could lead to discontent. Instead of murmuring at the loss of those indulgences, which long habit had almost converted into necessaries of life, she blessed God for the enjoyment of such a state of health, as none of the luxuries of wealth could purchase; and for which, those who possessed them so often sighed in vain. Considering all the events of her life as ordered under the wise dispensation of Providence, she looked to the subordinate situation in which she had been placed, as a school in which it was intended that she should learn the important lesson of humility, and when she looked back, it was for the purpose of enquiring, how she had fulfilled the duties of the lot assigned her.

She was now for the first time in her life completely her own mistress; but she was already sensible, that the idea of living completely independent of the will of others is merely visionary, and that in all situations, some portion of one's own will must necessarily be sacrificed. She saw that the more nearly people approached each other in their habits and opinions, the less would the sacrifice be felt; but while she entertained a hope of being able to do more good in her present situation than she could in any other, she resolved to remain where she was. "Surely," said she to herself, "I must be of some use to the children of these good people. They are ill brought up, but they do not seem deficient in understanding; and if I can once convince them of the advantage they will derive from listening to my advice, I may make a lasting impression on their minds."

While engaged by these reflections, as she busily pursued her work, she was startled by a sudden noise, followed by an immediate diminution of light; and on looking up, perceived her window all over bespattered with mud. A tittering laugh betrayed the aggressors, and directed her attention to the side where they stood, and from which she knew they could not retreat without being seen. She therefore continued quietly on the watch, and in a little time saw Jean and her younger brother issue from the spot, and hastily run down the bank that led to the river.

Mrs Mason had been for above twenty years employed in studying the tempers and dispositions of children; but as she had never before seen an instance of what appeared to be unprovoked malignity in the youthful mind; she was greatly shocked at the discovery, and thought it incumbent on her to inform their mother of the incident, and to give her opinion of it in the plainest terms.

Mrs MacClarty perceiving that Mrs Mason had something extraordinary to communicate, stopped her wheel to listen, and when the window was mentioned, asked, with great anxiety, whether it was broken? "No," said Mrs Mason, "the mud they threw at it was too soft to break the glass; it is not to the injury done the window that I wish to call your attention, but to the dispositions of your children, for what must the dispositions be, that lead them to take pleasure in such an act.''

"Hoot," said Mrs MacClarty, "is that it a'? ane wou'd ha' thought the window had been a' to shivers, by the way you spoke. If it's but a wee clarted, there's no sae muckle ill done. I tald ye it was nonsense to be at sae muckle fash aboot it; for that it wou'd na' get leave to bide clean lang.''

"But if your children were better taught," said Mrs Mason, "it might get leave to bide clean long enough. If the same activity which they have displayed in dirtying it, had been directed into proper channels, your cottage might have been kept in order by their little hands, and your garden, and all about your doors, made neat and beautiful. Children are naturally active, but unless their activity be early bent to useful purposes, it will only lead them into mischief. Were your children" –

"Hoots," said Mrs MacClarty, peevishly, "my bairns are just like other folks'. A' laddies are full o' mischief. I'm sure there's no a yard i' the town where they can get a flower or apple keepit for them. I wonder what ye would ha' said, if ye had seen the minester's yets the day after they were painted, slaked and blacket a' owre wi' dirt, by the laddies frae the schule?''

"I would have said," returned Mrs Mason, "what I said before, that all that bent to mischief in the children, arises from the neglect of the parents, in not directing their activity into proper channels. Do you not think that each of these boys would, if properly trained, find as much amusement in works that would tend to ornament the village, or in cultivating a few shrubs and flowers to adorn the walls of their own cottages, as they now appear to find in mischief and destruction? Do you not think, that that girl of yours might have been so brought up, as to have had more pleasure in cleaning a window of her father's house, than in bedaubing it with mud? Allowing the pleasure of being mischievously active, and the pleasure of being usefully active, to be at present equal; do you think that the consequences will not be different? 'Train up a child in the way he should go,' says Solomon, and depend upon it, that in the way you train him he will go, whether you desire it or no. If you permit a child to derive all his pleasure from doing ill to others, he will not, when he is grown up, be inclined to do much good. He will even, from his youth, be conscious of deserving the ill will of his neighbours, and must of course have no good will to them. His temper will thus be soured. If he succeeds in life, he will be proud and overbearing: if he does not, he will become sulky, and morose, and obdurate."

"Weel," said the farmer, who had been listening to the latter part of the conversation, "its a true that ye say; but how is it to be helpit? Do ye think corrupt nature can be subdued in ony other way than by the grace of God?"

"If I read my Bible right," returned Mrs Mason, "the grace of God is a gift which, like all the other gifts of divine love, must be sought by the appointed means. It is the duty of a parent to put his children upon the way of thus seeking it; and, as far as it is in his power, to remove the obstacles that would prevent it."

"The minister himsell cou'd speak nae better," returned the farmer. "But when folks gi' their bairns the best education in their power, what mair can they do?"

"In answer to your question," replied Mrs Mason, "I will put one to you. Suppose you had a field which produced only briers, and thorns, what method would you take to bring it into heart?"

"I would nae doubt rute out the briers and thorns, as weel as I cou'd," returned the farmer.

"And after you had opened the soil by plowing, and enriched it by the proper manure, you would sow good seed in it, and expect, by the blessing of heaven, to reap, in harvest, the reward of your labours," said Mrs Mason.

"To be sure I would," said the farmer.

"And do you imagine," said Mrs Mason, "that the human soul requires less care in cultivating it, than is necessary to your field? Is it merely by teaching them to say their questions, or even teaching them to read, that the briers and thorns of pride and self-will will be rooted up from your children's minds?"

"We maun trust a' to the grace of God," said the farmer.

"God forbid that we should put trust in ought beside," returned Mrs Mason: "but if we hope for a miraculous interposition of divine grace, in favour of ourselves, or of our children, without taking the means that God has appointed, our hope does not spring from faith, but from presumption. It is just as if you were neither to plow, nor sow your fields, and yet expect that Providence would bless you with an abundant crop."

"But what means ought we to use, that we do not use?" said the farmer. "We send our bairns to the schule, and we take them to the kirk, and we do our best to set them a gude example. I kenna what we could do mair."

"You are a good man," said Mrs Mason, with complacency; "and happy will it be for your children, if they follow your example. But let us drop all allusion to them in particular, and speak only of training up youth to virtue, as a general principle. By what you say, you think it sufficient to sow the seed, I contend for the necessity of preparing the soil to receive it, and say, that without such preparation, it will never take root, nor vegetate."

"I canno' contradict you," returned the farmer; "but I wish you to explain it better. If you mean that we ought to give our bairns lessons at hame, I can tell you we have not time for it, nor are we book-learned eneugh to make fine speeches to them, as the like of you might do: and if we were, I fear it wad do little gude."

"Believe me," replied Mrs Mason, "set lessons, and fine harangues, make no part of my plan of preparation, which consists of nothing else than a watchful attention to the first appearances of what is in its nature evil, and whether it comes in the shape of self will, passion, or perverseness, nipping it in the very bud; while, on the other hand, I would tenderly cherish every kindly affection, and enforce attention to the feelings of others; by which means I would render children kind-hearted, tractable, and obedient. This is what I call the preparation of the soil: now let us see the consequences. When a child who has been accustomed to prompt and chearful obedience, learns to read the commandment, *honour thy father and thy mother*, will he not be more apt to practise the duty then inculcated, than one who had from infancy indulged in contrary habits? And what doth the gospel teach? doth it not urge us to subdue all selfish and vindictive passions, in order that we may cherish the most perfect love to God and man? Now if we have permitted our children to indulge these passions, how do we prepare them for practising the gospel precepts? Their duty to God and man requires, that they should make the best use of every power of mind and body: the activity natural to youth is a power included in this role and if we permit them to waste it in effecting mischief, and in destroying or disturbing the happiness of others, can we say that we are not counteracting the express will of our Divine Master? How can we flatter ourselves, that with such habits the divine precepts will make much impression on their minds?"

Before Mrs Mason had finished her speech, her voice was drowned in the noise of a violent quarrel that had taken place between the farmer's two elder sons. Perceiving that the dispute would not be easily settled, she retired to her room; but was overtaken in the passage by Mrs MacClarty, who said in a whisper, "I houp ye'll say naething o' Jenny's playing the truant frae the schule. Her father manna ken o't, he wad be sae angry."

"Alas," said Mrs Mason, "you know not how much you are your child's enemy! but I shall be silent."

Chapter IX

Domestic Rebellion

Mrs Mason enjoyed the reward of her exertions, and of Grizzel's labour, in a night of sweet and uninterrupted repose. She was awoke at early dawn by the farmer calling his sons to get up, to prepare for the labours of the day; and looking out, beheld the clouds already decked in the colours of the morning, inviting her to the most glorious sight on which the eye of man can look. The invitation was not given in vain, she rose and dressed herself; and taking her staff and crutch, she sallied from her room, earnestly wishing to escape observation.

The young men, in no hurry to obey their father's summons, were still in bed. On passing through the dark passage where they slept, she could not help wondering at the perverted ingenuity, which could contrive to give to the sleeping rooms of a country house, all the disadvantages which attend the airless abodes of poverty in the crowded lanes of great and populous cities.

From the length of time that the outer door had been shut, the closeness of the house had become very unpleasant to her lungs. Welcome therefore was the reviving breeze of morning! Welcome the freshness of the coming day, which now burst upon the senses. It was not, indeed, until she had removed some paces from the house, that she fully felt its influence, for while near the door, the smell of the squashy pool, and its neighbour, the dunghill, were so powerful, as to subdue the fragrance of earth's fruits and flowers.

Having taken the road towards the river, she, on its first turning, found herself in full view of the waterfall, and was arrested by admiration at the many beauties of the scene. Seating herself upon a projecting rock, she contemplated the effulgent glory of the heavens, as they brightened into splendour at the approach of the lord of day; and when her eyes were dazzled by the scene, turned to view the living waters, pouring their crystal flood over the craggy precipice, shaded by the spreading boughs of birch and alder.

The good woman's heart glowed with rapture: but it did

not vainly glow, as does the heart, or the imagination of many a pretender to superior taste; for the rapture of her heart was fraught with gratitude. She saw the God of nature in his works, and blessed the goodness which, even in the hour of creation, ordained, that they should not only con-tribute to the use, but add to the enjoyments of the human race. "The eye is never satisfied with seeing, nor the ear with hearing," and he who implanted these desires, has he not mercifully provided for their gratification? What are all the works of man, what all the pomp and splendour of monarchs, compared with the grandeur of such a scene? But the sights that are designed by man, as proofs of his creative skill, are only to be seen by the rich and great; while the glorious works of God are exhibited to all. Pursuing this thought a little farther, it occurred to Mrs Mason, that all that is rare, is in general useless; and that all that is most truly valuable is given in common, and placed within the reach of the poor and lowly. "Let the poor then praise Thee!" she exclaimed. "Let the lowly in heart rejoice in thy salvation. Let us rejoice in the light which shines from on high to illumine the soul, as thy sun illumes the earth! O that man would praise the Lord for his goodness, and for his mercies to the children of men."

While Mrs Mason was thus indulging the grateful feel-ings of her heart, by sending up her tribute of praise to the Almighty Giver of all good, her ears were suddenly assailed by the harsh sound of discord; and on moving a few steps, discovered, that a violent dispute had taken place between the farmer and his eldest son. In the hopes of making peace, she advanced towards them, but before she turned the corner, she paused, doubting whether it were not better to take no notice of having heard the fray. The voices stopped, and proceeding, she saw the farmer hastily unsaddling a horse; and the son at the same moment issuing from the door, but pulled back by his mother, who held the skirt of his coat, saying, "I tell ye, Sandie, ye manna gang to anger your father."

"But I sal gang," cried Sandie, in a sullen tone. "I winna be hindered. I sal gang, I tell ye, whether my father likes or no."

"Ye may gang, ye door loon," says the father, "but if ye do, ye sal repent it as lang as ye live."

"Hoot na," returned the mother, "ye'll forgie' him, and ye had as weel let him gang, for ye see he winna be hindered!"

"Where is the young man for going to?"asked Mrs Mason.

"Where sud he be for gain' to, but to the fair?" returned the mother; "it's only natural. But our gudeman's unco particular, and never lets the lads get ony daffin."

"Daffin!" cried the farmer; "is druckenness daffin! Did na he gang last year, and come hame as drunk as a beast! And ye wad have him tak the brown mare too, without ever spearing my leave! saddled and bridled too, forsooth, like ony gentleman in the land! But ye sal baith repent it: I tell ye, ye'se repent it."

"O, I did na ken o the mare," said the too easy mother.

"But is it possible," said Mrs Mason, addressing herself to the young man, "is it possible that you should think of going to any place, in direct opposition to your father's will? I thought you would have been better acquainted with your duty, than to break the commands of God, by treating your parents in such a manner."

"I am sure he has been weel taught," said the mother; "but I kenna how it is, our bairns never mind a word we say!"

"But he will mind you," said Mrs Mason, "and set a better example of obedience to his brothers and sisters, than he is now doing. Come, I must reconcile all parties. Will you not give me your hand?"

"I'll no' stay frae the fair for naebody," said the sullen youth, endeavouring to pass; "a' the folk in the Glen are gain', and I'll gang too, say what ye wull."

Mrs Mason scarcely believed it possible that he could be so very hardy, until she saw him set off with sullen and deter-mined step, followed by his mother's eye, who, on seeing him depart, exclaimed, "Hegh me! ye're an unco laddie."

The farmer appeared to feel more deeply, but he said nothing. Grasping the mane of the mare, he turned to lead her down the road to his fields, and had advanced a few steps, when his wife called after him, to enquire what he was going to do with the saddle, which he carried on his shoulders? "Do wi' it!" repeated he, "I have naething to do wi' it!" Then dashing it on the ground, he proceeded with quickened pace down the steep.

"Wae's me!" said Mrs MacClarty, "the gudeman taks Sandie's doorness mickle to heart!"

"And is it any wonder, that he should take it to heart!" said Mrs Mason. "What can be more dreadful to a parent than to see a son, setting out in life with such dispositions? What can be expected of one who is capable of such undutiful behaviour?"

"To be sure," said the goodwife, "the lad's unco willfu'. There's nae gude in hindering him, for he maun ay tak his ain gait. But a' lads are just the same, and the gudeman shou'd na be sae hard on him, seeing he's yet but young."

"Mistress!" hollowed the voice of Grizzel from the house; "I wish ye wad come and speak to Meg. She winna be hindert putting her fingers in the kirn, and licking the cream."

"If I were at you," cried Mrs MacClarty,"I'd gar you" –

She was as good as her word; and in order to show Mrs Mason the good effect of her advice, she ran that moment into the kitchen, and gave her daughter a hearty slap upon the back. The girl went a few steps farther off, and deliberately applied her tongue to the back of her hand, where part of the cream was still visible.

"Go! ye idle whippy!" said her mother, "and let me see how weel ye'll ca' the kirn."

"I winna kirn the day," returned Meg; "I'm gain' to milk the kye. Jean may kirn, she has naething else to do."

"I'm ay set to kirn," says Jean, whimpering. "I never saw sic wark. I tell ye, I wonna kirn mair than Meg. Grizzy can milk the cows hersel'. She does na' want her help."

"But girls," said, Mrs Mason, "when I was a little girl like either of you, I never thought of chusing my work; I considered it my business to follow my mother's directions. Young people ought to obey, and not to dictate."

"Hear ye that!" said Mis MacClarty: "But Jean will gang to the kirn I ken, like a good bairn, and she sal get a dad o' butter to her bread."

"But I wonna haet frae the hairing knife," said Jean, "for the last I got stack i' my throat."

"Bless me!" cried Mrs Mason, in amazement, "how does your butter come to be so full of hairs? where do they come from?"

"O they are a' frae the cows," returned Mrs MacClarty.

"There has been lang a hole in the milk sythe, and I have
never been at the fash to get it mended, but as I tak ay care
to sythe the milk through my fingers, I wonder how sae
mony hairs win in."

"Ye need na wonder at that," observed Grizzel, "for the
house canna be soopit but the dirt flees into the kirn."

"But do you not clean the churn before you put in the
cream?" asked Mrs Mason, more and more astonished.

"Na, na," returned Mrs MacClarty, "That wad no be
canny, ye ken. Naebody hereabouts would clean their kirn,
for ony consideration. I never heard o' sic a thing i' my
life."

Mrs Mason found it difficult to conceal the disgust which
this discovery excited; but resolving to be cautious of giving
offence by the disclosure of her sentiments, she sat down
in silence, to watch the farther operations of the morning.
While Jean was slowly turning the churn with unwilling
hand, her mother was busily employed in making the
cheese. Part of the milk destined to that purpose was
already put upon the fire, in the same iron pot in which the
chickens had been feasting, and on which the hardened
curd at which they had been picking, was still visible
towards the rim. The remainder of the milk was turned into
a large tub, and to it that upon the fire was added, as soon
as it was of a proper heat. So far, all was done well and cle-
verly. Mrs MacClarty then took down a bottle of runnet,
or yearning, as she called it; and having poured in what she
thought a sufficient quantity, tucked up the sleeve of her
gown, and dashing in her arm, stirred the infusion with
equal care and speed.

"I believe, cousin," said Mrs Mason, hesitatingly, "I
believe – you forgot to wash your hands."

"Hoot!" returned the goodwife, "my hands do weel
enough. I canna be fashed to clean them at every turn."

"But you go about your work with such activity," rejoined
Mrs Mason, "that I should think it would give you little
trouble, if you were once accustomed to it; and by all that I
have observed, and I have had many opportunities of observation, I believe that in the management of a dairy, cleanliness is the first, the last, the one art needful."

"Cleanly!" repeated Mrs MacClarty; "nae ane ever said
that I was na' cleanly. There's no' a mair cleanly person i'

the parish. Cleanly, indeed? Ane wad think ye was speaking to a bairn!"

Mrs Mason offered a few words in explanation, and then retired to her own apartment, to which she saw it would be necessary to confine herself, in order to enjoy any tolerable degree of comfort. She therefore began to consider how it might be rendered more airy and commodious; and after dinner, observing that the farmer's mind still brooded on his son's behaviour, she gladly introduced the subject of her projected alterations, hoping thus to divert his thoughts into another channel. The first thing she proposed, was to have hinges for the frame of the window, that it might open and shut at pleasure. To this, the farmer said, he should have no objection, only that "he ken'd it wad soon be broken to pieces, blawing wi' the wind."

"O, but you mistake me," said Mrs Mason. "I intend that it should be fastened when open with an iron hook, as they constantly fasten the cottage windows in England."

"And wha do ye think wad put in the cleek? returned he. "Is there ane think ye aboot this hoose, that wad be at sic a fash?"

"Why what trouble is there in it?" said Mrs Mason. "It is only teaching your children to pay a little attention to such things, and they will soon come to find no trouble in them. They cannot too soon leam to be neat and regular in their ways."

"Ilka place has just its ain gait," said the goodwife; "and ye needna think that ever we'll learn your's. And indeed to be plain wi' you, cusin, I think you have our mony fykes. There did na ye keep Grizzy for mair than twa hours yesterday morning, soopin and dusting your room in every corner, and cleaning out the twa bits o' buird, that are for naething but to set your feet on after a'."

"But did you know how dirty they were?" said Mrs Mason.

"Hoot! the chickens just got their meat on them for twa or three ouks, poor wee beasties! the burds war a wee thought clarted wi' parritch, but it was weel dried on, and ye wadna' been a bit the war."

"But are the boards the worse for being scoured?" asked Mrs Mason; "or would they have been the worse, if they had been scoured when you took them from the chickens, or, while they were feeding on them?"

"O, to be sure it wad ha' been an easy matter to ha' scour't them then, if we had thought of being at the fash," returned Mrs MacClarty.

"In my opinion," rejoined Mrs Mason, "this *fear of being fashed* is the great bar to all improvement. I have seen this morning, that you are not afraid of work, for you have exerted yourself with a degree of activity that no one could excel; yet you dread the small additional trouble that would make your house cheerful, clean, and comfortable. You dread the trouble of attention, more than the labour of your hands; and thus, if I mistake not, you often bring upon yourself trouble, which timely attention would have spared. Would it not be well to have your children taught such habits of attention and regularity, as would make you more easy, and them more useful, both to themselves and you?"

"As for my bairns," returned Mrs MacClarty, "if they pleasure me, they do weel eneugh."

"There's a great spice o' gude sense in what Mrs Mason has said though," said the farmer; "but it's no easy for folk like us to be put out o' their ain gait."

In truth, Mrs MacClarty was one of those seemingly good-natured people, who are never to be put out of their own way; for she was obstinate to a degree; and so perfectly self-satisfied, that she could not bear to think it possible, that she might in any thing do better than she did. Thus, though she would not argue in favour of sloth and dirt in general, she nevertheless continued to be slothful and dirty, because she vindicated herself in every particular instance of either, and though she did not wish that her children should be idle, obstreperous, disobedient, and self-willed, she effectually formed them to those habits, and then took credit to herself for being one of the best of mothers!

Mrs Mason had discernment enough to see how much pride there was in that pretended contentment, which constantly repelled every idea of improvement. She saw that though Mrs MacClarty took no pains to teach her children what was truly useful, she encouraged, with respect to them, an undefined sentiment of ambition, which persuaded her, that her children were born to rise to something great, and that they would in time overtop their neighbours. Mrs Mason saw the unhappy effects which this would infallibly produce, upon minds brought up in ignorance; she therefore resolved to do all in her power to obviate the consequences; and from the opinion she had formed of the farmer's sense and principles, had no doubt of his co-operating with her in the work of reformation.

While musing on this subject, as she sat by her window in the twilight, she saw the two younger lads run hastily past; and soon heard from their mother such an exclamation of sorrow, as convinced her they had been the messengers of bad news. She therefore speedily proceeded *but*,* and there she found the poor woman wringing her hands, and lamenting herself bitterly. The farmer entered at the same moment; and on seeing him, she redoubled her lamentations, still calling out, "O Sandy! Sandy! O that I should ha lived to see this day! O Sandy! Sandy!"

"Sandy!' repeated the alarmed father, "what is the matter wi' Sandy? for God's sake, speak. Is my son gane? is he killed?"

"No, no, he's war' than killed! O that I shou'd have seen this day!"

"Speak, Robert," said Mrs Mason, "you can tell what has befallen your brother, let your father know the truth." Robert was silent; but the youngest boy eagerly came forward, and said, that "Jamie Bruce had brought word that Sandy was aff to be a soger."

"And where did you see Jamie Bruce?" asked his father.

"It was Rob that spoke wi' him; it was na me," said the little boy, hanging down his head.

"Where cou'd you, Rob, meet Jamie Bruce?" said the farmer. "Did not I send you to the West Croft? how cou'd you then see ony ane comin' frae the fair? Speak, sir! and tell truth, I desire you."

"I just thought I wad gang a wee while up to the road to see the folk coming frae the fair, before I gaid to the Craft," returned Robert. "I kent there wad be time eneugh."

---

* The English reader is referred to Horne Tooke for the etymology of this word. [E.H.]

"Aye," said the father, sighing; "its just the way wi' ye
a! ye just do what ye like yoursel's! Now, see what comes o
it! Here's Sandy done for himsel' wi' a vengeance! He too
wad do naething but what he liked! see what he'll mak o' it
now, but to be tied up to a stake, and lashed like a dog! a
disgrace, as he is, to us a'! I wou'd rather he had ne'er been
born!"

"Alace! gudeman," cried the poor mother, weeping
bitterly; "alake! hae pity on me, and try to get him aff."

"It will do nae gude,"says her husband, in a softened
accent, and wiping a tear which stole down his cheek, "it
will do nae gude, I tell ye. We shall never have comfort in
him while we live, for he is ane that will never be advised.
Ye ken he never minds a word we say – yet I canna think o'
his being made a reprobate."

"He need not necessarily be a reprobate in the army,"
said Mrs Mason. "I should hope his principles will preserve
him from that; and if he behaves well, he will be treated
kindly, and may come in time to be promoted. But you are
not yet certain that he is enlisted. The person who gave
the information may himself have been misinformed. Make
inquiry into the fact, and then take the steps that, on consideration, appear to be most prudent and judicious."

The gleam of hope which was presented in these words,
revived the spirits of the disconsolate parents; and the
father in haste set off for the village, to learn to a certainty
the fate of his untoward son.

Evening was now far advanced. The cows, which the boys
should have brought home to have milked, were still lowing
in the West Croft; and when Mrs MacClarty desired
Robert to go for them, she obtained no other answer, than
that "Grizzy might gang as weel as him." Grizzy was busy
in washing up the dishes wanted for supper, and which
had remained unwashed from breakfast time till now:
they had been left to the care of Meg, who had neglected
them, and by this neglect made the task more difficult to
Grizzy, who was therefore in very bad humour, and began
loudly to complain of Meg, and Rob; who in their turns
raised their voices in defence, and mutual accusation. The
din of the squabble became insufferable. Mrs Mason retired
from it with horror; and shut herself up in her room, where
she meditated, with deep regret, on the folly of those who,

having been placed by Almighty God in situations most favourable to the enjoyment of peace, and the exercise of virtue, are insensible to the blessing; and by permitting their passions to reign without controul, destroy at once both peace and virtue.

Chapter X

Containing a useful Prescription

"He's gane!" said the farmer, as he opened the cottage door. "It is just as I kent it wou'd be. They enticed him wi' drink, and then, when his senses war gane, they listet him."

"And sal I never see him mare!" cried his wife. "Wull ye no try to get him aff? maun my bairn gang wi' they loons and vaigabonds, and do at their bidding, what he ne'er wad do at oors! O! it will break my heart!"

"No," says the farmer, "I canno' think o' it! I maun try. Gang, Rob, and saddle the mare. I canna' ride lang at a time fur this rhumatic; but whan it comes, I'll light and walk. It is a fine night, and I may be there lang before the break of day. O Mrs Mason! little do our bairns think o' the sorrow they bring upon oor hearts!"

"I hope," said Mrs Mason, "all your children now present will take warning, and learn to submit themselves betimes to the duty of obedience: and that you will both enforce that duty, as you are enjoined by God to do. Take comfort, then, and assure yourself that this event may turn out in the end to be a blessing."

The farmer said he trusted in God that it might be so; and, having provided himself with what money he thought necessary, he, with a heavy heart, departed.

On the following day, many of the neighbours come to enquire for Mrs MacClarty; and on hearing that the farmer had gone alone, they all expressed a good-natured concern, saying, that he might have been sure there was not a man in the place, who would not willingly have gone with him, had he mentioned his intention. By noon-time he was expected back, but eight in the evening came, and still there was no appearance of his return. Mrs Mason now became truly uneasy, and was doubly distressed, as Mrs MacClarty seemed to depend on her for comfort. She proposed asking some of the neighbours to set off on horseback for intelligence, and sent to several; but they all declined the expedition as unnecessary, assuring her, that the farmer must have gone on to the head-quarters of the recruiting party, which were at a town about twelve miles from that in which the fair had been held. This assurance tended, in some degree, to lessen their alarm. They went to bed; but after passing a watchful and sleepless night, arose to fresh anxiety; for the first thing they heard was, that a man had passed through Glenburnie, who had seen Sandie at _____ with the recruiting party the night before, and that the farmer had not been there. Jamie Bruce, who had brought the first account of Sandie from the fair, now offered to go in search of the old man, for whose fate all had, from this intelligence, become anxious. He had scarcely been gone an hour, when Meg came running in from the door, where she had been idling all the morning, and exclaimed, that her father was coming down the loan in a cart.

Mrs MacClarty starting up at the news, flew out to meet her husband; her cousin followed in great agitation, and soon perceived that the poor man was too ill to reach the house without assistance. Friendly assistance was at hand, for the cart was already surrounded by the neighbours; but all were so anxious to have their curiosity gratified, relative to the cause, that not one thought of offering a hand, until their questions had been answered. Mrs Mason at length, by her remonstrances, restored silence, and got the people to help the poor sufferer to his bed, on which he was no sooner laid, than his wife flew to give him a dram of whisky, which she had been taught to consider as the only cordial for fatigue. But Mrs Mason observing how very feverish he appeared, begged her to desist, and at the same time hastened the preparation of a dish of tea, which having prevailed on him to swallow, she addressed the people who crowded round his bed, entreating they would leave him to the repose, of which he stood so much in need. This was not a matter so easily to be accomplished: for so eager were they all engaged in conversation, that among so many louder tongues, her voice had little chance of being heard.

"Hech! me," cries one, "I never heard o' sic a thing i' my life!"

"I have gane to the Lammas fair, these thirty years," says another, "an' ne'er heard tell o' ony body being robbet, in a' my days."

"But I mind o' just sic anither thing happening to auld John Robson, when he came frae the fair o' Glasgow, ae night," said the shoemaker.

"Glasgow!" exclaimed two or three of the women, "Glasgow, by a' accounts, is an unco place for wickedness: but then wha can wonder, whar there's sae mony factories."

"There is muckle gude, as weel as ill in't, Janet," returned the shoemaker.

Mrs Mason, perceiving the dispute likely to grow warm, again entreated them to remember, how much their poor neighbour stood in need of sleep. Her efforts to establish quietness were all exerted in vain. No sooner did one set of people go away, than another set poured in. All in their enquiries, equally friendly, equally loud, and equally loquacious; unfortunately, discovering that the poor man was still awake, the most forward teized him with questions; from his replies to which, it appeared, that as he had reached within half a mile of the town, he was met at a lonely part of the road, by two men, habited like sailors, and who, as he afterwards learned, had been seen begging at the fair, where, to excite compassion, they had pretended to be lame. He was then leading his horse, which they seized by the bridle, and rudely demanded money to drink. He gave them a sixpence; but they said it was not enough, and with many imprecations demanded more. While he hesitated, they knocked him down, and beat him dreadfully with their sticks. They then took from him the old pocketbook, in which he had put the notes intended for his son's release, and left him senseless on the ground. A little before day-break he so far recovered, as to be able to raise himself; and looking round for his mare, perceived her grazing by the road side at no great distance. With much pain, and great difficulty, he reached the town, and went to the public house, to which he had been directed, as the quarters of the sergeant: but on arriving there, had the mortification to find, that the sergeant and his recruits had set off at midnight for the head-quarters, and that consequently all hopes of obtaining his son's dismissal were at an end.

He was, however, advised to send in pursuit of the robbers; and having obtained a warrant, lent his mare to the constable, who promised that he should have his money before night; but night came on, and neither constable nor mare returned. He felt himself in the mean time grow worse and worse; and as soon as day appeared, resolved to return home. Ill as he was able to walk, he had, by resting every other step, got forward to the entrance of the Glen; where, finding that his strength entirely failed him, he took refuge in the first cottage; and, anxious to get to his own home, procured a cart, in which he proceeded as has been related.

He was now very ill indeed. The pain in his head and limbs becoming every minute more violent, while the encreased flushing in his face gave evident proof of the fever which burned in every vein. The only precaution which the good people, who came to see him, appeared now to think necessary, was carefully to shut the door, which usually stood open; and as a large fire was burning in the grate exactly opposite to his bed, the effect was little short of suffocation. Mrs Mason perceived this, and endeavoured to remedy it, but in vain. The prejudice against fresh air appeared to be universal. Neither could she get any creature to understand, how much harm the din of so many voices was likely to occasion. Mrs MacClarty, who, from being accustomed to speak to her children in an exalted pitch, in order to enforce attention, had herself contracted a habit of speaking loud, was quite insensible to the noise that now buzzed in the ear of her sick husband; and would on no account run the risk of offending any of her neighbours, by refusing them admittance to his bedside.

The fever in consequence encreased. Mrs Mason seeing that it was likely to be attended with danger, proposed sending for the doctor; but Mrs MacClarty acceded to the general opinion, that it would be *time eneugh* to send when he became worse.

"But if you wait until he becomes worse," said Mrs Mason, "it may then be too late. A fever may be stopped in the beginning, which, if permitted to go on for a couple of days, it maybe impossible to cure. We at present are ignorant of the nature of the fever with which your husband is attacked, and may therefore administer what is improper. I have no notion of drugs doing much good in any case; but what I want to have advice for, is, to be put upon the proper way of managing his disorder. You are, by the advice of your neighbours, giving him a variety of things, which, for aught you know, may all have opposite properties; and though they may each have done good in some instances, may all be equally unfit in the present. Take my advice, so far at, least, as, until you send for a doctor, give him nothing but plenty of cooling drink."

"Na, na," returned Mrs MacClarty, "I ha' nae sic little regard for my gudeman, as to gie him naething but water and sour milk whey, as ye wad hae me. What has done gude to ithers, may do gude to him, and I'm mistaen if auld John Smith hae na as mickle skeel as ony doctor amang them."

Auld John Smith just then arrived, and, after talking a great deal of nonsense about the nature of the disorder, took out his rusty lancet, and bled the patient in the arm, at the same time recommending a poultice of herbs to be applied to his head, and another of the same kind to his stomach, desiring, above all things, that he might be kept warm, and get nothing cold to drink.

Poor Mrs Mason was greatly shocked to see the life of a father of a family thus sported with, by an ignorant and presuming blockhead: but found that her opinions were looked upon with the eye of jealous prejudice; and that while she continued the advocate of fresh air, and cooling beverage, she must lay her account to meet with opposition. In spite of auld John Smith's infallible remedies, the farmer became evidently worse. When he was past all hope, the doctor was sent for, and on seeing him, and inquiring into the mode of treatment he had received, solemnly declared, that if they had intended to kill him, they could not have fallen on a method more effectual. He did not think it probable that he would live above three days; but said the only chance he had, was in removing him from that close box in which he was shut up, and admitting as much air as possible into the apartment. After giving some further directions concerning the patient, he warned them of the infectious nature of the disease, and mentioned the necessity of taking every precaution against spreading so fatal a disorder. Without listening to what was said in reply, he mounted his horse, and was out of sight in a minute.

No sooner did the fatal sentence, which the doctor had pronounced, reach the ears of the unhappy wife, than she gave way to utter despair. The neighbours, who had been watching for the doctor's departure, poured in to comfort her: but Mrs Mason resolving to make a vigorous exertion in behalf of the poor man's life, represented, in strong terms, the necessity of an immediate compliance with the doctor's directions; and proposed that all should go home but those who could lend assistance, in removing him to her room; when as she had now got the window to open, he would at once have air and quiet. To this proposition a violent opposition was made by all the good people assembled; in which Mrs MacClarty loudly joined, declaring "she wou'd never see her gudeman turned out o' his ain gude warm bed into a cauld room. She cou'dna bear the thoughts o' ony thing sae cruel."

"Is it not more cruel," said Mrs Mason, "to let him remain here, to be stifled to death by the bad air, which now surrounds him, and which no one can breath in safety? By removing him, he has at least a chance of recovery: here he can have none."

"If it's the will o' God that he's to dee," said Peter Macglashon, who was the oracle of the parish, "its a' ane whar ye tak him: ye canna hinder the will o' God."

"It is not only the will of God, but the *command* of God, that we should use the means," said Mrs Mason. "We should do our utmost, and then look up to God for his blessing, and for resignation to his will. When we do not make use of the reason he has bestowed upon us, we are at once guilty of disobedience and presumption."

"That's no soond doctrine," said Peter, "it's the law of works."

"No," returned Mrs Mason, "it's the law of faith, to which we shew our obedience by works. If, contrary to the command of God, we run upon our own destruction, or permit the destruction of a fellow creature, we do not shew faith, but contempt. Every one of you here present, who comes to lend assistance to the family, is performing an act of charity and benevolence, such as God has commanded us to perform to each other; but whoever comes without that intention, and knowing that he can be of no use, puts his life to needless risk, and, by tempting Providence, commits an act of sin."

"Say ye sae," said limping Jacob the Presenter, rising from the seat he had just taken by the bedside, "ye speak with authority, I maun confess. But how can ye prove the danger?"

"It is easily proved," replied Mrs Mason. "You know that

God has ordained, that life should he preserved by food
taken into the stomach, and air breathed into the lungs. If
poison is put into our food, we all know the consequence.
Now it has been clearly proved, that poisonous air is
equally fatal to life as poisoned food. By the breath of
persons in fever, and other infectious diseases, the air is
thus poisoned; and hence arises the necessity of admitting a
current of air to carry off the infection."

"But, madam," said a pale-faced man, "if that were true,
the air that gaed out, wad poison a' the toon. What say ye
to that?"

"I say," returned Mrs Mason, "that if you were to take
an ounce or two of arsenic, and put it into that dram glass
full of water, you would run the immediate risk of your life
by swallowing it; but that if you were to dissolve the same
quantity in yonder tub with ten gallons of water, the risk
would he diminished, and that if you were to put it in the
river, all the people of Glenburnie might drink of the water
without injury. The bad air which surrounds our poor
friend in that close bed, is the arsenic in a glass of water: it
cannot be breathed with impunity. Had he been placed, as
I at first recommended, the greater quantity of air would
have diminished the danger; but let us still do what is in
our power, to remedy the evil."

"I never heard better sense in my life," said the pale-faced
man; "if either me or my wife can do you any good, we
shall stay and help you: if no, we shall gang hame, and
remember you in our prayers. I shall never forget what you
have now told us as lang as I live."

"I have nae faith in't," said Peter Macglashon; "it's a'
dead works; and if I warna sae sick, I wad gi her a screed o'
doctrine; but I kenna what ails me, I'm unco far frae
weel."

Peter then went off, and all the rest of the people, one
by one, followed his example. In a short time the pale-faced
stranger returned, and addressing himself to Mrs Mason,
said, "that though he was but a stranger in Glenburnie, yet
as he was the farmer's nearest neighbour, he thought it his
duty to offer his services to the utmost, in the present situation of the family; and that though he was now convinced
of the danger, he would willingly encounter it to be of use."
He had, he said, "lately suffered much from sickness him-

self, and therefore he knew how to feel for those that suffered." There was something in this man's manner that
greatly pleased Mrs Mason, and she frankly accepted his
kind offer, pointing out where his assistance might be essentially useful to Mrs MacClarty, who, oppressed with fatigue,
had, by her persuasion, gone to take a little rest. While she
was speaking to him, the minister of the parish came in.
He had but just returned from a long journey, the only one
he had taken for many years, and though much tired, no
sooner heard that he had been sent for in his absence to
visit a sick parishioner, than he instantly proceeded to
administer comfort to the distressed. Learning from Mrs
Mason the state of insensibility to which the sick man was
now reduced, he desired his children to be called, in order
that they might benefit by the impression which such
serious acts of devotion are calculated to make; and when
they were assembled, he, with solemn fervency, supplicated
the God of all mercy and consolation, in behalf of the sufferer and his afflicted family. While he spoke, tears flowed
from the eyes of the most insensible, and Mrs Mason was
not without hope, that the spirit of obedience, which he
prayed might henceforth fill the hearts of the children,
would be seen in its effects: and that, sensible of the misery
which self-will and obstinacy had produced, they would
learn to reverence their Creator, by keeping the passions
which opposed his law under due subjection.

Chapter XI

An escape from earthly cares and sorrows

Mrs Mason's apprehensions concerning the consequences of the infectious air, were too effectually realised. While the farmer yet hovered on the brink of death, his wife, and Robert his second son, were both taken ill; and great reason there was to fear, that the fever might go through the whole family. By means of the surgeon, who was immediately sent for, an account of Mrs Mason's distressed situation reached her friends at Gowan-brae, and no sooner were they informed of it, than the car was dispatched for her with a trusty servant, by whom Miss Mary wrote, earnestly entreating her not to permit any scruples to prevent her compliance with their request.

Mrs Mason might indeed have been well justified in leaving a house where she had not now a bed to sleep on; she having insisted upon Mrs MacClarty's occupying her's.

Had Mrs MacClarty continued in health, she would have gone without hesitation; because she saw that her mind was too full of prejudice, to permit her to reap any benefit from one who had the advantage of more experience than herself; but now that the poor woman was in a state of suffering, and incapable of giving any directions, she would on no account leave her. Having returned a grateful answer to her friends at Gowan-brae, she dismissed their messenger, and proceeded in arranging the business of the family, with all the prudence and activity which become natural to minds that have been long accustomed to exertion. She was no longer troubled with useless visits from the neighbours, whom she had partly offended, and partly terrified, by her discourse on the nature of infection. Peter Macglashon, her great opponent, had taken to his bed on going home, and was now dangerously ill of the fever, and auld John Smith and his wife had happily been affronted by sending for the doctor. So that few now came near the house, excepting William Morison, the pale-faced stranger, whom we have already mentioned, and Peggy his wife, a very clever sensible woman. All the village indeed offered their services, and Mrs Mason, though she blamed the thoughtless custom of crowding into a sick room, could not but admire the kindness and good nature with which all the neighbours seemed to participate in the distress of this afflicted family.

The minister and his niece were particularly attentive. The former paid Mrs Mason a daily visit, and as often as circumstances would permit, performed the sacred offices of his function in devout and fervent prayer. The latter came in person to solicit Mrs Mason to sleep at the manse, but William Morison and his wife had anticipated her in the offer of a bed, and as their house was near at hand, she preferred going there, especially as Peggy had undertaken the management of Mrs MacClarty's dairy, and also the preparation of all the viands. Meg and Jean were sent to assist her in these offices; but she found them so obstinate and unmanageable, that they were rather a hindrance than a help. Nor was Grizzy of much greater use. Strong and active as she was, she seemed to feel every thing a trouble that she was desired to do; and though she would have lifted a heavy burden without murmuring, grumbled sadly at being desired to rince a few cups or basons, and still more at the fatigue of putting them in their proper places. This was, however, insisted upon by Mrs Mason, under whose directions all was preserved in order. In the attendance on the persons of the sick, she was assisted by an old woman of the village, but all the medicines were administered by her own hands. She was anxious to have Robert removed from the dark and airless passage in which he lay; but he so violently opposed the measure, that she could not get it effected; so that she was obliged to leave him to his fate; and after the third day the doctor gave little hopes of his recovery. As to his poor father, his death had been for some time hourly expected, but towards the evening of the twenty-fourth day, he appeared somewhat to revive. His senses returned, and observing Mrs Mason by his bedside, he asked her for his wife and children. On his repeating the question, Mrs Mason found herself under the painful necessity of informing him of the situation of his wife and son: to which he made no other answer, than that they were in the hands of a merciful God, and in life and death he submitted to his will.

On the minister coming in, he spoke to him in the same strain of pious resignation. "I know," he said, "that my hour is at hand, but though I walk through the valley of the shadow of death I will fear no evil, knowing that the Redeemer of the world has paved the way. He will guide his flock like a shepherd, and none that believe on him shall be lost." After much conversation of the same kind, in which he strongly evinced the faith and hope of a Christian – that faith and that hope, which transforms the death-bed of the cottager into a scene of glory, on which kings and conquerors might look with envy, and in comparison of which, all the grandeur of the world is contemptible – he desired to see his daughters and his little boy. They came to his bedside, and with a feeble and broken voice he spoke to them as follows:

"My dear bairns, it is God's will that I should be taken frae you; but God can never be taken frae you, if you learn by times to put your trust in him; and pray for his spirit to subdue the corrupt nature in your hearts. I have grievously wranged you, I maun confess; the thoughts of it is heavy on my heart. For though I weel knew the corruption that was in your natures, I did not teach you to subdue it, so as to put you in the way of God's grace, which is promised to the obedient. It has pleased God to punish me for this neglect. Through the mercies of the Saviour I hope for pardon; but I cannot die in peace till I warn you of the consequences of continuing in a contentious and disobedient spirit. If it pleases God to spare my dear wife" – here his feelings overpowered him, and his voice was so choked by sobs, that it became quite inarticulate. All remained profoundly silent; and at length the dying man so far recovered as to be about to proceed, when the door, which at his desire had been shut, flew suddenly open; and Sandie, with hasty and tremulous steps, ran in, crying, "Hide me, hide me, mother! for God's sake find out some place to hide me in!"

"Sandie!" exclaimed the dying man, "is it indeed my son, my son Sandie? Thank God, I sal see him ere I die, to gie him my blessing. Come, Sandie, winna ye come to me? Dinna be frightened. Ye have cost me sair; but God kens how truly I forgie you: come and tak my blessing."

Sandie uttered a deep groan; and hiding his face with

both his hands, fell prostrate at his father's bed-side. The minister raised him up, and bade him take comfort.

"Comfort!" cried he, "Oh, there's nae comfort for me; I have been the death of my father: is it not me that has brought his gray hairs wi' sorrow to the grave?"

"But your father has forgiven you," said the minister; "he is ready to give you his blessing."

"And will you bless me?" said Sandie, "O my father, I dinna deserve your blessing; but let me anes mair hear your voice."

"God Almighty bless you, my son, and give you a heart to serve him, and to walk in his ways." – "Is it not Sandie that I hear," cried his mother, rushing to the bedside, and clasping her son in her arms. "O Sandie, what have ye brought upon us a'?"

There was no time to answer, for the exertion was so much beyond her strength, that she would have fallen life-less on the ground, had, not her son prevented it, by clasp-ing her to his breast. "My mother! Have I killed my mother too!" exclaimed the affrighted youth, hanging over her with a look of inexpressible horror.

"Yes," uttered a loud and rough voice from behind, "you would rather kill twenty mothers than fight the French; but (swearing a horrid oath) you shan't find it so easy to get off next time, my lad." Two others sprung forward at the same moment, and laid hold of their prisoner, who was too much stupified by the variety of emotions to make any resistance, or even to utter a single word.

"Gentlemen," said the minister, gently laying his hand upon the hand of the foremost, as it eagerly grasped the young man's shoulder, "there is no occasion to use any vio-lence. You are, I suppose, in the performance of your duty, and I give you my word, you shall here meet with no resis-tance; but in the name of the parents who gave you birth, I conjure you to act like men, and not like savage brutes."

"We are no savages," returned the foremost, "we are his Majesty's soldiers, and come to execute his Majesty's orders on the body of this deserter, who will be tried and shot as sure as he stands there."

"It may be so," said the minister; "only give him a few minutes to take leave of his dying parents."

"O my poor mother," cried Sandie, "must I be torn from

you; what, what shall I do? Wretch that I am, it is me, me that has brought you to the grave."

"You will indeed injure her by this agitation," said Mrs Mason; "carry her back to her bed, these men will assist you in the office, for I see they are not strangers to humanity."

"God pity the poor woman," said the corporal, "I shall give her all the help in my power." So saying, he would have taken her from Sandie's arms, but could not prevail on him to part with his burden, though his knees trembled under him, while he carried her through the passage to Mrs Mason's room, where she was put to bed. She instantly became delirious, and in her raving, called out, that the house was on fire, and that she and her children would perish in the flames, then springing up, she caught her son by the arm, continuing to cry, help, help, in a wild and mournful voice, till her strength was exhausted, and she again sunk upon her pillow. The feelings of her son may perhaps be imagined, but cannot be described: nor were any of the by-standers unaffected by the scene. Even the rough soldier, though little accustomed to the melting mood, felt all the sympathies of his nature working in his breast. He was not, however, forgetful of his duty; for while Mrs Mason was administering a cordial to the poor mother, he drew his prisoner from the room. On Mrs Mason's returning to the outer room, she found him standing over his father's bed; his eye fixed upon the altered countenance of the dying man, who, since the entrance of the soldiers, had never shewn any other sign of sensibility, than the utterance of a faint groan. He was now speechless, but his hands were lifted up in the attitude of prayer. "Come, my brethren," said the minister, "let us unite our prayers to those of the departing spirit. The deathbed of a good man is the porch of heaven. Angels and archangels are now joint witnesses with us of this solemn scene. To him in whose hands are the issues of life and death, let us lift the voice of supplication, that living, we may live to him, and dying, we may he received into his glory." The imposing solemnity of the scene, aided the views of the venerable pastor, in making a deep impression upon his audience. His prayer, though delivered in language the most simple, had all the effects of eloquence upon the heart, and in the breasts of the hardy veterans, touched some cords which had, but for this adventure, lain for ever dormant. Far from hurrying away their prisoner with brutal violence, they patiently waited until he had attained some degree of composure; and then respectfully addressing the minister, they begged that he would exhort the young man, not to resist them in the performance of their duty. Mr Gourlay, sensible of the reasonableness of their request, went up to Sandie, who was then gazing in speechless sorrow on his father's corpse. After speaking with him for a few minutes, he took his hand, and turning to the chief of the party, "here, friend," said he, "I commit to your care this bruised reed, and I am persuaded you will treat him with humanity. Go in peace: in all circumstances perform your duty with the courage that becomes an immortal spirit; and whatever doctrine may be preached to rouse your bravery, believe me, that even in the field of battle, *it is only a good man that can die with glory.*"

Chapter XII

The doctrine of Liberty and Equality stripped of all seditious import

The morning of the day on which the farmer was to be buried, was rendered remarkable by the uncommon denseness of an autumnal fog. To Mrs Mason's eye it threw a gloom over the face of nature, nor when it gradually yielded to the influence of the sun, and slowly retiring from the valley, hung, as if rolled into masses, midway upon the mountains, did the changes thus produced excite any admiration. Still, wherever she looked, all seemed to wear the aspect of sadness. As she passed from Morison's to the house of mourning, the shocks of yellow corn spangled with dew-drops, appeared to her to stand as mementos of the vanity of human hopes, and the inutility of human labours. The cattle, as they went forth to pasture, lowing as they went, seemed as if lamenting, that the hand that fed them was at rest; and even the Robin-red-breast, whose cheerful notes she had so often listened to with pleasure, now seemed to send forth a song of sorrow, expressive of dejection and woe.

The house of the deceased was already filled with female guests: the barn was equally crowded with men, and all were, according to the custom of the country, banqueted at the expence of the widow and orphans, whose misfortunes they all the while very heartily deplored. Mrs Mason's presence imposed silence upon the women, but, in the barn, the absence of Sandie, who ought to have presided at his father's funeral, was freely descanted on, and the young man either blamed or pitied according to the light in which his conduct happened to be viewed. Various reports concerning him were whispered through the throng; but of his actual situation, all were evidently ignorant. Amid rumours so various and contradictory, none knew what to believe: all, however, agreed in lamenting, that so respectable a man as the farmer, having two sons grown up to manhood, should nevertheless have his head laid in the grave by a little boy. The poor child, on whom the office of chief mourner thus devolved, looked grave and sad, but he was rather bewildered than sorrowful; and in the midst of the tears which he shed, felt an emotion of pleasure from the novelty of the scene.

At length Mr Gourlay rose, and all was hushed in silence. Every heart joined in the solemn prayer in which the widow and the orphan were recommended to the throne of grace. The bier was then lifted. From the garden, to which she had retired apart from the crowd, Mrs Mason viewed the solemn procession, which, as the rocks reverberated the dismal note of the church-bell, tolling at measured intervals, slowly proceeded to the destined habitation of the dead. Casting her eyes upon the rustic train who followed, she could not help contrasting the outward circumstances of this solemnity, with those that had attended the last event of a similar nature in which she had been interested. She had seen her noble master conducted to the grave in all the splendour befitting his high station. Many were the lofty plumes that adorned his stately hearse; rich and brilliant were the banners and trophies that waved over it. Horses and their riders, clad in all the insignia of woe, (the horse and the rider being equal strangers to the sentiment) had lent their imposing influence to the spectacle, while a long train of empty carriages, distinguished by coronets and armorial bearings, gave notice to the gazers, that the dust which was about to be consigned to worms, was of high and illustrious descent. But there neither friend nor neighbour were to be seen. There, with the exception of a few faithful servants, all the actors in the solemnity were engaged in performing a part in which they had no interest.

Here all were interested.

The hoary headed elders, who had the place of honour next the corpse, thought as they looked on it, on the unblemished life of him who had been so long their associate in its duties; and wept for the man in whom they hoped their children's children would have found a friend. The distant farmers, who had bought and sold with him, paid the tribute that was due to his character and integrity; while those with whom he had lived in the constant intercourse of kindness, and good neighbourhood, betrayed, in their countenances, the sorrow of their hearts.

She continued to gaze after the mourners, till an angle

of the wall of the church-yard intercepted her view; soon
after all was still. The last toll of the bell died away upon
the distant hills, and gave place to a silence particularly
solemn and impressive. It denoted the conclusion of that
ceremony which returns dust to dust. "Where now,"
thought she, "are the distinctions of rank? Where those
barriers, which in this world separate man from man? Even
here sorrow only embalms the memory of the righteous.
When selfishness is silent, the heart pays its tribute to
nought but worth. Why then should those of lowly station
envy the trappings of vanity, that are but the boast of a
moment, when, by piety and virtue, they may attain a distinction so much more lasting and glorious? To the humble
and the lowly are the gates of Paradise thrown open. Nor
is there any other path which leads to them, but that which
the gospel points out to all. In that path may the grace of
God enable me to walk; so that my spirit may join the
spirits of the sanctified – the innumerable host, that out of
every tribe, and nation, and language, shall meet together
before the throne of the Eternal, to worship, and give
praise, and honour, and glory, to Him that liveth for ever
and ever."

From these solemn meditations, Mrs Mason was called
to witness the reading of the farmer's will. He had performed the duty of an honest man in making it while he
was in perfect health; wisely thinking, that if he deferred it
till the hour of sickness, he might then neither have the
ability nor inclination to give his mind to worldly cares.

To his wife he bequeathed a free cottage in the village,
and an annuity which he considered equal to her wants. To
each of his younger children he left the sum of forty
pounds, and to his eldest son the farm, burthened with the
above provision for the rest of the family. In case the elder
son should chose to go abroad, or enter into business, the
farm was to go to the second, and the elder to have only a
younger child's portion. By a clause in the will, the widow
was to retain possession of the farm till the Candlemas after
her husband's death. So much more consideration had this
humble cottager for the feelings of a wife, than is often
shewn in the settlements of the rich and great!

The minister, who read the will, addressed himself in
finishing it, to the friends and neighbours who were present;

and proposed, that they should alternately lend their assistance, in managing the business of the harvest for the
widow and her family. The proposal was readily agreed to
by the men; while Mrs Mason, on her part, cheerfully
undertook the superintendence of the household work and
dairy, until her cousin should be so far recovered as to be
able to resume the task.

As soon as all the strangers were dismissed, Mrs Mason
informed her cousin of the arrangements that had been
made, with which she appeared perfectly satisfied.
Depressed by grief and sickness, she still considered her
recovery as hopeless, and submitted to her fate with that
species of quiescence, which is often a substitute for the
true spirit of resignation.

Chapter XIII

The force of Prejudice

It appeared extraordinary to Mrs Mason, that she should have been so long forgotten by her friends at Gowan-brae. Nearly a fortnight had now elapsed since Mr Stewart's last visit; and though he had been invited to the funeral, he had neither come nor sent any apology for his absence, which appeared the more unaccountable from the circumstance of his having been seen that very day riding full speed on the road to the market town. Certain that neither Mr Stewart nor Mary could be actuated by caprice, she feared that some misfortune had befallen them; but though every day added to her anxiety, she had no means of relieving it, all hands being now engaged in getting in the harvest, and she was too wise to torment herself by shaping the form of uncertain evils. She had indeed no leisure for such unprofitable work: every moment of her time being fully occupied in managing the business of the family, or in attendance on the invalids, who though now recovering rapidly, were still so weak as to require her constant care.

The business of the family had never been so well conducted as since its mistress had been incapacitated from attending to it. By the effects of forethought, order, and regularity, the labour was so much diminished to the servant, that she willingly resigned herself to Mrs Mason's directions, and entered into all her plans. The girls, though at first refractory, and often inclined to rebel, were gradually brought to order, and finding they had no one to make excuses for their disobedience, quietly performed their allotted tasks. They began to taste the pleasure of praise, and encouraged by approbation, endeavoured to deserve it; so that though their tempers had been too far spoiled to be brought at once into subjection, Mrs Mason hoped that, by steadiness, she should succeed in reforming them.

Mrs MacClarty, who was not so changed by sickness, or so absorbed in grief, as to be indifferent to the world and its concerns, fretted at the length of her confinement, which was rendered doubly grievous to her, from the hints she occasionally received of the new methods of management introduced by Mrs Mason, which she could on no account believe equal to her own. Her friend and benefactress became the object of her jealousy and aversion. The neighbours, with whom she had cultivated the greatest intimacy, encouraged this dislike; and on all their visits of condolence, expressed in feeling terms, their sense of the sad change that had taken place in the appearance of the house, which they said was "now sae unco, they wad scarcely ken it for the same place."

"Aye!" exclaimed the wife of auld John Smith, who happened to visit the widow the first evening she was able to sit up to tea, "aye, alake! it's weel seen, that whar there's new lairds there's new laws. But how can your woman and your bairns put up wi' a' this fashery?"

"I kenna, truly," replied the widow, "but Mrs Mason has just sic a way wi' them, she gars them do ony thing she likes. Ye may think it is an eery thing to me, to see my poor bairns submitting that way to pleasure a strainger in a' her nonsense."

"An eery thing, indeed!" said Mrs Smith; "gif ye had but seen how she gard your dochter Meg clean out the kirn! outside and inside! ye wad hae been wae for the poor lassie. I trow, said I, Meg, it wad ha' been lang before your mither had set you to sic a turn? Aye, says she, we have new gaits now, and she looket up and leugh."

"New gaits, I trow!" cried Sandy Johnstone's mother, who had just taken her place at the tea table; "I ne'er kend gude come o' new gaits a' my days. There was Tibby Bell, at the head o' the Glen, she fell to cleaning her kirn ae day, and the very first kirning after, her butter was burstet, and gude for naething. I am sure it gangs to my heart to see your wark sae managed. It was but the day before yesterday, that I cam upon madam, as she was haddin' the strainer, as she called it, to Grizzy, desiring her a' the time she poured the milk, to beware of letting in ane o' the cow's hairs that were on her goon. Hoot! says I, cows' hairs are canny, they'll never choak ye." "The fewer of them that are in the butter the better!" says she. "Twa or three hairs are better than the blink o' an ill ee," says I. "The best charm against witchcraft is cleanliness," says she. "I doubt it muckle," says I, "auld ways are aye the best!"

"Weel done!" cried Mrs Smith. "I trow ye gae her a

screed o' your mind! But here comes Grizzy frae the market; let us hear what she says to it."

Grizzel advanced to her mistress, and with alacrity poured into her lap the money she had got for her cheese and butter, proudly at the same time observing, that it was more by some shillings than they had ever got for the pro- duce of one week before that lucky day.

"What say you?" cried the wife of auld John Smith, "are the markets sae muckle risen? That's gude news indeed!"

"I did na say that the markets were risen," returned the maid; "but we never got sae muckle for our butter, nor our cheese, by a penny i' the pund weight, as I got the day. A' the best folks in the town were striving for it. I cou'd ha' seld twice as muckle at the same price."

"Ye had need to be weel paid for it," said Sandy John- stone's mother, "for I fear ye had but sma' quantity to sell."

"We never had sae muckle in ae week before," said Grizzy; "for you see," continued she, "the milk used aye to sour before it had stood half its time, but noo the milk dishes are a' sae clean, that it keeps sweet to the last."

"And dinna ye think muckle o' the fash?" said Mrs Smith.

"I thought muckle o't at first," returned Grizzy; "but when I got into the way o't, I fand it nae trouble at a'."

"But how do ye find time to get thro' sae muckle wark?" said the widow Johnstone.

"I never," answered Grizzy, "got thro' my wark sae easy in my life; – for ye see Mrs Mason has just a set time for ilka turn; so that folk are never running in ane anithers gait; and every thing is set by clean, ye see, so that it's just ready for use."

"She maun hae an unco airt," said Mrs MacClarty," to gar ye do sae muckle, and think so little o't. I'm sure ye ken how you used to grumble at being put to do far less. But I did na bribe ye wi' haff-croon pieces, as she does."

"It's no the haff-croon she gae me, that gars me speak," cried Grizzy; "but I sal always say, that she is a most dis- creet and civil person, ay, and ane that taks a pleesur in doing gude. I am sure, mistress, she has done mair gude to you, than ye can ere repay, gif ye were to live this hunder year."

"I sal ne'er say that she has na been very kind," returned Mrs MacClarty; "but thank the Lord, a' body has shewn kindness as weel as her. Its no lessning o' her to say, that we hae other friends forby."

"Freends!" repeated Grizzy. "What hae a' your freends done for you, in comparison wi'' what she has done, and is e'now doing for you! Aye, just e'now, while I am speaking – But I forgot that she charged me no to tell."

"Is na' she gane to Gowan-brae?" said Mrs MacClarty, "What gude can she do me by that?"

"Aye," cried Mrs Smith, "what gude can the poor widow get by her gaen to visit amang the gentles! Did na I see her ride by upon the minester's black horse, behint the min-ester's man, and the minester himsel' ridin' by her side?"

"She's no gane to Gowan-brae tho'," returned Grizzy, "nor the minester neither; I ken whar they're gane to weel eneugh."

"But what are they gane about?" asked Mrs MacClarty, alarmed, "Is ony thing the matter wi' my puir Sandy? for my heart aye misgi'es me about his no comin' to see me."

Grizzy made no answer. The question was again repeated in an anxious and tremulous voice, by her mistress, but still she remained silent.

"Alake!" cried Mrs Smith, "I dread that the sough that gaed through o' his having deserted, had some truth in't, tho' William Morison wad na let a word be said at the bur-ial."

"O woman! for pity's sake speak," said the widow, "Is na my bairn already lost to me? Wharfor than will ye not tell me what has happened, seeing it canna be war than what has already befaln me!"

"I promised no to tell," said Grizzy, "but since ye will ha' it, I maun let ye ken, that if Sandy be not doomed to death this very day, it will be through the exertions of Mrs Mason."

"Doomed to death" repeated the widow; "my Sandy doomed to death! my bairn, that was just the very pride o' my heart! Alace! alace! his poor father!"

A kindly shower of tears came to the relief of the poor mother's heart, as she uttered the name of her husband; and as she was too much weakened by sickness to struggle against the violence of her emotions, they produced an hysterical affection, which alarmed those about her for her life. Her life was however in no danger. Soon after being put to bed, she became quite composed; and then so strongly insisted upon being informed of every particular relative to her son, that Grizzy was compelled to give a faithful account of all she knew.

"Ye have thought," said she, "that your seein' Sandy while you were in the fever was but a dream; and Mrs Mason thinking it best that ye shou'd continue in the delusion, has never contradickit ye. But it was nae dream; your son was here the very day his father died; and ye saw him, and faintet awa' in his arms."

"Wharefor than did he leave me?" exclaimed the widow; "Wharefor did he na stay to close his father's eyes: and to lay his father's head i' the grave, as becam the duty o' a first-born son?"

"Alace!" returned the damsel, "ye little ken how sair the struggle was ere he could he brought to part frae the lifeless corpse! Had ye seen how he graspet the clay-cauld hand! Had ye heard how he sobbet over it, and how he begget and prayed but for another moment to gaze on the altered face, it wad hae gane near to break your heart. I'm sure mine was sair for the poor lad. And then to see him dragged away as a prisoner by the sogers! O it was mair pitifu' than your heart can think!"

"The sogers!" repeated Mrs MacClarty, "What had the vile loons to do wi' my bairn! the cruel miscreants! was there nane to rescue him out of their bluidy hands."

"Na, na," returned Grizzy, "the minister geed his word that he shou'd na be rescued. And to say the truth, the sogers behaved wi' great discretion. They shewed nae signs of cruelty; but only said, it would na' be consistent wi' their duty, to let their prisoner escape."

"And what had my bairn done to be made a prisoner o'!" cried the widow.

"Why ye ken," returned Grizzy, "that Sandy was ay a wilfil' lad; so it's no to be wondered at, that whan he was ordered to stand this gait, and that gait, and had his hair tugged till it was ready to crack, and his neck made sair wi' standing ajee, he should tak it but unco ill. So he disobeyed orders; and than they lashed him, and his proud stamach cou'd na get o'er the disgrace; and than he ran aff, and hade himsel three days in the muirs. On the fourt day he cam here; and than the sogers got hand o' him; and they took him awa' to be tried for a deserter. So ye see Mrs Mason than got the minester to apply to the Captains, and the Coronels, aboot him; but they said they had resolved to make an example o' him, and naething cou'd mak them relent. So a' that the minester said, just gaed for naething; for they said, that by the law of court marshall he maun he shot. Weel, a' houp was at an end, when by chance Mrs Mason fand out, that the major of the regiment was the son of an auld freend o' hers, ane that she had kent and been kind to whan he was a bairn; and so she wrate a lang letter to him, and had an answer, and wrate another; and by his appointment, she and the minester are gane this very day to bear witness in Sandy's favour, and I wad fain houp they winna miss o' their errand."

The suspense in which poor Mrs MacClarty was now involved, with respect to her son's destiny, appeared more insupportable than the most dreadful certainty. The stream of consolation that was poured upon her by her loquacious friends, only seemed to add to her distress. She made no answer to their observations, but with her eyes eagerly bent towards the door, she fearfully listened to the sound of every passing footstep. At length the approach of horses was distinctly heard. Her maid hastily ran to the door for intelligence; and the old woman, whose curiosity was no less eager, as hastily followed. The poor mother's heart grew faint. Her head drooped upon her hands, and a sort of stupor came over her senses. She sat motionless and silent; nor did the entrance of the minister and Mrs Mason seem to be observed. Mrs Mason, who at a glance perceived that the sickness was the sickness of the mind, kindly took her hand and bid her be of good cheer, for that if she would recover, all her family would do well.

"Is he to live?" said Mrs MacClarty, in a low and hollow voice, fixing her eyes on Mrs Mason's as if expecting to read in them the doom of her son.

"Give thanks to God," returned the minister, "your son lives; God and his judges have dealt mercifully with him and you."

On hearing these blessed words, the poor agitated mother grasped Mrs Mason's hand, and burst into a flood of tears.

The spectators were little less affected; a considerable time elapsed before the silence that ensued was broken. At length, in faultering accents, the widow asked, whether she might hope to see her son again?

"Is he no' to come hame," said she, "to fill his father's place, and to take possession o' his inheritance? If they have granted this, I will say that they have been mercifu' indeed, but if no" –

"Though they have not granted this," returned the minister, "still they have been merciful, aye most merciful. For your son's offences were aggravated, his life was in their hands, it was most justly forfeited, yet they took pity on him, and spared him, and are you not grateful for this? if you are not, I must tell you, your ingratitude is sinful."

"Oh! you ken na' what it is to hae a bairn!" returned Mrs MacClarty in a doleful tone. "My poor Sandie! I never had the heart to contradick him sin' he was born, and now to think what command he maun he under! But I ken he'll ne'er submit to it, nor will I ever submit to it either. We have enough o' substance to buy him aff, and if we sell to the last rag, he shall never gang wi' these sogers, he never shall."

"You speak weakly, and without consideration," rejoined the minister. "Your duty as a parent, is to teach your children to obey the laws of God, and of their country. By nourishing them in disobedience, you have prepared their hearts to rebel against the one, and to disrespect the other. And now that you see what the consequence has been to this son, whom ungoverned self-will has brought to the very brink of destruction, instead of being convinced of your error, you persist in it, and would glory in repeating it. Happily your son is wiser, he has profited by his misfortunes, and has no regret but for the conduct that led to them."

"He was enticed to it," cried Mrs MacClarty. "He never wad have listed in his sober senses."

"Who enticed him to disobey his father, by going to the fair?" returned the minister. "It is the first error that is the fatal cause of all that follows; so true it is, that when we leave the path of duty but a single step, we may by that step be involved in a labyrinth from which there is no returning. Be thankful that your son has seen his error, and that he has repented of it, as becomes a Christian; and let it be your business to confirm these sentiments, and to exhort him, by his future conduct, to retrieve the past, so shall the blessing of God attend him wherever it may be his destiny to go."

"And whare is he to go?" said Mrs MacClarty. "To the East Indies," returned the minister. "To-morrow he will be on his way for that fine country, from which he may yet return to gladden your heart."

"Alace, my heart will never be gladdened mair!" said the poor widow, weeping, as she spake.

Mrs Mason was moved by her tears, though vexed by her folly; and therefore spoke to her only in the strain of consolation. But Mr Gourlay, incensed at the little gratitude she expressed for her son's deliverance, could not forbear reminding her of the predicament in which he so lately stood, and from which he had been rescued by Providence through the agency of Mrs Mason. In conclusion, he exhorted her to be thankful to God for having given her such a friend.

"The Lord will bless her for what she has done!" cried Mrs MacClarty.

"The Lord has already blessed her," returned the minister; "for a heart filled with benevolence is the first of blessings. But," continued he, "she has it still in her power to render you more essential service than any she has yet performed."

"Say you sae," cried Mrs MacClarty, eagerly.

"Yes," returned Mr Gourlay, "for if you will listen to her advice, she will instruct you in the art of governing your children's passions, and of teaching them to govern themselves, and thus, by the blessing of God, she may eventually be the means of rescuing them from a sentence of condemnation – more awful than the most awful that any human tribunal can pronounce."

The widow felt too much respect for her pastor to dispute the truth of his observation, though she probably entered a silent protest against its obvious inference. She, however, thanked him for his kind intentions, and he immediately after took his leave.

Chapter XIV

By the terms of his father's will, Robert, on his brother's leaving the kingdom, became the legal possessor of the farm. He wanted three years of one-and-twenty; but as his mother agreed to assist him in its management, it was thought, for the interest of the family, that he should succeed to it without delay.

No sooner was this point settled, than the young man, who had ever shewn a sulky antipathy to Mrs Mason, began to treat her with a rudeness that was too marked to be overlooked, nor did he receive any check from his mother for his bearish behaviour, except when she now and then, in a feeble tone, exclaimed, "Hoot, Robby, that's no' right." The girls, too, who had just began to appear sensible of the advantage of those habits of diligence and decorum, to which Mrs Mason had introduced them, were no sooner under their mother's direction, than they relaxed into indolence, and became as pert and obstreperous as ever. Mrs Mason saw that the reign of anarchy was fast approaching. She likewise saw, that her presence, which retarded it, was considered by all the family a restraint; she therefore determined to come to an explanation on the subject, and as soon as possible to change her quarters.

In pursuance of her design, Mrs Mason took the very first opportunity of speaking to Robert and his mother; and after reminding them, that the term agreed on between her and the late farmer, as a trial of her plan, had nearly expired, she informed them, that, for reasons on which she should not now enter, she thought it best for both parties, that her stay should not extend beyond it. Robert looked surprised, and even vexed; but it was the vexation of pride. He, however, remained silent. His mother, though much at a loss in what way to take Mrs Mason's notice, thought it necessary to speak for both; but she did not speak much to the purpose. Jealous of Mrs Mason's superior sense, and at the same time, conscious of the obligations she owed to her unwearied benevolence, she felt her presence as a burthen; but not being able to trace the cause of this feeling to its true and real source, which was no other than her own ignorance and pride, she durst not, even to herself, own that she disliked her.

"I'm sure," said she, – "I hope – I'm sure – for my part – I say, I'm sure – that, as far as I ken, we have done a' in oor poo'er to mak ye comfortable; but to be sure I ay thought it was nae place for you. Our ways were a' sae different, though I am sure ye ha' been very kind; I'm sure we're a' sensible o' that; but young folk dinna like to be contradicted; they're no ay sae wise as ane wau'd wish them; but they're just neeber-like. I'm sure if it's ony thing they have said that gars ye think o' leaving us, I canna help't; but I hope ye'll no blame me; for I'm sure Robby kens how often I have said, that they ought a' to be civil to you."

"What need ye be clashing sae mickle about it," cried Robert, interrupting her; "we did weel eneugh before she cam, and we'll do weel eneugh when she's gane." So saying, he went away, banging the door after him with even more than usual violence.

Mrs Mason took no notice of his behaviour; but unwilling to continue a conversation so little agreeable, she went to her own room, which she had for the last ten days seldom quitted but at the hour of meals. Disappointed in the hopes she had formed, of finding a home in the house of her kinswoman, and mortified by the seeming neglect of the family at Gowan-brae, on whose friendship she had depended with undoubting confidence, her spirits were inclined to sadness; but she would not give way to the depression. Recollecting how mercifully all the events of her life had hitherto been ordered, she chaced away despondency by trust in God; and resolving to act to the best of her judgment, fearlessly left the consequences to his disposal.

After some consideration, she resolved to apply to William Morison and his wife to take her as a lodger. They were poor; and therefore the small sum she could afford to pay, might to them be particularly useful. They were humble, and therefore would not refuse to be instructed in matters which they had never before had any opportunity to learn. She might then do good to them and to their children; and where she could do most good, there did Mrs Mason think it would be most for her happiness to go.

No sooner did she give a hint of her intention to Morison and his wife, than she perceived, from their brightened looks, that she had judged truly in imagining, that her offer would be received with joy. These poor people had been sorely visited by affliction; but their good principles and good sense had taught them to make a proper use of the visitation, in checking the spirit of pride and presumption. Their resignation to the will of God was cheerful and unfeigned, and therefore led to redoubled efforts of industry, but their exertions had not as yet effectually relieved them from the extreme poverty to which they had been reduced. After gratefully acknowledging their sense of Mrs Mason's kindness, in giving their house a preference, and declaring how much they deemed themselves honoured by having her beneath their roof, they looked at each other, and paused, as if struck by the sudden recollection of some invincible obstacle. Mrs Mason perceived their embarrassment, and asked the cause.

"What makes you hesitate?" said she. "I am afraid you think seven shillings a-week too little for my board and lodging; but you know I am to find my own wheaten bread, and my own tea, and" —— "O Madam, you are o'er generous," cried Peggy, interrupting her; "you give o'er mickle by a great deal, but still I fear, that in winter we may not he able to make things comfortable to you. Were it in summer, we should do weel eneugh."

"Then why not in winter?" said Mrs Mason; "I shall advance money to buy coal if that be all."

"Don't speak of it, Peggy," said William, gently pulling his wife's sleeve; "though it be winter, we shall do weel eneugh, there's nae fear."

"Na, na, gudeman," returned Peggy, "you're no sae strong yet as to be able to sleep without a bed through the winter in this cauld house; it manna be."

"Without a bed!" cried Mrs Mason; "Why should he be without a bed?"

"Why, Madam," said William, "since my wife has let the cat out o' the bag, as the saying is, it's as weel to tell you the truth. We have not a bed in the house but one; and that was bought for us by gude Mr Stewart of Gowan-brae, at the time that a' our furniture was rouped aff frae our house, at *****."

"Had we been now as we were then," cried Peggy, "how comfortable should we have made Mrs Mason. She should have had no more to do but just to speak her wishes."

"I don't fear being comfortable enough as it is," said Mrs Mason; "but what is become of the bed I slept on for so many weeks, and which you so kindly offered for my accommodation during all the time of Mrs MacClarty's illness?"

"O the want of a bed was nothing then," returned Peggy, "the weather was warm, and some weel-laid straw did us vastly weel: for my own part, I could put up with it all the year through; but my gudeman has been so weakly since he had the rheumatism, that I would he feared for his being the war' o't."

"And did you really put yourselves to such a shift, in order to oblige me?" said Mrs Mason. "What kindness! what delicacy in concealing the extent of the obligation! It grieves me to learn, that hearts so warm should have experienced misfortune; and by the hint you gave of selling off your furniture on leaving *****, I fear your circumstances have not been so prosperous as I heartily wish them."

"Since my misfortunes have been in some measure brought on by my own indiscretion, I ought not," said William, "to complain."

"Indeed, Madam; he does himself wrang," cried Peggy, "he never was guilty o' ony indiscretion in his days; but just only trusted o'er far, to the honesty and discretion of a fause-hearted loon, that cheated mony a man that kent mair o' business than he did. It was nae fau't o' William's, that the man was a rogue, yet he blames himsel in a way that vexes me to hear him."

"I do blame myself," said William, "for had I been contented to go on with my business, as my father did before me, on a scale within my means, my profits, though small, would have been certain. But I wished to raise my wife and bairns above their station; and God, who saw the pride of my heart, has punished me."

"If you only risked your own," said Mrs Mason, "your ambition was blameless, and your exertions, laudable."

"Alas! madam," returned William, "no man that enters into what they call speculations in business, can say that he risks only his own: he risks the money of his friends, and of his neighbours, and of all who, from confidence in his honesty, give him trust or credit. Grant that neither friend nor neighbour had suffered – and I hope to God that in the end none will suffer a farthing's loss by me – yet how can I answer to my conscience, for the ruin I have brought upon my wife and children? Nay, Peggy, you must not hinder me to speak. You ken that had your honest father seen what has happened, it you'd ha' brought his gray hairs wi' sorrow to the grave. He told me that he gi'ed ye to me wi' better will than to a richer man, because be kent that I loved ye weel, and wou'd ay be kind to ye, and that the siller he had gathered wi' meikle care and toil, I wou'dna lightly spend upon my pleasure – O I canna bear to think on't! When I look round these bare wa's, and see what I have reduced you to, I think mysel little better than a villain!"

Peggy hastily brushing away a falling tear, held out her hand to her husband, saying, with a smile – "Ye maun be an unco sort o' villain, William, for I wou'd rather beg my bread wi' you through the warld, than be the greatest lady in the land! But what will Mrs Mason think of us?"

"I think," said Mrs Mason, "that you are a worthy couple, and that you deserve to be happy, and will be happy too, in the end – not the less so perhaps for having known misfortune."

"O that you could gar my gudeman think sae!" cried Peggy; "I'm ay telling him, that if he wou'dna tint heart, we ha' tint naething. We are yet but young, we ha' promising bairns, gude health, and the warld for the winning; what should we desire mair! Could we but contrive to make the house fit to receive you, I should have no fears for the future. You would bring a blessing with you, I'm sure you would."

Mrs Mason obviated every difficulty, by saying, that she meant to furnish her own apartment, and after a little further conversation, in which every thing was arranged to mutual satisfaction, she set out on her return to the farm, animated by the delightful hope of having it in her power to dispense a degree of happiness to her fellow creatures. As she slowly proceeded homeward, an elderly man, mounted on a good horse, prepared for carrying double, passed her on the road, and having stopped a minute at Mrs MacClarty's door, turned again to meet her. On coming up, he said he was sent by Mr Stewart of Gowan-brae, with his and Miss Mary's compliments, to beg that she would do them the favour of going there to dinner, and that they should send her back in a few days. Observing that Mrs Mason hesitated concerning what answer she should give, the faithful old servant proceeded to enforce the message, by telling her that he was sure it would do them good to see her – "for I am far mista'en, madam," said he, "if they dinna stand in need o' comfort."

"Has any misfortune befallen the family?" asked Mrs Mason, anxiously.

"I kenna, madam," returned the servant, "whether it can be weel called a misfortune; for a marriage may be a vexation to ane's friends that's nae misfortune in the end." "And Miss Stewart has occasioned this vexation, I suppose?" said Mrs Mason.

"Ye guess right," returned the old man; "she has made a match to please hersel', and as she has brewed sae she maun drink; but my poor master taks it sair to heart; and it is e'en hard enough that the bairn should cross him maist, that he never crossed in his life."

Mrs Mason made no reply, but directing him to the stable to put up his horse for half an hour, said she should then be ready to accompany him. Having informed her cousin, in friendly terms, of the arrangements she had made with the Morisons, and assured her of the continuance of her kindness and good will, she quickly made what little preparations were necessary for her departure; and was on the road to Gowan-brae before Mrs MacClarty had recovered her astonishment.

As Mrs Mason rode from the door, Robert made his appearance. His mother on seeing him, burst into a violent flood of tears, and accused him as the cause of her losing the best friend that she ever had in the world – "one who," she said, "was a credit to her family, and an honour and a credit to them all." She reminded him of all that she had done for them in sickness – how she had attended his dying father – what exertions she had made to save his brother's life – what care she had taken of the family – how little trouble she had given, and how generously she had paid for the little trouble she occasioned. "And now," cried she,

"she'll be just the same friend to the Morisons she has been to us! I wou'dna wonder that they got every farthing she has in the warld. Scores o' fine silk goons, and grand petticoats and stockings; and sic a sight o' mutches and laces as wou'd fill twa o' Miss Tweedy's shop! Ay, ay, the Morisons will get it a', and a' her money forebye! They'll no be the fools to part wi' her that we ha' been; they're o'er cunning for that!"

Robert, who, in his treatment of Mrs Mason, had had no other end in view than the immediate gratification of his own bad temper, was enraged at this representation of the advantages which his neighbour's family were likely to derive from the event. Far, however, from acknowledging that he had been to blame, he insolently retorted on his mother, and poured on her a torrent of abuse. The poor woman attempted to speak in her own justification; but her voice was drowned in the louder and more vehement accents of her hopeful son. She had then no other resource but tears, and bitterly did she weep – bitterly did she lament herself. Her tears and lamentations aggravated the stings of conscience in Robert's heart; but where the passions are habitually uncontrouled, the stings of conscience have no other effect than to increase the irritation.

Had Mrs MacClarty been capable of reasoning, how would her soul have been wrung with remorse, had she then said to herself – "*There was a time when this boy's passions might haw been subdued, when, with a little care, he might have learned to controul them!*"

Chapter XV

A Marriage, and a Wedding

Mrs Mason had no sooner entered the gate leading up to Gowan-brae, than her kind friends were at the door ready to receive her. "You are very good," said Mr Stewart, as he conducted her to the parlour, "you are very good in coming to us after our apparent neglect of you, in circumstances that called for a double portion of attention; but when you know all that has happened, you will forgive us."

"I do know all, my good sir," returned Mrs Mason; "your trusty old Donald has told me enough, to shew me how fully your time has been occupied. I feel for the vexation you have suffered, but it is past, and I trust all may yet go well."

Mr Stewart shook his head. "We had better not speak of it," said he, in a melancholy voice. "Well, we shall not speak of it then," said Mrs Mason, "I had rather speak of the boys. When did you hear of them? When are they to have a holiday at Gowan-brae?"

Having thus given a turn to the conversation, she endeavoured to keep it up with cheerfulness; and so far succeeded, that a stranger would have thought all the party in excellent spirits.

After dinner, as soon as the servant who attended them had left the room, Mr Stewart became absent and thoughtful. A pause ensued in the conversation, during which Mary kept her eyes anxiously fixed upon her father. Starting at length from his reverie, he turned to Mrs Mason, and said, "it was now time to give her a full account of all that had taken place, but that he found he must leave the task to Mary. I have not patience to go over it," said he; "but I wish for your advice, and you must therefore know all. I shall be back by the time Mary has finished the recital, and in the mean time must speak to my labourers."

"My dear father!" said Mary, looking wistfully after him, as he left the room – "My dear good father will never be happy again!"

"With such a daughter as you, how can he be unhappy?" said Mrs Mason. "Your duty and affection will soon make

him forget the disappointment he has had in your sister,
and perhaps this match of hers may not turn out so ill as he
apprehends."

"Oh it cannot turn out well," said Mary. "How can any
match turn out well, that begins as this has done; by
wounding the heart of so good, so kind a father!"

"Young women seldom argue in this way now-a-days,"
returned Mrs Mason. "Love is, in the creed of sentiment,
and of plays, and novels, a sufficient excuse for the breach
of every duty, both before marriage and after it."

"I believe I am as capable of a strong attachment as my
sister is," said Mary; "but I could not love a man without
first esteeming him, and I could not esteem the man, who,
in pursuance of his own selfish purposes, led me into the
guilt of ingratitude, falsehood, and dissimulation."

"But you know, my dear, that in every clandestine correspondence, art and dissimulation are absolutely indispensable,"
said Mrs Mason.

"And therefore," cried Mary, "I abhor every thing clandestine. But perhaps I think worse of Mr Mollins than he
deserves. You shall read my sister's letters, and judge for
yourself."

"I shall read them afterwards," said Mrs Mason; "but
wish you in the mean time to give me some account of what
has happened, that I may be prepared to speak upon it with
your father. Where did your sister meet with Captain
Mollins? Who is he? What do you know of his character,
or what did she know of it? It is of those particulars that I
long to be informed."

"It is," replied Mary, "in her intimacy with Mrs Flinders,
that all our vexations have originated. Yet Mrs Flinders
meant no harm to Bell, but the contrary. She is a vain
shewy woman, and liked to have a young person of Bell's
appearance in her train; for you know that my sister has
naturally a genteel air, and such a taste in dress as sets it off
to the best advantage. She was much admired by all the
gentlemen who visited at Mount Flinders; but though taken
notice of when there by many of the first people in the
country, I know not how it was, but no one endeavoured to
keep up the acquaintance, except officers, and students,
from Edinburgh, and such sort of people who were in the
country only by chance. Still every one spoke of the great

advantage and happiness of her being honoured with the friendship of so fine a lady as Mrs Flinders; for excepting my father, I do not know a person in the country that makes such a distinction between being genteel, and being respectable, as would lead them to decline for their children an introduction to whatever was beyond their station. I confess I thought my father's objections the effects of prejudice, and entertained a hope, that Bell would make a conquest of some man of fortune. With this view, I rejoiced in the prospect of her being seen to such advantage at the races. I did not know that Captain Mollins was to be of the party; for though he was much at Mount Flinders, his acquaintance with the family was so merely accidental, that it did not warrant his being treated as an intimate.

"You will find by my sister's letters how much she was intoxicated by the gay and brilliant scene to which she was introduced at Edinburgh. The attention she met with, was indeed sufficient to turn a wiser head; for she danced at the balls with lords and baronets, and was constantly in the parties of a fine lady, a Mrs Spurton, whose equipage was described in the newspapers, as the finest that had ever appeared. Bell spoke of this lady as the intimate friend of Mrs Flinders, and the most charming of human beings. Her husband too was a delightful man, intimately acquainted with the first nobility, and quite regardless of expense. Mr and Mrs Flinders were thrown entirely into the background by this still more brilliant pair; but Captain Mollins, who was a prime favourite of Mr Spurton's, gained not a little in Bell's opinion, from the avowed friendship of so great a man.

"As my sister had no one but me to whom she could communicate the overflowings of her heart, she gave me a full description of the events of each successive day; and from the delight with which she dwelt on the compliments paid to her beauty by men of superior rank, I had no suspicion of Mollins being all the time a favoured lover. Nor do I believe he would have proved so at the last, had any of the lords she danced with stepped forward as declared admirers. But alas, they one by one took leave; and in ten days after the last of the races, their own party was the only one that remained in Edinburgh. It was then that Bell, for the first time, communicated to me an account of the embarrassment in which she had involved herself, by contracting debts for articles of dress, which she said it was absolutely impossible to do without; and which, by Mrs Flinders's advice, she had taken from the most fashionable milliner and mantua-maker in town. Mrs Flinders, indeed, told her, that genteel people never paid in ready money, and that many young ladies never paid their bills at all, or entertained a thought of paying them, till they were married: but Bell's early prejudices upon this subject had been so strongly impressed, that she could not easily reconcile herself to this new doctrine. Her pride was mortified at being obliged to implore the forbearance of tradespeople, at whose expense her vanity had been fed, but the dread of exposing to her father the extent of her extravagance, compelled her to submit to the mortification. Her gay friend laughed at her scruples; and reminding her of the independent fortune of which she was to come into possession at her marriage, advised her by all means to hasten the period of her emancipation. The independent fortune to which Mrs Flinders alluded, and which, in the zeal of her friendship, she always represented as very considerable, is in fact no more than fifteen hundred pounds. I always considered the exaggerated reports which Mrs Flinders spread of it, as ill-judged kindness; but my sister viewed it in a different light, and was evidently pleased with the fiction from which she derived a momentary addition to her consequence. How far Mr Mollins was deceived by these representations I know not; but his attentions, which seemed during the race-week to have been rather slackened, became now more assiduous than ever. This you will perceive, from the hints incidentally scattered through these letters; but nothing they contain, would lead one to suspect that they had then formed any serious engagement. I was the less suspicious of this, because I was persuaded that Bell would be too proud of having made a conquest of a man of rank and fortune to conceal a circumstance so flattering. At length, in a few hasty lines, written to inform me, that she was next day to set off on a jaunt to the Highlands with the Spurtons, Flinders, and Mr Mollins; she so far let me into the secret, as to say, that 'she approached the crisis of her fate, and that she would soon be either the most miserable, or the happiest of human beings.'

"I could not conceal this circumstance from my father, who was far from partaking of the sanguine hopes I entertained of the result. He did not doubt that Mollins was a man of fortune; but he thought the match unsuitable: and declared, that in his experience, he had never seen any unions so productive of happiness, as those that were cemented by a correspondence in circumstances and views, not only between the parties themselves, but extended to their friends and connections. While we were still debating this point, as we sat at breakfast the following morning, my father received a letter, which he read with such marks of agitation and dismay, as quite appalled me. He threw it to me when he had finished, and hiding his face with both his hands, burst into tears. I eagerly looked at the signature, but the name was unknown to me. The contents briefly stated – that respect for my father's character induced the writer to inform him, that his daughter was on the brink of ruin. That, by the vain and foolish pair, under whose protection he had unfortunately placed her, she had been introduced to society the most contemptible. A gambler of the name of Spurton, and his wife the kept-mistress of a man of quality; and that these worthless people had betrayed her to a needy adventurer, to whom even her small fortune was a consideration sufficient to tempt him to the darkest deed of villainy, that of sacrificing a young woman's happiness, and a worthy father's peace.

"On reading this letter," continued Mary, "I boldly pronounced it the work of an incendiary, and entreated my father to be comforted, as I could prove it to be, at least, partly false. That the Spurtons are persons of irreproachable character, I can have no doubt, said I. How else could they get into the society of people of rank and fortune? Were he a gambler, and she a woman of doubtful reputation, do you think that ladies and gentlemen of undoubted character would have gone to their balls, or been partakers of their splendid festivals? Yet that they did so I can prove, for at one of these balls Mr Spurton introduced a lord to my sister, and called him his particular friend! This of itself is conclusive testimony in their favour. I then endeavoured to persuade him, that all the information given concerning

Mr Mollins was equally false and malicious; and that
though he might be vain and extravagant, and have a thousand faults, he was doubtless a man of fortune, and well
received by the world."

" 'But may he not be the villain to seduce my daughter's
affections, and bring her to ruin and disgrace?' said my
father.

"Of that I replied I had no apprehensions, I too well
knew my sister, to fear that her affections would ever be
seduced by love. On the contrary, I was convinced that the
man who could most certainly gratify her ambition, would
still have in her heart the decided preference.

"By these arguments, I in some degree tranquillized my
father's mind; but his anxiety, to prevent my sister from
taking any irretrievable step, induced him to set off for
Edinburgh without delay. Learning on his arrival there, that
the Flinders's had set out with the intention of going by
Perth to Blair in Athole, he took the same route. At every
inn on the road, he, in answer to his inquiries, received
such intelligence as left no room to doubt that he should
speedily overtake them, but by the time he reached Perth,
he was too much fatigued to pursue the journey on horseback. He therefore was obliged to order a chaise; and as
soon as it could be got ready, proceeded by Dunkeld to
Blair and from Blair onward all the way to Inverness. There
at the door of the head inn he saw the three carriages,
whose route he had so diligently traced; but what was
his disappointment on finding that they were filled with
strangers.

"The strangers were not destitute of humanity; and perceiving how deeply he was chagrined, endeavoured to
soothe and tranquillize his spirits. In this they were kinder
than his own child, whom, soon after he entered Perth, on
his return, he saw, talking from the window of the inn, to a
gentleman, who stood in the street below. As the chaise
drew up, she caught the glance of her father's eye, and
retreated, uttering a screaming exclamation; Mollins, to
whom she had been talking, running at the same time into
the house. You may imagine how my father was agitated.
He involuntarily pursued his way up stairs to the room
where Bell was. As he entered, she threw herself into a chair
by the window, and either fainted, or pretended to faint.

"In the name of goodness, what is the meaning of all this?"
said my father, addressing himself to Mrs Flinders, who
was holding her smelling-bottle to my sister, who was supported by Captain Mollins.

"'Why, Miss Stewart,' cried Mrs Flinders, 'what can be
the matter with you? It is only your father! Bless me, poor
dear, what weak nerves you have! Pray, Sir, speak to her,
tell her you are not angry. Indeed Miss, your papa is not
displeased with you. Your papa is' –

"'She best knows whether I have cause to be displeased
with her,' said my father, gravely. My sister opening her
eyes, looked expressively at Mollins, who seemed in great
confusion, and as if undetermined what to do. At length,
holding up Bell's hand, which was folded in his, and turning
towards my father, he stammered out, 'You see, sir, you
perceive, sir, this lady, sir, this lady is my wife.'

"'And who are you, sir?' cried my father, indignantly.

"'I, I, I, sir, am a gentleman,' returned Mollins. 'O yes,
sir,' cried Mrs Flinders, 'we all know that Captain Mollins
is quite a gentleman; a man of fortune too. Miss Stewart
has had great luck, I assure you, but it was very sly of her
to get married without telling me.'

"My father, without taking any notice of Mrs Flinders,
advanced towards Bell, and taking her hand in a solemn
manner – 'Isabell,' said he, 'infatuated girl that you are,
listen to me, I conjure you. By the laws of this country, you
have it now in your power, by acknowledging a marriage
with this man, to fix yourself upon him as his wife. But
think, I beseech you, before you ratify the sentence of your
own misery. For what but misery can be the consequence
of a union, which substitutes *a falsehood* for the marriage
vow, and which, by the manner of it, proclaims to the
world, that the woman had ceased to respect herself!'

"Mollins here began to bluster, but my father silenced
him, and proceeded, while Bell wept, and sobbed aloud.
'My Isabell, my dear child, have I then been so unkind a
father, that you should thus break from my arms, to rush
into the arms of, you know not whom? But I mean not to
upbraid you. I only mean to tell you, that, however faulty,
nay however guilty you may have been, your father's arms
are still open to receive you, and that peace still waits you
in your father's house.'

"'Pray sir,' cried Mr Flinders, interrupting him; 'pray think of your daughter's character; after Mollins's declaration, it would be ruined, absolutely ruined.'

"'And will such a marriage as this wipe out the stain?' returned my father. 'Is it not saying to the world, that after having sacrificed delicacy and modesty at the shrine of folly, she stooped to solder her reputation by a falsehood? No, no. If she is thus sunk, thus degraded, let her, by humility and penitence, purify her own heart, and mine shall be open to receive her. Come my child, my Isabell; come to that home where no upbraidings' –

"'Sir,' interrupted Mollins, to whom Mr Flinders had been all this time making signals to speak, 'Sir, I claim this lady as my wife. Heaven and earth shall not separate us; for am I not her husband? Say my love, my dearest, fairest creature, are you not mine in the eye of heaven?'

"'Speak at once,' cried my father, "are you that man's wife?'

"'Yes,' returned Bell, in a voice scarcely audible; and giving her hand to Mollins as she spoke.

"'Poor misguided child!' said my father, 'may you never have cause to repent of the rash act, though it sends a knell to your father's heart.'

"He then turned to go, but was surrounded by the Flinders, and the other people, all calling out, that he must not leave them in ill will, but stay and be reconciled, and dine with them comfortably. Mrs Flinders was flippantly urgent, saying, that she was sure it would be very hard if he bore any resentment against her, for that she had treated his daughter like a sister.

"'I can have no resentment,' he returned, 'against any of this party; for I never feel resentment, where I have not previously felt respect.' So saying, he quitted them, and went to another room.

"In the evening he received a note from my sister, entreating to be admitted. I shall give you a particular account of all that passed at some other time; it is enough at present to say, that they consented to remain with him at Perth, until they could be regularly married, which they were on the following Monday; after which they came all together to Edinburgh, where my father had scarcely arrived before he was seized with a return of what we here

call a rose fever, a disorder to which he has been often subject. I set off for Edinburgh immediately on hearing of his
illness, and found him much distressed in spirits, but not,
the physician assured me, in any danger. He told me, that
Mr Mollins had been very attentive to him; and that from
all he had seen, he thought him a good natured, vain, silly
fellow. I was glad to find him thus far reconciled, and said
all in my power to persuade him that all might yet turn out
better than he expected. He assured me, that he was as willing to hope as I was, but that he could as yet find nothing
to rest his hopes upon. 'As yet,' said he, 'I neither know
what, nor who he is: but as he never, upon any occasion,
gives a direct and explicit answer to any question, I am at a
loss to determine, whether the ambiguity of his expressions,
arises from a confused intellect, or from a desire of conceal-
ment. The behaviour of your sister too, gives me great
uneasiness. She keeps aloof from me, as if I were her
enemy. Alas! how little have I deserved this of her!'

"The first time I was alone with my sister," continued
Mary, "I endeavoured to expostulate with her, on the
impropriety of keeping at such a distance from her father,
and treating him with such reserve. But she immediately
flew into a passion, and said that, her father had used both
her and Mr Mollins extremely ill; and that if Mr Mollins
had taken her advice, he would never have spoken to him
again, after the vile aspersions he had thrown upon his character, by seeming to doubt that he was a gentleman. Mr
Mollins, she said, despised such base insinuations; and as
his friend Lord Dashmore justly observed, he knew too
much of the world to be surprised at the mean and vulgar
notions of those who knew nothing of life or manners.
For her share, she expected to meet with a great deal of
envy and ill-nature, and she saw she should not be disappointed.

" 'My dear sister! how thoughtlessly you speak!' returned
I. 'Were you married to the greatest lord in Christendom,
I should not envy your good luck. But is it not natural, that
your father should wish to know the real circumstances
and situation of your husband, and does it not seem strange
that either of you should wish to conceal them from him?'

" 'Mr Mollins has a right to act just as he pleases,' cried
my sister. 'I hope no one will dispute that! but I can tell

you, he has not so little spirit, as to submit to be questioned. He despises such meanness. No wonder, living, as he has done all his life, in the first of company.'

A great deal more passed, to as little purpose, my sister getting more and more angry as she spoke. We were interrupted by Mr Mollins, who entered holding two open letters in his hand, which he presented to my sister with a careless air, though vexation was visibly painted on his countenance.

" 'You must give them to your father, my love!' said he, forcing a smile, 'for you know these are his business, not mine!'

" 'Ah dear Mollins,' cried Bell, looking at the contents of the letters, 'you know not how you would oblige me, by settling these trifles. I will rather want the diamond earrings, indeed I will. I will rather do any thing than speak to my father now, he is so peevish and so cross.'

" 'But I tell you I can't, upon my faith, my love, I can't,' returned Mollins, 'my Steward has run off, and I know not when I may get a remittance. I would not tell you before for vexing you, though it is of very little consequence; for I shall not lose more than a few hundreds by the rascal. But it puts me to present inconvenience. Pray ask the old gentleman for a hundred pounds at once. It will oblige me. Pray do, and these bills shall be paid directly.'

" 'A hundred pounds!' cried Bell; 'Why my dear Mollins, I imagine you believe my father thinks as little of a hundred pounds as you do.'

" 'O the old curmudgeon!" cried Mollins; "I forgot what a close hanks he is, but your sister here will coax him into it; I know he can refuse her nothing.'

"It were in vain to attempt describing to you what I suffered; when worn out by their teizing and urgent importunity, I at length was prevailed on to speak to my father on the subject of my sister's unpaid bills. I anticipated all that he would feel upon the occasion; for though I well knew, that no one regards money less for its own sake than he does, I likewise knew that few consider extravagance in a light so serious as that in which he views it. He considers it as the parent of every vice, and the grave of every virtue; and has therefore laboured to impress a just abhorrence of it upon our minds. You may then imagine what an effect the knowledge of my sister's extravagance produced upon him. It instantly possessed him with an idea of her levity, and want of principle, which it is impossible to eradicate, and from which he forebodes the most shocking conse- quences. Had she deigned to make proper concessions, she might perhaps have lessened the impression; but she affects to ascribe all he says to the meanest motives, and in return for all his tender anxiety for her honour and happiness, speaks to him with the haughty air of a person who has been deeply injured. In short, though my father paid all the expences of their living with him in Edinburgh, and all the debts my sister had contracted, he got no thanks: but, on the contrary, seemed to have rather given offence, than con- ferred obligation. I believe I have mentioned that, by the terms of my grand-father's will, the sum of fifteen hundred pounds was to be paid to her the day of her marriage. Mr Mollins seems to despise this paltry fortune, as scarcely worthy his acceptance. Yet, would you believe it, he, on my father's speaking to him on the subject, the day after we returned home, absolutely refused to permit two thirds of this to remain in trustees hands, for the benefit of my sister, and insists on having the whole paid down to him, on the terms of the will! This circumstance – but here comes my father, who will tell you all about it himself."

"Well, Mrs Mason, Mary has by this time given you a full account of our vexation," said Mr Stewart. "It may be explained in a few words. My daughter will be one of the many victims, to the epidemical frenzy, which has of late spread through our country, the desire of shining in a sphere above our own. People who labour under this disease, mistake show for splendour, and splendour for happiness, and while their pulses throb with the fever of vanity, think no sacrifice too great, to procure a momentary gratification to its insatiable thirst. From the palace to the cottage, the fever rages with equal force, sweeping before it every worthy feeling, and every solid virtue. O my friend! could we but look into the interior of all the families in the kingdom, what scenes of domestic misery would present themselves to our view, all originating in this accursed passion for gentility!"

"I believe, indeed," said Mrs Mason, "that, with regard to my own sex at least, the love of dress, and desire of admiration, have ruined hundreds, for one that has been brought to misery through the strength of other passions." "True," replied Mr Stewart. "But it is not to that silly vanity that I alone allude; it is to that still sillier ambition of figuring in a higher station, which destroys all notions of right and wrong, rendering vice and folly, if gilded by fashion, the objects of preference, nay of high and first regard. What could my daughter Bell have thought of such a silly fellow as Mollins, if he had been the son of a neighbouring farmer?"

"Indeed, my good sir," returned Mrs Mason, "there is no accounting for fancies of young people – one sees such marriages. So – "

"Believe me," interrupted Mr Stewart, "such matches may always be accounted for. No unsuitable or incongruous marriage ever yet took place, but where there was some wrong bias in the mind, some disease lurking in the imagination, which inflamed the vanity in that very way which the marriage promised to gratify. Had Bell's passion for wealth been born of avarice, she would have despised this Mollins: but a man, who lived among lords and ladies, was in her eyes irresistible. It is this propensity that will be her ruin. Yes, my good friend, I see it plainly. Their vanity is greater than their fortune can support. Mollins acknowledges that he is already embarrassed. He will soon be more so: they will live beyond their income, in order to keep up with the gay and giddy fools whose steps they follow. Bell's beauty, her levity, her want of fixed and solid principle, – O, Mrs Mason, what a shocking view does it present! I see her ruin before me. Night and day it haunts my imagination. A foreboding voice incessantly whispers, that if she ever returns to her father's house, she will return dishonoured and disgraced. O may I ere then be laid beside her angel mother in the silent grave!"

After a considerable pause, Mrs Mason addressed herself to the afflicted father. She could not in conscience say, that his fears were groundless, but she endeavoured to chequer them with hope, assuring him, that the time would come when his daughter would learn to prize the blessings of domestic happiness, and that the good principles she had imbibed in youth, would, in the meantime, prevent her from straying far from the path of duty. At Mr Stewart's request, she promised to remain at Gowan-brae, until Mr and Mrs Mollins returned from Mount Flinders, and then to take an opportunity of speaking to Mrs Mollins on the subject of her future plans.

Chapter XVI

An unexpected Meeting between old Acquaintances

Mrs Mason had spent a full week at Gowan-brae, before the quiet of the well-ordered family was interrupted by the return of the new-married pair. They at length came accompanied by Mr Flinders, who with Mr Mollins went immediately into Mr Stewart's business room, Bell meantime going into the parlour. On seeing Mrs Mason, she drew herself up haughtily, with a look expressive of surprise: and in return to her salutation, dropped a very distant curtsey. The good woman perfectly understood the meaning of her behaviour; but not at all discomposed by it, she placidly resumed her work.

"Well," said Mary, "I suppose your time has been pleasantly spent at Mount Flinders, that you have staid so much longer than you intended."

"One's time is always spent pleasantly there," returned Bell. "How can it be otherwise with people, who always keep company with people of fashion like themselves. It is some advantage, indeed, to have such neighbours! so gay, and so agreeable! and we have been so happy! do you know we have never sat down to dinner till six o'clock, nor gone to bed till past three in the morning."

"Then," said Mary, smiling, "you dined at the same hour that our plowmen dine all the winter; and as to going to bed at three in the morning, the shepherd has kept still genteeler hours than you, for I believe that during the last week he has never gone to bed till day break."

"I wonder how you can talk of such vulgar wretches," returned Mrs Mollins. "If you would but do yourself justice, you might soon rise out of the low sphere in which you have been buried. You ought now to aspire to something superior. I am sure I shall always be happy to assist you; and, with Mr Mollins's connections, you may get into the genteelest society when you please. Do you know that Lord Dashmore has been two days at Mount Flinders, and paid Mr Mollins and me such attention! he has invited us to spend our Christmas at Dashmore Lodge. Won't it be charming? But his Lordship has quite a friendship for Mr Mollins. They played together at billiards all morning; and Mr Harry Spend assured me, that Mr Mollins was by far the more graceful player of the two: But every one observes what a fine figure Mr Mollins has."

"But, my dear Bell, did not Mr Mollins tell my father, that business called him immediately to England? How is it then that he contrives to spend his Christmas at Dashmore Lodge?"

"How little you know of genteel life!" cried Mrs Mollins. "Do you think that men of fashion tie themselves down to rules of going here or there to a day, as my father does? Mr Mollins ought to be sure to visit his estate in Dorsetshire this winter, but a few weeks delay can be of no consequence. And besides was he to go there at Christmas time, he must entertain all his neighbours, which he says would be a great bore; so he thinks it better to put it off till they have gone up to Parliament, and then he will leave me at Bath, and take a dash down by himself. But I hear the gentlemen coming in; pray don't say that I mentioned" –

At that moment the door opened; and Mr Stewart entered, saying, with a disturbed air, that his daughter's presence was necessary, and that he wished Mrs Mason and Mary to accompany her to his writing chamber. While he spoke, Mr Flinders softly came up, and laying his hand upon his shoulder, "I wish, Mr Stewart," said he, "I really wish I could persuade you to consent with cheerfulness. You cannot fail to offend Mr Mollins by betraying such a want of confidence in his honour. Has he not promised, on the word of a gentleman, to make a settlement on Mrs Mollins suitable to his fortune."

"Where is his fortune!" cried Mr Stewart, peevishly. "He may carry it all on his back, for aught I know to the contrary."

"I do assure you, you wrong my friend Mollins greatly," replied Mr Flinders. "Mr Spurton told me he had hunted over his estate in Dorsetshire many times, and that his father kept the best pack of hounds in the country. Do you think my dear Sir, that if I had not known him to be a man of fortune" –

"Pho!" said Mr Stewart, "if he is a man of fortune, why

should he scruple to secure to my daughter, this small sum?"

"Because you see, my dear Sir, to settle formally such a trifling matter would be, in his opinion, a sort of disgrace; and besides, I dare say he wants money."

"I dare say he does," said Mr Stewart, drily, "and he must have it too. But I shall take all here witness to my intentions." Mr Stewart then advanced to Mrs Mason to give her his arm, while Mr Flinders, Mrs Mollins, and Mary stepped before them into the other room.

Mollins, who, as they entered, was sitting at the table, leaning his head upon his hand, apparently buried in thought, roused himself on seeing them, and was about to speak with his usual flippancy; when perceiving Mrs Mason, he started, and momentarily changed colour, his complexion quickly varying from the pale hue of ashes to the deepest crimson.

Mrs Mollins observing her husband's confusion, went up and whispered to him, "I don't wonder at your being surprised, my dear, to find such people here; but don't appear, to mind it; my father has such odd notions!"

"Does she know me?" cried Mollins, eagerly; "has she told you that she knows me?"

"No," said Mrs Mason, who overheard the question; "Mrs Mollins does not know that I have ever had the honour of seeing you; perhaps if she had, – But you and I shall talk of that another time, Mr Mollins. We are here I understand just now upon business. I hope I may tell Mr Stewart, that you are willing to settle his daughter's fortune in any way he pleases."

"You are very good, Mrs Mason," cried Mollins in great confusion; "you were always good, I – I shall be guided by and entirely – only – only promise – you know what I mean – you" –

"I do know what you mean," said Mrs Mason, "and I shall promise to be your friend if I find that you deserve it." Then, without taking any notice of the exclamations of surprise and astonishment that were bursting from every tongue, she invited Mr Mollins to a private conference in the adjoining room. In about half an hour they returned, and Mr Mollins, addressing himself to Mr Stewart, said, that as Mrs Mason had convinced him of the propriety of signing the papers he had shewed him, he was now willing to do it immediately. The papers were signed and witnessed in solemn silence, Mr Flinders biting his lip all the while; not knowing what to make of the sudden turn which the appearance of Mrs Mason had given to the business. He began to entertain some unfavourable suspicions with regard to Mollins; but recollecting the obligations he had been under to him for introducing him to two lords and a sporting baronet at the cockpit, gratitude sealed his lips, and he took leave without any apparent diminution of regard.

"I am glad that he is gone!" cried Mary. "We may now speak freely, and I am sure we all long to know how you and Mr Mollins comes to be so well acquainted. My sister won't say so; but I see she is dying to hear."

"I want to hear nothing about it," cried Mrs Mollins; "but I know you always take a pleasure in mortifying me, I know you do."

"Bell," said Mr Stewart, "if Mr Mollins has no acquaintances of whom he need be more ashamed, I congratulate you. I rejoice at least that I shall now have an opportunity of knowing how and what your husband is; for I confess that" –

"And what should you know of any one, at Gowanbrae?" cried Mrs Mollins. "I am sure if it was not for seeing the Court Calendar at Mount Flinders, I should not have known the names of above twenty people in my life. But you have such a hatred to strangers, and such a prejudice against any one that is in the least genteel, that I believe you would rather have seen me married to a shoemaker than to a gentleman."

"You had better not speak against shoemakers, my dear," said Mrs Mason, "as you happen to be nearly connected with several of them. I have on my feet at the present moment a pair of shoes made by your father-in-law, and I never wore better in my life, and though I believe he never was out of his native village, he is a very honest man."

"Mr Mollins's father a shoemaker!" cried Bell; "I wonder what you will say next. I declare I am quite diverted." She then burst into an hysterical laugh, which ended in a passionate flood of tears. Poor Mary, who was really sorry for her sister, endeavoured to sooth the raging storm, but was repelled with indignation; and Mrs Mason, who better knew how to treat such cases, begged her to desist until the tempest had spent itself. She then drew near, and in a gentle voice said, "believe me, I should hate myself, Mrs Mollins, if I could take pleasure in distressing you, but I have thought it better that you should know the truth, than expose yourself to ridicule, by speaking of your husband's family, or of his circumstances, or situation, in such a tone as that you latterly assumed."

Mrs Mollins, who was now quite exhausted, uttered a deep groan. Then after a few heavy sobs, cried, "If I have been deceived, I shall never see him again. No, I shall never live with him. I shall die sooner – Oh!" – then covering her face with her hands, she again wept bitterly.

"My dear Bell," said Mr Stewart, taking her hand affectionately, "you are still my child. Your father's house will be ever open to you. But remember the vows that are upon you. You have bound yourself by ties that are indissoluble as they are sacred, and though your husband were the lowest, nay even the worst of mankind, your fate is bound in his."

"But her husband is neither the one nor the other," said Mrs Mason. "He is, as I have told you, the son of an honest tradesman, who lives in a small village in Yorkshire and – "

"And – and – the – the estate in Dorsetshire, how did he come by it?" sobbed Mrs Mollins.

"He came by it," said Mrs Mason, "as people who forsake the direct path of truth come by all they boast of, telling one falsehood to support another; a species of lying, which, as it goes under the appellation of quizzing, or humming, is often mistaken for wit."

"Scoundrel! villain" cried Mr Stewart vehemently.

"Nay, my good sir, be not so violent, said Mrs Mason. "He has been wrong, but he has been led step by step into error, and I really hope his heart is not corrupted. I think it is a proof of it, that he has permitted me to tell all I know concerning him without disguise."

Mr Stewart beckoning to her to proceed, she thus continued.

"When I first saw him, he was about ten or twelve years old, and had obtained great praise for managing the horse he rode at our village races. I did not see the race, but I saw the little fellow when he came to my lady for his reward. She liked his appearance, and engaged him for a page; for she had always two that attended in the drawing-room, dressed in coats covered with lace. Jack was a great favourite with all the house. He was indeed a very good-natured boy, but got spoiled among the servants; and as he grew too tall for a page, my lady, when he was about six-teen, got him into one of the offices about court as an under clerk. His salary was very small, but as he had a great am-bition to be a gentleman, he was highly delighted with the promotion, and might have gone on very well, had he not been led to gambling in the lottery. He had at one time, as we were told, pawned all his clothes, and was on the very brink of desperation, when fortune turned, and he got a prize of about 1500 pounds. The sum appeared to him immense: he gave up his employment, and, purchasing a commission in a newly raised regiment, commenced his career as a gentleman, and man of fashion. One good trait still remained; he did not forget his friends in this change of circumstances, but sent fifty pounds to his old father, and presents to his mother and sisters, who still speak of him as the best hearted creature in the world."

"Then there some good in him!" cried Mr Stewart. "O yes, there must be some good in him. Come, he is not so bad as I thought, after all."

"Indeed there is good in him," said Mrs Mason. "He has only been led astray by vanity, and the foolish wish of being thought a great man. Had he been contented to rest upon his character for respectability, he would never have been otherwise than respectable, but his ambition to be genteel led him into the society of the showy and the dissi-pated, among whom he soon spent all his money, and when his regiment was disbanded, he found himself so much in debt, that he was obliged to leave England, and having met with the Flinders's at Bath, came down to this country, where he hoped to retrieve his fortune by a lucky marriage. In order to support the appearance of a gentleman, he bor-rowed money on his half pay, and having once been asked, whether he belonged to the Mollins's of Mollins Hall, in Dorsetshire? he resolved to acknowledge the relationship, and accordingly gave himself out for head of the family.

You now know as much as I do, excepting with respect to a snare into which he was led by a gambler of the name of Spurton, whom he met at Edinburgh, and which might have led to fatal consequences. But from these he is now happily rescued. I must, however, in justice to poor Jack, say a few words more. He sincerely loves your daughter: and as he was in quest of a fortune far greater than hers, he would never have married her, but from motives of affection. He at first indeed was made to believe, that she was a great heiress; for so Mrs Flinders gave out; and before he was undeceived, his affections were engaged to her, so that they are, in this respect, exactly upon a footing."

"They are in every respect upon a footing," cried Mr Stewart. "If his father is an honest tradesman, what is her father but an honest farmer. Believe me, I am quite relieved. You have taken a weight off my heart, Mrs Mason, by your account. If he has sense to apply to business, I shall put him in the way of doing it, and all may yet be well. Go, Mary, and bring him to us. I believe the poor fellow is ashamed to shew his face."

Mary went out, and soon returned, leading in her brother-in-law, who wore indeed a very humbled and mortified aspect, and though much cheered by the reception given him by Mr Stewart, he seemed evidently afraid to approach his wife, who, with averted face, sat sad and dejected, twisting the string of her apron in the corner. Some days elapsed before she could be brought into spirits; but the absolute annihilation of all her vain hopes and aspiring views, had already produced a salutary effect upon her temper.

Of all the plans of life that were suggested to Mollins, that which seemed most agreeable to his wishes, was an employment in the West Indies, which he knew it was at present in the power of Mr Flinders to procure for him. But an application to Mr Flinders would necessarily he productive of explanations so mortifying, that it was vehemently opposed by Mrs Mollins, who said she would rather starve than be so looked down on by Mrs Flinders, who now respected her, because she thought she was married to a man of fortune.

"And if Mrs Flinders respects her friends only on account of their fortunes, I would not give a pinch of snuff for her respect," cried Mr Stewart.

"O it is not fortune that Mrs Flinders minds," said Mrs Mollins; "it is only being genteel and stylish – and – and all that."

"And what right has Mrs Flinders to be genteel, and stylish, and all that, except from fortune?" returned Mr Stewart. "Who are those Flinders? Are they not the grandchildren of old Winkie Flinders, that kept the little public house at the end of the green loan? And was not the father of this Flinders transported for hen stealing? and did he not marry a planter's widow, and defraud her children, who, for aught I know are now begging their bread, while this Flinders, and his cousin, who was a broken milliner, are revelling in the fortune that should by right have been theirs."

"O dear sir, you have such a memory for these things. But you know that nobody minds them but yourself; and that all the great people court Mr and Mrs Flinders, both in town and country."

"Yes, yes," said Mr Stewart, "the vulgar of all ranks are mean and selfish. But don't mistake me, Bell; I do not despise the Flinders's on account of their want of birth, but on account of their paltry attempts at concealing the meanness of their origin by parade and ostentation. It is them, and such as them, who, by giving a false bent to ambition, have undermined our national virtues, and destroyed our national character; and they have done this, by leading such as you to connect all notions of happiness, with the gratification of vanity, and to undervalue the respect that attends on integrity and wisdom."

After some further discussion, the application to Mr Flinders was agreed on; but it failed of the expected success, so that poor Mollins would still have remained unprovided for, had it not been for the friendship of his wife's cousin, the honest manufacturer, whose attentions she had treated with such contempt. By the interest of this worthy man, an employment under government was obtained for Mollins, on condition that he and his wife should live in retirement, far from those temptations to extravagance, which experience had proved they were so little able to resist.

Chapter XVII

Receipt for making a thorough Servant. Thoughts on Methodism

Mrs Mason having, with difficulty, at length prevailed on Mr Stewart to consent to her departure, and having heard from the Morisons, that every thing was ready for her reception, took the opportunity of the first fine day to set out on her return to Glenburnie.

It was hard frost; but though the air in the shade was keen and piercing, its keenness was unfelt when in the kindly rays of the soul-enlivening sun. Mrs Mason, though she had not the eye of a painter, or connoisseur, enjoyed in perfection the pleasures of taste, in as far as they arise from feeling and observation, and considering all the beauties of nature as proofs of the divine beneficence, the contemplation of them always served to increase her confidence in the protection of the Almighty, of whose immediate presence they were to her a sacred pledge. To a person thus disposed, every change of season has some peculiar charm, and every object appears placed in a point of view, in which all that is lovely is seen to most advantage. She had no doubt that the air of cheerfulness which the bright sky diffused over the face of nature, imparted a sensible delight to all the animal creation; and saw with pleasure, as she passed through the farm of Gowan-brae, the out-lying cattle, roused from their cold beds, and dressing their shaggy sides, by rubbing them against the silver stems of the weeping birch, whose pendant branches shivered over the frozen stream. The little birds, who, during the late storms, seemed to have been annihilated, were now heard chirruping in every sheltered nook, or seen in flocks lightly flitting from field to field. As the day advanced, the plants on the sunny side of the road, glittering with dew drops, exhibited a fine contrast to the part that was still in shade, where every bushy brier and scrambling bramble were clothed in feathery frostwork.

"Yes," said Mrs Mason, as she cast her eyes over the dazzling prospect, "Yes, all the works of God are good and beautiful: all the designs of Providence must terminate in producing happiness and joy. The piercing cold of winter prepares the earth for the production of its summer fruits; and when the sorrows of life pierce the heart, is it not for the same benevolent purpose? When they are never felt, how many are the noxious weeds that over-run the soil! Let me then be thankful for the wholesome correctives that have been sent in mercy. Neither winter, nor poverty, are without their days of sunshine, their moments of enjoyment. See that of children upon the ice! Heaven bless the merry elves! how joyously they laugh and sport, and scamper, little caring how keen the cold wind may blow, so that it brings them the pleasure of a slide." Mrs Mason pursued the train of her reflection till she arrived at Morison's cottage; where she was received with a cordial welcome, to the comforts of "a blazing ingle, and a clean hearth-stane." On examining her own apartment, she was delighted to find that every thing was arranged to her wish, and far beyond her expectations; nor could she persuade herself, that her room had not undergone some very material and expensive alteration. This striking improvement was, however, merely the result of a little labour and attention; but so great was the effect thus produced, that though the furniture was not nearly so costly as the furniture of her room at Mrs MacClarty's, it appeared in all respects superior.

Mrs Morison was highly gratified by the approbation bestowed upon her labours; and pointing to her two little girls, told Mrs Mason how much they had done to forward the work, and that they were proud to find her pleased with it. Mrs Mason thanked them, and presented each with a ribbon as an encouragement for good behaviour; assuring them at the same time, that they would through life find happiness the reward of usefulness. "Alas," said Mrs Morison, "they must be obliged to work: poor things, they have nothing else to depend on!"

"And on what can they depend so well as on their own exertions?" replied Mrs Mason, "let them learn to excel in what they do, and look to the blessing of God upon their labours, and they may then pity the idle and the useless."

"If you could but get my poor gudeman to think in that way," said Peggy, "your coming to us would indeed be a blessing to our family."

"Fear not," said Mrs Mason; "as his health amends, his spirits will return, and in the good Providence of God he will find some useful opening for his industry. Who ever saw the righteous man forsaken, or the righteous man's children either, so long as they walked in their father's steps? But now I most give some directions to my two little handmaids, whose attendance I shall take week about. I see they are willing, and they will soon be able to do all that I require."

"I'll answer for their being willing," cried their mother, looking fondly at the girls, "but ye winna tak it ill, if they should no just fa' at ance into your ways."

"If they are willing," said Mrs Mason, "they will soon learn to do everything in the best way possible. All I want of them is to save themselves trouble, by getting into the habit of minding what they have to do. Any one who is willing may soon become a useful servant, by attending to three simple rules." – "To three rules!" cried Peggy, interrupting her, "that's odd, indeed. But my gudeman maun hear this. Come, William, and hear Mrs Mason tell our lassies a' the duties of a servant."

"I fear the kail will be cauld before she gets through them all," said William, smiling, "but I'm ready to listen to her, though it should."

"Your patience wont be long tried, said Mrs Mason; "for I have already told your girls, that, in order to make good servants, they have only to attend to three simple rules." – "Well, what are they?" said the husband and wife, speaking both at once.

"They are," returned Mrs Mason. "*To do every thing in its proper time; to keep every thing to its proper use; to put every thing in its proper place.*"

"Well said!" cried William; "and as I live, these same rules would mak a weel ordered house! my lassies shall get them by heart, and repeat them ilka morning after they say their prayers."

William kept his word; and Mrs Mason finding that she would be supported by the parents, did not despair of being truly useful to the children, by conveying to them the fruits of her experience. Mrs Morison was a neat orderly person and liked to see her house and children what she called *well red up*: But her notions of what was necessary to comfort

fell far short of Mrs Mason's; neither had she been accustomed to that thorough-going cleanliness, which is rather
the fruit of habitual attention, than of periodical labour;
and which, like the pure religion, which permits not the
accumulation of unrepented sins upon the conscience,
makes holiday of every day in the week. Mrs Morison was
a stranger to the pride which scorns instruction. She did
not refuse to adopt methods that were better than her own,
merely because they were new, and strange, nor, though
she loved her children as fondly and as dearly as any
mother in the world, did she ever defend their faults. But as
their children were early inspired with a desire to please,
they did not often stand in need of correction, and stood
more in awe of their father's frown, than those who have
been nurtured in self-will, stand in awe of a severe beating.

Mrs Mason had not been many weeks a resident in the
family, till the peculiar neatness of William's cottage
attracted the notice of the neighbours. The proud sneered,
at what they called the pride of the broken merchant; the
idle wondered how folk could find time for sic useless
wark; and the lazy, while they acknowledged that they
would like to live in the same comfort, drew in their chairs
to the fire, and said, they *cou'd na be fashed*.

The air of cheerfulness which was diffused around him,
had a happy effect upon William's spirits, but the severity
of the winter was adverse to the recovery of his health. The
rheumatism, which had settled in his left arm, had now rendered it entirely useless, and thus defeated all his schemes
of getting into employment. The last sale of his effects had
been so productive, that his creditors were paid 17s. in the
pound; but the remainder of what was due to them lay
heavy on his heart; and notwithstanding his efforts at resignation, the thoughts of what his wife and children must
suffer from the pressure of poverty, drew from his bosom
many a deep-drawn sigh.

The more Mrs Mason saw of William, the more deeply
did she become interested in his situation; and as no
scheme occurred to her that was likely to improve it, she
resolved to consult her good friend the minister, whose
mind she knew to be no less active than benevolent. An
invitation to dine at the manse was therefore gladly
accepted of, and scarcely had she taken her seat, until the

subject was introduced, and William's affairs became the topic of conversation. Miss Gourlay expressed great concern, but recollecting that she had forgot to give directions for making sauce for the pudding, left the room in the middle of Mrs Mason's speech. Her uncle, though he listened with great attention, made no other reply, than by saying, that he should be better able to speak upon the subject after dinner; adding, with a smile, that "he never talked well with a hungry stomach."

The nice roast fowl and boiled beef and greens being at that moment placed upon the table, prevented all reply; but when the cloth was removed, and grace said, and the glasses filled, Mr Gourlay, looking significantly after the sturdy lass who had attended, said, "Well, madam, now the hurly burly's done, we may, without fear of interruption, enter on the business of poor Morison, whom I from my heart wish to serve. I have thought of a plan for him, which, if he has no objections to it, will keep him above want. What would you think of his becoming schoolmaster?" "I should think well of it," replied Mrs Mason, "if nothing more were to be required of him than teaching writing, arithmetic, and reading English."

"Nothing more shall he required of him," replied Mr Gourlay. "We have suffered enough from the pedantry of a blockhead, who piqued himself upon *hic, hæc, hoc,* and who, though he has no more pretensions to being a scholar than my horse, is as proud as he is stupid.

"Until he came into the office, the school of Glenburnie had always maintained a respectable character; and the instruction which our youth received at it, was, as far as it went, solid and useful. But in the twelve years that it has been kept by Brown, it has, I verily believe, done more harm than good. It could not, indeed be otherwise; for it was an everlasting scene of noise, riot, and confusion."

"I should have thought, sir, that your authority would have been sufficient to introduce better regulations. Is not the parish school in some measure under your controul?"

"No," replied Mr Gourlay, "controul is, in this country, out of the question; nor do I believe that, if it were permitted, it would answer any good purpose; for who would embroil themselves, by opposing the pride and perverseness of an obstinate blockhead, unless when zeal was whetted by personal animosity? And under such malign influence, controul would soon be converted into an engine of oppression."

"But might not your advice, sir," –

"Advice! Surely, my good madam, you must know too much of the world to imagine, that a self-sufficient pedant will ever he advised. No Pope of Rome, in the days of papal power, was ever more jealous of his title to infallibility than the schoolmaster of Glenburnie. I once, and only once, endeavoured to persuade him how much he would abridge his own labour, and facilitate the improvement of his scholars, by adopting a regular method of teaching, and introducing certain rules into his school. But if I had attempted to take from him his bread, he could not have been more indignant, nor considered himself more deeply injured. He never forgave me; and I really believe that the grudge he entertained against me, was the primary motive of his leaving the kirk, and running after these enthusiasts among whom he has now commenced preacher."

"I have no doubt of it whatever," returned Mrs Mason; "for, as far as my knowledge extends, I have observed pride to be the ruling principle with all those pretenders to extraordinary sanctity."

"Ah, madam," said Mr Gourlay, "pride is a powerful adversary; it never fails to find out the weak part, and is often in possession of the fortress, while we are employing all our care to guard the outworks. If these enthusiasts do some mischief, by leading weak people into error, they likewise are, I doubt not, in some instances, the means of doing good. If they are the means of exciting us, who are the regular shepherds of the flock, to greater vigilance, they will do much good."

"Pardon me, sir," said Mrs Mason, "if I have the boldness to differ from you: but indeed I have seen so much malignity, so much self-conceit, and presumption, among these professors of evangelical righteousness, that I should suppose their doctrines were at war with the pure morality of the Gospel."

"The spirit of party must be ever adverse to the spirit of the Gospel," replied Mr Gourlay; "and in as far as sects are particularly liable to be infected by party spirit, in so far are they injurious to the Christian cause. But to confess

the truth, the church, as by law established, is too often
defended on the same narrow principles; nor, when the
defence of it is made a party question, do I perceive any difference in the fruits. In both instances they equally taste of
pride, the parent tree."

"But is it not proper to expose the errors into which
these visionaries betray weak minds?" returned Mrs
Mason.

"Very proper," said Mr Gourlay, "so that it be done in
the spirit of charity. Calmly and wisely to point out the
source of bigotry and enthusiasm, were an employment
worthy of superior talents; but men of superior talents feel
too much contempt for weakness, to undertake the task,
or at least to execute it in such a manner as to answer any
good purpose. Men of talents pour upon these enthusiasts
the shafts of ridicule, and attack their doctrines with all the
severity of censure, but they forget that all enthusiasts glory
in persecution. It is in the storm that men most firmly grasp
the cloak that wraps them, whatever be its shape. Would
we induce them to let go their hold, we must take other
methods, we must shew them we can approve as well as censure, and that it is not because we envy the eclat of their
superior zeal, or are jealous of their success in making converts, but because we honestly think they have taken an
erroneous view of the subjects in question, that we venture
to oppose them. Difficult, I confess, it is to gain access to
minds that are embued with a high opinion of their own
superior sanctity, and wrapped in the panoply of self-
conceit; but I am convinced that much might have been
done to stop the progress of methodism, by setting forth,
in strong and lively terms, the sin and danger of exalting
any one point of the Christian doctrine, so as to make it
pre-eminent, to the disparagement of the other Gospel
truths, and to the exclusion of the gospel virtues. We are
too rash in accusing such persons of hypocrisy. Hypocrites
may in all sects find shelter; but I believe in my conscience,
that few, if any, of their founders, or most zealous friends,
have been actuated by any other principle than honest,
though misguided zeal, – a zeal, the natural effect of having
fixed the attention exclusively on one point, until its importance is exaggerated beyond all bounds. We know, that
whatever occupies the imagination will enflame it; but so

wisely has the divine giver of light and life adapted the light of revelation to our present condition, that against this weakness of our nature, an ample provision is made, in the equal importance given to all the various truths revealed as objects of faith, and by accepting, as the only test of our sincerity, such a degree of moral purity as it requires our utmost vigilance to preserve. But this bears hard on human pride, and human pride is fruitful in resources. By picking out particular passages, and giving to them such explanation as may afford a basis for peculiar tenets, pride is gratified; and when it can thus form a party, and obtain distinction, the gratification is complete. Whether in religion or in politics, all the individuals who compose a party become, in their own minds, identified with the party they have espoused. Pride, in this way, operates without alarming the conscience; hence the zeal of methodists in making converts. Nor, when we preach against them in the same spirit, are we one whit better than they. It is not for the safety of our church establishments, nor for their honour, that we ought to sound the alarm, but for the integrity of the whole Gospel truths, which are torn and disfigured by being partially set forth, to the great danger of weak minds, the subversion of sound faith, and the detriment of pure morality."

The conversation was here interrupted by the entrance of one of Mr Gourlay's parishioners; a circumstance which affords us a favourable opportunity of concluding the present Chapter.

Chapter XVIII

Hints concerning the Duties of a Schoolmaster

The day after her visit to the minister, Mrs Mason took the first opportunity of speaking to Morison of the scheme which had been suggested. The colour which shot across his pallid cheek, and the animation which lighted up his languid eye, as he in mute attention listened to the proposal, shewed how deeply it interested him. His joy was, however, dashed by diffidence. He had not been trained to the business of teaching, and feared that it required abilities superior to his. While he expressed his thanks, and intimated his apprehensions, with a simplicity and candour peculiar to his character, his wife, who sympathised more deeply in his gratitude than in his fears, exhorted Mrs Mason, never to mind what her gudeman said of himself; for that it was just his way, always to think lowlier of himself than he need do. "I am sure," continued she, "that not a lord in all the land writes a more beautiful hand; and as for reading, he may compare wi' the minister himsel'! the kittlest word canna' stop him." Observing Mrs Mason smile, she paused, and then good-humouredly added, "I canna expect every ane to think as highly of my gudeman as I do, but I am sure I may safely say, that baith for learning and worth, he's equal to a higher post than being school-master o' Glenburnie." "You are perfectly right," cried Mr Gourlay, who had entered unobserved by any one; "and I believe we are all of the same opinion with regard to your husband's merit. Nay, you need not blush at having praised him, unless indeed you are ashamed at being so unfashionable a wife."

"O sir," returned Peggy, blushing yet more deeply, "we have nothing to do with fashion, but I hope we shall be grateful to God and our friends for all their kindness, and that you will prevail on William not to put from him such an advantage as this blessed offer."

William fearing that Mr Gourlay would misinterpret the reluctance hinted at, eagerly declared how joyfully he should accept the employment, did he consider himself fully qualified for discharging its duties, but that his want of experience in the art of teaching, destroyed his confidence, and rendered him hopeless of success.

"And it is upon that very circumstance that my hopes of your success are founded," replied Mr Gourlay. "You are not, I imagine, too proud to be advised?" "No, indeed sir, I am not," cried William. "Then, as you are not wedded to any particular method, you will honestly enquire, and candidly follow, what appears to be the best, nor obstinately refuse to adopt improvements that have been suggested by others, when their utility has been placed beyond a doubt. I do not say that you are at present qualified, I only say, that, by candid enquiry, and vigilant attention, you will soon become qualified for the discharge of an office, the duties of which are in my opinion seldom understood. A country schoolmaster, who considers himself hired to give lessons in certain branches of learning, and when he has given these, thinks he has done his duty, knows not what his duty is."

"And what, sir, if I may take the liberty of asking, what, in your opinion, is the nature and extent of the duties incumbent on the schoolmaster who would conscientiously discharge his trust?"

"As a preliminary to the answer of your question," replied the pastor, "let me ask you, what is the end you aim at in sending your children to school?"

"I send them," returned William, "in order that they may learn to read and write, and cast accounts; all of which they might, to be sure, have learned from me at home, but not so well, because I could not have given them their lessons so regularly."

"That is one reason, to be sure," said Mr Gourlay, "and a good one; but why do you wish them to be instructed in the branches you have mentioned?"

"I wish them to learn to read," returned William, "that their minds may be enlarged by knowledge, and that they may be able to study the word of God; and I have them taught to write and cast accounts, that they may have it in their power to carry on business, if it should be their lot to engage in any."

"That is to say," replied Mr Gourlay, "that you are

anxious to give your children such instruction as may enable them faithfully to discharge their religious and social duties; your object is laudable: but it is not merely by teaching them to read and write that it is to be accomplished. If their minds are not in some degree opened, they will never use the means thus put into their hands; and if their hearts are not in some degree cultivated, the means of knowledge will lead them rather to evil than to good. Even as to the art of reading, the acquirement of it will be useless, if the teacher has confined his instructions to the mere sounds of words, especially where these sounds are very different from those which we are accustomed to use in conversing with each other." "I confess, sir," said William, "I never could find out the reason, why all the children at our schools are taught to roar, and sing out what they read, in such an unnatural tone; but as the custom is so universal, I thought there surely must be some use in it; and indeed I know many people who think it would not be decent, nor proper, to read the Bible without something of the same tone."

"Nothing can be more absurd than such a notion," returned Mr Gourlay; "for if we sincerely respect the word of God, we ought to do all in our power to render it intelligible to ourselves and others. How else can we expect to profit by the instruction it conveys? The mere sound, without the sense, will do us no more good than a tune on the bagpipe. Yet if we are once taught at school to connect notions of piety with certain discordant accents, it is ten to one if we ever get so far quit of the impression, as to pay attention to the religious truths that are delivered with a natural and proper accent, while the greatest nonsense and absurdity, if conveyed to our ears in a solemn drawl, will pass for superior sanctity. It thus becomes easy for fools and hypocrites to impose on the credulity of the multitude."

"But, sir," said Mrs Mason, "it is not by fools and hypocrites alone that these false tones are made the vehicles of instruction. Of all the excellent sermons given us by the gentlemen who assisted at your preachings, how few were delivered with that propriety, as to do full justice to the sentiments they conveyed."

"I cannot deny the truth of your observation," returned

Mr Gourlay. "It is to be regretted that those who have early engaged in the study of the learned languages, seldom consider the art of reading English an object worthy their attention. They therefore are at little pains to correct the bad method so generally acquired at country schools. With regard to our peasantry, the effects of that bad method are still more unfortunate; it frequently renders their boasted advantages of education useless. This would not be the case, did the schoolmaster consider it his duty to teach his pupils to read with understanding, and carefully to observe whether they know the meanings and import of the words they utter. This they never can do, if they are not taught to read distinctly, and as nearly as possible in the tone of conversation. Nor is this all: in order to reap instruction from what they read, their minds must be in a state to receive it. Were this attended to by the parents at home, the schoolmaster would have an easy task; but instead of bestowing this necessary preparation, there seems to be, from the palace to the cottage, a combination among parents of all descriptions, to nurture in the minds of infants, all those passions which reason and religion must be applied to subdue.

"The schoolmaster who lends his endeavours to remedy this evil, renders a more important service to the community, than is in the power of any other public functionary. It should therefore be his first object, to train his pupils to habits of order and subordination, not by means of terror, but by a firmness which is not incompatible with kindness and affection."

"But how," said Morison, "without punishment, can order and subordination be enforced? and will not punishment beget terror, and terror beget aversion? I should think that a severe schoolmaster never could be beloved, and fear a lenient one would never be obeyed. This is my great difficulty."

"Did you ever know of a child complain of being punished, when sensible that the punishment was just?" replied Mr Gourlay. "No, there is a sense of justice implanted in the human mind, which shews itself even in the first dawn of reason, and would always operate, were it not stifled by the injudicious management of parents, who do not punish according to justice, but according to caprice. Of this the schoolmaster, who follows a well-digested plan, will never be guilty. He will be careful to avoid another common error of parents, who often, by oversight, lead their children to incur the penalty, and then enforce it, when in reality it is they, and not the children, who ought to pay the forfeit. I should pronounce the same sentence on the Master, who punished a boy at school, for playing, or making noise, if it appeared that he had provided him with no better employment. This is the great fault in all our country schools. The children spend three fourths of their time in downright idleness, and when fatigued with the listlessness of inaction, have no other resource, but in making noise, or doing mischief."

"But surely, sir," said William, "the master can not hear them all say their lessons at once?"

"True," replied Mr Gourlay, "but while he hears one, may not the others be at work the while? I will shew you a book written by one Mr David Manson, a schoolmaster in the north of Ireland, which contains an account of what he calls his play-school; the regulations of which are so excellent, that every scholar must have been made insensibly to teach himself, while he all the time considered himself as assisting the master in teaching others. All were, thus at the same time actively engaged, but so regulated, as to produce not the least confusion or disturbance.'"*

---

* At the period Mr Gourlay delivered this harangue, the improvements made by Mr Joseph Lancaster, in the method of instruction, were unknown. Had Mr Lancaster's book then been published, it would doubtless have been referred to, as containing the best digested plan that the ingenuity of man has hitherto been able to invent, for facilitating, and perfecting the work of instruction. The author is far from intending to detract from the praise so justly due to Mr Lancaster, by observing how far he had, in some of his most important improvements, been anticipated by the schoolmaster of Belfast. David Manson's extraordinary talents were exerted in too limited a sphere to attract attention. *He* consequently escaped the attacks of bigotry and envy; but the obscurity which ensured his peace, prevented his plans from obtaining the notice to which they were entitled; nor did their acknowledged success obtain for him any higher character, than that of an amiable visionary, who, in toys given to his scholars, foolishly squandered the profits of his profession. A small volume, containing an account of the school, rules of English grammar, and a spelling dictionary, is, as far as the writer of this knows, the only memorial left of a man, whose unwearied and disinterested zeal in the cause of education, would, in other circumstances, have raised him to distinction. [E.H.]

Mr Morison expressed great satisfaction, in having such assistance offered him, with regard to the method of teaching; and begged Mr Gourlay still farther to oblige him, by giving his opinion on the moral instruction which it was the duty of a schoolmaster to convey.

In reply to this, Mr Gourlay observed, that the school in which the greatest number of moral habits were acquired, would certainly be the best school of moral instruction. "Every person capable of reflection attaches great importance to what we call good principles," continued the worthy pastor; "now what are good principles, but certain truths brought habitually to recollection, as rules of conscience, and guides of conduct? Our knowledge of all the truths of revelation, can be of no further use to us than as they are thus, by being habitually referred to, wrought into the frame of our mind, till they become principles of action and motives of conduct. By a mere repetition of the words, in which these truths are conveyed, this will never be effected. The teacher, therefore, who wishes that his instructions may have the force of principles, must endeavour to bring the truths he inculcates, into such constant notice, that they may become habitual motives to the will. In a school where there is no order, no subordination, a boy may read lessons of obedience, and self government, day after day, without having any impression made upon his mind. Has he learned to steal and to tell lies; occasional punishment will not be sufficient to enforce the principles of truth and honesty. In order to convert sincerity and integrity into abiding habits of the mind, the love of these virtues must he strengthened by a conviction of the degree in which they are estimated by God and man. Falsehood and dishonesty must be rendered objects of abhorrence; and this they will soon become, if constantly and regularly attended by shame and disgrace. This comes to be the more incumbent on the schoolmaster, because (I am sorry to say it) lying is too generally considered by the poor as a very slight offence, or rather indeed as an excusable artifice, often necessary, sometimes even laudable. It is truly shocking to find the prevalence of this vice in a country, that boasts of the degree of instruction given to the poor. But where shall we find the tradesman, on whose word one can depend with confidence? Is it among the enthusiasts, who

pretend to the greatest portion of religious zeal? No. Go to
the next town, and bespeak a pair of shoes of one of these
saints; will he not solemnly promise, that they shall he
made by a certain day, while he in his conscience, knows,
they will not then have had a single stitch put into them? So
it is with tradesmen in every branch of business. And has
this want of probity no effect upon the moral character? Is
it consistent with the belief our being accountable to the
God of truth? And were the doctrine of our being thus
accountable, wrought into our minds, as an abiding principle, would it be possible that it should have no greater
effect upon our actions? Remember, that in being called to
the office of instruction, you are bound to do all that is in
your power to lead the little children unto Him who
declared, that for this end he came into the world, to *bear
witness to the truth*. With this impression constantly upon
your mind, you need be under no apprehensions concerning the success that will attend your labours."

Morison warmly expressed the gratitude he truly felt for
the instructions of his good pastor; and declared himself
convinced, by his arguments, of the nature and extent of
the duties he had to perform, but that, so far from being
deterred, he was more inclined than ever to undertake the
task, provided Mrs Mason would become his coadjutor in
the instruction of the girls, for which she should have half
the salary of the school. To this proposal Mrs Mason cheerfully agreed; and as the heritors had, with one consent,
determined to leave the choice of a schoolmaster to the
minister, Morison soon received a regular appointment to
the office, orders being at the same time issued to prepare
the school-house, and the premises attached, for the reception of his family.

While the repairs were under consideration, Mrs Mason
received a visit from Mr Stewart, who gladdened her heart,
by a letter which had been directed to his care. At the first
glance she saw that it had come from Italy, and that the
cover had been directed by Lady Harriet Bandon. The tears
of joy which burst from her eyes, prevented her for some
moments from proceeding to read the contents. They were
such as increased her emotion of gratitude and tenderness.
She clasped her hands, and, looking up to heaven, blessed
the God of mercies, for having preserved the family to

whom she was devoted in attachment, and for having bestowed on them such hearts, as would render them blessings to the world. She then shewed Mr Stewart the letter, which contained the most cordial assurances of the never-ceasing regard and affection of her beloved pupils, and a short account of their tour; and special injunctions to send them, in return, a particular account of her health, and of all that had happened to her since they parted. A postscript added by Mr Meriton, requesting that she would lay out the remittance he inclosed of twenty pounds, in doing all the good that such a trifle could effect. By thus putting it in her power to gratify her benevolence, the writer well knew he was affording the most delicate proof of his regard. As such, Mrs Mason received it; but she now found that Mr Stewart was commissioned to make the comfort of her situation a first object of attention. Her annuity was to be increased, if necessary, to even double the sum at first promised her, but she declined accepting any more than was sufficient for the purchase of some additional articles of furniture, for the habitation to which she was soon to remove.

The house allotted to the village-teacher was large, but so ill planned, as to be incommodious and uncomfortable. The alterations suggested by Mrs Mason removed these objections, and were favourable to her plans of order and cleanliness. A useless appendage, which projected by the back-door entrance, and which had hitherto been the receptacle of dirt and rubbish, was converted into a nice scullery, where the washing of clothes or dishes was carried on, so that the kitchen was kept always neat and clean. The two little girls had now acquired such a taste for neatness, and such habits of activity, that they not only took unwearied pains to make every thing appear to the best advantage in the kitchen and parlour, which were often liable to be seen by strangers, but were so orderly and regular in their exertions, that, from the garrets downwards, not a pile of dust found a resting-place, where it might remain unmolested.

Those who had known the house in its former condition, were amazed at the transformation; and could scarcely believe that such a change could be effected without the help of enchantment. Nor was it to the inside of the house that the transformation was confined; without doors, it was

perhaps still more remarkable. The school-house being set
back from the street, left an area of the width of ten or
twelve yards in front of the house, and on this convenient
spot, the former incumbent had erected a pig-sty, and piled
up a nasty dunghill. Every shower of rain washed part of
the contents into the unpaved foot-path, through which the
children paddled ancle deep in mud up to the school-room
door. But they were used to it and no one in the village
had ever objected to the inconvenience.

Morison having removed the incumbrances, sowed the
area with grass-seeds, and round it made a border to be
filled with flowers and shrubs. It was then railed in, leaving
a road up to the school, and an entrance, by a neat wicker
gate, to the front door of the dwelling-house. Planting,
watering, and rearing the shrubs and flowers, which orna-
mented the borders of the grass-plot, became the favourite
amusement of the elder school-boys; and being the reward
of good behaviour, was considered as a mark of favour
which all were ambitious to obtain. The school-room had
been left in a ruinous condition. The tables and benches
broken or disfigured; the plaister in some places peeled off
the walls, and in others scrawled over with chalk or ochre,
the panes of the windows broken, and stuffed with rags;
and the floor covered with such a thick paste of dirt, that it
was not till after much hard labour, the pavement was rendered visible. All was now put in complete repair, and the
first of May the school opened with forty scholars. The
twenty-five boys, and the fifteen girls, who made up this
number, came pouring in pell-mell, in the disorderly
manner to which they had been formerly accustomed; and
observing that the desks and benches were not yet placed,
they were proceeding in groups rudely to seize on them;
but were arrested by the master, who commanded silence in
a tone of such authority, as forced attention. Having
formed them into a circle round his chair, he explained to
them, that the school was henceforth to be governed by
rules, to which he would exact the most complete obedience; and then examining the boys as to their respective
progress, he formed them into separate classes, making the
girls meantime stand apart. The boys were then led out of
the school, that they might make their entrance in proper
order. Those of the first class taking the lead, were directed

how to clean their feet upon the scraper, and well bound wisps of straw, which served instead of matts. They next placed for themselves their forms and benches, opposite a double slip of wood fixed to the wall, marked No. 1, and stuck full of pegs, for their hats to hang on; the second and third classes marched in, each in their turn, and took their places in equal order. Mrs Mason, meanwhile, allotted to the girls their proper stations near her chair at the upper end of the school room, where they were concealed from view by a screen, which formed a sort of moveable partition between them and the boys.

At first several of the children were refractory, and many symptoms of a mutinous disposition appeared, but by patience and perseverance, all were so completely brought into subjection, that by the time the minister visited the school, at the conclusion of the first month, all the plans he had suggested were completely carried into execution. Each of the three classes were, according to Manson's method, divided into three distinct orders, viz. landlord, tenants, and under-tenants. The landlord prescribed the lesson which was to be received as rent from his tenants: Each of the tenants had one or two under-tenants, who were in like manner bound to pay him a certain portion of reading, or spelling lesson; and when the class was called up, the land-lord was responsible to the master, as superior lord, not only for his own diligence, but for the diligence of his vassals. The landlord who appeared to have neglected his duty, or who permitted the least noise or disturbance in his class, was degraded to the rank of an under-tenant. It became, therefore, his interest not to permit any infringe-ment of the rules. When these were in any instance broken, it became his duty to inform the master, who called the culprit before him, attended by the landlord and tenants of his class. If the tenants who formed his jury found him guilty of the charge, sentence of punishment was immedi-ately pronounced: if idleness was the crime, the culprit was obliged to sit in a corner, having his eyes blindfolded, and his hands tied across: if disobedience had been proved against him, he was imprisoned in a large chair turned to the wall: and if noise, he was obliged to carry a drum upon his back round the school. Nor after punishment did a boy immediately regain his rank; he was obliged to sit apart

from his companions the whole of the following day, without being permitted, while in disgrace, to look upon a
book. All the lads, especially those who were at a more
advanced period, found this species of punishment more
intolerable than any manual chastisement that could have
been indicted; and the consequence of this was highly
favourable to the Master's views. Mr Gourlay having examined the state of each class, distributed to the landlords
and head-tenants, the premiums, provided by Mrs Mason,
who devoted to this use part of the money sent by Mr
Meriton. These consisted of light hoes, small spades, and
other implements of gardening, together with parcels of
flower seeds suited to the season of the year. He next visited
the girls school, where, extraordinary as it may appear,
Mrs Mason had encountered greater difficulties than had
occurred to Morison in the execution of his task. She had
indeed, since her residence in Glenburnie, frequently
observed, that the female children of the poor had far less
appearance of intelligence and sagacity than the males of
the same age; and could no otherwise account for this, than
by supposing that their education had been more neglected.
This, as far as schooling was concerned, was not the case;
but while the boys, by being constantly engaged either in
observing the operations that were going on without doors,
or in assisting in them, had their attention exercised, and
their observation called forth, the girls, till able to spin,
were without object or occupation. After the first week, the
labour of the wheel became mechanical, and required no
exertion of the mental faculties. The mind, therefore,
remained inert, and the power of perception, from being so
long dormant, became at length extinct. The habits acquired
by such beings were not easily to be changed; for nothing
is so intractable as stupidity. But Mrs Mason having discovered the root of the disease, judiciously applied the proper
remedies. It was her first care to endeavour to rouse the
sleeping faculties. To effect this, she not only contrived
varieties of occupation, but made all the girls examine and
sit in judgment on the work that was done. Considering the
business of household work, not merely useful to girls in
their station as an employment to which many of them
would be devoted, but as a means of calling into action
their activity and discernment, she allotted to them, by

pairs, the task of cleaning the school-rooms; and on Satur-
day, the two girls who had best performed the duties
assigned them, were promoted to the honour of dusting
and rubbing the furniture of her parlour. As to the rest, the
morning was devoted to needle-work, the afternoon to
instruction in reading; but whether at the needle or book,
she rendered their tasks easy and cheerful, by the pleasant-
ness of her manners, which were always kind and
affectionate.

When Mr Gourlay distributed the rewards prepared for
the girls, whose behaviour had been most approved, he
expressed great approbation at their progress, and particularly noticed their improvement in personal neatness and
good-breeding, which assured him of the attention they
were likely to pay to the instruction of their teacher in
points still more essential; and concluded by giving a suitable exhortation.

Conclusion

Mrs Mason had not been many months in her employment
of schoolmistress, when she received a great addition to
her consequence in the eyes of her neighbours, by the
accession of Mr Meriton to the estate and title of Longlands, on the sudden decease of his elder brother. The amiable disposition of this young nobleman left no room to
doubt of his gratitude to the preserver of his life, and the
instructress of his infancy. The friendship of Mrs Mason
was therefore considered of great importance by those who
in any way depended on the favour or protection of their
superior lord. But even where there was no interested
motive, the use which she had already made of his bounty,
and the certainty that she would have the means of doing
still farther good, had a wonderful effect in increasing the
opinion of her wisdom. Of all the people in the village, it
was to poor Mrs MacClarty alone, that this opinion came
too late to be of any use. When she observed the thriving
appearance of the Morisons, and how fast they were rising
into notice and respect, her heart was torn between envy
and regret. Far was she, however, from imputing to herself
any blame; she, on the contrary, believed all the blame to
rest with Mrs Mason, who was so unnatural as to leave her
own relations, "and to tak up wi' straingers, who were
neither kith nor kin to her;" nor did she omit any opportunity of railing at the pride of the schoolmaster's wife and
daughters, who, she said, "were now sae saucy as to pretend
that they cou'd na sit down in comfort in a house that was
na' clean soopet." She for a time found many among the
neighbours who readily acquiesced in her opinions, and
joined in her expressions of contempt; but by degrees the
strength of her party visibly declined. Those who had their
children at school were so sensible of the rapid improvement that had been made in their tempers and manners, as
well as in their learning, that they could not help feeling
some gratitude to their instructors; and Mrs Mason having
instructed the girls in needle-work, without any additional
charge, added considerably to their sense of obligation.

Even the old women, who during the first summer had most bitterly exclaimed against the pride of innovation, were by mid-winter inclined to alter their tone. How far the flannel waistcoats and petticoats distributed among them, contributed to this change of sentiment, cannot be positively ascertained; but certain it is, that as the people were coming from church the first fine day of the following spring, all stopped a few moments before the school-house, to inhale the fragrance of the sweet-brier, and to admire the beauty of the crocuses, primroses, and violets, which embroidered the borders of the grass-plot. Mrs MacClarty, who, in great disdain, asked auld John Smith's wife "what a' the folks were glowering at?" received for answer, that they were "leuking at the bonniest sight in a' the town," pointing at the same time to the spot.

"Eh!" returned Mrs MacClarty, "I wonder what the warld will come to at last, since naething can serve the pride o' William Morison, but to hae a flower garden whar' gude Mr Brown's middenstead stood sappy for mony a day! he's a better man than will ever stand on William Morison's shanks."

"The flowers are a hantel bonnier than the midden tho', and smell a hantel sweeter too, I trow," returned Mrs Smith.

This striking indication of a change of sentiment in the most sturdy stickler for the *gude auld gaits*, foreboded the improvements that were speedily to take place in the village of Glenburnie. These had their origin in the spirit of emulation excited among the elder school-boys, for the external appearance of their respective homes. The girls exerted themselves with no less activity, to effect a reformation within doors, and so successful were they in their respective operations, that by the time the Earl of Longlands came to take possession of Hill Castle, when he, accompanied by his two sisters, came to visit Mrs Mason at Glenburnie, the village presented such a picture of neatness and comfort, as excelled all that in the course of their travels they had seen. The carts, which used formerly to be stuck up on end before every door, were now placed in wattled sheds attached to the gable end of the dwelling, and which were rendered ornamental from their coverings of honey-suckle or ivy. The bright and clear glass of the windows, was seen to advantage peeping through the foliage of the rose-trees,

and other flowering shrubs, that were trimly nailed against
the walls. The gardens on the other side were kept with
equal care. There the pot-herb flourished. There the goodly
rows of bee-hives evinced the effects of the additional nourishment afforded their inhabitants, and shewed that the
flowers were of other use besides regaling the sight or smell.
Mrs Mason, at the request of her noble benefactors, conducted them into several of the cottages, where, merely
from the attention paid to neatness, all had the air of cheerfulness and contentment. She was no less pleased than were
the cottagers at the expressions of approbation which were
liberally bestowed by her admiring friends; who particularly
noticed the dress of the young women, which, equally
removed from the slovenliness in which so many indulge
on working days, as from the absurd and preposterous
attempts at fashion, which is on Sundays so generally
assumed, was remarkable for neatness and simplicity. Great
as was Mrs Mason's attachment to the family of Longlands,
she would not consent to relinquish her employment, and
go to reside at Hill Castle, as they proposed she should
immediately do. She continued for some years to give her
assistance to Morison in conducting the school, which was
now increased by scholars from all parts of the country;
and was amply repaid for her kindness by the undeviating
gratitude of the worthy couple and their children, from
whom she experienced a constant increase of friendship
and affection.

The happy effects of their joint efforts in improving the
hearts and dispositions of the youth of both sexes, and in
confirming them in habits of industry and virtue, were so
fully displayed, as to afford the greatest satisfaction to their
instructors. To have been educated at the school of Glenburnie was considered as an ample recommendation to a
servant, and implied a security for truth, diligence, and honesty. And fortunate was the lad pronounced, whose bride
could boast of the tokens of Mrs Mason's favour and
approbation; for never did these fail to be followed by a
conduct that insured happiness, and prosperity.

The events that took place among her friends while Mrs
Mason remained at Glenburnie shall now he briefly
noticed. The first of these was Rob MacClarty's taking to
wife the daughter of a smuggler, a man of notorious bad

character, who, it was said, tricked him into the marriage. Mrs MacClarty's opposition was violent, but abortive, and ended in an irreconcilable quarrel between her and her son. On being turned out of his house, she went with her daughters to reside at a country town in the neighbourhood, where the latter were employed by a manufacturer in flowering muslin. Their gains were considerable, but as all they earned was laid out in finery, it only added to their vanity and pride. Meg was, in her 17th year, detected in an intrigue with one of the workmen; and as her seducer refused to marry her, she was exposed to disgrace. Leaving to her mother the care of her infant, she went to Edinburgh to look for service, and was never heard of more. Jean's conduct was in some respects less culpable; but her notions of duty were not such as to afford much comfort to her mother's heart.

At Gowan-brae all went on prosperously. Mr Stewart had the happiness of seeing his daughter, Mary, united to an excellent young man, who had a handsome property in his immediate neighbourhood, and farmed his own estate. His sons turned out as well as he could possibly have expected. And Mr and Mrs Mollins, though not all he could have wished, were more reasonable and happy than he had at one time any grounds to expect they would ever be.

In the second year of his keeping school, Morison had the heart-felt happiness of paying to his creditors the full amount of all he owed them; and from that moment he seemed to enjoy the blessings of life with double relish. Mrs Mason perceiving that his daughters were now qualified to succeed her in the charge of the school, at length acceded to the wishes of her friends, and took possession of the pretty cottage, which had been built for her by Lord Longlands, in the midst of the pleasure grounds at Hill Castle. In that sweet retreat she tranquilly spent the last days of a useful life; looking to the past with gratitude, and to the future with the full assurance of the hope, which is mingled with peace and joy.

Extract of a Letter

Addressed to the Author of *The Cottagers of Glenburnie*

Madam,

It appears very surprising, that, well acquainted as you evidently are with the past and present state of the families about Glenburnie, you should nevertheless be so ignorant of the history of Jean MacClarty, as not to know that she some years ago married a cousin of her own, and that they keep a well known inn on the _____ road. As their circumstances are, I fear, in a declining state, and as it may be in your power to avert their utter ruin, by inducing travellers to give a preference to their house, at which none, alas! now stop, but from dire necessity, I shall be at pains to furnish you with such an exact description of it, as cannot fail to be instantly recognized.

I might begin by mentioning the slovenliness apparent about the entrance, the dirty state of the door-steps, &c.; but as this is not altogether peculiar to this inn, it might serve to mislead you. I shall, therefore, conduct you into the passage, the walls of which seem to have been painted at the time the colour called *Paris mud* was so much in fashion. The pavement and the stairs have a still blacker ground-work, over which lies a coat of sand, which answers the purpose of a register, and enables them to measure the size of every foot that treats the carpets of the adjoining rooms, as you will perceive on entering the best dining-room, into which you will, of course, be conducted. You will imagine on entering it, that you have immediately succeeded to a company who have been regaling themselves with rum-punch and tobacco; but you need not scruple to occupy the room on that account, as I assure you the smell is perennial, and has been so carefully preserved in its original purity, that you will find it all seasons of the year the same. The floor is completely covered with carpet, but what that carpet covers can only be conjectured, the nails with which it is fastened to the floor having never been removed: and this circumstance, together with the black dust which lies in heaps around the edges, and works up through the thinner parts of the fabric, has led many to suppose that a manufactory of charcoal is carried on below! The tables you will find still more worthy your attention. On those that have been much in use, you will observe many curious figures traced in ale, &c. bearing a striking resemblance to the *Lichen Geographicus*, well known to botanists. The chairs you will probably find it advisable to dust before sitting down, and this will be done with great alacrity by the sturdy lass, who, barelegged, and with untied nightcap, and scanty bedgown, will, soon after your arrival, hurry into the room with a shovelful of coals as kindling for your fire. As there will, on this occasion, be an absolute necessity for removing at least part of the immense pile of white ashes with which the grate is filled, and which have remained undisturbed since the room was last in use, I would hint the propriety of keeping at a due distance from the scene of action; but when the bars have been raked, I would recommend it to you not to suffer the farther removal of the ashes, as, if you are any way squeamish, I can assure you they will be of use as a covering to the hearth, especially if your immediate precdecessors have been fond of tobacco.

In the article of attendance, you will find this inn to be no less remarkable than in the particulars above described. The waiters are of both sexes, and all are equally ingenious in delay. It is a rule of the house, that your bell shall never be answered twice by the same person; and this is attended with many advantages. It, in the first place, gives you time to know your own mind, and affords you an opportunity, in repeating your orders to so many different people, of making any additions that may in the interim have occurred. It, in the next place, keeps up the character of the house, by making you believe it to be full of company; and lastly, it provides an excuse for all the mistakes that may be made in obeying your directions. If you dine at Mrs MacClarty's, I shall not anticipate the pleasure of your meal, farther than to assure you, that you may depend on having here the largest and fattest mutton of its age that is any where to be met with, and that though it should be roasted to rags, the vegetables will not be more than half boiled. I cannot forbear warning you on the subject of the

salt, which you will conclude, from its appearance, to be
mixed with pepper, but I am well informed that it is free
from all such mixture. As to the knives and forks, spoons,
plates, &c. it is needless to tell you that they are in excellent order, as you will at a glance perceive them to have
been recently wiped. In order to obtain a complete notion
of the comforts of this excellent inn, you must not only
dine, but sleep there: in which case you must of necessity
breakfast before leaving it, as, at whatever hour you rise,
the carriage will not be got ready till you have taken that
meal. Nor must you expect that breakfast will be on the
table in less than an hour from the time of your ordering
it, even though all the fore-mentioned waiters should, in
succession, have told you it would be up in five minutes.
At length one bustles in with the tea equipage, and toast
swimming in butter. After this has had half an hour to
cool, another appears armed with the huge tea-kettle,
which he places on the hearth, while he goes in search of
your tea. Another half-hour passes, during which you
repeatedly ring the bell, but to no purpose. By the time
you are in despair, the bare-legged wench runs in, bearing
the tea-caddie in her black hand, and saying, she has been
but this moment able to get it from her mistress. Her mistress you need not expect to see; as she makes a point of
never appearing to ladies, not being in dress to be seen
among them; and being, moreover, greatly troubled with
weak nerves.

If you are so unfortunate as not to have a travelling carriage, I hope you will not travel this road in rainy weather;
as the glasses of Mr MacClarty's chaises were all broken at
an election, about two years ago, and have not been yet
repaired. This will account for the heap of wet straw at the
bottom of the carriage, which, as it is never changed, must
of course smell somewhat fusty. The linings are likewise in
a very bad condition; but on the stuffing of the cushions,
time has made little alteration: and as you may be curious
to know of what materials it is composed, I am happy to be
able to inform you, having been at the trouble to dissect
one on purpose; when, to my great astonishment, I found,
instead of the usual quantity of tow and horse-hair, an
assemblage of old ropes, every piece of which was so in-
geniously knotted, as to evince in how many useful pur-

poses they had been employed, before they reached their destined state of preferment.

My earnest desire of rendering an essential service to the daughter of my old friend Mrs MacClarty has, I am afraid, led me to trespass too long upon your patience; but the preference shewn by travellers for the inn at the next stage, will be a sufficient apology for my partiality; and account for the dread I entertain of the impending ruin which threatens to overwhelm this last branch of the old and respectable stock of the MacClartys. When I inform you, that the rival inn is kept by a scholar of Mrs Mason's, you will quickly perceive that my fears are not without foundation: and yet I must own, the reason of the preference given to it by the public, appears to me to imply a contradiction. Why are people of fortune so fond of travelling, but on account of the variety it affords? And when one finds at an inn, as at that which I now speak of, the same neatness, cleanness, regularity and quiet, as at one's own house, the charm of variety is surely wanting. Yet these innkeepers thrive amazingly. They indeed trust nothing entirely to the discretion of servants. They super-intend all that is done in every department with their own eyes; and as any injury that happens to furniture, carriages, &c. &c. is instantly repaired, the saving in tear and wear must be considerable. Add to this, what is saved in the article of attendance by method, and in the article of food by good cookery, and you will not wonder that they should prosper. Alas! I fear they will continue to prosper, and that their example will soon be too generally followed, and com-plete the ruin of my unfortunate friends.

I remain, &c.

from
Letters on the Elementary
Principles of Education
(2 vols, 1801)

Editor's note

Letters on the Elementary Principles of Education was by far the most successful of Hamilton's works of non-fiction, and it is the cornerstone of her theories of education and moral development. It might not be the most intellectually ambitious of her books – she was perhaps more innovative in *Agrippina*, in which she attempts to apply the theories sketched out in the Letters to a reading of classical history, and more far-ranging in her philosophical interests in *Popular Essays* – but it is unapologetic in its assumption that a basic knowledge of the philosophy of mind developed by John Locke and his successors is essential to everybody who has any interest in education and in its refusal to talk down to the female readers it is addressing. The unnamed female "friend" who is the nominal recipient of the letters is a fiction that reinforces Hamilton's insistence that, despite the philosophical content, her intended audience was ordinary middle-class women. The book is, by any standards, a major intervention in the late eighteenth- and early nineteenth-century debates about female education, something that makes it a little surprising that it received so little attention in twentieth-century criticism. Like Mary Wollstonecraft in *A Vindication of the Rights of Woman* (1792), Hamilton is exploring the ways in which she sees society as educating women into triviality and folly. Her conclusions are not always the same as Wollstonecraft's, but her insistence upon the damaging effects of contemporary educational practice has much in common with the work of her more famous contemporary.

Where Hamilton's educational writing differs most markedly from that of almost all her female contemporaries is in her dependence upon both Locke's theories of the association of ideas and the moral philosophy being argued out by mainly Scottish philosophers from the mid-eighteenth century forward. At times, the book reads almost like a survey and critique of late Scottish Enlightenment thought (with the – admittedly – major exception of the work of David Hume, whom Hamilton apparently did not especially

admire). The two dominant influences, however, are
Thomas Reid (1710–1796) and Dugald Stewart (1753–
1828); Hamilton repeatedly and approvingly quotes their
philosophical essays, and her central argument about education is in harmony with (and influenced by) the ideas in
both the first volume of Stewart's *Elements of the Philosophy
of the Human Mind* (1792) and his *Outlines of Moral Philosophy* (1793). The later work, a handbook for University of
Edinburgh Students based on Stewart's lectures, anticipates
(but inverts) the structure that Hamilton uses in Elementary
Principles, beginning with a study of the intellectual powers
of the mind, then moving on to an analysis of the formation
of moral principle. Even more generally, Stewart's summary
of "the object of Moral Philosophy," which he states is
"to ascertain the general rules of a wise and virtuous conduct in life" (*Outlines*, 12), is echoed in Hamilton's comment that "the business of education" is "[t]o qualify a
human being for the true enjoyment of existence (see p. 261
of this edition).

Hamilton also structures her book in much the same
way as the philosophers who influenced her did their arguments, beginning with basic principles and building from
there. That formal structure is of course lost in excerpts, a
fact that leads to some distortion of her work, as it is a vital
part of Hamilton's argument that education is progressive
and cumulative, and that unless one understands the most
basic principles, one will be left with an inadequate conception of more complex ideas. She insists upon the importance of this grounding in the basics in the cases of both
educator and pupil, something that leads her to be particularly scornful of attempts to make children appear prodigies
of knowledge through rote memorization of facts when
they have no grasp of the underlying concepts. Perhaps in
part as a result she appears rather more sceptical of the
Lancaster-Bell system in this book than she does in Glenburnie, where it underpins to some degree the ideal school
run by Mrs Mason. This scepticism in fact predates *Elementary Principles* and is not by any means confined to the effects
of rote learning on the training of the intellect; in *Memoirs
of Modern Philosophers*, Hamilton includes an episode in
which her hero, on a walking tour in Scotland, is both
amused and dismayed by his encounter with a child who is

able to parrot the catechism but who is all too obviously entirely ignorant of the meaning of her words. Such a child, Hamilton argues, will be left bereft of principle, as it has nothing but meaningless words to guide its behaviour and actions. The result will be an adult who is driven by prejudice and habit rather than reason, precisely the situation in which both Mrs MacClarty and Lady N———— (in "The Story of the Tame Pigeon") find themselves.

The first volume of *Elementary Principles* focuses on moral principles, or what Hamilton calls the education of the heart; the second examines the training of the intellect. The excerpts printed here include two complete letters from each volume, in each case focusing on subjects that are particularly relevant to the arguments that she develops in less theoretical form in Glenburnie. Benevolence is the most basic principle that Hamilton thinks it necessary to instill in children; as she makes clear in these letters, she believes that it should be cultivated from the earliest infancy and that it underlies all other virtues. The sullen, stubborn children in Glenburnie are, clearly enough, illustrations of what Hamilton sees as the results of failing to cultivate the benevolent affections, but as the second letter demonstrates, Hamilton sees parental failure in this matter as laying the groundwork for serious social disorder. The process by which Hamilton moves from an account of a spoilt child to a diagnosis of the ways in which disregard for women is both sympton and cause of the failure of her society to be truly Christian is characteristic of her work throughout this book: her interest is in the proper education of children, but she wants to make very clear that failure to achieve that goal has ramifications far beyond the individual or the household. The first letter from the second volume sets out Hamilton's theory of mind and explains, more clearly than the first letter of the first volume, the structure of her work. It also reinforces what we might now call the feminist elements of her thought, as she insists upon women's ability to master philosophical theory. Even her refusal to dabble in "metaphysics" is not so much a concession that there are aspects of philosophy that women are unable to pursue as it is a quiet attack on the men who lose themselves in what Hamilton saw as the wilder reaches of fancy. Once again, her arguments here are in line with those of Stewart, who

informed the University of Edinburgh students for whom
he wrote *Outlines of Moral Philosophy* that moral philosophy
extended only so far as man could reason by "the un-
assisted light of nature" (12). The final letter printed here,
on taste and imagination, is the most general in its relevance
to Hamilton's educational thought. The question of the role
of taste in the formation of the intellect and character was
one that preoccupied the thinkers of the Scottish Enlightenment; Hamilton's assumption, like that of Stewart and
Archibald Alison (whom she also cites) is that proper taste
is guided by and reflective of good judgement and careful
observation. In Glenburnie, Mrs Mason's ability to appreciate the landscape around her, like Mrs MacClarty's indifference to scenery, is an important indication of character, a
point explored here in considerably more detail. Likewise,
Bell Stewart's obsession with fashion is, according to the
arguments developed in this letter, a failure not just of taste
but also, and more importantly, of moral judgement. Most
generally, this letter suggests the degree to which, for
Hamilton, the various faculties of the mind are inextricable:
aesthetic failure is also a failure of both the intellect and
the affections.

There were some complaints about Hamilton's intellectual ambition in *Elementary Principles*. As late as 1858, the
educational writer William Ross, rather missing the entire
point of the book, was grumbling that Hamilton should
have concentrated less on the principles and more on her
educational methods. Nonetheless, as Hamilton proudly
noted in letters to friends (reprinted in Benger), her philosophical interests did nothing to harm the book's reception,
as it was an immediate success. Originally published in one
volume (as *Letters on Education*), it was reprinted and
expanded in the same year. It had gone into a fifth edition
by 1810, which was the last to appear in Hamilton's lifetime, though a sixth was printed in 1818. It received three
separate printings in America (in Alexandria VA, Phila-
delphia, and Boston) and was also translated into French
and German.

Letter VII
Associations Producing Benevolence

State of Infancy favourable to the Cultivation of the
benevolent Affections. – Tendency of every Passion to
produce Passions of the Class to which it belongs. –
Malevolent and dissocial Passions inspired by the
Gratification of Self-Will. – Examples.

Having attended to those associations which inspire devotional sentiment, or the love of God, let us now proceed to the consideration of the associations by which the spirit of benevolence and philanthropy is made to diffuse its divine and abiding influence over the human heart.

Benevolence, in a general sense, includes all the sympathetic affections by which we are made to rejoice in the happiness, and grieve at the misery, of others. It disposes the mind to sociality, generosity, and gratitude, and is the fountain of compassion and mercy. All the qualities belonging to benevolence have a tendency to produce peace and complacency in the breast, so that the happiness of the individual as well as of society is intimately concerned in their cultivation. The passions which it inspires are all of the amiable class, as love, hope, joy &c.; and these passions in their turn increase the dispositions to benevolence, a disposition for the growth and nourishment of which in the state of infancy the goodness of Providence has made ample provision.

The helplessness of the infant state is protracted in man to a period far beyond that of other animals; and this helplessness, by inspiring compassion and tenderness in the breast of adults, has a powerful tendency to keep alive the spirit of benevolence in the human heart. Wherever human policy has counteracted the wise designs of nature by taking children from their parents at an early age, and separating them into a different society, for the purpose of education, the sympathetic affections have become extinct; a striking instance which occurs in the history of ancient

Sparta, where the murder of infants was, in certain circumstances, not only enjoined by the laws, but permitted by
the parents without the least remorse.

Luxury, which is ever at war with nature, has, perhaps,
in no instance done a greater injury to the interests of
benevolence, than by introducing as a fashion that premature separation of children from their parents, which the
Spartan legislature enjoined as a duty. If the exercise of
parental tenderness softens the heart, so as to render it emi-
nently susceptible of all the sympathetic and social affections, it is the interest of society that the objects of it
should not be suddenly removed from the parental roof.

According to the wise provision of nature, the fond
endearments of parental love not only increase the benevolent feelings in the breast of the parent, but produce a disposition to them in the breast of the child, which is soon
made sensible of the source from whence its happiness is
derived. A judicious parent will take advantage of the
circumstance, to encourage the growth of benevolence in
the infant mind.

The pleasures they receive from others, naturally incline
children to sociality and good-will; and were they, while
they receive them, always made sensible of their own helplessness, they would at the same time be inspired with the
feelings of generosity and gratitude. But the tenderness of
parents so seldom is judicious, that the wise provision of
nature for inspiring children with benevolence is commonly
rendered abortive, and, instead of the amiable dispositions
arising from love and gratitude, the seeds of moroseness,
anger, revenge, jealousy, cruelty, and malice, are often pre-
maturely planted in the little heart.

Let us examine into the cause of this. And here the doctrine of association presents us with a clue, by means of
which we may easily explore the labyrinth.

Nature early impels the mind to seek for happiness;
but before the dawn of reason and experience, the judgments concerning it must be erroneous. In infancy, all
ideas concerning it are comprised in the gratification of
will; the propensity to this gratification is encouraged by
frequent indulgence, till every notion of happiness becomes connected with it. The idea of misery becomes
consequently associated with disappointment; and how far

these associations may affect the mind, by producing the malevolent passions, will appear evident on a very little reflection.

We have already remarked, that the painful sensations make a more vivid as well as a more lasting impression than the pleasurable; from which it evidently follows, that the happiness derived from the gratification of *will* can never bear any proportion to the misery occasioned by its disappointment. Where the propensity to this gratification is strengthened by indulgence, the frequent repetition of disappointment will deeply impress the mind with the feelings of resentment and thus render it liable to the reception of all the malevolent passions connected with it; while the pleasurable sensation occasioned by indulgence will produce no other effects than to augment the desire of future gratification.

An admirable illustration of this doctrine is given by Hartley, who, after observing that the gratification of self-will, if it does not always produce pleasure, yet is always so associated with the idea of pleasure in the mind, that the disappointment of it never fails to produce pain, proceeds as follows: "If the will was always gratified, this mere associated pleasure would, according to the present frame of our natures, absorb, as it were, all other pleasures; and thus, by drying up the source from whence it sprung, be itself dried up at last; and the first disappointments would be intolerable. Both of which things are observable in an inferior degree, both in adults and in children after they are much indulged. *Gratifications of the will without the consequent expected pleasure, disappointments of it without the consequent expected pleasure, are here particularly useful to us.* And it is by this, amongst other means, that the human brought to a conformity with the Divine, which is the only radical cure for all our evils and disappointments, and the only earnest and medium for obtaining everlasting happiness."

By the above reasoning, which I think conclusive, it evidently appears that were the constant gratification of will possible (which, in the present state of things it certainly is not) it would only tend to make the being so gratified miserable. The constant gratification of self-will must necessarily exclude the exercise of all the passions. Where success is

certain, hope can have no existence; nor can joy be produced by attaining that which is considered as a right. Let
hope and joy be excluded from the human mind, and where
is happiness?

Further, the habitual gratification of will not only pre-
cludes the grateful passions of hope and joy, but tends to
produce all the unamiable and hateful passions and dispositions of the human heart. Anger, peevishness, and pride,
are almost, without exception, produced by the constant
gratification of every wayward desire. The first is the father
of revenge and cruelty, the second, of displacency and discontent, and the third, of arrogance, ingratitude, and contempt. Think of this, ye mothers, who, by a weak and blind
indulgence of the infant will, lay the foundation of future
vice and misery to your ill-fated offspring!

Were the happiness of the *child* and the happiness of
the *man* incompatible, so that whatever contributed to the
latter must be deducted from the former, the overweaning
indulgence of parents might be excused, and the common
apology, viz. "that as life is uncertain, the poor things ought
to be permitted to enjoy the present," accepted as satis-
factory. But may we not appeal to every person who has
had the misfortune to live for any time with a family of
spoiled children for a sanction to our assertion, that the
gratification of will has only been productive of misery.

In the career of indulgence the fondest parents must
somewhere stop. There are certain boundaries which folly
itself will not at all times be willing to overleap. The
pain of the disappointment that must ensue, will be intolerably aggravated by the discordant passions preceeding
indulgence.

A child, whose infant will has been habituated to the discipline of obedience, submits to disappointment, as to
inevitable necessity with cheerfulness. Nor will disappointment to such an one so frequently occur, a wholesome
check having been early put upon the extravagance of
desire. Whilst, on the contrary, the satiety consequent
upon the fruition of every wish sets imagination to work to
find out new and untried sources of pleasure. I once saw a
child make itself miserable for a whole evening, because it
could not have the birds that flew through the garden, to
play with. In vain did the fond mother promise that a bird

should be procured to-morrow, and that it should be all his own, and that he should have a pretty gilded cage to keep it in, which was far better than the nasty high trees on which it now perched. "No, no, that would not do; it must be caught now; he would have it now, and at no other time!"

"Well, my pretty darling, don't cry," returns Mamma, "and you shall have a bird, a pretty bird, love, in a minute;" casting a significant look on her friends, a she retired to speak to the servants. She soon returned with a young chicken in her hand, which she covered so as not to be immediately seen.

"Here, darling, is a pretty, pretty bird for you; but you must not cry so. Bless me, if you cry at that rate, the old black dog will come and fetch you in a minute. There now, that's my good boy! now dry your eyes, love, and look at the pretty bird."

At these words little master snatches it from her hand, and perceiving the deception, dashes it on the ground with tenfold fury. All now was uproar and dismay till the scene becoming rather too oppressive, even for the mother, a servant was called, who took the little struggling victim of passion in his arms, and conveyed him to the nursery. Such are the effects of the unlimited indulgence of self-will! Yet this fond mother persuaded herself that she obeyed the dictates of pure affection! Had she, however, been accustomed to reflect upon the motives that influenced her conduct, she would have found selfishness in this instance the governing principle.

Parental affection has been described by many philosophers as a refined species of self-love. Considered merely an *instinct*, it undoubtedly is so. But the same instinct in the brute creation only leads to the care and protection of their young, and, I may add, to the education also; the care of the dams in this particular, both in the feathered and four-footed race, being well known. But never does it lead to a false and dangerous indulgence.

Were parental affection in man, as in the brute creation, merely instinctive, instinct might be trusted to as an unerring guide. But to man the higher gift of reason is granted, and therefore in him instinct is feeble and uncertain. And yet by mere instinctive tenderness do parents permit themselves to be governed, in opposition to the dictates of that reason which should teach them true affection ought to study the *real* and *permanent* happiness of the beloved object.

It is not uncommon for parents, while they forego the exercise of their own reason, to trust to the future reason of their children for counteracting the effects of their injudicious management. But does experience justify their confidence? I believe every person who has traced the rise and progress of the passions in individuals will answer in the negative.

The frequent recurrence of any passion even in our earliest years, begets a tendency to that passion, till it is strengthens into a habit, and becomes as it were interwoven with the constitution. How difficult, how next to impossible, it is then to conquer, all can witness! Reason may govern, and religion may in some measure subdue it, so as to prevent its excess to the prejudice of society; but by nothing less than a miracle can it be totally eradicated from the breast. The more worthy the heart, the more delicate the conscience, the more bitter will be the sensations of regret and self-abhorrence which a person liable to the dominion of passion, and at same time under the influence of principle, must frequently endure. How many are the agonizing tears shed in private by the irascible! while, perhaps, the sudden ebullition of wrath that brought them forth, may have fixed a dagger in the heart of a friend doomed there to rankle for ever. And yet anger, being a passion which quickly vents itself by explosion, and is then annihilated, is less generally obnoxious than peevishness or pride which have no crisis, but which continue to operate without rest or interval.

Which of these passions will be most powerfully excited when by the early indulgence of will, and the frequent disappointments inevitably consequent upon such indulgence, depends, perhaps, upon the organization or constitution of the infant. In robust habits the passion of anger is most frequent; while in the, more delicate, peevishness is commonly generated. By pride both are aggravated to an extreme degree; for pride, restless as a jackal, is perpetually on the hunt to find food and nourishment for these tormentors. At every disappointment of the self-will that has been accustomed to habitual indulgence, pride takes the alarm, and calls on anger or peevishness to revenge the injury.

And here it is worthy of remark, how the passions act and re-act upon each other. The frequent gratification of will engenders pride, and pride augments the desire for the gratification of will, till it becomes insatiable. Hence the love of power predominates, and hence a disposition to tyranny appears to be inherent in the mind of man. Many, alas! are the tyrannical husbands and fathers that have been formed in the nursery!

The unamiable passions, like the lean kine in Pharoah's dream, which devoured the goodly, have a strong tendency to destroy the amiable. Indeed, they are, in a great measure, incompatible with each other. The social affections are kept alive by a sense of mutual dependence and mutual obligation. But pride acknowledges no dependence; and arrogates to itself all the attentions and good offices of others, not as a matter of favour, but of right. Hence, while it is ever ready to take offence at the slightest neglect, it is never warmed by kindness into gratitude.

Observe the boy who has been a mother's darling, and to whom his sisters have from infancy been obliged to do homage. How often are their endeavours to please him received with contempt, while the most trifling offence is aggravated into an injury. Follow him into the world. There, alas! mortification and disappointment attend his steps, for there no one regards him in the light in which he has been taught to regard himself. No one comes up to his ideas of propriety in their conduct towards him. If favoured by fortune he may, indeed, meet many flatterers, but he will never make a friend. The irritation to which he is perpetually exposed will by degrees expel feelings of benevolence from his heart; and, perhaps, even the parent, to whose fond indulgence he owes his misery, may be the first to feel the effects of his malevolence and ingratitude.* Indig-

---

* The just and striking point of view in which Dr. Moore has placed this subject in the life of Zeluco, must speak more forcibly to the heart than volumes of reasoning. It is a picture which every mother ought to study. But, alas! where is the mother whose fond partiality will allow her to see one feature of Zeluco in her own spoiled darling? [E.H.]

nant at the world, which he thinks in league to torment and vex him, he perhaps resolves to make himself amends in the tranquility of domestic life, and makes choice of such a partner as he imagines will be most obsequious and obedient. Dreading the control of reason he carefully avoids a woman of cultured mind; and is, perhaps, made sensible, when too late, that it is not always the most weak who are the most conformable. In his family, however, he resolves to rule; and there he does rule with despotic sway. Perhaps he meets with a partner who is led by love of peace and sense of duty, to study the gratification of his will in the most minute particulars. But his will becomes too capricious for gratification. The passions which he has indulged are incompatible with the enjoyment of satisfaction, tranquility, or contentment. The gratification of these passions may wound his conscience, and irritate his feelings, by a sense of having inspired hatred or contempt in the breasts of others, but can never bring peace to his heart. The pleasure of making others miserable has little in it of the nature of felicity.

Yet may we sometimes observe the wife of such a man as I have here described, endeavouring, by means of unlimited indulgence, to excite the very same passions and propensities in the breast of her son, of which she has felt the fatal consequences in the husband; as if she resolved to revenge on some other innocent woman the misery she has herself endured! – Her daughter-in-law may share her fate, and probably imitate her example; and thus may pride, cruelty, and injustice, be reproduced in the family *ad infinitum*!

As the operations of reason are slow, and her induction liable to error, it has pleased the Almighty Creator to make not only reason, but the passions themselves, our school-masters in virtue. Every passion whose inordinate gratification is inimical to the happiness of others, is likewise inimical to our own felicity; while the grateful and benevolent passions and affections of our nature bring in the exercise pleasure, and on reflection peace. Is it not then, a sufficient argument against producing, by early indulgence, a predominant desire for the gratification of self-will, to shew that the instruments employed by this desire to procure its gratification are all of the unworthy class? The love of power has other servants besides anger, cruelty, arrogance, and resentment. Selfishness often stoops to seek the aid of cunning; and I have known the happy art of objecting to whatever was proposed by others, and of finding fault with every thing that did not originate in the objector, employed with as much effect in procuring the uncontrolled gratification of self-will, as any of the irrascible passions. But compare the happiness which results from this gratification with that which springs in a generous and benevolent heart when conscious of having made a sacrifice for another's good. How different the sensations, how different their effects upon the mind! The selfish and unsocial satisfaction produced by the former, so far from tranquillizing the mind, seems only to prepare it for fresh ebullitions of spleen and peevishness; while the latter diffuses the sweet serenity of cheerfulness and complacency over the whole soul. These opposite dispositions have each a natural tendency to lead to a repetition of the same sort of conduct by which they were severally produced; the progress of vice and virtue resembling the laws of gravitation in regard to accelerated motion. The truth of this may be illustrated by innumerable instances. But these must occur to the recollection of every reader; for little must they have been observant of human character, who have not traced the progress of vicious or virtuous propensities in the minds of those around them.

The malevolent passions produced by frequent irritation, the certain consequence of great indulgence, appear at first but as a small cloud that occasionally overcasts the mental horizon, and which, it is hoped, the sun of reason will dispel. But, alas! it soon grows too thick for the sun of reason to penetrate. During the sprightliness of youth, it may often brighten into transient gleams of generosity and affection, but if not repelled by the strength of religious principle, it returns in ten-fold darkness, till at length, having extinguished all the amiable and all the endearing qualities of the heart, it spreads its gloomy wings over the soul, and rages in all the horror of a perpetual tempest.*

---

* Upon the principle which I have here unfolded, it is observed by Lord Kames, that "A passion founded on a peculiar propensity subsists generally for ever, which is the case of pride, envy, and malice; objects are never wanting to inflame the propensity into a passion." – Elements of Criticism, vol. i. p. 122. [E.H.]

The benevolent affections, on the contrary, are like the soft and gentle light of morning, as described by the poet:

> At first faint gleaming on the dappl'd East,
> Till far o'er ether spreads the widening glow;
> And from before the lustre of her face,
> White break the clouds away.

The longer the mind has enjoyed the sweet tranquillity of benevolence, the more unwilling will it be to give admission to the turbulent passions which are destructive of peace; and the more frequently it has rejoiced in the consciousness of having conferred felicity on others, the more will it be disposed to a repetition of acts of benificence, charity, and mercy. Of what importance, then, is the early management of children; since upon it, in a great measure, depend the vice and virtue, the happiness and misery, of the world! And yet this is the period consigned to the care of ignorance and folly!

Before the period assigned for the commencement of education, such a propensity to the malignant passions is frequently generated in the infant mind, as not all the pains of the most careful and judicious preceptors can ever after eradicate. And here I may safely appeal to all who are concerned in the education of youth; let them say, how often they have been able to conquer the spirit of self-will, with its attendant passions, pride, arrogance, anger, resentment, peevishness, and ingratitude. If these are not stifled in the birth, they may afterwards be cut in pieces by the rod of chastisement, but, like the Polypus, they will preserve the vital principle, and be immediately re-produced.

How much of the tendency to passion may be referred to physical causes, it is not for me to examine; it is sufficient for my purpose to shew, that they are often produced by an early and indiscreet indulgence of self-will. That this indulgence generates pride, we know from experience. That the disappointment of its gratification, after the habit of indulgence produces the violent and ungrateful passions, is likewise evident. And that the frequent recurrence of any passion produces a disposition to that and similar passions, has been, I hope, clearly and satisfactorily proved.

To prevent any mistake that may arise from my strenuous inculcation of the necessity of the early control of self-will, I think it necessary to observe, that if injudicious indulgence become injurious to the mind, in consequence of the frequent irritation it occasions, (which is obvious from the fretfulness observable in all spoiled children;) it follows, that injudicious severity, by producing a similar irritation, must be equally injurious to the disposition. But do we not often see the one follow the other? A poor child, accustomed to have every thing he cries for, will sometimes cry for things Mamma may not choose to give, and persevere in crying, till he exhausts her patience, and then he is to be whipped! People first indulge children for their own pleasure, and then chastise the poor infants for the natural consequence of that indulgence; and it is, perhaps, difficult to say, which injures the temper the most. "You must not touch this! Don't do that!" are injunctions ever in the mouth of a foolish mother, who, nevertheless, permits *this* to be touched, and *that* to be done, with impunity till some petty mischief is accomplished, which she considers of consequence, though impossible for the child to make the distinction, and then he must again be whipped!

Self-will grows so rapidly upon indulgence, that a capricious humour is its unavoidable consequence. This caprice, when it becomes troublesome and unmanageable, is likewise punished by a whipping, and to this whipping does the mother appeal as a sufficient testimony that she does not spoil her child! If it be possible, and that it is possible I have had ample proofs, by an early habit of implicit obedience to prevent all this whipping, would not the mother, as well as the child, be the happier for it? Even in the nurse's arms may a notion of the necessity of this obedience be obtained.

The prohibitions of a parent ought to be judicious, but they ought to be decisive. When they are made to from earliest infancy, they will not often be controverted. A salutary check will thus be put upon the gratification of will, and the wish for that gratification will thus become habitually subordinate to the will of the parent. This requires only steadiness and self-command; but steadiness and self-command are seldom the virtues of young mothers and nurses; and yet without these there are no hopes that the education of a child will ever be conducted upon consistent principles.

The idea of obedience ought to be early and firmly associated with ideas of security and happiness. And here again
the imbecility and helplessness of infancy afford us the
means of effecting our salutary purpose. Entirely dependent
on the wisdom and experience of others, to guard them
from the dangers to which they are hourly exposed,
children might be easily made to learn the advantage of
obedience, and they infallibly would learn it, if obedience
were properly enforced. Were all prohibitions *made absolute*
and the necessity of issuing them guarded against as much
as possible, so that they should not often occur, it would go
far towards rendering obedience natural and easy, for it
would then appear a matter of necessity, and as such be
submitted to without reluctance.

I was some years ago intimately acquainted with a
respectable and happy family, where the behaviour of the
children excited my admiration. One morning, on entering
the drawing-room, I found the little group of laughing
cherubs at high play round their fond mother, who was
encouraging their sportive vivacity, which was at that time
noisy enough, but which on my entrance she hushed into
silence by a single word. No bad humour followed. But as
the spirits, which had been elevated by the preceding
amusement, could not at once sink into a state of quiescence, the judicious mother did not require what she knew
could not, without difficulty, be complied with; but calmly
addressing them, gave the choice of remaining in the room
without making any noise, or of going their own apartment,
where they might make what noise they pleased. The eldest
and youngest of the four preferred the former, while the
two others went away to the nursery. Those who stayed
with us amused themselves by cutting paper in a corner,
without giving any interruption to our conversation. I
could not refrain from expressing my admiration at their
behaviour, and begged to know by what art she had
attained such a perfect government of her children's wills
and actions. "By no art," returned this excellent parent,
"but that of teaching them from the very cradle an *implicit submission*. Having never once been permitted to disobey me, they have no idea of attempting it, but you see,
I always give them a choice, when it can be done with
propriety; if it cannot, whatever I say they know to be a

law, like that of the Medes and Persians, which altereth not."

The happy effects of this discipline were soon rendered more conspicuous, during the very long illness of this amiable mother, who, when confined to her chamber, continued to regulate her family through the medium of her eldest daughter, then a child of eleven years old.

Affectionate as obedient, this amiable girl not only attended her mother's sick bed with the most tender assiduity, but acting as her mother's substitute towards her little brothers and sisters, directed their conduct and behaviour; and was obeyed with the same unmurmuring submission as if their mother had herself been present. Was her mother so ill as to render noise particularly injurious – all was, by her care, hushed to silence. She invented plays for the little ones that would make no disturbance, and taught them to speak in whispers. It was sufficient reward for their forbearance, to be told by her that Mamma sent them a kiss and thanked them for their goodness, *and that she had been the better for it*. What a foundation was here laid for the operation of benevolence!

Let us compare this with the behaviour of an indulged child, to whom the gratification of self-will had become habitual, who had never been taught to submit to aught but force, and to whom submission was consequently hateful, exciting all the painful emotions of anger, indignation, and resentment. I have known such a child make use of a parent's illness as a means of procuring the gratification of all its capricious humours; when, seeing the pains that were taken to prevent noise, it would on the least opposition cry out, "if you don't give it me this minute, I'll roar!" and accordingly she would roar till she had what she wanted.

What are the dispositions which, in the latter case, must have naturally been inspired? To the pleasing associations attached to the gratification of self-will the idea of inflicting pain upon others must likewise be attached. What a foundation for that cruelty which is always allied to a tyrannical disposition! Nor is this all. The exultation consequent upon thus carrying her point, must have engendered pride; and pride, by aggravating opposition into injury, brought forth anger and resentment; and from the extravagance of childish humours, this opposition must frequently recur, so that these hateful passions must soon gain the strength of habit, and a propensity to them be for ever fixed and rooted in the disposition.

Let us suppose the same indulgence continued through the early stages of youth in the fond hope that reason will conquer passion, as the child advances to maturity.

Were the nature of passion, with regard to the influence it has upon the judgment properly attended to, I believe this fond hope would be soon annihilated. On a mind under the dominion of passion the calm suggestions of reason can have little influence, supposing the calm suggestions of reason possible in such circumstances. But it is not possible; for to a mind under the dominion of the selfish passions that appears to be just and reasonable, which is in reality unjust and unreasonable in the last degree; because the ideas of *just* and *reasonable* are all by pride associated with the idea of the gratification of self-will.* Does it not hence appear evident, that the farther such a person as I have been describing advances in life, the more firmly will the dominion of passion be established in the heart? Reason will, indeed, be soon taught by experience to discern the necessity of governing, or at least of disguising, these feelings in the company of strangers or superiors. But if this restraint be not of sufficient duration to induce a habit of self-government, and if that habit be not strengthened and confirmed by motives of religion, occasional restraint will only serve to increase the impetuosity of passion.

The salutary effect of long continued restraint upon the irascible passions is a strong argument in favour of the cultivation of that politeness, which, though too often a fictitious substitute of true gentleness, is yet favourable to the cultivation of the reality. Were the same laws of politeness which govern our intercourse with strangers, always observed

---

* The reasonings of the traffickers in human misery, the self-interested abettors of the Slave-Trade, may with propriety be referred to as an illustration of my present argument. The imagination, inflamed by the passion of avarice, aggravated by pride and ambition, sees it just and reasonable that one part of the species should inflict upon another every kind and degree of misery that human nature can sustain, in order to gratify the avarice, pride, and luxury, of a few worthless individuals! [E.H.]

in the more familiar intercourse of domestic life, it would prove a sovereign antidote against the frequent recurrence of those jars and wrangles, by which the happiness of many families is destroyed. True politeness consists not merely in a strict adherence the forms of ceremony: *it consists in an exquisite observance of the feelings of others, and an invariable respect for those feelings.* By this definition, it claims alliance with benevolence, and, may sometimes be found as genuine in the cottage as the court. A spurious species, adulterated by pride, is, however, in far more common use; and this, being too costly for home consumption, is usually worn with our best clothes, and like them, reserved for particular occasions; nor does the casual restraint it puts upon the feelings, essentially promote the cause of virtue. To it, indeed, society is indebted for all its charms; and in this consideration would surely be sufficient to recommend its constant practice at home as well as abroad, did not self-will and its unruly train of passions interpose. To self-will the restraint imposed by politeness is intolerable. Pride has no respect for the feelings of others, but imperiously demands universal attention to its own. The least, even imaginary, omission of this attention brings forth resentment, either expressed in the sullen tone of peevish discontent, or in the louder notes of brawling anger. In the familiar intercourse of domestic life a thousand opportunities daily occur for exciting these passions, by the petty oppositions which self-will has to encounter; and where all the members of a family are equally eager for its gratification, the scenes of discord that ensue are horrible. But supposing that only one, one darling child, in whom these passions have been fostered by indulgence, should be subject to their influence, I fear it will be quite sufficient to destroy the charm of domestic harmony. When this has been so repeatedly wounded, as to call aloud for a remedy, the only one that presents is that of sending the child to school. There it is hoped, the passions will be subdued, and the mind opened by education to the control of reason. How far this hope is likely to be justified by the event, is worthy of our consideration. But this must be reserved for another Letter, the present has already too far exceeded its bounds.

Adieu.

Letter IX
Associations Destructive of Benevolence

Pernicious Effects of Parental Partiality. – Of Ridicule. –
Of Contempt for the Female Character.

The disposition to benevolence is sown and nourished in the grateful soil of family affection. Where children are educated upon sensible principles, so that their wills are not perpetually clashing with each other, mutual affection must naturally spring from sympathy in each other's joys and the pleasure derived from each other's society. But this affection is too often nipped in the bud by the canker of parental partiality.

Children are so far conscious of their *rights*, as to feel that they have an equal claim to the parent's tenderness and affection. Where this claim is not allowed, and capricious fondness singles out some particular objects on which to lavish its regards, it never fails to produce the worst consequences both on the favoured and neglected parties. In the former it engenders pride and arrogance, in the latter it brings forth indignation and hatred; and destroys the sense of justice in both. It too often happens, that personal defects, or personal charms, occasion this unfortunate bias in a mother's mind. Sometimes that briskness which is so frequently mistaken for genius, or that slowness which is confounded with stupidity, becomes an excuse for partiality or dislike; and sometimes no excuse is attempted, but the sensible one, that "it is a feeling which cannot be helped!"

Whatever may be the motive assigned for partiality to a favourite, or for dislike to an unfavoured child, the mother who indulges her feelings with regard to either, may be assured she is guilty of a crime of no light dye. She, in the first place, breaks the bonds of family affection, and sows the seeds of discord among her children, which, as they

grow up, produce envy, jealousy, and a perpetual recurrence of strife. Home is thus made a scene of displacency
and discontent; than which nothing can be more inimical to
the feelings of benevolence.

If the injury done to the rest of her offspring make a
slight impression on the mother's heart, the injury done to
the favourite by her ill-judged partiality is surely worthy
her attention. Let the partial mother consider, that she is
not only perverting the heart of her beloved darling by the
introduction of all the passions connected with pride and
arrogance, but by rendering him an object of jealousy and
envy, is begetting towards him the hatred and aversion of
those to whom in after-life he ought naturally to look for
solace and support; that she may be the means of depriving
his youth of the blessings of fraternal affection, and his old
age of the consolations of fraternal sympathy.

Nor is it the affection and good-will of his own family
alone of which she robs him. No one can regard a spoiled
child but with feelings of dislike. The faults which good-
nature would over-look, the blemishes which compassion
would regard with tenderness, become odious and revolt-
ing, when seen in the object of blind and doting partiality.
Can a mother compensate by her endearments for thus
depriving her child of the good-will of brothers, sisters,
relations, and friends?

The child who finds itself the object of dislike to every
one besides, will, it is true, be induced to cling to her to
whom alone it perceives itself an object of affection, and
this exclusive preference is so pleasing to self-love, that a
weak mother is sufficiently gratified by the expression of it,
without troubling herself to examine the principles from
which it flows.

In families where connubial harmony has not survived
the honey-moon, where mutual esteem and mutual complacency have given place to the little jealousies of prerogative
and the splenetic humours of contradiction, it is no uncommon thing to see the well-being and happiness of
children sacrificed to the spirit of contention. I have lately
heard of an instance in point, where two fine children have
been the victims of this disunion of sentiment and affection.
The boy, the mother's darling, has had his temper com-
plently ruined by her indulgence; while his resentful pas-

sions are perpetually irritated, not subdued, by the severity of the father. This severity is revenged in turn by the mother on the father's favourite, the poor little girl being always whipped by her, whenever father has bestowed upon the boy a similar chastisement. What are the dispositions, what the sentiments, that must thus be inevitably inspired? The love towards the parent who indulges, must be unmingled with esteem, respect, or veneration, and associated merely with ideas of selfish gratification, while towards the other parent, the sense of injustice will operate to the production of sullen hatred and slavish fear. Thus pride and displacency, selfishness and malevolence, will be cherished in the infant bosom; till an habitual tendency to all the passions and affections against which it is the peculiar duty of a parent to guard, will be fatally introduced, leading their victims to vice and misery.

The feelings of benevolence will neither be uniform nor extensive in their operation, unless they are supported by a strong sense of justice. For this end the necessity and propriety of practising the rule of "doing as they would be done by," ought to be early and forcibly inculcated on the minds of children; and as opportunities of inculcating it daily and hourly occur, they ought never to be passed in silence.

When a child has received pleasure from the complaisance of a companion, or been gratified by any act of kindness or generosity an appeal ought instantly to be made to his feelings, and the duty of contributing in a similar manner to the happiness of others, enforced at the moment when the mind is in a proper tone for the exercise of the sympathetic affections. When he has received any hurt or injury, instead of soothing his angry passions by taking part in his quarrel, the opportunity ought to be seized for recalling to his mind the petty injuries he may have inflicted on a companion on some former occasion, and thus inspiring him with a regard for the feelings of others.

An early and deep-founded sense of justice is the proper soil wherein to nourish every moral virtue. Nor is it more essential towards the culture of the heart, than of the understanding. When we come to investigate the faculty of judgment, we shall have a fuller view of its important consequences. At present I shall only urge the necessity of paying a strict attention to those early habits and associations, by which the sense of justice is diminished or destroyed.

I have already endeavoured to point out the danger of permitting young persons to attach ideas of contempt to any person, on account of involuntary defects, peculiar manners, or peculiar sentiments. Wherever contempt is felt, it must be accompanied with a consciousness of superiority; and if this consciousness of superiority be built upon a bad foundation, pride and arrogance are the inevitable consequences.

What, then, shall we say for those parents, who encourage their children in a practice by which all the feelings of contempt, pride, and arrogance, are inspired and cherished? You will here anticipate my mention of mimickry and ridicule, which is often applauded in children as a proof of wit, while in reality it is the worst of folly.

Ridicule is a sacred weapon which ought never to be lightly wielded. When applied to as the means of exposing sophistry, it is sanctioned by truth and justice; though even then the person who dares to use it, ought to be assuredly purified from every sinister motive.

By children it can never be applied to any useful purpose; while, from the particular light in which it places the object of it to their imaginations, the judgment is perverted, and the nice feelings of moral justice compleatly destroyed.

Children who are brought up at great schools, seldom, I believe, escape this vice. The under-teachers at such seminaries are, in general, considered as buts at which the darts of ridicule may be lawfully shot. Thus the infant wit is whetted by malignity; the mind is corrupted, and rendered callous to every generous sentiment, while obstinacy and self-conceit lead to all the errors of presumption.

Would we implant the sense of justice in the heart, we must vigilantly guard it against those prejudices which effectually check its growth, and prevent its ever coming to maturity. Of this nature, in my opinion, are those which originate in the early distinction that is made between the sexes, from which boys acquire ideas of an inherent superiority, grafted on pride, and supported by selfishness.

The foolish partiality which some mothers evince towards their male offspring, is sometimes such as would induce a spectator to think they have embraced the opinion vulgarly attributed to Mahommed, and have been taught to believe that men only have souls, and that the female children whom God has sent them, have been brought into the world for no other purpose than to contribute to the pleasure, and submit to the authority, of the lords of the creation. Were this, indeed, the case, it would still behove the tender mother to consider, that till the age when decided and incontrovertible superiority in every natural endowment was unequivocally displayed, a boy might be taught to respect the feelings of the companion in the sister, without injury to his inherent dignity, and that the early sense of justice thus acquired would produce habits of urbanity highly favourable to his happiness as well as to his virtue.

Christian mothers cannot for their partiality plead the same excuse that may be offered in favour of the Mahommedan. She who believes her daughters and her sons to be equally born heirs of immortality, equally favoured in the sight of the Most High, equally endowed with all that can exalt and ennoble human nature – the means of grace, and the hope of glory; she who considers eternal misery as the consequence of vice, and eternal happiness as the reward of virtue; cannot shew the preference of superior regard and affection on account of sex, independently of mental qualification, without a manifest dereliction of religious principle. Yet so powerful are first impressions, so strongly rooted are the prejudices of our education, that not even religion itself, no, not in minds where it is deeply cherished, can prevail against them. These are the tares which the enemy has sown while we slept, which will continue to grow up with the wheat till the great and general harvest. Alas! who can tell how many of the opinions we now so fondly cherish, may be found in the number? "By far the greater part of the opinions on which we act in life, are not (says Stewart) the result of our own investigations, but are adopted implicitly in infancy and youth, upon the authority of others. When a child hears either a speculative absurdity, or an erroneous principle of action, recommended and enforced daily by the same voice which first conveyed to it those simple and sublime lessons of morality and religion, which are congenial to its nature, is it to be wondered at, that in future life it should find it so difficult to eradicate prejudices which have twined their roots with all the essential principles of the human frame." That a contempt of the female nature, and an overweaning conceit of the essential superiority of that of the male, is of the number of these hereditary prejudices, will, I imagine, be no difficult matter to prove.

Though as it is a prejudice that has "twined its roots," not only with the essential principles, but with the strongest passions of his nature, the hopes of eradicating it must be faint and remote.

The obstinacy of prejudices received from early associations is commonly in proportion to the mixture of truth with error. Had nature, indeed, made no distinction in the mental endowments of the sexes, the prejudice alluded to would long since have yielded to conviction; but the distinction made by nature, which is merely such as to render each sex most fit and capable to fulfil the duties of its peculiar sphere, confers neither superiority on the one, nor degredation on the other. Of all that is truly worthy, of all that is truly estimable, in the sight of God and man, both sexes are capable alike. Excited to similar virtue by similar motives, exposed to similar temptations by passions and frailties, would it not be wise, if, instead of strengthening these passions by mutual jealousy concerning objects of comparatively small importance, they endeavoured to be mutually instrumental in the support of each other's virtue? This, I am convinced, would be much more commonly the case, were it not for the prevalence of that prejudice which teaches even boys to regard females with contempt, as beings of an inferior order.

All the prejudices which originate in early association, are for a time deemed obvious and incontrovertible truths, discovered by the light of nature. Thus, while the West-Indian planter judges the jetty skin of the negro a mark of inferiority inscribed by the hand of the Great Creator, to point out the immensity of the distance between him and his sable brethren; the African, seated under the bentang tree of his native village, and listening to the tale of the stranger, regards the white skin of the European with disgust and horror, as the signet of nature stampt with the character of cruelty and cunning. Thus does man, in every nation, and in every stage of society, from the associations his infancy attach to the weakness arising from the more delicate structure of the female frame ideas of contempt and inferiority.

In order to analyze this prejudice, it is necessary to trace it to its source, that is to say, to the *savage state* in which it evidently originated; for in the savage state bodily strength gives an indisputable title to superiority. Man is, in this state, distinguished from the brute chiefly by the possession of improveable faculties; but this is latent treasure, of which he is long insensible, and while undiscovered, he is, in some respects, beneath his brothers of the field. The lion brings not his weaker mate into a state of slavish subjection, but inspired by instinct, lays at her feet the spoils his strength and courage have procured; while the savage, his inferior in all but pride and cruelty, treats the miserable partner of his hut with contumelious disdain and rigorous oppression. The poor female, subdued by habitual wretchedness to habitual submission, acquiesces in her miserable destiny; and while she teaches her daughters to submit with cheerfulness to the doom of slavery, she inspires her sons with savage notions of their own comparative importance, and glories in the first indications of their haughtiness and ferocity; dispositions with which she associates the ideas of strength and valour, which comprise all that is in her view great and honourable.

As society advances in its progress towards civilization, the mental powers begin to rise into importance; but the associations of contempt, which the inferiority with regard to physical strength, had originally generated, continue to operate, and debar females from those opportunities of improvement which gradually open on the other sex. Thus we still find in many nations of Asia, where society is advanced to a considerable degree of refinement, this refinement entirely confined to the men; the women being still destined to all the miseries of ignorance and slavery. Thus throughout the world, while man advanced in knowledge and science, from merely physical to rational life, women were doomed to remain stationary; till the distance between the sexes was deemed as great with regard to mental endowments in the civilized state, as it had been with respect to personal strength in the savage.

A lively picture is given by the Eastern writers, of the consequences of this continued degradation of the female character. It is, however, worthy of remark, that the vices of which they uniformly accuse women, are the vices of slaves; and that while innate depravity is by them constantly attributed to the sex, the cause of this depravity is never once hinted at, though it must be sufficiently obvious to every unprejudiced mind.

A more enlightened policy than was ever known to Oriental wisdom, elevated the European nations of antiquity to nobler sentiments and more enlarged views; but so deeply rooted are the prejudices of early association, nourished by habit, and strengthened by the pride of power, that neither legislator, philosopher, priest, or poet, appears to have been superior to their control. The prejudices of the savage state, with regard to women, continued to operate on the enlightened sages of Grecian and Roman world; though, in the intercourse of social life, the minds of the females of Greece and Rome acquired a degree of improvement, which elevated their sentiments to high notions of honour and virtue. The improvement was casual, the effect transient. The virtue that is merely the effect of imitation, cannot be expected to survive its model. Never taught to consider themselves as having inherent interest in the cultivation of their faculties, they learned to value their virtues and accomplishments, not as intrinsically their own, but as shedding a lustre on the house from which they sprung, or on that to which they were allied. Virtues built on such a shallow foundation might be brilliant, but could not be comprehensive or durable. It was, however, the only foundation which the pride of man, in the most advanced state of human knowledge, allowed for female virtue; nor did it ever enter into the heart of the most philanthropic sage to place it on the same foundation as his own.

That to which human philanthropy and human wisdom were unequal, was accomplished by Divine.

Were there no other proofs of the superiority of our blessed Saviour to the wisest of the sons of men, his superiority to the prejudices of his age, and country, and sex, and situation, would, I think, be sufficient to prove him more than human.

By making the purification of the heart, and the subjugation of the passions, alike the duty of all, he broke down the barriers which pride and prejudice had placed between the sexes. He elevated the weaker, not by the pride of intellect, but by the dignity of virtue. He changed the associations of honour and esteem from the *nature of the duty* to its due performance; and promised eternal life as the reward not of great talents or elegant accomplishments, not of valour, or of renown, or of worldly wisdom, but of a pure faith, producing a pure heart and undefiled conscience.

So far did this doctrine operate, that wherever it was embraced, it procured for women, as heirs of immortality, a degree of respect to which the philosophy of Greece and Rome had never elevated them.

But the doctrine of Christ was embraced nominally by millions, who remained strangers to the spirit of its precepts. It was made to bend to human passions and human prejudices, with which it was blended, as to become distorted and disgraced. The instructions which our Saviour and his Apostles addressed indiscriminately to the poor and to the rich, to the learned and the ignorant, to *men* and to *women*, were supposed, in process of time, to be incomprehensible to all but the priesthood, who arrogated to itself the privilege of explaining them. The explanations being generally tinctured by prejudice, and not unfrequently by prejudices of the impurest sort, originating in the selfish passions, were opposed, contested, censured; till the passions were enflamed into resentment, and both parties become infinitely more zealous for the establishment of their own particular explanations, than for the diffusion of the spirit of the Gospel. Had that spirit continued to preserve its influence on the human heart, great is the alteration which would have undoubtedly been produced on human character. But instead of subduing the passions that opposed it, these passions were enlisted in support of what was called by its name. Prejudices, which the example and doctrines of our Divine Master would have completely overthrown, became thus in a manner sanctified by their alliance with superstition; and selfishness continued to justify injustice. That the prejudices of the savage state should continue to prevail in the ages of barbarism, when the light shed by the Christian dispensation was veiled in impenetrable darkness, is not surprising; but that these prejudices should continue after this veil was removed, appears a little extraordinary, though the cause may easily be ascertained.

When the light of science began to illumine our long benighted hemisphere, and the art of printing diffused those treasures of knowledge which had been an useless deposit in the hands of ignorance and superstition, an enthusiastic admiration of the writings of the ancients was generally inspired. Devoted to the study of heathen wisdom, men forgot, or lightly esteemed, the fountain of truth; they beheld it agitated by theological controversy, and polluted by theological prejudice, and turned from it with disgust; not permitting themselves to examine, whether a stream so polluted could have its source in Divine perfection. – The consequence has long been, still is, and may long continue, fatal to the cause of sound morality and virtue.

However the study of the classics may have opened the understanding, enlarged the views, and elevated the sentiments, of men; it is to be feared, that many prejudices have flowed from the same source, which are inconsistent with and inimical to the spirit of the religion we profess, prejudices which are at variance with the whole tenor of our Saviour's precepts, and which occasion a perpetual and manifest inconsistency between the practice and profession of Christians. These prejudices have thrown a shade of ignominy over the mild glories of humility, meekness, and mercy, and exalted pride and revenge into the rank of virtues. They have substituted the love of glory for the love of truth, emblazoned the crimes of ambition with the lustre of renown, and taught man to prefer the applause of a giddy multitude to the approbation of his God. By introducing false associations of regard and preference with adventitious circumstances, altogether foreign to the moral character, as learning, strength, valour, power, &c. they have destroyed the just criterion of human worth, and given to situation which marks the nature of the duty to be performed, that respect which is morally due to the just performance of duty. These prejudices have all an evident tendency to continue and perpetuate the ideas of sexual superiority, which infallibly have been destroyed by the morality of the Gospel. They have gratified the pride of man at the expence of his virtue.

With a contempt for the female sex, on account of this fancied inferiority, has been associated a contempt for those moral qualities which are allowed to constitute the persecution of the female character. Meekness, gentleness, temperance, chastity, that command over the passions which is obtained by frequent self-denial; and that willingness to sacrifice every selfish wish, and every selfish feeling, to the happiness of others, which is the consequence of subdued self-will, and the cultivation of social and benevolent affections; are considered as feminine virtues, derogatory to the dignity of the manly character. Nay, further. By this unfortunate association has religion itself come into disgrace; devotional sentiment is considered as a mere adjunct of female virtue, suitable to the weakness of the female mind, and *for that reason*, disgraceful to the superior wisdom of man. At the thought of *judgment to come*, women, like Felix, may learn to tremble; and, in order to avert the chastisements of Divine displeasure, may study the practice of that righteousness and temperance recommended by the Apostle to his royal auditor. But while the Christian graces are associated with that contempt which the idea of inferiority inspires, neither righteousness, nor temperance, nor judgment to come, will be considered as worthy of consideration in the mind of man.

This unhappy prejudice is in some respects far less injurious to the female than to the male. The obedience which they are taught to pay to authority, the submission which they are made to bow to arrogance and to justice, produce habit of self-denial favourable to disinterestedness, meekness, humility, and generosity; dispositions which are allied to every species of moral excellence. And so seldom do these amiable dispositions fail to be produced by the subjugation of self-will, in females who have been properly educated, that in combating the prejudice which throws contempt upon the female character, I shall be found to plead the cause of the other sex rather than of my own. – Every prejudice founded in selfishness and injustice inevitably corrupts the mind, and every act of tyranny resulting from it debases the human character; but submission for "conscience sake," even to the highest degree of tyranny and injustice, is an act, not of meanness, but of magnanimity. Instead of murmurmg at the circumstances under which they are placed, women ought early to be taught to turn those very circumstances to their advantage, by rendering them conducive to the cultivation of all the milder virtues. And this they would not fail to do, unless they were made to participate in those prejudices which I have humbly attempted to explain, and to expose.*

By far the greater part of those who have hitherto taken upon them to stand forth as champions for sexual equality, have done it upon grounds that to me appear indefensible, if not absurd. It is not an equality of moral worth for which they contend, and which is the only true object of regard, nor for an equality of rights with respect to the Divine favour, which alone elevates the human character into dignity and importance; but for an equality of employments and avocations, founded upon the erroneous idea of a perfect similarity of powers. Infected by the prejudices which associate ideas of honour and esteem with knowledge and science, independent of moral virtue, and envious of the short-lived glories of ambition, they desire for their sex an admission into the theatre of public life, and wish to qualify them for it by an education in every respect similar to that of men. Men scoff at their pretences, and hold their presumption in abhorrence; but men do not consider, that these pretences, and that presumption, have been caught from the false notions of importance which they have themselves affixed to their own peculiar avocations. Taught from

---

* The testimony of the African travellers, Ledyard and Park, may with propriety be adduced in support of what has been advanced. "I have always remarked," says Ledyard, (whose words are repeated by Mr Park) "that women in all countries are civil and obliging, tender and humane; that they are ever inclined to be gay and cheerful, timorous and modest; and that they do not hesitate, like men, to perform a generous action. Not haughty, not arrogant, not supercilious; they are full of courtesy, and fond of society: more liable in general to err than man, but in general also more virtuous, and performing more good actions than he. To a woman, whether civilized or savage, I never addressed myself in the language of decency and friendship, without receiving a decent and friendly answer; with man it has often been otherwise. In wandering over the barren plains of inhospitable Denmark, through honest Sweden, and frozen Lapland, rude and churlish Finland, unprincipled Russia, and the wide-spread regions of the wandering Tartar; if hungry, dry, cold, wet, or sick, the women have ever been friendly to me, and uniformly so: and to add to this virtue (so worthy the appellation of benevolence), these actions have been performed in so free and so kind a manner, that if I was dry, I drank the sweetest draught, and if hungry, I ate the coarse morsel with a double relish." [E.H.]

earliest infancy to arrogate to themselves a claim of inherent
superiority, this idea attaches itself to all the studies and
pursuits which custom has exclusively assigned them. These
prejudices operating likewise on the minds of women, it is
not surprising that those who perceive in themselves a capacity for attaining as high a degree of intellectual eminence,
should aspire to be sharers in those honours which they
have been taught, by the pride of men, to regard as supreme
distinction. Were both sexes guarded from the admission
of early prejudice, and taught to value themselves on no
superiority but that of virtue, these vain and idle jealousies
would cease; man would become more worthy, and woman
more respectable. Were these prejudices annihilated, the
virtues of temperance and chastity would not in the mind
man be associated with ideas of contempt, as merely proper
to be observed by the inferior part of the species, nor
would habits of licentiousness be considered as a light and
venial evil, but regarded with the same horror which is happily still attached to female depravity.

Of the licentiousness of one sex, however, the depravity
of the other is the natural and certain consequence. Accustomed to acquiesce in the idea of man's superiority in all
wisdom and perfection, women cease to respect those laws
of decency and reserve, which they perceive the glory of the
other sex to set at defiance. They learn to consider the
restrictions of chastity as the fetters of worldly prudence;
and as those to whom they are accustomed to look up as
beings of a superior order, scoff at that religion which teaches purity of heart as well as manners, they likewise learn
to regard it with contempt. The *believing wife* is, from the
prejudices of early association, considered as too much
inferior, in point of intellect and intelligence, to have any
chance of converting the *unbelieving husband*; while a thousand to one are in favour of the unbelieving husband's
perverting the believing wife!

If such are the consequences of sexual prejudice, it
behoves every parent who is anxious for the temporal and
eternal happiness of the beings entrusted to her care, to
guard against its introduction into the infant mind. For this
end, she must carefully and conscientiously maintain a
strict impartiality in the distribution of favour and affection. There must be no separate rules of discipline; no sys-

tem of individual and partial indulgence, nor partial restriction, nor partial exemption; but one law of propriety, decency, modesty, and simplicity; one rule of humble submission and cheerful obedience. Boys and girls must equally be made to perceive that there is but one path to approbation and esteem, *the path of duty*; and made to feel that they are approved of and esteemed on no other principle.

I can see no good reason why, in early life, their tasks and instructions should not be the same. Is it because the superior portion of reason supposed to be inherent in man is so very evidently equal to the government of his passions, that we think we may safely neglect in infancy the culture of his heart? Or has the instinctive faculty of imitation proved so efficient a guide to the other sex; has it always so certainly led to the performance of the important duties assigned to females in civilized society; as to justify us in withholding from them the advantages of mental cultivation? Such seem to have been the opinions on which the common practice has been founded. But before we implicitly adopt them, it is surely proper to ascertain, whether they have originated in prejudice, or have been justified by long and ample experience.

The pride and arrogance which we acquire from early ideas of inherent superiority, is greatly increased by the premature distinction that is made between the pursuits and avocations, and those of girls. The trifling accomplishments to which the girls are devoted, they despise as irrational; while consciousness of the superior dignity of that species of knowledge into which they are early initiated, augments their supercilious disdain, and increases the idea of the distance that is placed between them. They soon cease to tolerate them as companions but regard them as incumbrances both troublesome and despicable.

In men of little minds this early-acquired contempt for the female character takes deep and lasting root. It is an everlasting source of consolation to their pride, and a happy excuse for the exercise of a selfish tyranny over the unfortunate females of their families. Where the mind is enlightened and the heart is generous, this early prejudice will cease to operate; but its strength is not always in proportion to the weakness of the character. To what, but to this early prejudice, can we ascribe the conduct of some

men of sense, in the most important concern of life? Having
never experienced any pleasure in female society but
through the medium of passion, by passion only are they
guided in the choice of a connexion sacred and indissoluble.
Passion is short-lived, but when passion is no more, a
sense of common interest, habit, and necessity, happily
unite their forces to keep off wretchedness. Without their
powerful aid, how miserably must existence drag on in the
society of a person with whom there is no intercourse of
intellect, no interchange of sentiment, no similarity of taste,
no common object of pursuit, no common subject of conversation! To be tied to one week of such society would be
misery. What, then, shall we say to those who voluntarily
tie themselves to it for life? To the children of such marriages the contempt for the female character is inevitable. It
is with them hereditary sentiment, confirmed by the father's
conduct, and the mother's folly. In such families, it may
easily be supposed, that a distinction will soon be made
between the boys and girls; a distinction, which, if it prove
injurious to the male, is no less fatal to the female mind.

By the early associations above described as inimical to
manly virtue, girls learn to place the virtues recommended
to their practice on an improper basis; not founded on
immutable truth, but on worldly notions of prudence and
propriety. It is in reality *manners*, not *morals*, which they
thus acquire. Opinion is the idol they are taught to worship.
Opinion is their rule of life, their law of virtue; and fashion,
their only test of propriety. Hence we behold decency out-
raged in the dress and behaviour of women, who assume
the appellation of virtuous! We behold modesty depending
on the caprice of fashion; and by the ease with which it is
plucked up by the roots at her decree, we may judge of the
lightness of the soil in which it was planted.

By these early associations which render opinion the test
of truth, the female mind is so much perverted, as to render
it in some degree dangerous for us to rise above the prejudices of education. For want of proper notions of the
immutability of moral truth, females who have had sufficient strength of mind to emancipate themselves from the
dominion of opinion, have sometimes been seen to despise
the virtues they had in early life learned to associate with
it, and to pique themselves on a dereliction of the peculiar

duties of their sex and station. From these examples plausible arguments have been formed against the cultivation of the female mind. But a more enlarged view of the subject would afford different conclusions. If, by a defective education, opinion has been made the only rule of virtue; whenever a deference for opinion is got the better of, so as no longer to operate on the mind, the notions of virtue attached to it must of course be annihilated. Where a judicious care has been exercised in the cultivation of the moral and intellectual faculties in early life, the respect for virtue is placed on a permanent foundation. The female who is taught an early and habitual respect to the laws of God and conscience, will never learn to despise the duties of her sex and situation. And she whose whole primary desire is to approve herself to these, may cultivate her reason with safety, for never will it lead her astray from the path of duty.

By the early distinction that is made between the sexes, the idea of a distinct and separate code of morality is inevitably inspired, and if the consequences of this idea be such as I have represented them, it surely behoves parents to consider how the evil may be avoided. Let them examine, whether the early separation which now takes place, under the sanction of fashion assuming the name of delicacy, be absolutely necessary; and whether the artificial manners which are prescribed to girls from the cradle, be a real advantage of such vast importance to their future well-being, as to be an equivalent for sense and virtue. Far am I from considering the preservation of female delicacy as a matter of slight importance; but it is in the purity of the heart, and not in deference to public opinion, that I would fix its basis. To guard the purity of the heart from spot or blemish is, in a private family, brought up under the eye of a judicious parent, no difficult task.* But the purity that depends solely on innocent ignorance, is liable to be soiled on the slightest exposure. It may be contaminated by

---

*There is no point in which the conduct of servants towards children ought to be more severely scrutinized, than in that to which I now allude; for in none do I believe it more generally reprehensible. Would we have delicacy fixed in the heart, infancy itself treated with decency and respect. [E.H.]

chance, and receive a lasting stain through the medium of a natural curiosity. It is not by mere ignorance of evil, that genuine delicacy can be inspired. If pains be not taken, at an early period of life, firmly to associate the ideas of personal delicacy and personal decency with the ideas of propriety and to attach ideas of shame and remorse to the smallest breach of the laws of decorum, our pupils may remain personally unpolluted from principle, but they will have little chance of being numbered with the "pure in heart."

It is, I am well convinced, only by attaching ideas of disgust and abhorrence to every circumstance, and every idea, which can soil the purity of the imagination, that we can hope to inspire that species of delicacy which, like the beautiful armour which nature has bestowed upon some plants and flowers, is at once a guard and ornament. Let it be firmly fixed in the mind, let it be strengthened by frequent communication with the Author of all purity and all perfection, and we need entertain no apprehension that it will injured by learning, or contaminated by science. Often, I fear, is this delicacy a stranger to the hearts of those who nevertheless assume its appearance. But where it is only assumed, it will, like other parts of dress, obey the decrees of fashion, and be reserved for particular occasions; whereas the sensibility arising from unsoiled purity is seen

> In all the thousand decencies that flow
> From every word and action.

The delicacy that is produced by association, and confirmed by religious principle, will be found as superior to the spurious sort born of association and sentiment (which is often only another word for affectation) as reality is to fiction. The former is unalterable and undeviating, while the latter is ever liable to be contaminated by the contagion of example, and to vary with situation and circumstances.

Modesty has been, with much truth and propriety, represented as the first ornament of the female mind, but it may be questioned, whether both sexes have not been injured by considering it as a *sexual* virtue. Why should not boys be inspired with the feelings of delicacy as well as girls? Why should the early corruption of their imagination be deemed a matter of light importance? What do we gain by attaching ideas of manliness and spirit to depravity of heart and manners? Alas! many and fatal are the errors which may be traced to this unfortunate association! Let it be the endeavour of my friend to guard her sons from its pernicious effects, and may they in their future lives evince, that dignity of conduct, elevation of sentiment, and refinement of taste, are connected with modesty, purity, and virtue!

Adieu.

Volume 2

Letter I

On the Necessity of obtaining a Knowledge of the Intellectual
Faculties, in order to their proper Cultivation. – How this
Knowledge is to be acquired. – Futility of endeavouring to
cultivate the Faculties out of the Order prescribed by Nature.
– A short Analysis of the Plan to be pursued. – Reflections.

My Dear Friend,

Having endeavoured to point out the necessity of paying
an early and unremitting attention to the active powers of
the human mind, it now remains for me to attempt an
examination of the principles upon which we ought to proceed in the Improvement of the Intellectual Faculties. If we
admit, as a fundamental principle, *that the true end of education*
is to bring all the powers and faculties of our nature to the highest
perfection of which they are capable; it evidently follows, that
an adequate knowledge of these powers and faculties is
necessary towards the accomplishment of the end we have
in view. The diffusion of this species of knowledge would
doubtless correct many errors, both in theory and practice;
and did it once become general among those with whom
the first years of life are commonly spent, would produce
consequences of the utmost importance to society.

But where are we to search for this desirable information?
Must we turn to the voluminous works of philosophers,
and there seek for this hidden treasure, amid all the rubbish
and conjecture and hypothesis? Such a task would be, to
the generality of our sex, impossible: nor were it possible,
would it be attended with much advantage.

To explore the nature of the human mind is, indeed, the
proper object of metaphysical enquiry; but few philosophers have been at sufficient pains to discriminate and ascertain the different degrees of certainty that attend their
discoveries. With all that is speculative or conjectural upon
this subject we have properly no concern; but happily for
us, we may derive an adequate knowledge of all that is true
and certain by means of reflection and observation.

"We take it for granted," says the venerable Reid, "that, by attentive reflection, a man may gain a clear and certain knowledge of the operations of his own mind: a knowledge no less clear and certain than that which he has of an external object, when it is set before his eyes. Another source of information upon this subject is a due attention to the course of human actions and conduct. The actions of men are effects; their sentiments, their passions, and their affections are causes of those effects; and we may, in many cases, form a judgment of the cause from the effect. Not only the actions, but even the opinions, of men, may sometimes give light into the frame of the human mind. The opinions of men may be considered as the effects of their intellectual powers, as their actions are the effects of their active principles. Even the prejudices and errors of mankind, when they are general, must have some cause no less general; the discovery of which will throw some light upon the frame of the human understanding."

Fortified by such authority, I need not scruple to aver, that by reflection upon the operations of our own minds, and attentive operation of the conduct and opinions of others, we may attain all the information that is absolutely requisite for us upon the subject in question; and that the greatest advantage to be derived from the disquisitions of the learned is the leading our minds to a more attentive reflection and observation than we might otherwise be inclined to bestow. "The understanding," as Mr Locke beautifully observes, "like the eye, whilst it makes us see and perceive all other things, takes no notice of itself; and it requires art and pains to set it at a distance, and make its own object." This "art and pains" are implied in serious reflection; and to this reflection it is the object of these volumes to call the guardians of the rising generation.

Let it not be imagined, that I mean to engage my sex in the nice subtleties of logic or metaphysics. It is not for the purpose of exercising their minds in speculation, that I exhort them to the species of inquiry alluded to; but it is to enable them to discharge, with fidelity and honour, the momentous duties to which Providence has been pleased to call them.

Parents are the agents of the Most High in extending the blessing of existence. But in giving life to a new race of

beings is their agency at an end? Ought they not still to consider themselves as the instruments of the Deity, employed
by Him to train up a certain portion of his rational offspring
to capacity for the enjoyment of that felicity which He has
prepared, for those who love Him? In all that we know of
his decrees, we behold a provision for the gradual improvement and final perfection of the human race. In this benefi-
cent plan parents have the privilege of co-operating.
Glorious privilege! Who that had a sense of its importance
would sacrifice it at the shrine of vanity, or relinquish it at
the suggestion of selfish indolence?

To mothers is entrusted the care of rational beings in
the most important period of their existence; the springs of
human conduct are in their hands. From them must the
nascent passions and affections of the heart receive their
direction; by them must the germ of intellect be taught to
expand; by them must the foundation be laid of all that is
great and good, and admirable, in human character. These
are the important privileges by which our sex is honoured;
these are the duties to which it is called. Let not assistance
towards the due performance of them be despised, however
humble the hand that offers it.

In entering upon the Cultivation of the Understanding,
it is necessary to premise, that I do not intend to prescribe
any particular course of study, or to point out the best
methods of instruction in any branch of learning or of
science. To those, therefore, who confine their views solely
to the acquirement of this or that accomplishment, my
observations will necessarily appear dull and uninteresting,
because totally destitute of rules that may facilitate the
attainment of their particular object.

It is observed by an authority to which I am always proud
to refer, that "to instruct youth in the languages and in the
sciences is comparatively of little importance, if we are in-
attentive to the habits they acquire, and are not careful in
giving to all the different faculties, and all their different
principles of action, a proper degree of employment.
Abstracting entirely from the culture of their moral powers,
how extensive and difficult is the business of conducting
their intellectual improvement! To watch over the associations which they form in their tender years; to give them
early habits of mental activity, to rouse their curiosity, and

to direct it to proper objects; to exercise their ingenuity and invention; to cultivate in their minds a turn for specula-tion, and at the same time preserve their attention alive to objects around them; to awaken their attention to the beau-ties of nature and to inspire them with a relish for intellec-tual enjoyment; these form *but a part* of the business of education, and yet the execution even of this part requires an acquaintance with the general principles of our nature, which seldom falls to the share of those to whom the instruction of youth is commonly entrusted."*

The sketch that is here drawn by a masterly hand, will better explain to you my notions upon the subject of intel-lectual improvement than the most laboured definition. Still I must agree with the enlightened author, that these particulars but a part of the business of education:

They are but a few of the necessary means that must be employed in accomplishing our great end.

To qualify a human being for the true enjoyment of exis-tence, the highest cultivation of the intellectual powers will not be sufficient, unless these powers be properly directed; this direction they must receive from the bias that has been given to the desires and affections of the heart. If these desires and affections have been corrupted by improper indulgence, or perverted and depraved by means of power-ful impressions made upon the tender mind; we may give our children knowledge, we may give them learning, we may give them accomplishments, but we shall never be able to teach them to apply these acquirements to just or noble purposes.

To explain and to urge the importance of giving such a direction to the active powers of the mind, as is agreeable to the precepts of divine philosophy, was the particular object of my first Series of Letters. But though my view was there chiefly directed towards the Culture of the Heart, it was impossible to entirely to separate subjects in them-selves united, as not to blend my ideas of the early culti-vation of the mental powers with what I advanced on the cultivation of the affections. The subjects, indeed, ought

---

* *Elements of the Philosophy of the Human Mind*, p. 24. [E.H.]

never to be considered as distinct; though, from our limited powers, it is necessary, in works of this nature, to view them in succession.

That the greatest perfection of which our nature is susceptible, consists in the capability of exerting, in an eminent degree, not one or two of the faculties with which Providence has endowed us, BUT THE WHOLE OF THESE FACULTIES; and of having the direction given to this exertion, under the constant influence of the pious and benevolent affections; I believe few will be inclined to deny. This is the perfection after which we ought incessantly to labour; of this perfection it has pleased the Deity to give us an example, in Him, who, in compassion to our infirmities, *took not on him the nature of Angels,* that is to say, gave us not an example of perfection beyond the grasp of our present faculties to conceive, or of our present powers to imitate.

In the character of our blessed Savior we behold the union of the intellectual and moral powers of man in their most exalted state of perfection; nor is it doing justice either to his example or his precepts, to keep our eye fixed upon one part of the character, while we neglect the other. His precepts and example are never at variance, while he taught the necessity and advantage of improving every talent with which Heaven has entrusted us, he displayed every faculty of the human mind exerted in the cause of piety and virtue. To give our children such a partial and imperfect education, as shall render them inclined to bury their talents in the earth, is to act directly contrary to the commands of Him, who gives them with an express injunction that they may be occupied.

As the body is composed of a variety of organs, of which each is equally necessary to the well-being of the whole, so the mind is a compound, if I may so speak, of a variety of faculties, none of which can be defective, without enfeebling or injuring the rest. The lungs are not more necessary to the functions of the heart, than accurate conception to sound judgment. The circulation of the blood is not more necessary to the animal economy, than memory is to the mental. But memory depends upon attention; the accuracy of conception has the same source: and if both are not duly exercised by means of the perceptions, neither will attain perfection.

Where any one of the faculties has attained a manifest ascendancy, the character will be imperfect, unhappy in itself, and useless to society. This irregular shoot is some-times dignified by ignorance with the name of *genius*; but genius is not the partial vigour of a single faculty, – it implies the possession of all the powers of the mind in an eminent degree. The new combinations which genius pro-duces, either in literature or in the arts, are the production of vigorous conception and sound judgment; aided by the creative power of imagination, and modelled by taste. Where any of these appear to be wanting, the inventions of genius must be proportionally defective. To suppose that genius can exist without them, is absurd.

The same want of reflection leads into other errors, which are frequent causes of disappointment. In the present state of refinement, the cultivation of Taste is an object of much importance: in the education of young ladies, it indeed often appears to be the only object that is deemed worthy of attention. To ascertain the best and most certain method of cultivating this faculty will, therefore, I doubt not, be considered as a very desirable object. If these Letters are read with attention, I hope the discovery will be made. I do not despair of convincing the most incredulous, of the utter impossibility of cultivating Taste, without the previous cultivation of the leading faculties. It is here, how-ever, necessary to premise, that by Taste, wherever the word occurs, I invariably mean that faculty of the mind, whereby we are enabled to *perceive*, and to *feel*, whatever is beautiful or sublime in Nature or in the Arts. It is necessary to give this definition, because the term is often applied to denote *predilection*; and this application of it has given rise to much confusion, not only in colloquial language, but in the writings of some ingenious authors. A predilection for music or painting may be acquired by means of habit and of association; but these are inadequate to the production of the *emotions of Taste*, which have their origin in other sources. All animals that have nice perceptions, are capable of acquiring a predilection for certain sounds or colours, but the emotions of Taste are peculiar to the human race, and even in man are confined to the circle of the cultivated.

The same faculties which must unite their operations in

order to render the mind susceptible of the emotions of
sublimity or beauty, are equally necessary to the imagination. An early and partial cultivation of this faculty is an
evil pregnant with so much mischief, that it cannot be too
severely deprecated. To it are we indebted for those thousand extravagances in opinion and in conduct, which extort
the pity of the wise, and the censures of the severe. To it
we owe the motley absurdities, which, under the name of
Novels, deprave the Taste, and corrupt the affections, of
the youthful heart, and in the early incitement that is given
to the imagination, while judgment is suffered to lie
dormant, we see the reason why such books are read with
avidity and delight. A predilection for the wild and extravagant must be the inevitable consequence of introducing
trains of thought, made up of unnatural combinations, at a
period when the mind has obtained few accurate ideas,
and the judgment has been but little exercised.

The imagination that is not regulated by judgment is pernicious in exact proportion to its strength. It presents to
the mind's eye a false glass, through which no object is seen
in its natural size and just proportion. All is distorted;
though, by the glare of false colouring, the deformity
escapes detection. Thus, by injudicious management, is that
faculty which, under proper regulation, is the ornament
and blessing of our present state, converted into a source of
error and delusion. Thus what was intended for our happiness is rendered productive of misery, and confusion is
introduced into the works of God!

Nor is the partial cultivation of the faculties confined to
taste and imagination. Upon a strict investigation of this
important subject, I am afraid we should find, that it is no
uncommon thing to attempt the cultivation of the
reasoning faculty without having paid any regard to the culture of those by which, in the order of nature it is preceded.
Have we no abstract reasoners who shew a deficiency in
judgment? No metaphysicians who betray the absence of
that common sense which has sound judgment for its basis?
Is it not to the neglect of the judging faculty, that we must
attribute the favourable reception which the crude dreams
of speculative visionaries meet with from the young? How
should they detect sophistry, whose minds have never been
exercised on truth?

Where the judgment has not been duly cultivated, it is in vain that we endeavour to lead the mind to general reasoning; on such minds the sciences, that afford the most powerful aid to the faculty of abstraction, are lost. Those who know what assistance is to be derived from a knowledge of mathematics in this particular, are apt to envy such as have been favoured with opportunities of making this acquirement. But on what numbers is this useful branch of science totally thrown away! By how few is it made use of as a means of further improvement! Without the cultivation of judgment, the means will ever be rested in as the end. The knowledge of various languages opens a rich and inexhaustible mine to the cultivated understanding, but if judgment do not lend its assistance, the ore will never be extracted. While we devote the most precious years of life to the study of languages, it is surely proper to take some precautions against the possibility of so much pains proving utterly abortive. Let it be remembered, that to be able to construe Greek and Latin is one thing, and to be inspired with a taste for classical literature is another. The first, you will perhaps say, is sufficient to qualify your sons for the professions to which you destine them. But who, in any profession, ever rose to distinguished eminence without taste and judgment?

Is a taste for classical literature acknowledged to be an accomplishment worthy of a gentleman? Do not flatter yourself it will ever be acquired, without accuracy of conception, and soundness of judgment. Nor will these be sufficient, if pains be not at the same time taken to fix such associations as may introduce habits of thinking favourable to the cultivation of sentiment. How much this is attended to at great seminaries, I leave it to parents to enquire. Let them reflect on the nature of the human mind, and consider which of its faculties are likely to receive improvement, where hundreds of bad and good are promiscuously mingled. Where the time of boys is so entirely at their own disposal, that of the four-and-twenty hours but two or three at the utmost are spent under the master's eye; of the remainder, when we deduct what is employed in the important business of purveying, in quarreling, and in play, we shall find little left for the purposes of voluntary improvement. But unless much previous pains have been bestowed,

how can we expect that boys completely left to their own
disposal, goaded to idleness and dissipation by example,
incited by the same means to sensual gratification, and destitute of guide or monitor, should voluntarily betake themselves to improvement? Such instances are, I believe,
sufficiently rare; and wherever they occur we may be
assured that the foundation had been laid at home. Where
this is wanting, all that can, from the nature of things, be
acquired at school, is merely a verbal knowledge of the languages. The mind will not certainly at this active season
remain stationary: it will be sharpened by suspicion; its
sagacity will be called forth by selfishness, and the experience of fraud, deceit, and perfidy, will give a premature existence to the feelings of indignation, jealousy, and
revenge. It is there evident, that where boys are to be sent
to great schools, an uncommon degree of previous pains
is necessary, in order to secure them from all the fatal
consequences of such a plunge, and to enable them to
reap all the benefit which such institutions are calculated to
produce.

If, in analysing the faculties of the human mind, we find
that Providence has made a manifest distinction between
the sexes, by leaving the female soul destitute of the intellectual powers, it will become us to submit to the Divine
decision. But if, upon enquiry, we find that no such partiality has been shewn by Heaven; it is incumbent upon us to
consider, by what right we take upon us to despise the gift
of God. When we neglect the cultivation of the faculties
which He has to graciously bestowed, can we flatter ourselves that we act in concert with our Almighty Father? Let
us examine the mode of education adopted at our great
boarding-schools, and say, which of the faculties of the soul
it has a tendency to improve? Let us reflect on the manner
in which education is too often conducted at home, and
pronounce how far it is calculated to bring to perfection
those high intellectual endowments with which Heaven has
entrusted us? Could it be proved, that the rational faculties
are indeed useless to the sex; and that the duties to which
they are called, as intelligent and accountable beings, as
daughters, sisters, wives, mothers, and members of society,
could be equally well performed by means of those powers
which they have in common with the brute creation; then

might the higher faculties of the soul be neglected with impunity.

To the wretched beings who are destined to be shut up in the zenanas of Eastern despots, reason would be not only an useless, but a cruel gift. The accomplishments, however superficial, which can help to amuse the listless hours of hopeless captivity, ought by them to be prized as a resource from wretchedness. Considering themselves in no higher light than as mere objects of sensual appetite, it is to this point that their whole endeavours will necessarily be directed.

> Bred only and completed to the Taste
> Of fretful appetence – to sing, to dance,
> To dress, and troll the tongue, and roll the eye –
> Yet empty of all good, wherein consists
> Woman's domestic honour and chief praise.*

Such education to women so destined is perfectly appropriate; and the sole inconsistency which we can detect in the Eastern system, is in permitting their sons, as well as daughters, to pass the most important period of youth under the tuition of such degraded beings. By them are the seeds of moral depravity effectually sown; and sloth, and ignorance, and pride, and self-importance, with every species of corruption, become the inheritance of the children committed to their care. Such are the consequences that must necessarily follow, when those who are destined to instruct others are themselves destitute of instruction!

Where the chief aim in education is directed to any other point than the improvement of the intellectual and moral powers, an artificial character will be produced, which, neither guided by reason, nor inspired by any noble or generous sentiment, will be the mere puppet of opinion, and the creature of imitation. But if imitation is made to supply the use of reason, it is probable, that the early associations will be such as to lead the mind to chuse the brightest patterns of virtue? Alas! experience has fully proved the contrary. Experience shews us daily examples of the fatal consequences of carrying the system of *zenana* educa-

---

* Milton. [E.H.]

tion into practice, in a country where women are called to act an important part on the theatre of society. Without intellect there can be no principle, and without principle there can be no security for virtue.

In order to cultivate the intellectual faculties to advantage, it appears to me, that we ought to accompany Nature in her progress; and as she gradually unfolds the powers of the mind, that we should devote ourselves to the improvement of each faculty, in the order it is by her presented.

Assuming this as a principle, I shall proceed in the following Letters to examine, in the first place, the faculty of PERCEPTION; shewing the advantages that are to be derived from its assiduous cultivation, and the very great disadvantages that accrue from its neglect.

ATTENTION is the next subject that will naturally fall under our consideration. I shall be at some pains to illustrate its importance; and shall not scruple to advance upon it arguments which appear convincing to my own mind, though they are unsupported by the authority of others. If they are founded in truth, they will stand the test of investigation; if otherwise, I should be sorry to protract their fall.

CONCEPTION is the next faculty brought forth by Nature. By conception, I mean the ideas which we form of absent objects of sense, or of our past sensations. So much depends upon the vigour of this faculty, that I cannot be at too much pains to inculcate the necessity of its being cultivated with never-ceasing vigilance. I shall, therefore, do all in my power to urge the careful cultivation of this faculty, by an explanation of the important consequences to which it leads; and shall give you such hints with respect to its improvement, as, I hope, may be found of use to those who are concerned in the practical part of education.

The faculty of JUDGMENT is the next that will demand our attention. I shall trace its progress from its first dawn in the infant mind to its maturity; and though conscious that my abilities are inadequate to the magnitude of my subject, I shall do what in me lies to enforce its importance. To the neglect of this faculty, all the follies, and many of the vices, which abound among us, may be fairly traced. Where the judgment is sound and unperverted, the unruly desires and associations will not revel without control; but in order to the cultivation of sound judgment, it is not only necessary that the affections be uncorrupted, but that they be *early engaged on the side of truth.*

Having dwelt at large on the cultivation of Judgment, we shall then proceed to an examination of the faculty of ABSTRACTION. This faculty, though common to all, and susceptible of great improvement, is seldom cultivated to any perfection, but by the few whose course of studies has led them to cherish a turn for speculative enquiry. If general reasoning were indeed useful to none but the philosopher, we should leave the philosopher to enjoy it as his peculiar prerogative. But if it can be proved to be no less necessary in the conduct of life than in the speculations of philosophy, it becomes our business to endeavour to find out the means which are best adapted to its improvement. These the circumscribed limits of my present plan will not permit me to explain at large; neither are my abilities equal to such a task: but having proved the advantages which result from the cultivation of this faculty, the hints which I shall offer, may be sufficient to direct the mind in search of higher guides.

Subsequent to Abstraction I shall place what offers upon the cultivation of TASTE and IMAGINATION, because the faculty of Abstraction is necessary to both. A few hints concerning the necessity of cultivating power of REFLECTION will conclude the series.

And now, my friend, that I have laid before you a compleat view of the plan which it is my intention to pursue, you will be able in some measure to decide upon its propriety. Where I fail in the execution, candour will make allowances for the imperfections of one who makes no pretensions to superior abilities. Placed by Providence in a situation undisturbed by the pressure of life's cares, tho' by an experience of its sufferings called to serious reflection; blest with leisure, and early inspired with such a Taste for enquiry as gives that leisure sure full employment, I should have deemed myself highly culpable, if I had declined the task to which I was called by friendship, and urged by the hope which is dear to every generous mind – the hope of being in some degree useful. The arrogance and ambition of a dictator are alike foreign to my heart. But to be an humble instrument in routing my sex from the

lethargy of quiescent indolence, to the exertion of those
faculties which the bounty of a kind Providence has conferred; to be the means of turning the attention to those
objects which tend to the progressive improvement of the
human race; is a species of glory, to which, I confess, I am
not indifferent.

If in this way

> To covet honour be a sin,
> I am the most offending soul alive.

But lest I should be tempted to further egotism, I hasten
to assure you how much

I am yours, &c.

Letter X
Imagination and Taste

Imagination defined. – Necessity of its Operations being
guided by Judgment. – Illustrations. – Definition of Taste. –
Mistakes concerning the Cultivation of this Faculty, Union of
Conception and Judgment essential to its Cultivation. –
Illustrations.

My Dear Friend,

The necessity I feel myself under of compressing into the
limits of a single Letter the observations that occur to me
on the subjects of Imagination and Taste, will compel me to
be concise; I shall, however, endeavour to be as little ob-
scure as possible.

The word Imagination has great latitude in its application.
It is sometimes employed to denote simple apprehension;
it being very usual in common conversation to say, that we
cannot imagine how such a thing could happen, when we
mean, that we cannot conceive it. In this sense, you will
observe, that I have carefully avoided employing it. It is
sometimes likewise applied in a general way, to express the
operation of the mind in thinking; and in this incorrect
way of speaking, we frequently observe, that a thing occupies the imagination, when in reality it is the subject of
reflection.

Again; the term Imagination is sometimes made use of
in describing the intellectual pleasures and pursuits, in con-
tradistinction to those of sense. In this way it is applied by
Doctor Akenside, whose poem on the Pleasures of the
Imagination describes the employment of all the intellectual
faculties.

By Imagination, in the sense to which I have confined
myself, is understood that power of the mind, which is
exerted in forming new combinations of ideas. The power
of calling up at pleasure any particular class of ideas is properly denominated Fancy. A creative imagination implies

not only the power of fancy, but judgment, abstraction, and taste. Where these are wanting, the flights of imagination are little better than the ravings of a lunatic.

From the nature of this faculty, it is obvious, that it can be exercised but in a slight degree in childhood, the ideas being at that period too few in number to afford materials for new combinations; or should the attempt at forming them be made, they must, from the want of taste and judgment, be weak and imperfect. But long before the mind can combine for itself, the conceptions are sufficiently vigorous to enter with avidity into the combinations made by others. If these are artfully contrived as to interest the passions, or to excite the emotions of terror, hope, indignation, or sympathy, they become the most pleasing exercises of the juvenile mind, but if this exercise be frequently repeated, it will infallibly produce trains of thought highly unfavourable to the cultivation of those important faculties, without whose aid the creative power of imagination can never be exerted to any useful purpose.

While the mind is occupied in making observations on the nature and properties of the objects of sense, its train of thought is merely a series of simple conceptions; but these conceptions are the materials with which imagination is at a proper time to work. On these conceptions, too, does judgment begin its operations; by these, is it exercised into strength; and by such exercise alone it is, that it can ever attain perfection. These operations are, as I suspect, greatly retarded, and in some instances utterly prevented, by a premature disposition to make attempts at combination; the inevitable consequence of having the mind powerfully impressed by interesting fictions. After every such impression the train of thought flows for a considerable time in the same channel with the emotion that has been excited: and before judgment has attained the capability of directing its combinations, the images that are formed must of necessity be wild and incoherent. However incoherent they may be, they have such a tendency to increase the flow of ideas, and, of consequence, to augment vivacity, that such children appear to much greater advantage, than those whose faculties are cultivated in the natural order. But when both arrive at maturity, they who have laid in the greatest fund of clear, distinct, and accurate ideas, must possess a manifest advantage.

Were imagination (as is unfortunately too often supposed) a simple faculty, which could be exercised to advantage without the assistance of the other faculties, the methods usually taken to cultivate it would be judicious and effectual. But if it be in fact a compound of several other faculties, it necessarily follows, that its excellence depends on the degree of perfection, to which the faculties connected with it have arrived. The Iliad of Homer is a work of imagination; it exhibits a series of situations, perhaps more astonishing in their variety, harmony, and consistency, than any that human genius has ever produced; but does it not in every line give a proof of clear and vigorous conceptions, strong judgment, and profound reflection? When our own Shakespeare, whose elevated genius exhausted worlds, and then imagin'd new, pourtrayed the character of Caliban, (who is certainly a creature of the poet's imagination) did not judgment evidently guide the pencil, and lay on the colours? From the incomparable productions of these extraordinary men, we may justly infer, that all the faculties of the mind were by them possessed in an uncommon degree of vigour, and therefore conclude them to have been cultivated according to the order assigned by nature.

In a living author, whose remote situation will apologize for a comparison which would otherwise seem invidious, we see still further proof of our argument. In the power of imagination, (taken according to its simple definition) it is probable that Kotzebue does not yield to either of the poets above-mentioned. But what are the combinations which his genius has produced? I have no intention of turning critic, and therefore shall decline answering the question; but think it not out of my province to observe, that if a deficiency in the powers of accurate conception and sound judgment are laid to his charge, he has given us a clue to lead to the cause of this deficiency in his memoirs, where he describes his mother having, while he was yet a child, assiduously cultivated his imagination by the powerful emotions excited by romantic fiction. He tells us, "she was a woman of sensibility, and delighted in inspiring him with a taste for works of imagination, of which he soon grew enthusiastically fond." Of old Mrs Shakespeare we know nothing; but from the sound judgment exhibited in the works of her son, I think the probability is, that instead of being a woman of *sensibility*, (in the sense Kotzebue employs the term) she was a woman of plain good sense.

To produce a work of genius, the power of imagination must be possessed in a very eminent degree; but unless a certain portion of the same imagination be possessed by the reader, the works of genius will never be perused with delight. Nothing can be relished but in proportion as it is understood; and thoroughly to understand an author, we must be able, with the rapidity of thought, to enter into all his associations. This can never be done by those who possess a very limited stock of ideas. The beautiful allusions which at once illustrate and adorn the works of the learned, are lost upon those who are unacquainted with classical literature; and we may be assured, that many of the beauties of the ancient orators and poets are in like manner lost upon the learned of our days, from their ignorance of the associations which produced them. A small number of ideas will, indeed, suffice to pursue a simple narrative; and accordingly we find that narrative, either of real or fictitious events, is the only sort of reading which is relished by the uncultivated mind. Do we wish to inspire a taste for studies of a higher order? Then let us lay a solid foundation for such a taste in the cultivation of all those faculties which are necessary to the proper exercise of imagination. Let us by the exercise of the reasoning powers, as well as of the conception and the judgment, produce that arrangement in the ideas, which is alike favourable to invention and to action. In such minds the trains of associated ideas are, if I may to express myself, harmonized by truth. The ideas being numerous, distinct, and just, are called up in proper order, and as arrangement in our associations is the true key of memory, every idea that is wanted obeys the call of will. It is then that the power of imagination comes forth to irradiate the mind, and to give a new zest to the charm of existence. The combinations which it then presents, arranged by judgment, selected by taste, and elevated by the sublime ideas of Divine perfection, give an exercise to all the intellectual powers.

"What employment can he have worthy of a man, whose

imagination is occupied only about things low and base, and grovels in a narrow field of mean, unanimating, and uninteresting objects?" and such must ever be the case with him whose ideas are few, confused, and inaccurate; and who, while incapable of expanding his mind to embrace the forms of general and abstract truth, has habitually employed his imagination on the chimeras of untutored fancy; such a person must be "insensible to those finer and more delicate sentiments, and blind to those more enlarged and nobler views, which elevate the soul and make it conscious of its dignity. How different from him, whose imagination, like an eagle in her flight, takes a wide prospect, and observes *whatever it presents*, that is new or beautiful or important; whose rapid wing varies the scene every moment, carrying him thro' the fairy regions of wit or fancy, sometimes through the more regular and sober walks of science and philosophy."

"The various objects which he surveys, according to their different degrees of beauty and dignity, raise in him the lively and agreeable emotions of taste. Illustrious human characters as they pass in review, clothed with their moral qualities, touch his heart still more deeply. They not only awaken the sense of beauty, but excite the sentiment of approbation, and kindle the glow of virtue. While he views what is truly great and glorious in human conduct, his soul catches the divine flame, and burns with desire to emulate what it admires."*

The reveries of such a mind are not only delightfully amusing, but salutary and useful. On the gay pictures delineated by fancy, judgment, reason, and the moral sense, exert their powers of criticism, and thus the casual combinations of imagination are made a means of improvement to the heart.

I have known a young person, prone to indulge in the reveries presented by a rich and lively imagination, who acknowledged that it was by reflecting on these spontaneous effusions of fancy, that she became acquainted with the propensities and imperfections of her own temper and

---

* Reid. [E.H.]

disposition. In her dreams of future felicity, she found that the gratification of vanity was always included, or indeed formed the ground-work of the piece; she accordingly set herself to root out a propensity which she thus discovered to be predominant. When mortified by the pride of others, she found fancy immediately busied in forming scenes whereon she was to act the superior part, and to retort the mortification on those by whom her feelings had been wounded. Conscience took the alarm, and taught her to apply to the Throne of Grace for the Christian spirit of true humility. Thus was imagination rendered subservient to religion, judgment, and reason; and while it acts under such control, we may safely pronounce it the first of human blessings!

Where the imagination has been injudiciously stimulated at an early period, it has little chance of ever coming under this species of regulation. The attention having been habitually engaged in pursuing the dreams of fiction, loses a thousand opportunities of information and improvement, and the number of ideas must consequently be extremely circumscribed. The judgment having never been exercised on realities, can only compare ideas that are equally imperfect, and consequently be for ever liable to error. An expectation that the same causes should always produce similar effects, will, to the mind which has been exercised in fiction, be attended with the most fatal consequences, the real events of life succeeding each other in a very different train from that in which they are represented in such productions. The false associations that are thus produced in the mind, may not only mislead the judgment, but, as I have endeavoured elsewhere to shew, may effectually pervert the heart – sensibility excited by fictitious representations of human misery being very far from that genuine spirit of benevolence, that is actively exerted in alleviating the distresses which it cannot remove. Where the judgment has been strengthened by observation, and habits of active benevolence have been, in some measure, acquired, and confirmed by religious principle; then, indeed, the luxurious tear, called forth by the witching power of imagination, may be indulged with safety; for its source will not then be mistaken. But where by imagination sensibility has been brought into existence, to the woes of imagination will sensibility be confined; and far too sickly will be its constitution, to produce the active charities of life.

Taste is so intimately connected with imagination, that many of the observations applicable to the one will be found to reach the other. The emotion of taste, though simple in its operation, is derived from complex sources. Its very existence depends on the vigour of conception, and implies the exercise of judgment. Nor are these faculties alone equal to the production of this delightful emotion, as we may be convinced, by observing the numbers of persons who possess these faculties in an eminent degree, who, nevertheless, are incapable of experiencing the emotions of taste. Without a certain portion of sensibility, I believe, true taste is never found. How much this sensibility depends upon organization, I cannot presume to determine; but that it is seldom the boon of uncultivated minds, experience affords convincing proofs.

To perceive and to enjoy whatever is beautiful or sublime in the work of nature or of art, is the peculiar privilege of taste. Its emotions are accordingly divided by an author,* to whose elegant and judicious remarks I confess many obligations, into the *emotions of sublimity*, and the *emotions of beauty*.

"The qualities that produce these emotions, are to be found in almost every class of the objects of human knowledge, and the emotions themselves afford one of the most extensive sources of human delight. They occur to us amid every variety of external scenery, and among many diversities of disposition and affection in the mind of man. The most pleasing arts of human invention are altogether directed to their pursuit; and even the necessary arts are exalted into dignity by the genius that can unite beauty with use."

That a susceptibility to the emotion of taste does not altogether depend upon the original frame of our nature, is evident from its being entirely confined to minds possessing a certain degree of cultivation; whereas the emotions of surprise, joy, wonder, &c. are felt by all. Nor is the mind of the most cultivated at all times equally susceptible of these emotions. All must know, that there are moments

---

* See Alison on Taste. [E.H.]

when objects of sublimity or beauty make no impression. All must have experienced, that scenes which have at one period called forth the most vivid sensations of delight, have at another been viewed with the most perfect indifference.

The more deeply we examine this curious subject, the more fully shall we be convinced, that the emotions of taste entirely depend on the train of ideas which are called up in the mind by certain objects of perception. If the mind has not been previously furnished with a store of ideas that can be thus associated, the finest objects of sublimity or beauty will never give a pleasurable sensation to the breast. They may be viewed with wonder, with admiration, but will never produce emotions of sublimity or beauty.

The above observations may be further illustrated, by reflecting on the manner in which a taste for the beauties of nature in the material world, and for the beauties of poetry, enhance each other. A young mind, accustomed to the contemplation of rural scenery, is enraptured by the poetical descriptions which present a transcript of all that had so often charmed the imagination.

When Nature charms, for life itself is new.

The elevated sentiments and sublime ideas of the poet give, on the other hand, a number of new associations, which are henceforth called up by the scenes of nature, and become to the mind of sensibility a new and inexhaustible source of delight.

By the ideas associated with them, a thousand sounds that are in themselves indifferent, nay, some that are rather in their natures disagreeable, become pregnant with delight. I have for this last half hour been leaning on my elbow, listening to the distant tinkling of the sheep-bell, a sound so perfectly in unison with the surrounding scenery, as to appear enchantingly beautiful. Upon reflection, I believe it to be just such a bell as is tied to the pie-man's basket, which I have often in town deemed an execrable nuisance. The different emotions which it now excites can only be resolved into the different trains of ideas with which the sound is associated.*

---

*I once knew a lady who had been brought up in one of the most confined streets in the city of London, where her father had, by dint of

My narrow limits will not permit me to go into this subject at sufficient length, but the hints I have suggested, will,
if pursued with any attention, infallibly lead us to conclude,
that the foundation of the emotions of taste, with regard
to natural objects and to poetical description, must be laid
in distinct and accurate conceptions. By these must the
ideas be accumulated, which, by the laws of association, are
formed into distinct trains, which, like the genii of Adelin's
lamp, appear the moment the enchanter imagination is disposed to call them. Without some pains taken in the cultivation of the faculty of conception, we may learn to
criticize upon the laws of taste, but we shall never be
subject to its influence.

In creating a susceptibility to the emotions of taste, we
shall find a powerful assistant in devotional sentiment. The
mind that has been accustomed to associate the ideas of
Infinite Power, Wisdom, and Goodness with all that is
striking in the works of nature, must have a peculiar tendency to the emotions of sublimity and beauty. It is thus
that sensibility may be properly and effectually awakened.
The train of thought which devotional sentiment excites, is
so highly favourable to the cultivation of refined taste, that
I greatly question whether its emotions were ever excited
where sensibility had not been thus called forth. So necessary is it towards the perfection of the human mind, that
the cultivation of the affections should go hand in hand
with that of intellect!

It is no small incitement to the cultivation of taste, to
reflect, that the emotions of sublimity and beauty are connected, not only with our devotional, but with our moral
feelings. They coalesce not with any of the dissocial or
malevolent passions; and can never be experienced while the
mind is under their influence. By rendering the mind suscep-

---

industry, accumulated a large fortune. When complaining of her hard fate,
in being obliged upon her marriage to leave the metropolis for the dull
sameness of a country life, she drew a striking picture of the joys she had
unwillingly relinquished. "*There* (she said) she never knew what it was to be
lonely; for besides the bustle all day long in the street of carts and coaches,
there were forty coopers in the back-yard, who were knock, knocking,
from morning till night!" Does not this strongly evince the power of association in forming our ideas of harmony? [E.H.]

tible of the emotions of taste, we not only expand the circle
of human pleasures, but as every emotion, of which the heart
is capable, has a tendency to produce emotions that are in
the same key, we give an additional chord, if I may so express
it, to the harmony of the virtues.

To those who are by their situation in society exempted
from the cares and perplexities of business, it is of the last
importance to have a sufficient number of such objects and
pursuits, as may serve fully to occupy the time which is
thus left to their disposal. The intellectual powers have
little chance of being called forth, in any eminent degree,
where there are no difficulties to stimulate the energies of
the soul, and no object to rouze its activity. The love of
knowledge is, indeed, an active principle; and for that
reason cannot be too assiduously cultivated in the minds of
those who are born to the privilege of the *curse* of leisure:
but if to the love of knowledge we do not add a susceptibility to the emotions of taste, the mind will be apt to lan-
guish, and to seek resources in those fatal scenes of
dissipation, where every virtuous disposition and manly
sentiment are soon obliterated.

The emotions of taste are, I believe, particularly congenial to the female mind; but it deserves our serious
enquiry, how the common mode of female education aids
to cultivate, or to destroy, this natural susceptibility. When
we hear a mother speak of giving her daughters *a taste for
music, and a taste for painting*, we may, nine times in ten, conclude, that she means nothing more by the expression, than
exciting in her children an ambition to exhibit to advantage
their practical skill in these accomplishments. For this purpose, the methods generally adopted are obviously so
successful, as to render it unnecessary to suggest any
improvement.

With the idea of excelling in those accomplishments is
associated every idea of glory and approbation. To render
the road to excellence easy of access, diffidence and
modesty are banished from the youthful mind; the veil of
bashfulness is torn aside by vanity, and every art made use
of to render the gentle pupils callous to the public gaze.
Vanity, aided by example, and stimulated by ambition, does
wonders.

The attention is exerted in the art of imitation, and its

power is never exerted in vain. Where the best models are procured, the copies will in time be excellent. The Music-Master who has taste, will teach his pupils to make use of graces, which will serve as a succedaneum for that which he has it not in his power to confer; and rapid execution must inevitably be attained by unwearied application.

All this may, I confess, be accomplished without the cultivation of a single faculty of the mind, excepting those of perception and attention; but to confound this paltry art of imitation with the idea of Taste is no less absurd, than if we were to call the compositor, who arranges the types for an edition of Homer, the Prince of Poets!

The emotion of Taste with regard to musical composition, depends upon association no less than it does with regard to the other objects of our perceptions.

Single sounds, we well know, are accounted agreeable or disagreeable, according to the ideas which they excite. On examination we shall find that those which particularly strike us as sublime or beautiful, never fail to produce certain trains of ideas in the mind; which, if accidentally broken, the emotions of sublimity or beauty are annihilated. An instance or two will sufficiently elucidate this truth. What sound so sublime as a peal of thunder? The emptying of a cart of stones in the street may be mistaken for it, and, while the deception lasts, will produce the emotions of sublimity in their fullest extent; but let us discover our mistake, and what becomes of the emotions of sublimity? The melodious notes of the nightingale have been well imitated on the stage; but did they there produce the same emotions of beauty, as when heard in the stillness of the solemn grove?

Music, which is a continuation of sounds, may, from the various combinations of which it is capable, be rendered highly expressive of the tender, the plaintive, the melancholy, the cheerful, or the gay. It may be rendered elevating or depressing, soothing the soul to sadness, or exhilarating to the tone of pleasure. Now that every one of these various emotions are occasioned by the production of certain trains of ideas connected by the laws of association, I think no person of reflection will dispute. The person who is not susceptible of these emotions, may attain a knowledge of the laws of composition, and acquainted with the difficulty attending the execution of laborious passages, may admire the art of the performer; but this admiration is perfectly distinct from the emotion of taste. To obtain this species of applause, is the sole aim of a number of composers, whose ambition is amply gratified by the approbation of the vulgar many: but it is the man of real taste alone, who, either in his compositions or performance, can excite the emotions of sublimity or beauty.

That the number is so few, will not be matter of surprise, when we reflect that the person who would call forth the emotions of taste, either in the disposition of material objects, or in *any* of the fine arts, must be capable of entering into all those associations that are connected with the tones of mind which he wishes to produce. Whatever rudely breaks these trains of ideas, utterly destroys the effect. Every person of taste, who has heard the Messiah of Handel performed at Westminster-Abbey, and at the Play-House, must be sensible of the advantage with which this sublime composition was heard at the former place, where every object tended to produce associations in unison with the tone of the performance. At the Play-House these associations were forcibly broken, trains of discordant ideas obtruded themselves on the mind, and thus the effect was lost.

Why is our church-music in general so poor, so deficient in sublime expression, and so ill calculated to produce the sublimity of devotional sentiment? Why, but because the sublimity of devotional sentiment was unknown to the composers. Had the musical compositions of David happily been handed down to us, I make no doubt, we should have in them examples of the elevated and sublime in music, which would have harmonized with the tone of his own inimitable poetry.*

---

* I wish I could prevail on accomplished young ladies to consider the effect that would be produced by the exertion of their musical talents in places of public worship. Why should Church be the only place in which they are ashamed to let their voices be heard? Is it, that they think none should join in the praise of God, but such as are paid for it? Is it the theme that is unworthy of their talents, or the *place* that is unfit for their exertion; or is the audience too mean to be indulged with hearing the delicious melody of their fine voices? The cultivation of true taste would, I think,

From the tenor of these observations, I hope it has been made clear, that a taste for the fine arts can only be cultivated by the same means which must be employed to lay the foundation of taste in general, viz. a careful improvement of all the intellectual faculties. If the conceptions have not been rendered clear and accurate, and the attention rouzed to give them constant employment, so as to lay in a large stock of ideas upon every subject, if the judgment has not been exercised upon the agreement and disagreement of ideas; and if the powers of abstraction and imagination have not been called forth; it is impossible that the emotions of taste should ever be experienced. It is not by constantly practicing at a musical instrument, or by handling the pencil, that taste for painting or for music can possibly be acquired. But let the taste be fixed, and then by rendering your pupils capable of the practical part these accomplishments, you enlarge the sphere of their innocent enjoyments, and afford them the opportunity of communicating pleasure to others.

The mother who is superior to the chains of fashion, and who is capable of taking an extensive view of the probabilities of human life, as well as of weighing the talents of her children with accurate impartiality, will decide with wisdom and precision on the value of those accomplishments which must inevitably be purchased at the expence of a large portion of time and attention. Does the mind appear destitute of that energy which is necessary to give a zest to the intellectual pleasures, she will readily perceive the advantage which may be derived to such a mind, from having at all times the power of gratifying itself by an elegant and innocent amusement. But if her children possess sufficient intellectual vigour to find full employment from other sources, she will, perhaps, content herself with

---

teach the reverse of all this. Can songs of gratitude and praise proceed with more propriety from the lips of hirelings, than from those of youth and innocence, in the full enjoyment of life's best blessings? If uniting their voices to those of the assembled congregation in the house of God, be an act of humility; let it be remembered, that humility is a quality associated with all the feminine virtues, and that the expression of it must therefore be highly favourable to those associations, which produce the emotions of beauty. [E.H.]

cultivating in them that taste for the fine arts in general,
which will at all times ensure them the most exquisite
gratification.

To such minds sources of delight open on every side.
Every scene in nature presents some object calculated to
call forth trains of ideas, which either interest the heart, or
amuse the fancy. But if the time in which the mind ought
naturally to be employed in accumulating those ideas, be
devoted to acquiring a facility of execution at a musical
instrument, it is evident no such ideas can be called forth. I
once travelled four hundred miles in company with an
accomplished young gentleman, who made, in the course of
the journey, but one solitary observation, and that was
called forth by an extensive moorish fen, where he said he
was sure there was abundance of snipes! Read the observations of St. Fond, on going over the same ground, and
observe the rich variety of ideas presented to the man of
science by objects which are to the vulgar eye barren of
delight. Follow the elegant Gilpin through the same tour,
and mark the emotions which the various scenery of natural
landscape excites in the mind of the man of taste. Who that
is capable of weighing the value of the mind's enjoyments
in the scale of truth and reason, will not instantly perceive,
how much the balance preponderates in favour of those
who have such a rich variety of associations, when put in
competition with the superficially accomplished? Let
science and taste unite in the same mind, and you prepare
materials for a constant feast.

As painting is now become a fashionable accomplishment, little less generally cultivated than music, it may be
expected that I should make a few observations that may
particularly apply to it. It is a subject on which I have no
assistance from the writings of others; in what I say upon it
I have, therefore, no guide but my own feelings and my
own judgment, and in such circumstances it becomes me to
express myself with diffidence.

The pleasure we receive from painting appears to be
derived from two very unequal sources. The first, and greatest, is from the emotions of sublimity or of beauty; which
in painting, as in all other subjects, depend on the train of
associated ideas. The more perfect the work of the artist,
the more perfect the emotion; which is so powerful in a

mind of sensibility, that it must be permitted, in some degree, to subside, before we are capable of examining with minute attention the sources from which it is derived. These are various, as design, expression, colouring, &c.; but if these were not in perfect harmony with each other, we may be assured the emotion of taste would not be produced in any powerful degree.

The second source of pleasure in painting is the accuracy of imitation. This corresponds to the facility of execution the musical performer; both are sources of a certain degree of admiration and surprise, but are equally distinct from the emotions of taste. Where taste has not been previously cultivated, painting will never advance beyond an imitative art; and as the happy imitation of nature depends upon vigorous conception, it cannot be expected that those who have not had their conceptions exercised upon natural objects, can ever produce any imitations which will be worthy of even this inferior species of admiration. Masters may, indeed, give them rules of perspective, and teach them to daub on abundance of pretty colours with striking effect; but if taste be wanting, the lessons of a Raphael will be thrown away. Examples, on the other hand, are not wanting to shew what progress in this delightful art may be made with little instruction from masters, where real taste is guided by judgment and warmed by a brilliant imagination. I have the pleasure of knowing many ladies who do excel; but not one uncultivated mind is of the number.

Taste in the form of ornamental decoration, whether in articles of dress or furniture, is so much under the influence of the tyrant *fashion*, that it can no longer be stiled a simple emotion. Fashion depends so evidently upon association, that it must be traced to that source by the least reflecting mind: but the associations to which it owes its wonderful ascendancy, are merely those which connect the ideas of esteem and admiration with the splendour of rank and elevated situation. The form of dress that is worn by those we account patterns of gentility, is associated with the ideas of respect and admiration, which we are accustomed to cherish towards those of a certain rank; or with the ideas of a distinction still more flattering, which constitutes the glory of gay and youthful beauty. When the same form of dress descends to the vulgar, the change that takes place in our

associations strips it of its adventitious lustre, and affixes
to the very same object which had before called forth our
admiration, ideas of meanness and contempt.

If the sovereignty of fashion be so absolute, what use,
you will say, is there in cultivation of just and refined taste,
which cannot overturn her decrees?

Notwithstanding the influence which fashion has over
our opinions, taste has still a very important part to act,
and if true taste (of which judgment is a necessary consti-
tuent) were properly cultivated, all the evils arising from the
powerful influence of fashion would be completely done
away.

Taste rejects whatever is incongruous; it requires fitness
and harmony, and therefore taste will always reject the
affectation of singularity. It will always, for this reason,
adopt the mode of the present fashion; but it will adopt it
under such limitations as are agreeable to its general principles. Wherever cultivated taste prevails, one general sentiment, whether of simplicity or magnificence, will pervade
the scene. In the furniture of the house, in the economy of
the table, the same predominant idea will be expressed;
and every ornament will be rejected, that does not give
additional force to the expression. If inanimate objects can
be so disposed as to produce an undivided emotion, surely
the decorations of the human form ought to be able to produce the same effect. There true taste must revolt with inexpressible disgust from whatever does not perfectly
harmonize with the character. Where purity, modesty, and
virtue, dwell in the heart, it is not taste that will decorate
the form with the fleering dress of the wanton.

A knowledge of the principles of taste would teach our
sex to preserve the appearance of modesty at least, even if
the reality were wanting. In female beauty, I believe no one
will deny, that softness graced with dignity, modesty, gentleness, and purity, are ideas that perfectly harmonize with
the object. Let these associations be broken by discordant
images, and the emotion of beauty will be no longer felt.

"But," says Miss Pert, "young men are strangers to the
emotions of taste; to please them other associations must be
excited. By dressing in the stile of women of a certain description, we call up trains of ideas favourable to passion."

True, young woman; but know that she who glories in

this species of conquest, degrades herself beneath the rank of those she imitates, and stands upon the brink of a precipice, with nothing but a little pride betwixt her and destruction. Few, however, very few of the numbers who adopt modes of dress highly incongruous with sentiments of modesty, are influenced by any other motive than the desire of being in the very extreme of fashion. The cultivation of taste would modify this species of ambition in the young; and would lead those who have arrived at the sober autumn of life, to adopt that mode of decoration which harmonizes with the season.*

---

* If the principles of taste be such as they are here described; if fitness and congruity be constituents in their essence; it is to be feared that the leaders of the *beau monde* are not yet many steps removed from barbarism.

The false notions that have been entertained concerning Taste, have in many respects been injurious to society. By rendering the subject contemptible in the minds of the serious, they have prevented that investigation of its principles which would have brought them into general notice, and rendered their application universal. It is from the want of this investigation, that Taste has been considered as altogether unconnected with the subject of morals, though a very little reflection would be sufficient to point out their affinity. True taste would associate ideas of esteem and respect to all those qualities which are estimable and respectable; from the neglect of its cultivation, many of these qualities are held in contempt. What are the associations which evidently prevail in the minds of the young and the gay, with respect to the virtues of modesty, prudence, and temperance? Does it not obviously appear that ideas of glory are often attached to qualities directly opposite: and that such dress and manners are adopted as may best shew the strength of this association in the most glaring colours? To the eye of Taste each season of the year has its peculiar beauties: nor does the venerable oak, when fringed with the hoary ornaments of winter, afford a prospect less various or delightful, than when decked in the most luxuriant foliage. Is, then, the winter of life connected with no associations but those of horror? This can never be the case, until ideas of contempt are associated with ideas of wisdom and experience; associations which the cultivation of true taste would effectually prevent. Suppose the person who wishes to improve on Nature's plan, should apply to the artificial florist to deck the bare boughs of his spreading oak with ever-blooming roses; would it not be soon discovered, that in deserting Nature he had deserted Taste? It would be remembered, that the colouring of Nature, whether in the animate or inanimate creation, never fails to harmonize with the object: that her most beautiful hues are often transient, and excite a more lively emotion from that very circumstance. I leave the application to your own sagacity; and should sincerely rejoice, that the observations I have made, would lead to an examination of the principles on which they have been founded. [E.H.]

The principles of which I have here given an imperfect sketch, are of universal application. They extend not merely to the disposition of material objects, but have an important connexion with moral conduct and behaviour. It is in these principles that the laws of propriety originate. From them they derive authority; and the period in which fashion gives a sanction to such modes of conduct as the principles of taste condemn, is the epoch of depravity.

It may now be expected, that I should proceed to give some hints respecting the cultivation of taste and imagination; I shall not, however, swell the size of my letter by laying down rules, which the foregoing investigation must have rendered in some measure unnecessary. I have endeavoured to prove, that unless we have assiduously cultivated the faculty of attention, and directed it to such objects as may enlarge the stock of useful ideas; unless we have awakened the curiosity, invigorated the conceptions, and enlightened the judgment; we can have no hopes of introducing those trains of thought which are the loftiest exercise of imagination, or those associations which are the source of refined taste.

Where the preliminary steps have been taken, and Nature has granted to the character a common share of sensibility, the preceptor will find the cultivation of imagination an easy task. True taste is more difficult of acquirement. But where the first faculties of the mind have been duly cultivated, and the pupil is then directed to such subjects as are calculated to elevate the tone of feeling, and awaken the sympathies of the human heart, there is no doubt that the principles of taste will be understood, felt, and practised.

Should our efforts prove unsuccessful, it is in the neglect of the early associations we shall probably find the cause of our disappointment. If we have suffered pride, self-will, arrogance, hatred, envy, or any other malignant passion, to gain an ascendancy in the disposition, we need not expect that taste will be either felt or cultivated. Its emotions were never known to the selfish; they harmonize with the most generous feelings of our nature, and seek alliance with all the virtues!

Adieu.

from
*Memoirs of the Life of
Agrippina,
the Wife of Germanicus
(3 vols, 1804)*

Editor's note

Memoirs of the life of Agrippina is an ambitious book, but Hamilton's main innovation was not so much in her subject matter as in her experiments with genre. A number of women at the time had taken classical history as a subject; Hamilton's contemporary and acquaintance Mary Hays, for example, produced a collection of biographical sketches of notable women which featured accounts of both the elder and the younger Agrippina (*Female Biography: Or Memoirs of Illustrious and Celebrated Women, of All Ages and Countries*, 6 vols. London, 1803). There were also a number of retellings of classical history for children and young women (to which Hamilton alludes in her preface) although most of them were at some pains to make the subject into little more than a collection of unchallengingly didactic anecdotes, something not always that easy with Roman history. In one representative book, for example, readers are told that Sextus "threatened to kill" Lucretia "if she would not become his wife"; in another, the violent tale of Tullia, who triumphantly drove her chariot over the dead body of her father, is framed as an illustration of the dangers to children of indulging their "passion and pride".

Hamilton was attempting something rather different from bowdlerized classical history, as her preface to the volume makes clear. Her interest lies in showing the impact of culture and society on character and in exploring the ways in which a close study of historical biography can be used to develop or support theories about the development of the human mind. The preface is noteworthy not just for its explicit rejection of fiction as a method for exploring character and the passions but also for its reflections on biography as a genre. Writing less than a decade after the publication of James Boswell's best-selling but controversial *Life of Samuel Johnson* – which had been a target of criticism on exactly the grounds that Hamilton gives for refusing to choose a subject who was within living memory – Hamilton is contributing to contemporary debates about the theory and practice of biography, and, in doing so, she attempts to

expand the possibilities of the genre. For all her suspicion
of fiction, she is quite prepared to employ the techniques of
a novelist in rounding out her central character: rather than
employing Boswell's practice of minute documentation and
careful reporting of the subject's own words and ideas
(something clearly impossible with Agrippina in any case),
Hamilton employs invented situations and speeches, justifying them on the grounds that given what we know of the
culture and of the character, we can be reasonably confident that Agrippina would have said or thought something
along those lines. The result, she claims, is a work that will
illustrate the ways in which character is shaped by education and culture but that is grounded in fact, rather than
imagination. She was apparently encouraged by Dugald
Stewart, who read about half the book in manuscript, to
continue with the project of using biography for case
studies illustrating her theories of the development of the
mind; he suggested Locke as subject, while she expressed
interest in Elizabeth of Bohemia (daughter of James VI and
I) and Seneca. None of these books were ever started. Some
years after Hamilton's death, the novelist and biographer
Isaac D'Israeli wrote a rather bemused account of Hamilton's project, which he compared to Plutarch's Parallel
Lives, although he thought Hamilton was in "danger of displaying more ingenuity than truth," as he was dubious
about the amenability of classical history to a modern-day
version of such a project.

Given Hamilton's decision to write about Roman history
in the first place, however, Agrippina the Elder is perhaps
as close to an ideal subject as she could find. Hamilton was
particularly interested in the roles that women played in
society, and while there is not a great deal of source material for any of the women of early imperial Rome, there is
perhaps a little more information on Agrippina than most,
because of her rank and the extraordinary circumstances of
her life. She was the daughter of Marcus Vipsanius
Agrippa, the general who defeated Mark Antony at Actium,
and of Julia, the only child of the emperor Augustus. Her
husband Germanicus was the nephew of the emperor
Tiberius, the grandson of Mark Antony, and the great-
nephew of Augustus. Both Agrippina and Germanicus were
celebrated as exemplars of the old-fashioned Roman virtue,

and given their popularity – along with Germanicus' considerable military success in Germany – Germanicus might
have been able to take power when Augustus died, had he
not refused to challenge his uncle (and adoptive father)
Tiberius. Germanicus himself died, possibly by poison, not
long after Tiberius' succession, and Agrippina, who had
accompanied him to both Germany and the Middle East,
returned to Rome. She and her elder sons were persecuted
by Tiberius and all died in prison or exile. Her one surviving son, Caligula, became Tiberius' heir; her daughter,
Agrippina the Younger, eventually married Germanicus'
brother, the emperor Claudius, whom she was suspected of
poisoning in order clear the way for her son Nero to in-
herit. In Agrippina, Hamilton thus had as a subject a
famously virtuous woman who was celebrated for standing
firm against corruption and decadence, but who was also
the mother of two of the most notorious figures of the early
imperial era.

The passage from *Agrippina* printed here is one of the
most detailed examples of Hamilton's attempts to engage
readers' interest in the manner of a novelist but without
directly violating historical fact. The Ubians and Cattians
are historical Germanic tribes, and the story of Arminius,
one of the great German warrior heroes, appears in the
Annals of Tacitus. His rebellion against his father-in-law
Segustus, a Roman ally, and the flight and eventual capture
of his pregnant wife Thusnelda are also drawn from that
source, although, as Hamilton readily admits in her notes,
there are no historical grounds for assuming that Agrippina
and Thusnelda ever met. Indeed, there is nothing at all
known about Agrippina's time in a German village beyond
the simple fact of her having stayed there for a winter. Yet
Hamilton – as she demonstrates most straightforwardly in
her first novel, *Translations of the Letters of a Hindoo Rajah* –
was always fascinated by cultural difference, and in imagining Agrippina's bewilderment or disorientation as she
encounters the strange German customs described by
Tacitus, she is attempting to dramatize her contention that
ideas of virtue and honour are, to some degree, a matter of
culture. In the process, she is drawing not just on Tacitus,
but also, if less explicitly, on Scottish Enlightenment
theories of historical progress. Philosophers such as Adam

Ferguson, John Millar, and Dugald Stewart argued that "primitive" societies, whether modern or ancient, are always more or less the same, and as Hamilton juxtaposes the "politeness" and luxury of the Romans with the virtuous, strong-minded German women and the brave but indolent German men, she is echoing the distinctions drawn between metropolitan Britain and the Highlands in other writing of her day.

While Hamilton had some predictable worries that the subject was "too classical for a female pen," she was also sufficiently confident in her abilities as a writer to expect to earn a respectable sum for a book that she thought far more important and innovative than mere fiction could be. In a letter to her publisher, she states her terms as follows: "Two hundred pounds a volume – and one hundred more (ie. fifty on each volume) on the work's going to a third edition. Of this I shall beg [100 pounds] on the publication of the work, and the remainder as the sale of the work shall authorize before at the end of [sic] one year from the time it is published." She also instructed him to announce it in the following terms, ensuring that it could not be confused with a novel: "Memoirs of the elder Agrippina, being the commencement of a series of Comparative Biography illustrative of the principles of the human mind." (The book was published in three volumes; it is not clear what the final payment per volume turned out to be.) *Agrippina* was fairly well reviewed when it first appeared, although some critics appeared rather bemused by Hamilton's attempt to write at such length about a figure who makes only relatively limited appearances in works by Roman historians. The reviewer for *The Scots Magazine*, for one, thought that there "seemed something preposterous in three octavo volumes, devoted to the life of the elder Agrippina," but concluded that the work offered "very high gratification" to its readers. *The British Critic* was even more favourable, praising the "perspicuous and elegant language" of the book and its presentation of "such a connected view of the politics and parties of the courts of Augustus and Tiberius, as will not perhaps elsewhere be readily found." Even so, it was a little dubious about Hamilton's attempt to reinvent the genre of biography. The book did not sell well enough to go into a second edition until 1811, and Hamilton's experiments with biography inspired few, if any, imitators.

Preface

To point out the advantages which are to be derived from paying some attention to the nature of the human mind in the education of youth was the object of a former work; the Author's aim in the present is to give such an illustration of the principles that were then unfolded, as may render them more extensively useful.

In the task of instructing others many are indeed concerned; but the duties of self-instruction and self-government are imposed on all. Whoever can lend assistance towards the due performance of these important duties, may be considered as the benefactor of the human race; and from the approbation with which her feeble efforts have been hitherto honoured, the Author is convinced, that even those who bring their single mite into the treasury, shall in no way fail of reward.

Such a knowledge of the human mind as is to be obtained from observation and experience, appears to be placed within the reach of every one capable of reflection, and this reflection it is the aim of every moralist to excite, when he reasons upon the consequences of vice and virtue. But to those who wish to attain a knowledge of their own hearts, and are anxiously solicitous for their improvement, something more than general observations are requisite.

In order to the government of the passions, it is necessary to be acquainted with their origin and progress; a species of knowledge, to be derived not so much from a view of their consequences, as from an accurate observation of their gradual developement. In pursuing this enquiry, we ought not to be discouraged at finding it more complex than we at first view apprehended. The metaphysician may indeed separate the passions from each other, as the experimental philosopher separates the rays of light by the prism, and represents each singly to our view in one uniform colour. But in human character it is not thus that the passions are found to appear. Every passion, even that which predominates, is there seen blended with those which gave it birth, and with the passions and affections to which it has affinity: and it is by observing those affinities, that we are enabled to pronounce on the good or evil tendency of any particular passion. If pride, for instance, be a virtue, it will be found in connexion with, and productive of, affections of the benevolent class; if on the contrary it should appear allied to the malevolent and vindictive, we need not hesitate to pronounce it a dangerous inmate of the human bosom.

Convinced of the importance of throwing light upon a subject so universally interesting, and fully aware of the dislike which the young and unreflecting are apt to conceive against whatever appears in a didactic form, the Author formed the design of conveying the observations that had occurred to her, through a more agreeable medium.

She soon perceived that it was not by fiction her purpose could be accomplished.

A work of imagination, in which the characters are of the author's own creation, and in which every event is at his disposal, may be so managed, as to be admirably calculated to promote the reception of a favourite theory, but can never be considered as a confirmation of its truth. Nor will the theory built upon such a basis be of long duration; for though the brilliant illusions of fancy may affect the sensibilities of the heart, and so far captivate the understanding as to render it unwilling to exert itself in detecting the fallacy of arguments which have spoken so powerfully to the feelings, the charm will at length be broken, and then the system which had been supported by its influence, will inevitably sink into disgrace.

The characters of a work of imagination may, it is true, be drawn in exact conformity to nature, and placed in such situations as to afford a striking illustration of certain truths; but how are those who are little accustomed to make observations on human life to judge of the genuineness of the representation? They cannot appeal to experience, and if they refer to the feelings, it is but too probable that the decision will be erroneous. Should it even be otherwise, there is still reason to doubt whether the emotions produced by the narration of fictitious events will awaken those reflections upon the progress of the passions, for which the work may have been principally intended.

Where the effect produced upon the feelings is powerful,
all that is addressed to the judgment appears dull; nor is it
to be expected, that the young and ardent mind will receive
much improvement from lessons of wisdom, perused at a
moment,

> When hope and fear alternate sway the breast,
> Like light and shade upon a waving field,
> Coursing each other.

If from an interesting novel so little is to be expected, from
a novel void of interest we can hope for nothing; since,
however wise, however moral, it would have few readers.
The same sermon which a person of taste would listen to
with delight from the mouth of the preacher, would, if
delivered from the stage, appear intolerably dull. So necessary is it that the tone of mind should be in unison with the
object of attention! Hence arises the advantage which the
biographer possesses over the novelist. Amusement is
expected by the reader from both; but in sitting down to
peruse the memoirs of a fellow being, in whose past existence we have assurance; in whose eternal existence we have
hope, the expectation of amusement is chastened by the
solemnity of the ideas attached to truth. The emotions produced will, on this account, be probably less vivid, but the
impression made upon the mind, by a belief in the reality
of the scene will give a peculiar force to whatever is calculated to operate either as warning or example.

Such was the tenour of the arguments which determined the Author in favour of biography. What subject
to make choice of, was the question that next occurred;
and it must be confessed, that it was far from being easily
resolved.

To give the memoirs of those who have but lately
departed from the scene, and who still live in the hearts of
their friends and the memory of the public, may at first
view appear an easy task. Concerning them there seems to
be no difficulty in obtaining information. All the events of
their lives, their peculiar habits and sentiments, their joys
and sorrows, their frailties and their virtues, may be collected from the lips of living witnesses. But even with all
these sources of information at his command, the biographer who wishes to convey instruction to the living from

the grave of the dead, will find himself encompassed with many difficulties. The obstacles by which he is opposed, are, in some instances, such as sensibility will never attempt to surmount; and in others, of a nature which not even the united powers of industry and genius can overcome.

In the lives of persons who have filled a private station, exercising their talents and their virtues in the performance of the relative and social duties, there may be much to honour, and much to applaud; but there cannot, in the nature of things, be a sufficient variety of incident to attract attention. In the few instances where the memoirs of such persons have been given to the world, we accordingly seldom find more than a general eulogium on their characters; which, tho' it may leave an impression favourable to virtue, is not calculated to add much to our knowledge. Nor concerning those who have been placed in situations more conspicuous, who, in their lives were considered as the ornaments of their country, and whose names are universally known and venerated is it easy for the biographer to give such particulars as can alone convey a *full* idea of the character.

To trace the progress of an extraordinary mind from the first dawn of genius to maturity; to mark the circumstances from which it received its peculiar bent; to develope the sources whence the understanding derived its stores; and thus (if I may be allowed the expression), to pourtray the characteristic features of the soul, though a task that requires transcendent abilities for its accomplishment, is but a part of what the biographer is expected to perform.

Every individual, however high his intellectual attainments, is impelled by passions, and influenced by affections, which essentially affect his character and conduct. Without a compleat display of these, the delineation will remain imperfect; and yet completely to delineate them, is not in human power; for however possible it may be to trace the progress of talents, and to take the measure of the understanding, HE who made the heart can alone appreciate its frailties and its virtues. Their record is on high, but the memorial that remains is imperfect, and the manner of their growth has eluded observation. To special acts of benevolence many may indeed give testimony; but the secret trials of the heart, those exercises of patience, forbearance, and

the fortitude, by which it obtained a triumph over the selfish affections, are not of a nature to be disclosed.

In private life, the virtues are exercised by the temper,
dispositions, and sentiments of those with whom one is intimately connected. Wisdom is learned from experience;
and this experience is in many instances derived from the
errors of the individual, or from the errors and frailties of
those most dear to him. These are, these ought to be, for-
ever veiled from vulgar eyes.

The heart must be without a spark of delicacy or feeling,
that would voluntarily drag them into notice.

If in tracing the virtues of the illustrious dead we find it
so difficult to arrive at truth, how shall we dare to dip our
pencil in the darker shades? Is it from indifferent spectators,
from friends or foes that we shall take our colouring? Upon
whom, alas! can we depend? Casual observers are liable to
misapprehension; where there has been enmity, there will
be prejudice; and ill would it suit the tenderness of friendship to point out the blemishes which have been washed
with its tears, and to harrow up the faults which would
soon have been buried in oblivion!

Nor is it from what passes in conversation, when the
spirits are animated beyond the usual tone, and the mind is
influenced by associations which an intimate acquaintance
with every member of the company could alone explain,
that a just idea of the principles and sentiments of an individual is to be obtained. The observations which drop even
from persons of deep reflection, upon subjects casually
introduced, are not always to be received as conclusive
testimony of their serious opinions; far less ought the
expressions drawn forth by opposition in the warmth of
colloquial debate to be recorded as certain indications of
peevishness or irascibility. The writer who speaks from his
own knowledge, may doubtless, in his statement, be exceedingly correct; he may describe with faithful accuracy the
personal defects, the incidental weaknesses of a departed
friend and by his philosophical impartiality entitle himself
to rank with the investigator of nature,

> One who could peep and botanize
> Upon his mother's grave!

But with whatever avidity this species of information may

be received, we naturally revolt from the hand that offers it. It is also to be questioned whether all that could be learned from such disclosures of the secret transactions of private life, would in any degree compensate for the moral evils which would ensue, did such instances of breach of confidence become common. Intimacy would then be considered as a snare, and the companion of the social board dreaded as a spy, who was to report to the world the unguarded sallies of the moment.

Are we, then, it may be asked, to make no enquiries concerning the characters of those who have gone before us to the silent house? Should delicacy with regard to the feelings of surviving friends be permitted to silence the voice of truth? or respect for departed genius to cancel the remembrance of its follies, and to veil its crimes? On this general view of the question it becomes not the present writer to decide. It is enough for her to point out the difficulties which must be encountered by a mind not destitute of sensibility, in attempting to give a genuine likeness of any well-known character.

If uncertainty dwell upon the transactions of a recent period, it may be deemed fruitless to carry our researches into times that are now remote: and fruitless it must undoubtedly prove, if we confine our enquiries to the lives and characters of private citizens. Even of those votaries of science, or favourites of the muses, who have "built to themselves a name," how few are there concerning whom we can now obtain such information as would afford any addition to our knowledge of the human mind? Of such however it cannot be said, that "their memorial has perished with them." In their writings, they have left an evidence of their talents, whose testimony cannot be suborned; but still they do not afford sufficient data to the biographer, who is required to give an account of the actions, as well as of the sentiments. If he go to former ages in quest of materials, he can only hope to find them in the page of history; and the transactions that are there recorded, will, in the opinion of many, appear too far removed from the occurrences of common life, to convey instruction to those who aspire not beyond the sphere in which Providence has placed them.

To the writer of the following memoirs the objection

above stated did not appear so forcible as it has been by others represented. In order to get a clear insight into the nature of the passions, and the consequences arising from their indulgence, it is perhaps necessary that we extend our views beyond the station in which Providence has placed us. If human nature be our object, it is needless to confine ourselves to rank, or sex, or period of society, for we shall find it in every clime and situation invariably the same. The actions of a person of exalted rank may not, it is true, afford us any direct example, capable of application to the transactions of our limited sphere; but are we hence to infer, that an examination of the passions and opinions in which those actions originated, is without its use? To know how this man rose to power, and that achieved greatness, may be a fruitless speculation to the private citizen. But to know how far the attainment of the object of ambition tended to happiness; to ascertain the consequences of indulging the love of wealth, or power, or distinction, and all the passions with which they are connected; are objects in which all have an equal degree of interest. When the sphere of action is circumscribed, the passions must of necessity be subject to controul. It is in the rank soil of unlimited power that we are to look for these giant productions of the active principle: but let it be remembered, that though situation may lop some of the most luxuriant shoots, the root is still the same; and that human pride operates in the production of human misery as certainly in the bosom of the peasant as in that of the prince.

That the characters of those who stand on the dangerous pinnacle of greatness are peculiarly liable to misrepresentation, cannot be denied. Their errors are marks at which calumny delights to throw her darts, whilst flattery holds up her concave mirror to their slightest virtues. But as time advances, malice and flattery disappear; and from actions which have been scrutinized and canvassed by friends and foes, and received and acknowledged by facts as both parties, truth then endeavours to extract the evidence on which posterity is to pronounce its verdict.

It is, indeed, the conquerors and disturbers of the earth, to whose actions the attention of succeeding ages has been chiefly devoted; "for," as it has been well observed by a venerable historian, "it has unfortunately happened, the

Muse of History hath been so much in love with Mars, that she hath conversed but little with Minerva."*

The character of Agrippina must be considered as an exception to the above observation. By the masterly hand of Tacitus it has been delineated with a force and spirit, which gives the original to our eyes glowing with life and animation. The features are, indeed, so prominent, that the most unskilful artist could not fail of taking a likeness; and it is this consideration which has chiefly operated as an encouragement to what has been attempted in the following pages. The age in which Agrippina lived is likewise considered as a favourable circumstance. With the names of her contemporaries all are in some degree conversant. The most remarkable events of the period are so familiar even to the unlearned, that imagination can without difficulty enter on the scene, and be pleased to form an intimacy with objects which had hitherto been only indistinctly viewed, as from a distance.

In singling out the grand-daughter of Augustus as the subject of her first attempt at biographical sketching, the Author may perhaps have been influenced by impressions made upon the mind at that period of life when the feelings are usually stronger than the judgment: but though, on mature deliberation, she perceived that the choice was not without objections none occurred that were of sufficient force to induce her to relinquish the design.

In one whose range of information is, even when compared with many of her own sex, extremely limited, and who in classical learning vies not with a school-boy of the lowest form, an attempt to approach so near to classic ground, may have the appearance of presumption: but as the most enlightened are always the most liberal and candid, she has little reason to fear being thus interpreted.

In the memoirs of Agrippina, the learned reader will not expect to find any accession to his knowledge with regard to facts; though, when presented in a detached form, they may possibly, in some instances, give rise to reflections that did not before occur: nor will he be displeased to re-peruse even those more trifling anecdotes, which, by delighting

---

* Henry's Hist. of Britain, vol. iv. p. 9. [E.H.]

the youthful fancy, had served to sweeten the labours of his school day hours. In a work intended only for the learned, these might with propriety have been omitted; but as there are many readers of her own sex, who are only acquainted with the outline of Roman history, every minute circumstance which tended to render the scene familiar to the imagination, was essential to the Author's plan. In this respect, advantage might undoubtedly have been derived from the assistance of the artist; but by the author who aspires at having book approved on other grounds than the merits of its adventitious embellishments, such decorations will be rejected, as, while they do not essentially enhance the value of the work, add materially to its price.

It now remains to give some account of the materials that have been employed in the compilation of the following Memoirs. These have been chiefly taken from the records of antiquity; for though it was only through the medium of translation that these could be consulted, it appeared more advisable thus to apply to the source, than to seek for information from the compilers of modern history.

Mr Murphy's translation of the Annals of Tacitus, and the notes prefixed to that valuable performance have afforded almost the whole of the outline; occasionally assisted by Suetonius, in Mr Thomson's translation. For whatever related to Agrippina in Dio Cassius, or in V. Paterculus, the Author has been indebted to the kindness of two learned friends, who obligingly translated such extracts from each as they thought would be in anywise useful. In the description of manners and customs she has been assisted by the works of numerous writers, but where accuracy was required, has chiefly consulted the treatise of Mr Adams on Roman antiquities. To avoid swelling the page with a parade of quotations, authorities have never been referred to, except where the very words of the author are quoted; and it is believed that those who are most intimately acquainted with the original, will not be most forward to tax the Author with having exaggerated the features of the portrait, which, with feeble hand, she has attempted to delineate.

In the life of Agrippina, she has never departed from her authority; though where they were silent, she has endeavoured to fill the chasm in the manner that appeared most consonant to probability. The employment of Agrippina's leisure hours, her domestic avocations, society, &c. were circumstances which it suited not the dignity of history to record. But circumstances too trivial for history are essentially necessary to the biographer, who aims at exciting an interest for the subject of his memoirs in the reader's breast. General descriptions possess not a sufficient influence over the imagination or the feelings, to answer his purpose. "Where we do not conceive distinctly, we do not sympathize deeply in any human affection."*

If Agrippina may sometimes be found in scenes into which she was not followed by the historian, – the scenes themselves, every object with which they are filled, and every ornament by which they are decorated are faithfully copied from the most authentic describers of Ancient manners.

The period of Agrippina's residence in Germany, could not be passed over without some account of the native inhabitants. In a detached form, this account would have been disgusting to those to whom it was already familiar, and dull and uninteresting to the ignorant. By interweaving it with the narrative, it was hoped that it might be rendered acceptable to both. In a few other instances a similar liberty has been taken. How far the author has succeeded upon these occasions in keeping up the character of the heroine, by ascribing to her such sentiments and feelings as were perfectly appropriate, every reader will for himself determine.

Throughout the whole performance criticism may find much to censure, but it is hoped that candour will find something to applaud: and let those who are least willing to admit extenuation or apology for the Author's failures remember, that "to have attempted much is always laudable, even when the enterprise is above the strength that undertakes it."†

---

* Currie. [E.H.]
† Johnson. [E.H.]

[Volume 1, 256-289, and Volume 2, 14-22: Agrippina in a German village]

Agrippina meanwhile proceeded on her melancholy journey, rendered more irksome by having lost the company of her son, whose infantine prattle might have beguiled the heavy hours, and prevented her thoughts from dwelling on subjects that were anxious and perplexing. She was, it is true, surrounded by many faithful friends; and the nation of the Ubii, on whose territories she was about to enter, were devoted to her family; so that for herself she had nothing to apprehend. But she still trembled for her husband's safety: her spirits had not yet recovered from the agitation into which they had been thrown by the late transactions, and wherever she cast her eyes, the absence of Germanicus, like an east wind, gave a hardness to the outline of every prospect.

No sooner did the inhabitants of Ubiorum Oppidum receive notice of the honour intended them, than they hastened to meet their noble visitor; and to assure her of a proud and joyful welcome. To them Agrippina was endeared by ties which the Germans held most sacred. Originally inhabitants of the eastern side of the Rhine, the Ubians had incurred the displeasure of their German neighbours, by their attachment to the Roman cause. During Caesar's wars in Gaul they had placed themselves under his protection, and by adhering faithfully to the engagements they had then made, brought upon themselves the persecution of the Cattians, and the Suevii; by whom they would have been overpowered, had not Vipsanius Agrippa, at that time commander of the Roman armies, rescued them from destruction. Conducting them to the west side of the river, Agrippa there gave them a territory of sufficient extent, aided them in building their new city, and declared himself their patron and protector.

Ardently attached to the memory of their benefactor, the Ubians considered the honour conferred upon them by the presence of his daughter as one of the happiest events. Their honest gratitude appeared in every action: respectfully conducting Agrippina and her suite into their city, (for so the assemblage of ill constructed huts was called) the principal house was prepared for her reception, as well as the shortness of the notice would permit, and what was wanting in elegance was abundantly supplied in good will.

It was in situations like these that Agrippina fully experienced the advantage of having had her mind formed in early life to habits of simplicity. Taught to consider the slaves of luxury as under the most ignominious bondage, she carefully preserved her mind from its dominion; and by frequently submitting to voluntary privations, prepared herself for encountering with resolution those which the vicissitudes of fortune might render inevitable.

To Agrippina and her friends all was new and strange. In her progress with Germanicus she had indeed often seen the natives of the country; but the communication with them had till now been slight and distant. The tight dress of the men appeared in the eyes of the Roman ladies indelicate and offensive. That of the women was more graceful. A robe, though not of very flowing drapery, partially concealed their shape, leaving the arms and part of the bosom uncovered. The texture seldom varied. It was of coarse linen, adorned, according to fancy, with purple stains. "Our wives," said the chief in presenting his to the princess, "our wives are unadorned except with modesty. Their treasure is the affection of their husbands, and the reverence of their children. You who are a virtuous wife and happy mother will find them worthy your protection!"*

---

*From the time of Agrippina's retiring to Ubiorum Oppidum, till her return to the Roman camp, the only event recorded by the historians is the birth of her daughter. But though her part in the scenes that are in this chapter introduced, is merely conjectural, the description of German manners will be found so exactly to correspond with that given by Tacitus, that the picture may be depended upon as genuine. The adventures of Thusnelda are related likewise by the Roman historian in nearly the same terms as she is represented relating them to Agrippina; and therefore, tho' the interview between the German heroine and the Roman princess may never actually have taken place, the truth of history cannot properly be said to have been violated. Who now believes the long speeches which the historians have thought fit to put into the mouths of their princes and warriors were ever spoken? Are they not universally considered as a medium of illustration, more animated and therefore more impressive than any

Agrippina, returning a proper compliment, saluted the honourable matrons with great complacency. The feast being now prepared was served up according to the manner of the country, every one sitting at a separate table. The fare would not by a voluptuary have been considered tolerable. But though the mutton was newly killed and very ill broiled, the curds were excellent, and the wild apples, notwithstanding their acidity, were highly flavoured. Agrippina, though she never drank any thing stronger than water, had the curiosity to taste the liquor made from barley, which she had often heard spoken of as the favourite beverage of the Germans. Wine indeed the Ubians could now boast of, as the vineyards planted under the auspices of Agrippa, on the banks of the Rhine, had come to great perfection, and produced abundantly. But still many of them from long habit gave a preference to ale, which they drank in such quantities as to answer all the purposes of intoxication. The characteristic virtue of the women afforded sufficient evidence, that inebriety was a vice confined to the other sex; since excess is altogether incompatible with steady regularity of conduct.

The house destined to Agrippina was, like the others, surrounded with a small inclosure, for the Germans considered being overlooked by a neighbour as an infringement on freedom, and therefore even in their towns built each house apart. The slaves who attended the princess, were shocked at the homely furniture of her apartment, but she with better sense smiled at their distress, and though she could not help being incommoded by the smoke, which having no vent filled every part of the house, she neither gave way to fretfulness nor discontent.

Agrippina was not more surprised at the insensibility of the Germans to this inconvenience, than they in their turn were astonished how she could bear being troubled with the attendance of such a numerous retinue. This she discovered by means of one of the daughters of the Ubian chief, to whom as she had conceived a liking, she permitted

---

other mode in which the same ideas could have been conveyed? All that the critic requires, is, that nothing should be thus introduced which is not strictly characteristic. [EH]

the liberty of attending her toilette. "Is the lady lame," asked the young barbarian, "that she requires so much assistance? But if she has lost the use of her own limbs, why cannot one person reach what she wants? Why torment her with so many to do so very little. Alas, that one so great should be so helpless!"

The pride of the Roman was piqued at thus exciting only pity, where she expected admiration. "And has your mother then no slaves to attend her person?" asked Agrippina.

"O no;" replied the girl, "my mother is too proud to be dependent. Our slaves live in their own houses, and take care of their own families; they till the ground, and raise corn, and take care of the vineyards; but they do not come near us, we want none of their assistance."

Agrippina then discovered that all the household business was managed by its mistress and her daughters, without the assistance of servant or of slave; and that as nothing could be more disgraceful than a slothful performance of these necessary duties, the girls were from infancy brought up to diligence and activity. Indolence was the exclusive privilege of the men, who in time of peace passed the sluggish hours in sleep or gluttony. The hero who had in the field braved every danger, and whose active and enterprising spirit had sustained all the evils of fatigue and hunger, and want of rest, with a resolution amounting to insensibility, sunk on his return into listlessness; from which he was only to be roused by objects that applied to the passions.

Agrippina did not for some time see much of this, as her arrival had created a sufficient degree of interest to prevent the Ubians from sinking into torpour. To serve or amuse their illustrious visitor, was the object of every heart. In every house the feast was spread, and the strangers who poured in from the surrounding country to get a sight of the Roman princess, were welcomed with a spirit of hospitality which Agrippina had never before seen any thing to equal. As dancing was the amusement in which they took most delight, they naturally thought, that by an exhibition of this kind they should most highly gratify the Roman ladies, who, they were persuaded, had never witnessed any spectacle half so interesting. Agrippina cheerfully accepted the invitation, and with her friends and attendants, went at

the appointed hour to the place of entertainment, which
was a spacious lawn in the vicinity of the city. There, on an
eminence, a sort of throne had been prepared for her, to
which she was conducted by the Ubian chief, who had
enough of the Roman language to do the office of interpreter. A band of young men immediately made their
appearance, armed with swords and javelins, and dressed in
short tunics of white linen. "Here are fencers!" cried Agrippina on perceiving them, "pray to whom do these performers belong?" The chief, astonished at her ignorance,
replied, that the young men were all of noble birth, that
they were not to fence but to dance, for with the Germans
dancing was a martial exercise; that in honour to her they
were clothed with the garments which they now wore,
otherwise it was their usual custom to dance unincumbered
by clothes. As he thus spake, the performance commenced;
and Agrippina could not but admire the agility, grace and
elegance, that was displayed in every movement. The clashing of swords seemed at first to keep time with the music,
but the combat soon became more fierce; wounds were
given and received; and though, from the blood that flowed,
many were evidently very seriously hurt, none relinquished
his place, or appeared sensible to pain, but rather to go
through the evolutions of the dance with redoubled animation. Agrippina had been too much accustomed to the
amusements of the amphitheatre, to be shocked by this
spectacle; but could not forbear expressing to her companions her astonishment, that any who were of free birth
should thus expose themselves to unnecessary trouble. She
however took care to conceal her sentiments from her
entertainer, and distributed presents of golden chains and
bracelets among such of the performers as had most distinguished themselves in the martial dance.

On the following day, as Agrippina was walking through
the city, her attention was attracted towards a young man
of uncommonly dignified aspect, who was bound in chains,
and walking with a look of stern fortitude by the side of a
person who eyed him from time to time with an air of seeming exultation. On a nearer approach, she recollected having
seen both these youths in the dance of the preceding evening. The gold chains which she had given to each, were
now both worn by him who was leading the other into

captivity, and who appeared too much elated by prosperity to take notice of any surrounding object. On being stopped by her interpreter, whom she had ordered to enquire into the meaning of these extraordinary circumstances, they both lifted up their eyes, and on seeing Agrippina betrayed symptoms of confusion. Both were covered with blushes, but while the captive seemed to shrink from her inquisitive glance, the other, affecting a careless air, came forwards, and informed her attendant, that after partaking of the banquet which had been prepared for them the preceding evening, they had, according to the custom of their nation, amused themselves by gaming; that the young man his companion, after losing all that he had in the world, had staked the gold chain given him by the princess; and that likewise being lost, he had at length staked himself! You see the consequence, added he gaily, he is now my slave, and I am about to sell him to the highest bidder.

Agrippina was extremely shocked at this account, and after a moment's deliberation resolved to save the imprudent youth from the horrors of a fate so dreadful. Having learned the price that was fixed upon him, she desired both the young men to follow her to her house, where, with a frowning aspect, she delivered the money into the winner's hand, telling him at the same time never more to approach her presence. Mortified and abashed he slunk away, while his companion, released from his fetters, threw himself at the feet of his benefactress, and expressed by a flood of tears the feelings of gratitude which overwhelmed his heart.*

---

* It may be useful to the young reader to remark, that where the reasoning faculty is, either from want of cultivation, (as in the savage state) or from the indolence of luxury, (as in the refined) permitted to lie dormant, the mind must necessarily be impelled to seek relief from the wretchedness of vacuity, by whatever means it can be procured. To the person destitute of internal resources, the doom of earning his bread by the sweat of his brow is in reality a blessing. Constant employment on the objects of perception, if it do not much expand the reasoning powers, is in so far favourable to their improvement, as it keeps the passions in subjection, and gives a constant exercise to the faculty of attention, which, where it has no such opportunities of exertion, must be awakened by the aid of powerful stimulants. Here, as in many instances, the extremes of barbarism and of civilization may be observed to meet. Idleness is considered as his peculiar

Agrippina did not fail to give to Germanicus a very particular detail of all the circumstances that occurred to her observation. In every letter he repeated his injunctions to continue her remarks on the manners of the barbarians, and to use all the means in her power to obtain information concerning the meaning and origin of such customs as appeared to her most strange and unaccountable. But though indefatigable in her enquiries, it was but seldom that she met with satisfaction. Even in the civilised world customs are continued long after the circumstances in which they originated have ceased to operate, and are forgotten; but to a rude and simple people whatever is immemorial appears eternal. With regard to what was reported to her of the various superstitions of the natives, Agrippina was perhaps sufficiently credulous; but as the very situation of the groves in which the principal ceremonies of their religion was performed, was carefully concealed, it is not to be supposed that the accounts they gave of their sacred rites was to be depended on as genuine.

No circumstance in the behaviour of the Germans appeared to the polite Romans so entirely unaccountable,

---

privilege by the savage as much as by the fine gentleman: but idleness must necessarily produce ennui; and to get rid of such a troublesome companion, the same devices seem to have occurred to both. "To devote," says Tacitus in his account of the Germans, "both day and night to deep drinking, is a disgrace to no man; disputes, as will be the case with people in liquor, frequently arise; *and the quarrel often ends in scenes of blood!* Even without the exercise of liquor, in their sober moments, strange as it may appear! *they have recourse to dice, as to a serious and regular business,* with the most desperate spirit committing their whole substance to chance; and when they have lost their all, putting their liberty, and even their persons upon the hazard of the dye! *Such is the effect of a ruinous and inveterate habit!* They are victims to *folly,* and they call themselves *men of honour!*"

Unfortunate men! yet who shall say that *they* were without excuse. The light of science had never beamed on their benighted minds,

> Fair knowledge to their eyes her ample page,
> Rich with the spoils of time, did ne'er enroll.

They were necessarily, and not by choice, without object or pursuit that was capable of giving constant and ample employment to all the glorious faculties, with which nature had endowed them. For the barbarian, therefore, some apology may be made. [E.H.]

as their high respect for the softer sex. Augustus, observing that the women were considered as their dearest pledges, and that the idea of their being led into captivity was insupportable, demanded female hostages from the conquered tribes, as the most undoubted of all securities. The event did honour to his penetration; as they who had never considered their male hostages as of any consequence, were never known to break a treaty when female honour was concerned in its preservation. With these facts Germanicus was well acquainted. He had likewise witnessed the effects of the ardour inspired in the barbarians by the presence of these beloved objects of affection in many an engagement, where the men were urged on to the cruel conflict by the shouts of approbation sent up by their wives and daughters who surrounded the field. He had seen the combat at their instance oft renewed, and by their interference the glory of victory snatched from the Roman arms. But he knew not by what means the German women had obtained to so great an ascendancy, and would not lose an opportunity so favourable as the present for having his curiosity gratified.

The observations which Agrippina made, led (or might have led) her to conclude, that the esteem and respect in which the German women were held by their male relations, was as much the cause as the consequence of their superior merit. Conscious of having a character to support, they were impelled by the most generous motives to the exercise of all the virtues, on which their nation set the highest value. In war they accompanied their husbands to the field, and after the battle, it was upon them that the care of the wounded entirely devolved. They were the only surgeons, and by their skill in the art of healing supported that character of superior wisdom, which they had imperceptibly acquired. How it came to be acquired will be easily accounted for, when we reflect, that in the intervals of peace, while the other sex were engaged in gaming, drinking, and quarrelling, or in the indulgence of sloth, no less injurious to the mental powers, they were in their domestic avocations accustomed to the perpetual exercise of judgment. Hence, when questions of importance came to be discussed, they who were neither blinded by the fury of the passions nor the fumes, of intoxication, had an evident advantage over their impassioned lords; and were frequently enabled by their sagacity and discernment to penetrate into the probable consequence of events, in a way that to minds incapable of reflection appeared altogether extraordinary. The Germans had the good sense not to despise the judicious counsels of their female friends, but to rescue the pride of sex from the mortification of acknowledged inferiority; they ascribed the wisdom of which they availed themselves to the inspiration of the gods! Whether it was the old women only who were believed to be thus inspired, or whether illumination was particularly attributed to the young and beautiful, could not perhaps be easily ascertained; but neither in youth nor age did the German females disgrace the sacred character with which they were thus invested.

Agrippina, after her arrival at Ubiorum, was invited to the celebration of a grand feast, given by one of the principal chiefs in honour of his daughter's nuptials. A few days previous to the solemnity she went with a friend to pay a visit to the intended bride. They were received with the utmost respect by the mother of the family and her daughters, who, contrary to the expectation of the Roman ladies, were neither embarrassed by their presence, nor reluctant to satisfy their curiosity. In answer to the queries concerning the fortune of the bride, they were given to understand that marriages in Germany were not contracted from mercenary motives. "My daughter", said the mother of the bride, "has been sought by many chiefs, but she has preferred the son of our friend. The youth has proved himself deserving of her love, for in single combat he has slain three of the most valiant of the Suevii. She in the last war accompanied the other maidens to behold the battle, each resolved, should the enemy prove victorious, to die by her own hand, rather than submit to the conquerors, for never has any of our race survived their honour. Her gallant lover was crowned with glory, but he was deeply wounded in the bloody fray. Had she not been there, he must have perished. She flew like lightning to the spot where he lay gasping with fatigue and agony; she bound up his wounds, she administered cordials to revive his soul, and assisted by the damsels her companions in raising a shed of green boughs to keep out the scorching rays of the sun, she

attended him by night and day till his recovery was completed. When they came back from the war, he delivered
her the marriage presents in presence of her father and his
friends. By accepting them the match was made, and on the
day appointed for the wedding-feast when she will have
the return for his gifts prepared, she will be made his for
ever."

"And is what I have heard true?" said the sprightly friend
of Agrippina, "that there is here no chance of a second
husband?"

"A second husband!" cried the old woman with astonishment, "where should she find a second heart to bestow
upon him? We have indeed heard that at Rome women
have many hearts, or rather that by their conduct they
sometimes appear to have none; that there they commit
adultery with impunity, and that, by a something called
divorce, they even make adultery lawful. But these are
slanders not to be credited of the great nation; nor am I so
simple as to believe that women of exalted rank should ever
degrade themselves."

"Would to the gods!" cried Agrippina, "that every
Roman matron thought with you!"

The attendants of Agrippina were then ordered by their
mistress to produce the ornaments she had selected as a
present for the bride. These consisted of a white robe, an
embroidered girdle with a clasp, and a gold ring, such as
were given by the Romans to their brides at the ceremony
of betrothment. To these Paulina added the purple ribbon,
which it was the peculiar privilege of modest women to
wear.

"The gifts are precious to me," said the young German,
"they shall be preserved in my family for ever. To the latest
generation they shall be handed down, as a perpetual
memorial of the honour conveyed upon our house by the
daughter of Agrippa."

"But you must wear them yourself," said Agrippina,
"they were intended as a wedding-dress."

"No," replied the young woman, "such gaudy ornaments
are not befitting for a German; I should lose the respect of
my husband, did he think me capable of taking pleasure in
superfluous finery. He will glory in the gifts of the princess
as the pledge of her friendship, but he would blush to see

me expose myself by affecting to depart from the simplicity
of our nation."

Firm to her resolution the bride appeared on the day of
her nuptials clad in the usual attire. A chemise of blue and
white linen without sleeves descended to her feet, and being
drawn tight round the waist by a band of the same materials, displayed her shape to advantage. Her long yellow
hair, braided on her snowy forehead, was turned up behind,
and fastened at the top by a bodkin of white thorn. Her fine
complexion heightened by the blush of modesty gave to
her dark blue eyes a vivacity, which, if it did not equal the
brilliant lustre that sparkled in Agrippina's, was nevertheless expressive and beautiful. At the entrance of the small
lawn which surrounded the house, she received Agrippina
and her friends, and conduced them to the seats prepared
for them; from whence they could have a full view of
the exchange of gifts which constituted the marriage
ceremony.

The companion of the young chief first advanced with a
yoke of oxen, which were given to the bride to remind her
that the labours of the field were to be under her direction.
Having driven the oxen to the stalls prepared for them,
she returned and was met by the brother of the bridegroom, leading in his hand a horse fully caparisoned. "By
accepting this horse," said he, "you declare your resolution
of accompanying your husband wherever his fortunes may
lead him. You are to be his companion in war, the partner
of his toil and danger. You are to have but one country and
one fate."

The bride listened with attention, and by taking the reins
and leading off the horse evinced her acquiescence. The
bridegroom, who had been a pleased spectator of all that
had hitherto passed, now came forward. In his hands he
held a shield, a spear, and a sword. "These," said he, "are
the arms transmitted to me by my ancestors, they have for
several generations been, by every chief of our family given
to his bride, and faithfully kept by her till claimed by her
eldest son. By my mother were they presented to me in the
midst of the assembled chiefs, and by this act she declared
her life to be without stain. These arms are emblematical of
the husband's honour, which he commits in trust to the
partner of his bosom. They come unto your hands un-

polluted by a single stain; be it your care to preserve the sacred treasure, and to deliver it without spot or blemish to the son of our loves."

The bride received the precious deposit with modesty, but firmness, and then in her turn presented a helmet, a shield, a sword, and javelin; which, as her father in a short speech intimated, were intended to remind the husband that he was to be the protector of his wife and family. The shield being of very curious workmanship attracted the attention of Agrippina; it was handed to her for inspection, and on nearer view she found that it was composed of osier twigs, dyed of a variety of bright colours, and most curiously platted, so as to give in each of the four divisions a lively representation of some flower, or animal peculiar to the country in which the chief or his family had signalized their valour.

The feast for the numerous company was profusely spread; and was, as may be supposed, less remarkable for elegance or variety than for abundance. It had but just commenced, when two strangers appeared, who from their dress were known to belong to the Cattian nation. Neither their names or business were however asked. According to the German rules of hospitality, they were conducted in silence to the seat of honour, on the right hand of the master of the house, and regaled with the most dainty morsels.

There was something in the appearance of these youths which particularly attracted the attention of Agrippina. In the elder of the two an air of superiority was conspicuous; and the extreme delicacy of the features suited to ill with the complexion, as to create a doubt in her mind, whether it had not been embrowned by art. She had not yet among the barbarians seen a figure so graceful, or a deportment so dignified. Her curiosity was excited, and the silence of the strangers added to its force. Impatient of delay, she sent to the Ubian chief to beg that he would enquire the name and rank of his extraordinary guests. The old man appeared no less surprised than mortified by her request, and humbly entreated that she would not insist upon his dishonouring himself by a breach of hospitality. It was then explained to her, that by the established customs of Germany, to ask the name of a stranger was to imply a doubt of his right to your protection, and was therefore highly indecorous: nor was it proper for the stranger rashly to declare himself, since whether he was the son of a friend or a foe, he had an equal claim to attention.*

While Agrippina was holding this conference with her host, the strangers appeared to listen with interest to all that passed. The elder lifting his dark blue eyes which had hitherto been fixed upon the ground, darted on her a look of reproach, which affected her in the most sensible manner. Quickly entering into his feelings, she was ashamed of having indulged a curiosity which must have appeared to him to be reprehensible, nor could all the proud consciousness of superiority prevent her from being sensibly mortified at having violated the rules of propriety established by a rude unlettered people.

Agrippina heard nothing more of the strangers for several days. She had in that time been agreeably surprised by receiving an unexpected visit from the wife of Caius Silius, a lady to whom from infancy she had been attached by ties of the strictest friendship. Silius, who commanded one of the detached armies stationed on the frontiers, no sooner heard of the situation of Agrippina, than he sent his wife guarded by a proper escort to Ubiorum, to soothe by her presence the lonely hours of her friend. Since she was thought worthy of that title, Sosia Galla could not have been destitute of merit; she had already been endeared to Agrippina by many proofs of affection, and the kindness of the present visit served to rivet every tie of mutual attachment.†

---

* The spirit of hospitality appears in the progress of society gradually to decrease, in proportion as nations advance in refinement. "In countries," says Montesquieu, "where the people move only by the spirit of commerce, they make a traffic of all the humane and the moral virtues. The sentiments of the heart, the social affections, and even the dues of humanity, are there to be obtained only for money." The spirit of selfishness which extinguishes that of hospitality, is not confined to commerce; it is the never-failing attendant on luxury and refinement. [E.H.]

† Whether Sosia Galla, the wife of Silius, was sister or cousin of Asinius Gallus, does not clearly appear; but the part he took on a future occasion, when the unfortunate Sosia was, on account of her friendship for Agrippina, persecuted by Tiberius, leaves no room to doubt of their being connected; Asinius Gallus, by his marriage with Vipsania, was now the brother-in-law of Agrippina. If Sosia was his sister, she was the daughter

Sosia found the situation of Agrippina much more tolerable than she could have imagined. Her house had been
fitted up by the Roman artisans in a style of neatness and
comfort, and her apartments furnished according to the
Roman taste. Here, too, after the arrival of Sosia, she was
one morning, when engaged in conversation with her
friend, surprised by the sudden entrance of the two stranger
youths, who had at the marriage feast so much attracted
her curiosity. Observing in their looks the appearance of
perturbation and anxiety, she endeavoured to inspire them
with confidence by the kindness of her reception. After a
short pause, the elder thus addressed her: —

"You are the wife of a Roman, but the praises I have
heard bestowed upon your virtue inspires me with confidence. I do not however expect that you should protect me,
without knowing to whom that protection is extended, for
those of your nation understand not the claims of the
stranger."

Agrippina eagerly assured him, that she knew how to
respect the rights of hospitality, and that he might depend
on her protection. "My name is of no importance,"
returned the stranger, "but I will not impose upon you in
regard to my situation. This garb which I and my companion have assumed, belongs not to our sex. You see
before you an unhappy female, who flies from the vengeance of an offended father to the protecting arms of a
beloved husband.

"The chief from whom I sprung, and he to whom I have
been united, are equals in rank and in renown. They long
were friends, and when I gave my heart to the hero, my
father smiled upon our loves; but alas! no sooner did
discord enter into their councils, than he commanded me
to withdraw my affections from him to whom they had
irrevocably been engaged. Obedience was impossible; nor
could I be unfaithful to my vows without tarnishing my

---

of Asinius Pollio, the distinguished orator and confidential friend of
Augustus, whose name has been immortalized by Horace and Virgil.
Pollio's intimacy with Augustus must have introduced his children, even
in infancy, to the acquaintance of Agrippina. Hence, perhaps, the origin
of that strong attachment which they had for each other. [E.H.]

honour. My lover urged me to fulfil the promise that had once been sanctioned by duty, my heart impelled me to a compliance with his request; and at the moment when my father had promised me in marriage to a chief who was of his party in the quarrel, I eloped with the object of my affection, and became his wife. The rage of an incensed father still pursues me. Taking advantage of my husband's absence, he resolves to get me into his power. I have by means of this disguise succeeded in escaping from his emissaries, and could I be concealed under your roof till midnight, should have no doubt of being safe from their pursuit. I adjure you then by your love for the husband you adore, to assist in saving a wretched wife from the miseries of an eternal separation!"

Here the stranger paused; but though her voice was silent, her eyes continued expressively to convey her feelings to the soul of Agrippina. True generosity is prompt in its decisions. Agrippina did not hesitate to promise the desired protection, and immediately conveyed her guests to a place where they would be secure from all intrusion.

At the dead hour of midnight, Agrippina, faithful to her word, attended the fugitives. She urged their remaining in their present place of safety, till the husband of the stranger should be informed where his wife was now concealed, and could come to take her under his own protection. But the proposal was declined, and the German heroine, having thanked her benefactress with tears of genuine gratitude, departed in the assured hope of meeting her beloved lord at an appointed place before the dawn of day.

[from Vol. 2, Chapter 1; Germanicus brings Agrippina back to the Roman camp]

Tired of the inactive life which he here led [in the German village], Germanicus impatiently waited the return of spring, and as soon as the roads were passable hastened to the camp, accompanied by Agrippina and his children. He had concerted his plan of operations for the ensuing summer, and as a prelude, opened the campaign by a sudden irruption into the territories of the Cattians, a war-like people inhabiting an extensive district, known to the moderns by the names of Hesse, Thuringia, and Franconia.

The Cattians were divided by the spirit of party into opposite factions; part of the people adhering to Segestus, the friend of Rome and consequently of peace, though the greater number were attached to the cause of Arminius, the patriotic defender of German liberty.

While Arminius displayed all the savage virtues of a hero, Segestus even in that early stage of society, evinced the cold-hearted prudence of a politician. The hatred of these chiefs to each other was enflamed by mutual injury. While apparently united in the same cause, Segestus, by betraying the plans of Arminius to the Roman general, would have preserved the army of Varus, had not that unhappy man proudly despised the advice of the barbarian. Arminius in consequence triumphed, and Varus paid the forfeit of his pride and presumption; but the German hero could not pardon the treachery of his countryman.

Such was the state of affairs, when the Roman army appeared in the country of the Cattians, and with it all the accustomary accompaniments of havoc and desolation. Taken by surprise, and while their forces were unassembled, resistance was impossible; the stout and active saved themselves by flight, and swimming across the Edar gained the impenetrable shelter of the forest; but old age, and infancy, and weakness, were left exposed to the cruel rage of the invaders. The allies of the Cattians flew to arms, and in their ardour for revenge, risqued a battle with Germanicus, which ended, as might have been expected, in their total defeat.

It was some time before Germanicus could gain any intelligence concerning the situation of the rival chiefs; at length
an embassy from Segestus acquainted him, that unless
timely succours arrived to his assistance, he must fall a
sacrifice to his friendship for the Romans, for to that cause
alone did the crafty politician attribute the resentment of
Arminius, by whom, as he informed Germanicus, he was
now closely besieged. The son of Segestus was the bearer of
this message; and on being strictly interrogated, the youth
confessed that other causes, besides his father's attachment
to Rome, had excited the fury of Arminius. The beautiful
Thusnelda was, he said, the object of the present deadly dispute. Thusnelda was wife to Arminius, but she was the
daughter of Segestus. Her heart refused to share in her
father's enmity, she admired the spirit, she returned the
love of Arminius, and fled with the object of her affection.
But though her father's vengeance seemed to sleep, it at
length overtook the undutiful Thusnelda. "In vain," continued the youth,"had my sister disguised herself in the
habit of a young warrior, she was discovered, betrayed, and
brought to our fortress in the woods, which is now besieged
by the haughty Arminius, who burns with all the rage and
fury of resentment."

Agrippina soon discovered that Thusnelda was the stranger
to whom she had at Ubiorum extended her protection.
Time had not effaced the interest which she then had taken
in her fate. With sorrow, therefore, she now learned, that
Germanicus deemed it not consistent with his duty to
permit to Arminius the triumph of rescuing his affectionate
wife from the captivity in which she was held by her
offended father. The prince marched to the relief of
Segestus, and at the approach of the Roman army the indignant Arminius was forced to make a hasty retreat.

Segestus came out to meet Germanicus, attended by his
faithful adherents, and followed by a long train of captives,
among whom were several women of noble birth. Abhor-
rent at the idea of slavery, this mournful group in tears and
lamentations vented the bitterness of their souls. The wife
of Arminius alone preserved indignant silence. No tear
betrayed the weakness of her sex, no appeal to pity
acknowledged the power of the conqueror; pensive and
serene, she stood unmoved amid the clamorous grief of her

companions. She was now apparently far advanced in her pregnancy, and her whole deportment seemed to declare that the honour of Arminius should not be tarnished by any act of meanness in the mother of his child.

Segestus looked and spoke like a warrior who was a stranger to guilt or fear. He explained the motives of his conduct, as founded on a just sense of the interests of his country; declared his attachment to Rome; and supplicated the clemency of Germanicus with respect to a son who had at one time joined the party of Arminius, but who had repented of his error, and was worthy of forgiveness. "As for my daughter," said the chief, "she appears before you by necessity, and not by her own choice. I acknowledge it. It is yours to decide her fate. It is yours to judge which ought to have most influence, her husband or her father. She is with child by Arminius, and she sprung from me!"

If Germanicus had been at liberty to obey the generous impulse of sensibility, Thusnelda would without doubt have been restored to the arms of her husband. But the philanthropy which binds in its golden cords the individuals of adverse nations, beamed not on the pagan world: by customs of his enlightened country, Germanicus was compelled to treat the wife of Arminius as a captive doomed to perpetual bondage. We know little farther of her history; except that soon after her captivity she was delivered of a son, who, in his mother's arms, attended the triumph of Germanicus.

No rage ever equalled that of Arminius, upon being informed of these events. He flew from place to place rousing his countrymen to arms and vengeance; he represented the conduct of the Romans in the late instance as mean and dastardly in the extreme. "Behold!" he cried, "in the exploits of the Roman army the glory of a warlike nation! With mighty numbers they have led a woman into captivity! It was not in this manner that Arminius dealt with them. Three legions fell a sacrifice to my revenge. I am a stranger to the arts of traitors: I wage no war with women big with child. My enemies are worthy of a soldier, and sword in hand I meet them in the field of battle."

These severe truths excited less of remorse than indignation in the Roman breast. The defender of his country was in the eyes of his oppressors an incendiary, who, by

exposing their conduct to public view, incurred their ten-
fold hatred and resentment. The patriotic efforts of Arminius were, however, crowned with success. He engaged all
the neighbouring states in a league against the Romans, and
the abettors of Roman despotism. He declared Segestus a
traitor to his country, whose memory posterity would for
ever curse; since to him it was owing that the badges of
slavery had ever been seen in the land of liberty. He
reminded the people, that to other nations punishments
and taxes were unknown; but that these alone were happy
who were ignorant of the Romans. He conjured them, by
throwing off the yoke, to vindicate the rights of freedom;
and assured them, that by following where he should lead,
success would crown the glorious enterprise.

The spirit of the German chief was worthy of respect
and admiration. Nor could it have failed of producing
esteem in the generous mind of Germanicus, had the prejudices of education permitted him to view the conduct of a
barbarian through the medium of impartiality. Imperfectly
as Christianity has operated in conquering the pride of the
human heart, it has removed the barriers which before its
introduction separated man from man. The mean and
narrow policy of avarice and selfishness may still affect to
believe in radical distinctions, and teach us that complexion
ought to be the criterion of human sympathy; but these
sentiments are confined to the ignorant and the interested,
while the enlightened of every Christian nation consider the
inhabitants of the globe as the children of one common
parent. The benevolence of the Romans was bounded by
the limits of their territorial acquisitions. The same conduct
that constituted the virtue of a Roman citizen, was in one
of any other description criminal or presumptuous. Hence
the indignation of their historians against the heroic spirit
with which the love of liberty inspired our German ancestors: and hence the inveterate resentment with which the
mild and amiable Germanicus pursued the gallant Arminius.

from
*Letters, Addressed to the
Daughter of a Nobleman,
on the Formation of
Religious and Moral
Principle (2 vols, 1806)*

Editor's note

The nobleman's daughter who was the nominal recipient of these letters was Lady Elizabeth Bingham (1795-1838), the eldest child of the second Earl of Lucan. According to Benger, the Earl had made a considerable effort to persuade Hamilton to oversee the education of his children; she resisted from a desire to preserve her independence but finally, and with some reluctance, she agreed to spend six months setting up a programme of education and training the children's governess. Slightly more gossipy accounts are provided by Hamilton's contemporaries, who evidently found her decision to enter the Lucan household odd enough to warrant comment, as Lucan's reputation was dubious, at best, following his affair with and subsequent marriage to Lady Elizabeth Belasyse, whose first husband was the heir of the Duke of Norfolk (the Lucan marriage in turn broke down some years later). Agnes Porter, a governess with a strong interest in contemporary literature, wrote somewhat uneasily to a friend that *Elementary Education* "induced Lord Lucan to offer [Hamilton] by letter the care of his unfortunate children, with a carte blanche as to terms. She declined the situation, but his lordship came post to Edinburgh to prevail on her acceptance of his proposal. His daughter, a fine young lady, made use of entreaties and caresses for the same purpose, and Miss Hamilton accompanied them back. Her celebrity is great in Edinburgh, and her character is so highly estimated that every-one says it stands too high for calumny's envenomed arrows ever to reach." An acquaintance of Hamilton's, a Miss Ewbank of York, was apparently even more alarmed, as she wrote at some length in her journal of the extenuating circumstances that might make it more or less acceptable for Hamilton to work for such an employer, in the process turning the Lucan marriage into sentimental romance. (According to Miss Ewbank, the Earl and Countess had been in love before her first marriage, but were forced apart by their families; she was already corrupted by a loveless life of pleasure when they reunited, eventually leading her second husband to seek a separation in the interests of his children.) Miss Ewbank concludes that "from her works, & from public character he [Lucan] form'd his estimate of Miss Hamilton's worth, & in securing to his family such a friend, has made to them a noble recompense, for the bad Mother he gave them." Whether or not one takes seriously the sentimental tale sketched out in miniature by Miss Ewbank, Hamilton's initial reluctance to take the position seems justified, as her employment in the household was brief, although the circumstances of her departure and her reasons for publishing the letters are not entirely clear. Anne Grant, however, noted that the gossip in Edinburgh was that Hamilton had left because "Lord Ls conduct was not agreeable to her," and, no longer "on corresponding terms" with the family, Hamilton then turned to the press in order to maintain some contact with her former charge.

Unsurprisingly, the motives that Hamilton gives for publication are less sensationalized, if still a little odd. In the first letter, she explains to the eleven-year-old Lady Elizabeth that she has chosen to communicate through the public medium of a printed book rather than corresponding directly because, first of all, she could not expect that "letters in manuscript would be preserved with care" by so young a recipient and second, that the "benefit" of private letters would "have been exclusively confined" to Lady Elizabeth, even though Hamilton hoped to benefit the younger sisters as well (I. 4). Hamilton is here stretching to breaking point the fiction that collections of letters were merely a transcription of private exchanges between two individuals; Lady Elizabeth becomes more the excuse for than the recipient of these letters, as Hamilton somewhat tactlessly implies she can be trusted neither to value them properly nor to recognize their value to others. The point that the book is not in any sense a private exchange between teacher and an individual student is made even more strongly in the preface – directed to the general reader – in which Hamilton explains that as she didn't want to encounter resistance from the "peculiar opinions, or accidental prejudices" of other members of the Lucan household, she has kept "as much as possible to general views" (1. vii), something that inevitably depersonalizes the letters.

The obvious point of framing the arguments of the book as letters to an aristocratic pupil is that, in doing so, Hamilton is quietly puffing her own work, making clear that her educational views have been sought out by the elite. At the same time, however, she forestalls potential criticism about the violation of private confidences by making it very clear that the "private" letters to Lady Elizabeth are in fact nothing of the sort but are rather didactic essays in epistolary form. This was a point that *The British Critic*, in a generally highly favourable review, picked up on, observing that even if the letters are nominally to "a very young correspondent" they are meant for "the public at large." Indeed, its main complaint was that Hamilton was a little too attentive to maintaining the fiction that she was writing to an eleven-year-old child, complaining that she should have "avoided such childish appellations as Lady Elizabeth's papa [. . .] which are suited only to the nursery." Anne Grant, though generally an admirer of Hamilton, was even more unenthusiastic about the letters, on much the same grounds, commenting to a friend that while the letters worked to a degree as a "vehicle" for the expression of "very commendable" ideas, their effectiveness was marred by "frequent expressions of tender familiarity and fond and adulatory allusions to her pupils[,] seeming to indicate a greater degree of attachment to their preceptress [. . .] than could well take place in so short a period."

The excerpt printed below is a self-contained short story, intended, as Hamilton states directly in the following letter, to illustrate "an example of injustice, produced, not by the operation of any malignant passion, but merely by a deficiency in the point of firmness" (1: 161). As this comment makes clear, the almost cartoon-like villainy of Mrs Pegg, a one-dimensional wicked nurse, is not the real source of evil in this story; instead, the true wrong-doer is the beautiful, kind, and superficially virtuous Lady N_____, who is too morally indolent to think through or take responsibility for her own actions. In some ways, she is an upper-class version of Mrs MacClarty, protected by rank and wealth from the consequences of her moral obtuseness. The harm that she does, however, is even more far-reaching, as the hapless Tom is left physically destitute and morally adrift by her refusal to trouble herself with inquiries or the pursuit of justice. In making this point, Hamilton comes very close to denying Mrs Pegg a moral life of her own, as she blames Lady N———— for Mrs Pegg's tyranny, but even if the focus remains on Lady N————, Hamilton suggests that the errors both women make are parallel: if Mrs Pegg is unable to resist the combined temptations of ease and power (like Mrs Dickens in *Glenburnie*), Lady N———— is led astray by the temptations to indolence and irresponsibility held out by a society that equates upper-class femininity with a form of permanent childishness. In a world that assumes women should be under the guidance of men, the formation of independent moral character becomes very difficult for women, but Hamilton's message in this story is that neither gender nor class excuse one from ordinary human responsibilities.

The Daughter of a Nobleman, like *Agrippina*, was not one of Hamilton's more successful works. It went into a second edition in the year of its publication, but did not go into a third until 1814, which, aside from an 1821 American printing, was also the last. *The British Critic* thought the subject of the book much more valuable than that of *Agrippina*, but it was the only major periodical to review the *Letters*, which never achieved the success of either the novels or *Elementary Education*.

The Story of the Tame Pigeon

Some years before you were born, a deep and universal regret was excited by the premature death of the Earl of N., a nobleman who had the rare felicity of being very sincerely and very deservedly beloved. An eulogium upon his character given in one of the newspapers of the day concludes as follows: "His lordship is succeeded in his titles and estates by his only son, now in the third year of his age. The present earl and his sister, who is in her sixth year, are left to the sole guardianship of their amiable mother, a lady no less distinguished by exemplary virtue, than by her exquisite beauty, splendid fortune, and brilliant accomplishments."

This account of Lady N. was by no means exaggerated. She had hitherto performed all the duties of life in an exemplary manner. She had been an amiable daughter, a good wife, and a fond mother – but she had been neither one nor other from principle. She had only acted the part planned for her by others, and quietly gone on in the track into which she had fortunately been led.

For the sweetness with which she accommodated herself to the inclinations of her parents, and her husband, Lady N. had obtained much applause, and would have merited more than all the praise bestowed, had her obedience proceeded from a principle of duty; but it was in her the offspring of indolence and timidity. She yielded, not to gratify others, but to save trouble to herself. She consequently never had experienced the pleasure which glows in the breasts of the generous when conscious of having made a sacrifice of inclination to duty or affection.

Having been successfully guided by the wisdom of judicious parents, and of a sensible husband, Lady N. had always appeared to act with uncommon prudence; but when left solely dependent upon her own judgment, she found that she had been very imprudent in never having given herself the habit of exerting it. She had had what is sometimes called a religious education: – that is to say, she had learned a respect for the institutions of the church, had learned to repeat her creed, and say her prayers, and to keep clear of all gross offences. But even these best impressions were rather adopted as prejudices, than embraced as principles. In the formation of principles, the heart and the understanding unite; the adoption of prejudices is the work of the feelings and the imagination.

It has been observed of women, by a witty poet, (though in fact the observation is equally applicable to both sexes,) that

> They who are born to be controll'd,
> Stoop to the forward and the bold.

Indeed, in the very nature of things, they who must be governed will fall under the dominion of the worthless; for who but the self-interested and depraved will practise the arts necessary to obtain an ascendancy over the mind either of an equal or superior?

Those who do not select from esteem, or esteem from real and accurate observation, will be for ever liable to misplace their confidence. Such was the fate of Lady N. Her too great facility of temper rendered her an easy prey to the arts of the designing. Her principles were good; but they were not fixed in her mind with sufficient strength to be resorted to as the support and guide of her life. She thought it requisite for her to have some one on whom to lean, and indolently resigned herself to the first to whom chance happened to direct her.

Mrs Pegg, the person who, after the death of the Earl of N. had the boldness to aspire and to gain her lady's confidence, was a woman of very low origin, but of very insinuating address. By pretending a more profound degree of sorrow for the death of her late master than was at all consistent with probability, she made her first approaches to her lady's favour. The grief of Lady N. was unaffected and sincere. She was soothed by the apparent sympathy of the hypocrite, whose tears flowed still faster than her own, and considered them as an infallible proof of the strength of her attachment.

Lady N. was not deficient in understanding; but Mrs Pegg was as much her superior in talent as in artifice. Had her talents been guided by principle, she would indeed have been a valuable acquisition in any family; but her heart was corrupt and depraved: her talents were therefore employed to cheat, to circumvent, and to deceive. She soon penetrated into all the weaknesses of her lady's character, and with infinite dexterity turned them to her own advantage. Every thing at Castle N. was now placed under the control of this ambitious woman. So complete was the ascendancy she obtained over the mind of her too easy mistress, that she neither heard, saw, examined, nor judged, for herself. Every thing was left to Mrs Pegg. All the servants, even the old and attached domestics of the family, were, one after another, on various pretexts, dismissed. Some Mrs Pegg thought it dangerous to keep, because they knew too much of her real character; others were too unbending to be subservient to her wicked views: she therefore made use of the opportunity which constant access to her lady afforded, to prejudice her mind against them all.

Never, indeed, did Mrs Pegg make use of her influence for the advantage of any human bring. Never did she commend any one to her lady's favour on account of their real worth; or seek to lessen any one in her regard on account of any blemish in their moral character: all her motives were purely selfish. But if Lady N. had been possessed of the principles of justice, she would not have taken this woman's representations as sufficient evidence, neither would she have delegated to a mean and vulgar person that authority, for the due exercise of which, she was to be responsible at the tribunal of the Almighty.

The dread of giving herself trouble, would not then have appeared to her as a sufficient excuse for shrinking from those inquiries by which the truth would have been established; nor would she have considered herself justified in giving up her own judgment, where she was called upon by Providence to exercise it.

With respect to her children, Lady N. was still more seriously to blame. She doated upon them to excess. Yet she did not give herself any trouble in the formation of their minds. She trusted every thing to Mrs Pegg. "What could she do?" she said; "she never had been used to children, and did not know how to manage them; but happily Mrs Pegg had been used to them, and therefore could not fail to manage them properly!"

Their first notions of right and wrong were consequently imbibed from Mrs Pegg. Now it happened, that of right and wrong Mrs Pegg had no other rule or standard than self-interest. Whatever gave her trouble was punished as a fault of the first magnitude. Whatever did not interfere with her ease or convenience was passed without notice. No idea of the consequences which false and injurious impressions might have upon the future character, entered into her imagination; nor, if it had, would it have disturbed her peace. The children might be false, cruel, capricious, proud, or obstinate, with impunity, provided they paid a proper respect to her, and never failed to observe her special orders; but no sooner did they transgress in this respect, than they were punished with unmerciful severity; and so completely did she keep the poor infants under subjection, that they dared not utter a complaint.

The children believed that their mamma's apartments were haunted by a secret spy; and in truth they were so; for the unprincipled nurse, not contented with the possession of her lady's unbounded confidence, took care, by means of listening, to inform herself of all that was going forward. And such an adept had she become in this detestable practice, that a two-inch door was no obstacle in the way of her information. When she had, from any thing that passed, the slightest grounds for alarm respecting the continuance of her influence, she had immediate recourse to a method which she had ever found to be infallible. Lord N. or Lady Mary were, upon such occasions, the innocent sufferers.

As they were the objects, of their mother's doting fondness, their slightest indisposition engrossed her whole attention; and upon such occasions her sole dependence was placed on the care, the skill, the wonderful management of Mrs Pegg. No wonder, then, that Mrs Pegg should be sometimes induced to make to herself an opportunity of evincing her skill and dexterity in their recovery; and as she could do it at the expense of a little stomach sickness, the children were, perhaps, in reality, not much the worse for the experiment.

Mrs Pegg was not, however, always thus fortunate in being able speedily to remove the effects of her own treatment. When her young lord was in his fifth year, he was seized with an inflammation in his lungs, which had nearly cut short the slender thread of his existence. It is impossible to describe the confusion and dismay which reigned at

Castle N. during the anxious period of his danger. No eye
(at least so Lady N. believed) ever shut in sleep; no lips were
opened for any other purpose but to sigh. How much the
usual consumption of victuals was lessened, is best known
to the housekeeper; but certain it is, that among the numerous train of domestics and dependants at Castle N. there
were few who did not on this occasion feel deeply interested for their lady, or – for their young lord, or – for
themselves!

We may believe that Mrs Pegg would now act the part
of grief to admiration. She indeed appeared to be almost
distracted; but she did not now act a part: her terrors were,
for the first time, sincere. For, though her soul was of too
hard a texture to be susceptible of the tenderness of affection, the fond mother herself was not now more truly
anxious for her son's recovery than she was. Her attention
was not however solely engrossed by the little sufferer. Lady
Mary never experienced from Mrs Pegg so much tenderness
of endearment, or such unlimited indulgence as she now
experienced. She was only entreated not to speak of her
brother to her mamma; and she might have what she
pleased.

Mrs Pegg gave herself, in this instance, a great deal of
unnecessary trouble. The poor child's spirits had been too
effectually subdued by terror to betray any transaction
which it was Mrs Pegg's interest to conceal: nor did it, perhaps, enter into her mind to ascribe her brother's illness
to any other cause than that to which she had heard it
ascribed, viz. running across the lawn without his hat. But
though Lady Mary might not know, or might not chuse to
tell, I know, and I shall tell you how it really happened.

Mrs Pegg's standard of right and wrong has already been
explained. Now as the children could do nothing which produced so much trouble to her as soiling or tearing their
clothes, so no fault of which they were ever guilty, was
punished with half the severity. Lady Mary, being of a timid
and quiet disposition, was not nearly so apt to transgress
in this way as her brother, who, while he was in frocks, was
perpetually grieving Mrs Pegg's righteous spirit by stains,
and rents, most unfeelingly inflicted on her future per-
quisite. Nor when he exchanged the fragile muslin for the
stouter trousers, were her troubles at an end. Though he

could no longer tear, he still could soil; and in those elope-
ments into the garden or court-yard, which not all her vigilance could prevent, he would sometimes in running after
a butterfly slip his foot on the fresh dug mould, sometimes
in caressing a spaniel receive such a warm return of gratitude as left its visible effects behind; nor did he think of the
consequences, until he beheld the marks of his favourite's
paws upon the fair nankeen, which he would then most
willingly have exchanged for the coarsest linsey-woolsey
that ever little boy was clothed in.

It happened on a luckless day, when, as Lady N. dined
from home, Mrs Pegg intended saving herself the trouble of
dressing the children a second time, that Lord N. finding
himself unobserved, and hearing the voice of Tom the sta-
bleboy speaking to his tame pigeon, was tempted to slip
down the back stairs to share with Tom the pleasure of
feeding his Pet.

The pigeon was at first a little shy. It flew away at his
approach, but being lured back by Tom, it at length became
so familiar as to eat the corn which he scattered for it at
his feet. Tom assured him that when a little better
acquainted, it would eat from his hand with as little fear as
it now did from his. Lord N. was very ambitious to rival
Tom in the pigeon's favour, but in the eagerness of impetuosity he defeated his own purpose. The pigeon took fright
and retreated. He pursued. Snatching the hat full of corn
from Tom's hand, he followed the fugitive, coaxing it in
such sweet accents as but one other little boy in the wide
world could utter. The hard-hearted pigeon heeded not the
music of his voice. It walked on till, turning into an inner
court, it there took to its wings and flew to the top of the
opposite wall. Poor N. rushed on unconscious of his
danger, nor once perceived the heap of mud which had
been that morning raked from a sewer, and lay directly in
his way, and in which he would, the next moment, have
measured all his length, had it not been for the agility of his
companion, who, throwing himself before him, saved him
from falling farther than his knees. As he was not hurt, he
would have joined Tom in the loud laugh which he
instantly set up, had not the idea of Mrs Pegg presented
itself to his affrighted imagination, banishing all thoughts of
mirth and gladness from his mind. As he looked in sad

dismay on the woefully bespattered trowsers the roses for-
sook his cheeks, the ruby lips grew pale, and the long dark
silken fringes with which nature had adorned his seraph
eyes, were moistened with the tears of anguish. He stood
aghast and trembling; afraid to cry, lest his crying should
reach the ears of Mrs Pegg, and yet not able to refrain from
giving vent to the misery which swelled his little heart. At
length he took courage to turn his steps towards the house,
supported by Tom, who was now little less terrified than
himself, though he knew not for what; when all at once the
sound of Mrs Pegg's voice broke in thunder on his ears,
and her stately form was seen advancing towards them,
clothed in all the majesty of anger. Lord N. now screamed
outright; but unmindful of his emotion she took him by the
arm with one of those jerks which prove that dislocation
is not so easily accomplished as some weak persons may
imagine; and giving Tom a box on the ear which sent him
staggering to the other side of the court, hastily proceeded
with the culprit to her own apartment. How she stamped
and raged, and scolded, it is needless to describe, but as she
had stamped and raged, and scolded at offences of the same
kind before now, and as it proved without effect, she determined on a new method of punishment. Having stripped
the unfortunate delinquent of his soiled garments, she
put him in a corner, there to stand during the term of
her pleasure, and then calmly left him, in order to resume
the occupation in which she had been so disagreeably
interrupted.

It was in the month of May. The sun was hot, but the
east wind blew chill. The poor boy had thrown himself into
a heat running after the pigeon, which had been increased
by succeeding agitation, and from wearing coat and trowsers lined with flannel, he was now exposed, without
defence, to the piercing air of an open window. The consequences are not so surprising as his recovery appeared to
be to those best acquainted with his danger.

These consequences it is certain Mrs Pegg did not fore-
see, but she made no scruple of doing under the eye of
God, what she would not have done under the eye of her
mistress. And that she was conscious of doing wrong was
evident from the rage she was in on finding that the situation in which she had left Lord N. was discovered by little

Tom; who, deeply interested in the fate of his young master, and directed by his lamentations to the scene of punishment, had adventurously dared, by the assistance of a step-ladder, to peep in at the window, through which he hastily offered all the consolation in his power, by assuring Lord N. that the pigeon should be his own.

Letter IX

[Continuation of "The Story of the Tame Pigeon"]

When Lord N. was well enough to be taken out an airing, he went one morning with his mamma and sister, attended by Mrs Pegg, in the landau, and was standing up by his mamma's side looking over the carriage, when it stopped so suddenly as to throw him off his balance, with a violence that might have been fatal, had not Mrs Pegg's arm been ready to receive him.

The coachman at the same moment called loudly to some one to get out of the way. "No," replied the person spoken to, "I will not get out of the way. You may ride over me, you may trample me to death – but I will not stir till my lady promises to speak to me."

Lady N. stood up, and on looking out perceived a little boy kneeling in the middle of the highway, which was in that part only just sufficiently wide for the carriage. She called out to know who it was. "It is little Tom the stable-boy, please your ladyship," said the coachman, "he was turned away yesterday morning by your ladyship's orders."

"I gave no such orders," said Lady N. "Let the boy come here to speak to me."

"Bless me," cried Mrs Pegg, "I dare say Mr Ditto (the steward) has mistaken me. I told him yesterday that I was sure if your ladyship knew what a sad liar this little fellow was, you would not keep him another day about the house; but I did not say your ladyship had dismissed him – I wonder how he could mistake me."

"I wonder so too," growled the coachman; "I never knew Mr Ditto make blunders, nor did little Tom ever tell a fib in all his life, as I knows of."

Tom was by this time at the carriage-door, a piteous spectacle. Stripped of his livery, and having outgrown his former clothes, he had, in order to secure himself from the inclemency of the weather, fastened his old coat upon his back by bringing the sleeves round his neck, and tying them in a hard knot upon his breast, where they conveniently hung, as they now served the office of a handkerchief, in wiping the tears from his swollen eyes.

Lady N. could not but compassionate the little wretch. In a mild tone she desired him to tell what he wanted, but to be sure to speak the truth, for that she could not endure any one that told lies.

"No, my lady, Ize never told no lies since I was born, my lady. My lord there can tell you it was not I, was it, my lord? Pray tell your lady mamma; was it I that 'ticed you out the day you fell into the mud and dirtied all your clothes so? and when Mrs Pegg was so hugeous angry? Do pray speak, my dear sweet young lord, was it I?"

"No," said Lord N. looking wistfully up in his mother's face, "indeed, indeed mamma, it was not Tom's fault."

"I know not what you speak of, my dear child," said Lady N.

"I said so," cried Tom, "I said my lady knew nothing of the matter, I was sure and certain, my lady, that it was all a story of Mrs Pegg's own making, and that you never would have had the heart, my lady, to order her to twist off the neck of my pretty pigeon."

"You little abominable lying vagabond," said Mrs Pegg, lifting up her voice, and casting her indignant regards on the unfortunate outcast, "what is it that you dare to say of me?"

"I say," cried Tom, agitated with fresh emotion, "I say that you said as how that my lady said, that my lord caught cold by following of me; and that it was I that 'ticed him into the yard, and that it was by my lady's orders that you twisted off the head of my pretty pigeon. Lady Mary saw you do it; aye, she saw you do it, and she saw you throw the bloody head in my face too, and heard you tell me that I should be served in the same way myself. And she heard you say, too, that it was all my lady's orders. Did not you my Lady Mary? I am sure you will not say you didn't."

The poor Lady Mary sadly discomfited by this appeal, sat trembling and silent. Three times the truth rose to her lips, and a voice within her heart told her that she ought to give it utterance. But a glance from the eyes of Mrs Pegg silenced the feeble voice of conscience, and repelled the truth that sat upon the tongue. Lady N. looked at her daughter in surprise, "And do you know any thing of this, my love?" said she, taking her kindly by the hand.

"Do, pray tell," cried Mrs Pegg in a tone which Lady Mary perfectly well knew how to interpret, "did you ever see *me* do such a thing in your life? *Me* twist off the head of a tame pigeon! Do, pray tell, my dear, I *insist* upon your speaking."

Lady Mary was still silent.

"Bless you, dear sweet young lady, speak," cried Tom. "I am sure and certain you can't have forgotten."

"Was there ever such impudence!" cried Mrs Pegg in a voice half choaked with rage, "you little story-telling villain, I shall know who it is that has put you upon this." Then turning to Lady Mary, whose hand she at the same time seized with vehemence, "tell this moment insist upon it. Did you ever see me do such a thing?"

"No," faintly uttered the too timid Lady Mary; the consciousness of so flagrantly departing from truth and justice dying her face with crimson as she spoke.

"Now," cried Mrs Pegg, in exultation, "Now, my lady, I hope you will believe, I hope you see what a knave this is: if your ladyship chuses to listen to him all day you will have plenty of stories, I'll be bound for it."

"You know it is no story," said Tom, "indeed, indeed, my lady, it is no story; I have not a friend in the wide world, but God; and my mammy told me God would be my friend while I told the truth. Indeed, my lady, I don't lye, and if your ladyship's honour will let me go back to the castle, I will bring proof that I don't."

"What astonishing impudence!" cried Mrs Pegg, turning up the whites of her eyes, "I wonder how your ladyship can encourage such a depraved little wretch. I should hope your ladyship cannot possibly take his word against mine and Lady Mary's too! Shall I bid the coachman drive on?"

Lady N. silently assented. The coachman smacked his whip. The horses darted forward, and poor honest little Tom was left a helpless orphan, destitute and forlorn, to seek his way through a world in which he saw hypocrisy and falsehood triumph over innocence and truth; and in which he found the ear of the powerful to be only open to favourites and flatterers, even when justice and judgment lifted up the voice!

Had Lady N. been sensible of the fatal impression which her conduct at that moment made upon the mind of a fellow creature, – had she foreseen the consequences which ensued from depriving this, then innocent boy, of the confidence which he had been taught to put in the certain success of integrity, she would have been struck with horror! But though these consequences were too remote to be distinctly foreseen, she must doubtless be considered as responsible for them, in so far as she acted upon other principles than those which her heart and conscience most seriously approved.

She was in reality far from being satisfied that Mrs Pegg was free from blame, and far from being convinced that the boy said what was false; but she had not courage to pursue an enquiry, which, if it terminated to the disadvantage of her favourite, would disturb her own peace; and which, would at any rate give a sad shock to her poor nerves!

The principle of selfishness was in Lady N. more powerful than the principle of justice. She had from youth been accustomed to cultivate the one, for it is evident that it had become a habit of her mind; – and she had from youth been accustomed *only to talk* of the other, so that it had no real influence upon her conduct. Lady N. was mild, and amiable, and gentle, as heart could wish, yet here we see her guilty of an act of cruelty and oppression, of which a person of a less yielding disposition, and who had been actuated by steady principle would never have been guilty.

Even for the crimes into which Mrs Pegg was led, Lady N. was in a great measure accountable. Had she considered the influence she possessed as a trust received from God, a talent which she was bound to employ to the best advantage, she would not have deemed herself excusable in thus disposing of it. The ambition which led Mrs Pegg from crime to crime would have been crushed in its very birth. Her talents would have been employed in their proper sphere; and her merit, judged of, not merely according to the height of its artificial gloss; but by the rigid rules of truth and justice. The poor woman would by this means have escaped the misery into which she was afterwards led by the gradual but overpowering force of great temptations.

As to Lady Mary, we cannot but consider her as an object of pity. She had been told to respect truth, yet was

placed in a situation where to speak truth, required a degree
of fortitude beyond her strength. She had never been taught
the necessity of exerting it. But had religious principle been
implanted in her heart, she would have felt that it was less
daring to offend Mrs Pegg, than to offend her creator and
her judge. She would therefore at all events have run the
risk of incurring Mrs Pegg's displeasure, rather than soil the
pure integrity of her mind, by giving utterance to a wilful
falsehood. Granting that through timidity she had permitted herself to be inadvertently hurried into this grievous
error; she would, upon reflection, have hastened to repair
it, and by an ingenuous confession of the truth, have wiped
the stain from her conscience. Thus would the principles
of honour and humanity have been upheld by the principles
of religion.

Happy they who are taught the practice, while they are
initiated into the precepts of virtue! Happy they who at an
early period, have acquired sufficient resolution to adhere
with firmness to the principles in which they have been thus
instructed!

The fruits of this firmness of mind are so admirably
represented by a Latin poet, that I cannot better conclude
this letter than by transcribing a translation:

> The man whose mind on virtue bent
> Pursues some greatly good intent,
> With undiverted aim,
> Serene beholds the angry crowd,
> Nor can their clamours fierce and loud
> His stubborn honour tame.
>
> Not the proud tyrant's fiercest threat,
> Nor storms that from their dark retreat,
> The lawless surges wake;
> Nor Jove's dread bolt that shakes the pole,
> The firmer purpose of his soul
> With all its power can shake.

Appendix

Francis Jeffrey's review of
The Cottagers of Glenburnie
The Edinburgh Review, *vol. 12*
(July 1808), 401-410

[Francis Jeffrey], *The Cottagers of Glenburnie: A Tale &c.* By Elizabeth Hamilton, Author of the Elementary Principles of Education; Memoirs of Modern Philosophers, &c. &c. 8vo. pp. 402. Manners & Miller, Edinburgh; Cadell & Davies, London. 1808.

We have not met with any thing nearly so good as this, since we read the Castle Rackrent and the Popular Tales of Miss Edgeworth. This contains as admirable a picture of the Scotish [sic] peasantry as those works do of the Irish; and rivals them not only in the general truth of the delineations, and in the cheerfulness and practical good sense of the lessons which they convey, but in the nice discrimination of national character, and the skill with which a dramatic representation of humble life is saved from caricature and absurdity.

After having given this just and attractive description of the book, we have a sort of malicious pleasure in announcing to our Southern readers, that it is a sealed book to them; and that, until they take the trouble thoroughly to familiarize themselves with our antient and venerable dialect, they will not be able to understand three pages of it. To such as are engaged in that interesting study, we recommend it as a specimen of the purest and most characteristic Scotch which we have lately met with in writing; and have much satisfaction in thinking of the singular refreshment and delight which it must afford to our worthy countrymen abroad, by setting before them, in such clear and lively colours, those simple and peculiar manners with which their youth was familiar. This sentimental purpose it may serve well enough in its present form; but if Mrs Hamilton really wishes it to be of use to our peasants at home, (and we think it is capable of being very useful), she must submit to strike out all the scenes in upper life, and to print the remainder upon coarse paper, at such a price as may enable the volume to find its way into the cottage library. In order to encourage her to take this trouble, and to make the book known to clergymen and resident proprietors who have it in their power to introduce it where it may be of use, we shall make a short abstract of its contents, – giving due warning to our polite readers, that it relates to the comforts of real cottagers, and the best methods of rearing honest ploughmen and careful nursery-maids.

Mrs Mason, a native of Scotland, and a person of great worth and discretion, had lived long as a domestic in a noble and amiable family in England, where she had rendered herself unusually respectable by her faithful and zealous services. Having quitted this situation with a very slender annuity, she is naturally led to seek a retirement in her native country; and proposes to board herself with a cousin, who, she understands, is married to a small farmer in the vicinity of her birth-place. To Glenburnie, accordingly, she comes, under the protection of a worthy gentleman in the neighbourhood; and takes up her residence with her cousin Mrs MacClarty. Here the interest and the instruction of the description begin. Her habits of cleanliness and domestic order make her more than usually sensible of the discomfort of a Scottish cottage, and her long experience of the benefits of early steadiness in the management of children, render her more alive to the pernicious effects of indulgence and inattention. The object of the book is to make our peasantry sensible of their errors in these particulars, and to convince them with how little exertion they may be remedied. The picture of their actual practices and notions is drawn, as we have already said, with admirable liveliness and fidelity, and without any attempt to produce effect by the broad glare of exaggeration. Full credit is given for their real merits, and, even when their faults are displayed, the amiable or respectable traits in their character are brought forward along with them. Mrs MacClarty, who is the chief representative of the Scotish party, is extremely good tempered, active, and indulgent to her children; but altogether insensible of the disadvantages of dirtiness, and attached to old ways with so narrow and obstinate a bigotry, as to resent all attempts at the most obvious improvements. So she not only keeps her hands unwashed, and her butter full of hairs, but allows her children to take their own way so entirely in every thing, that her eldest son gets drunk and enlists, and her husband dies of a fever caught in striving to deliver him, and of suffocation occasioned by his wife's over-care of him. After a long and patient experiment, Mrs Mason finds her kinswoman incurable, and, quite disgusted with the filth and discord of her habitation, transfers her residence to the cottage of another villager, to whom she speedily communicates her own taste for neatness and regularity; and, having got the clergyman to concur with her in his appointment as schoolmaster, gradually introduces a reformation in the domestic economy and education of the whole neighbourhood.

There is no great merit, of course, in the *plan* of such a story; and of the execution, excellent as it is, we scarcely think it would be fair to give any considerable specimen, considering the small number of readers to whom the language can be intelligible. However, as we sometimes take the liberty to quote a page or two of Latin and Italian, we shall venture upon a few sentences, for the satisfaction of those who can judge of them. We may begin with Mrs Mason's *debut* in the Glen. She and her conductor are suddenly stopped, by finding a wooden bridge on the road broken down, and a cart overturned beside it. While they are contemplating this scene of disaster, they suddenly hear –

– 'a child's voice in the hollow exclaiming, "Come on, ye muckle brute! ye had as weel come on! I'll gar ye! That's a gude beast now; come awa! That's it! Ay, ye're a gude beast now." As the last words were uttered, a little fellow of about ten years of age was seen issuing from the hollow, and, pulling after him, with all his might, a great longbacked clumsy, animal of the horse species, though apparently of a very mulish temper. "You have met with a sad accident," said Mr Stewart; "how did all this happen?" "You may see how it happened, plain enough," returned the boy, "the brig brak, and the cart couppet." "And did you and the horse coup likewise?" said Mr St'ewart. "O aye, we a' couppet thegether, for I was riding on his back." "And where is your father, and all the rest of the folk?"

"Whar sud they be but in the hay-field? Dinna ye ken that we're taking in our hay? John Tamson's and Jamie Forster's was in a week syne, but we're ay ahint the lave." All the party were greatly amused by the composure which the young peasant evinced under his misfortune, as well as by the shrewdness of his answers; and having learned from him, that the hay-field was at no great distance, gave him some halfpence to hasten his speed, and promised to take care of his horse till he should return with assistance. He soon appeared, followed by his father, and two other men, who came on, stepping at their usual pace. "Why, farmer," said Mr Stewart, "you have trusted rather too long to this rotten plank, I think," (pointing to where it had given way), "If you remember the last time I passed this road, which was several months since, I then told you that the bridge was in danger, and shewed you how easily it might be repaired?" "It is aw true," said the farmer, moving his bonnet; "but I thought it would do weel enough. I spoke to Jamie Forster and John Tamson about it; but they said they wad na fash themselves to mend a brig that was to serve a' the folk in the Glen." "But you must now mend it for your own sake," said Mr Stewart, "even though *a the folk in the Glen* should be the better, for it. Bring down the planks that I saw lying in the barn-yard, and which, though you have been obliged to step over them every day since the stack they propped was taken in, have never been lifted. You know what I mean." "O yes, Sir," said the farmer, grinning, "we ken what ye mean well enough; and indeed, I may ken, for I have fallen thrice ow're them since they lay there; and often said they sud be set by, but we *cou'dna be fashed*" p. 130-133.

'This is an out-of-doors picture. In their way into the house, they had to wade through a kind of dunghill and filthy pool that was collected opposite to the door, and then stumbled over a great iron pot, in which a whole brood of chickens were feeding, in the dark passage. On their arrival,

'Mrs Mason soon saw, that the place they were in served in the triple capacity of kitchen, parlour, and bedroom. Its furniture was suitably abundant. It consisted, on one side, of a dresser, over which were shelves filled with plates and dishes, which she supposed to be of pewter, but they had been so bedimmed by the quantities of flies that sat upon them, that she could not pronounce with certainty as to the metal they were made of. On the shelf that projected immediately next the dresser, was a number of delf and wooden bowls, of different dimensions, with horn spoons, &c. These, though arranged with apparent care, did not entirely conceal from view, the dirty nightcaps, and other articles, that were stuffed in behind. Opposite the fireplace were two beds, each enclosed in a sort of wooden closet, so firmly built as to exclude the entrance of a breath of air, except in front, where were small folding doors, which were now open, and exhibited a quantity of yarn hung up in bunches, affording proof of the goodwife's husbandry. The portable furniture, as chairs, tables, &c., were all, though clumsy, of good materials; so that Mrs Mason thought the place wanted nothing but a little attention to neatness, and some more light, to render it tolerably comfortable. When the tea was about to be made, Mrs MacClarty stepped to a huge Dutch press, and having, with some difficulty, opened the leaves, took from a store of nice linen, which it presented to their view, a fine damask napkin, of which she begged her to make use. "You have a noble stock of linen, cousin," said Mrs Mason. "Few farmers houses in England could produce the like; but I think this is rather too fine for common use." "For common use!" cried Mrs MacClarty, "na, na, we're no sic fools as put our napery to use! I have a dizen table-claiths in that press thirty years old, that were never laid upon a table. They are a' o' my mother's spinning. I have nine o' my ain makin' forby, that never saw the sun but at the bookin washing. Ye needna be telling us of England!" "It is no doubt a good thing," said Mrs Mason, "to have a stock of goods of any kind, provided one has a prospect of turning them to account, but I confess I think the labour unprofitably employed, which during thirty years is to produce no advantage, and that linen of an inferior quality would be preferable, as it would certainly be more useful. A towel of nice clean huck-a-back would wipe a cup as well, and better, than a damask napkin." "Towels!" cried Mrs MacClarty, "na, na, we manna pretend to towels; we just wipe up the things wi what comes in the gait." On saying this, the good woman, to show how exactly she practised what she spoke, pulled out from between the seed tub, and her husband's dirty shoes, (which stood beneath the bench by the fire side), a long blackened rag, and with it rubbed one of the pewter plates, with which she stepped into the closet for a roll of butter.' p. 143-146.

The butter was full of hairs: and poor Mrs Mason's room littered with new shorn wool, hung with cobwebs, and without a window that could be opened. Her morning adventures, however, are more characteristic of the people.

'She awoke late, and on perceiving, when about half dressed, that she had in her room neither water nor hand-bason to wash in, she threw on her dimity bed gown, and went out to the kitchen, to procure a supply of these necessary articles. She there found Meg and Jean; the former standing at the table, from which the porridge dishes seemed to have been just removed; the latter killing flies at the window. Mrs Mason addressed herself to Meg, and after a courteous good-morrow, asked her where she should find a hand-bason? "I dinna ken," said Meg, drawing her finger through the milk that had been spilled upon the table. "Where is your mother?" asked Mrs Mason. "I dinna ken," returned Meg, continuing to dabble her hands through the remaining fragments of the feast. "If you are going to clean that table," said Mrs Mason, "you will give yourself more work than you need, by daubing it all over with the porridge; bring your cloth, and I shall show you how I learned to clean our tables when I was a girl like you." Meg continued to make lines with her fore finger. "Come," said Mrs Mason, "shall I teach you?" "Na," said Meg, "I sal dight nane o't. I'm gain' to the schul." "But that need not hinder you to wipe up the table before you go," said Mrs Mason. "You might have cleaned it up as bright as a looking-glass, in the time that you have spent in spattering it, and dirtying your fingers. Would it not be pleasanter for you to make it clean, than to leave it dirty?" "I'll no be at the fash," returned Meg, making off to the door as she spoke. Before she got out, she was met by her mother, who, on seeing her, exclaimed: "Are ye no awa yet bairns! I never saw the like. Sic a fight to get you to the schul. Nae wonner ye learn little, whan you'r at it. Gae awa like good bairns, for theres nae schul in the morn ye ken, its the fair day." Meg set off after some farther parley; but Jean continued to catch the flies at the window, taking no notice of her mother's exhortations, though again repeated in pretty nearly the same terms. "Dear me," said the mother, "what's the matter wi' the bairn! what for winna ye gang, when Meg's gane? Rin, and ye'll be after her or she wins to the end o' the loan." "I'm no ga'an the day," says Jean, turning away her face. "And wharfor are no ye ga'an, my dear?" says her mother. "Cause I hinna gotten my questions," replied Jean. "O, but ye may gang for a' that," said her mother; "the maister will no be angry. Gang, like a gude bairn." "Na," said Jean, "but he will be angry, for I did no get it the last time either."

'"And wharfor did na ye get it, my dear," said Mrs MacClarty in a soothing tone. "Cause 'twas unco kittle, and *I cou'd no be fashed;*" replied the hopeful girl, catching as she spoke another handful of flies. p. 164-167.

'Mrs Mason then makes some moral observations on disobedience, and renews her application for the means of ablution.

'"Dear me," replied Mrs MacClarty, "I'm sure you're weel eneugh. Your hands ha' nae need of washing, I trow. Ye ne'er do a turn to file them."

'"You can't surely be in earnest," replied Mrs Mason. "Do you think I could sit down to breakfast with unwashed hands? I never heard of such a thing, and never saw it done in my life." "I see nae gude o' sic nicety," returned her friend, "but its easy to gie ye water eneugh, though I'm sure I dinna ken what to put it in, unless ye tak ane o the porridge plates: or may be the calf's luggie may do better, for it 'ill gie you enough o' room." "Your own bason will do better than either," said Mrs Mason. "Give me the loan of it for this morning, and I shall return it immediately, as you must doubtless often want it through the day." "Na, na," returned Mrs MacClarty, "I dinna fash wi' sae mony fykes. There's ay water standing in some thing or others for ane to ca their hands through when they're blacket. The gudeman indeed is a wee conceity like yourself, an' he coft a brown bason for his shaving in on Saturdays, but it's in use a' the week haddin' milk, or I'm sure ye'd be welcome to it. I sal see an' get it ready for you the morn." p. 170, 171.

'These scenes are little more than ludicrous. The mismanagement of these good people, however, soon produces effects more seriously distressing; and these, too, are drawn by Mrs Hamilton with great effect and discrimination. Hearing a violent noise of quarrelling, Mrs Mason advances to inquire into the cause of it.

'The voices stopped, and proceeding, she saw the farmer hastily unsaddling a horse; and the son at the same moment issuing from the door, but pulled back by his mother, who held the skirt of his coat, saying, "I tell ye, Sandie, ye manna gang to anger your father." "But I sal gang," cried Sandie, in a sullen tone. "I winna be hindered. I sal gang, I tell ye, whether my father likes or no." "Ye may gang, ye door loon," says the father, "but if ye do, ye sal repent it as lang as ye live." "Hoot na," returned the mother, "ye'll forgie' him, and ye had as weel let him gang, for ye see he winna be hindered!" "Where is the young man for going to?"asked Mrs Mason. "Where sud he be for gain' to, but to the fair?" returned the mother; "it's only natural. But our gudeman's unco particular, and never lets the lads get ony daffin." "Daffin!" cried the farmer; "is Druckenness daffin? Did na he gang last year, and come hame as drunk as a beast? And ye wad have him tak the brown mare too, without ever spearing my leave! saddled and bridled too, forsooth, like ony gentleman in the land! But ye sal baith repent it: I tell ye, ye'se repent it." "O, I did na ken o the mare," said the too easy mother. "But is it possible," said Mrs Mason, addressing herself to the young man, "is it possible that you should think of going to any place, in direct opposition to your father's will? I thought you would have been better acquainted with your duty, than to break the commands of God, by treating your parents in such a manner." "I am sure he has been weel taught," said the mother; "but I kenna how it is, our bairns never mind a word we say!" "But he will mind you," said Mrs Mason, "and set a better example of obedience to his brothers and sisters, than he is now doing. Come, I must reconcile all parties. Will you not give me your hand?" "I'll no' stay frae the fair for naebody," said the sullen youth, endeavouring to pass; "a' the folk in the Glen are gain', and I'll gang too, say what ye wull." Mrs Mason scarcely believed it possible that he could be so very hardy, until she saw him set off with sullen and determined step, followed by his mother's

eye, who, on seeing him depart, exclaimed, "Hegh me! ye're
an unco laddie."

'The farmer appeared to feel more deeply, but he said
nothing. Grasping the mane of the mare, he turned to lead
her down the road to his fields, and had advanced a few
steps, when his wife called after him, to enquire what he
was going to do with the saddle, which he carried on his
shoulders? "Do wi' it!" repeated he, "I have naething to do
wi' it!" Then dashing it on the ground, he proceeded with
quickened pace down the steep. "Wae's me!" said Mrs
MacClarty, "the gudeman taks Sandie's doorness mickle to
heart!"' p. 195-198,

The dying scene of the worthy rustic, is described with
great feeling and effect, and at the same time with a scrupu-
lous attention to the peculiarities of national habits. The
funeral is equally good. The crowd of sincere mourners
feeding the house and the barn – the hoary headed elders
bearing the corpse, and the decent farmers coming in from
a distance to follow it to the grave. But it is more to our
purpose, to trace the effects of Mrs Mason's exertions to
overcome rooted prejudices.

'"Aye!" exclaimed the wife of auld John Smith, who happened to visit the widow the first evening she was able to
sit up to tea, "aye, alake! it's weel seen, that whar there's
new lairds there's new laws. But how can your woman and
your bairns put up wi' a' this fashery?" "I kenna, truly,"
replied the widow, "but Mrs Mason has just sic a way wi'
them, she gars them do ony thing she likes. Ye may think it
is an eery thing to me, to see my poor bairns submitting
that way to pleasure a strainger in a' her nonsense." "An
eery thing, indeed!" said Mrs Smith; "gif ye had but seen
how she gard your dochter Meg clean out the kirn! outside
and inside! ye wad hae been wae for the poor lassie. I trow,
said I, Meg, it wad ha' been lang before your mither had
set you to sic a turn? Aye, says she, we have new gaits now,
and she looket up and leugh." "New gaits, I trow!" cried
Sandy Johnstone's mother, who had just taken her place at
the tea table; "I ne'er kend gude come o' new gaits a' my
days. There was Tibby Bell, at the head o' the Glen, she fell
to cleaning her kirn ae day, and the very first kirning after,
her butter was burstet, and gude for naething. I am sure it
gangs to my heart to see your wark sae managed. It was but

the day before yesterday, that I cam upon madam, as she was haddin' the strainer, as she called it, to Grizzy, desiring her a' the time she poured the milk, to beware of letting in ane o' the cow's hairs that were on her goon. Hoot! says I, cows' hairs are canny, they'll never choak ye." "The fewer of them that are in the butter the better!" says she. "Twa or three hairs are better than the blink o' an ill ee," says I. "The best charm against witchcraft is cleanliness," says she. "I doubt it muckle," says I, "auld ways are aye the best!" "Weel done!" cried Mrs Smith. "I trow ye gae her a screed o' your mind!" p. 260-262.

'We cannot afford to console our readers with the counter-part to this picture, in the history of Mrs Mason's more successful efforts in the cottage of the schoolmaster. We give only the final result of them. Poor Mrs MacClarty per-sisted in deriding her newfangled whimsies, and omitted no opportunity of railing at the schoolmaster's wife, who she said –

' "was now sae saucy as to pretend that they cou'd na sit down in comfort in a house that was na' clean soopet." She for a time found many among the neighbours who readily acquiesced in her opinions, and joined in her expres-sions of contempt; but by degrees the strength of her party visibly declined. Those who had their children at school were so sensible of the rapid improvement that had been made in their tempers and manners, as well as in their learn-ing, that they could not help feeling some gratitude to their instructors; and Mrs Mason having instructed the girls in needle-work, without any additional charge, added con-siderably to their sense of obligation. Even the old women, who during the first summer had most bitterly exclaimed against the pride of innovation, were by mid-winter inclined to alter their tone. How far the flannel waistcoats and petti-coats distributed among them, contributed to this change of sentiment, cannot be positively ascertained; but certain it is, that as the people were coming from church the first fine day of the following spring, all stopped a few moments before the school-house, to inhale the fragrance of the sweet-brier, and to admire the beauty of the crocuses, prim-roses, and violets, which embroidered the borders of the grass-plot. Mrs MacClarty, who, in great disdain, asked auld John Smith's wife "what a' the folks were glowering

at?" received for answer, that they were "leuking at the
bonniest sight in a' the town," pointing at the same time to
the spot. – "Eh!" returned Mrs MacClarty, "I wonder what
the warld will come to at last, since naething can serve the
pride o' William Morison, but to hae a flower garden whar'
gude Mr Brown's middenstead stood sappy for mony a
day! he's a better man than will ever stand on William
Morison's shanks." "The flowers are a hantel bonnier than
the midden tho', and smell a hantel sweeter too, I trow,"
returned Mrs Smith. This striking indication of a change of
sentiment in the most sturdy stickler for the *gude auld gaits*,
foreboded the improvements that were speedily to take
place in the village of Glenburnie. The carts, which used
formerly to be stuck up on end before every door, were
now placed in wattled sheds attached to the gable end of
the dwelling, and which were rendered ornamental from
their coverings of honey-suckle or ivy. The bright and clear
glass of the windows, was seen to advantage peeping
through the foliage of the rose-trees, and other flowering
shrubs, that were trimly nailed against the walls. The gardens on the other side were kept with equal care. There the
pot-herb flourished. There the goodly rows of bee-hives
evinced the effects of the additional nourishment afforded
their inhabitants, and shewed that the flowers were of other
use besides regaling the sight or smell.' p. 394-398.

It would be extravagant to hope, that the mere perusal
of this, or any other narrative, should effect a reformation
which it truly represented as having been so laborious. But
a strong current of improvement runs at present through
all Scotland, and a much smaller impulse than would once
have been necessary, will now throw the peasantry within
the sphere of its action. Besides, *our* cottagers are reading
and reasoning animals; and are more likely perhaps to be
moved from their old habits by hints and suggestions which
they themselves may glean up from a book, than by the
more officious and insulting interference of a living reformer. It does not appear to us altogether visionary, therefore, to expect that some good may actually be done by
the circulation of such a work as this among the lower
classes of society; and therefore, we earnestly recommend it
to Mrs Hamilton to take measures for facilitating its admission into their economical circles. We have not taken any

notice of the story of Mrs Mollins, because we do not think
it is nearly equal in merit and originality to the picture of
the cottagers; and with regard to Mrs Mason's own history,
we think it is rather long and languid, and would be much
improved by abridgment. We would also take the liberty to
hint, that this part of the performance rather seems calculated to encourage a feeling of too great servility in the lower ranks, and to be liable, on this account, to a censure
which applies with particular force to Miss Hannah More's
productions in the Cheap Repository. The poor are quite
apt enough already to pay at least a due homage to wealth
and station; and we really do not think it particularly necessary to inculcate these vassal feelings in Scotland.

Gloss of Hamilton's Scots Terms

Note on the gloss: The meanings given here are solely those that Hamilton employs in the novel. If a word has another meaning in Scots (for example "fou," which would usually mean "drunk," not "full"), I have not included it.

A':	One, every, all
Ae:	One, a
Aff:	Off
Ahint:	Behind
Airt:	Art, cunning
Ajee:	Crooked
Alace / Alake:	Alas / Alack
Ane:	One
Anes:	Once
Auld:	Old
Aw:	All
Ay(e):	Always or yes
Bairn:	Child
Baith:	Both
Bicker:	A wooden bowl
Blacket:	Dirtied
Bluidy:	Bloody
Bonnier:	Prettier, more attractive
Bookin:	A type of lye used to bleach linen
Brig:	Bridge
Burds /Buird:	Boards, floor
Burstet:	Spoiled
But:	Outside or towards the outside of a building
Ca' the kirn:	Work the churn
Ca:	Dip (in water)
Canna:	Cannot
Canny:	Prudent, wise, good
Cauld:	Cold
Clarty / Clarted:	Dirty, dirtied
Cleek:	Hook or latch
Coft:	Bought

Conceity:	Vain
Coup / Couppet:	Overturn(ed), fell
Cousine / Cusine:	Cousin
Craft:	Croft; piece of land
Dad:	Dab; a little bit
Daffin:	Amusement; pleasure
Dee:	Die
Dight:	To wipe or clean
Dinna:	Do not
Dochter:	Daughter
Door / Doorness:	Dour; dourness
Eery:	Strange, uncomfortable
Eneugh:	Enough
E'now:	Enough
Fash /Fashed/ Fashious:	Trouble(d); bother(ed) / troublesome
Fause:	False
File:	Dirty, foul
For(e)by(e):	Besides
Fou:	Full
Frae:	From
Fykes:	Fidgets, fusses
Gait:	Way or manner
Gang, Gaed, Gaen, Gane:	Go, went, gone
Gar, Gard:	Make, make
Geed, Gi'ed:	Gave
Gif:	If
Glowering:	Looking, staring (without the connotation of sullenness)
Goon:	Gown
Gude:	Good
Gudeman:	Husband
Hadden', Haddin':	Holding, handing
Hade:	Hid
Haet:	Have it
Haff-croon:	Half crown; two and a half shillings
Hantel:	A great many
Hindert:	Stopped, prevented
Hinna:	Have not
Hoot:	An exclamation of mild protest or annoyance

Houp:	Hope
Ilka:	Each, Each one
Ill ee:	The evil eye
Ingle:	Hearth or fireside
Kail:	Cabbage or kale
Ken, kenna, kent:	Know, do not know, knew
Kick-shaws:	Fancy or delicate dishes
Kirk:	Church
Kirn:	Churn
Kittle / Kittlest:	Troublesome, most difficult
Kye:	Cows
Lave, the Lave:	Remnant or remainder
Leugh:	Laughed
Leuking:	Looking
Listet:	Enlisted (in the army)
Loan:	A strip of green or pasture land
Loon:	A boy or lad
Luggie:	A small basin or dish
Mair, Mare:	More
Maist:	Most
Manna:	Must not
Maun:	Must
Mickle / Muckle:	Much, a great deal, large
Middenstead:	Dunghill
Mony:	Many
Mutches:	Linen or muslin caps
Na:	Not, no
Neeber:	Neighbour
Noo:	Now
O't:	Of it
Owre:	Too, over
Ouk:	A week
Parritch:	Porridge
Pit mirk:	Fully dark
Poo'er:	Power
Puir:	Poor
Red up:	Tidied, cleared up
Rouped:	Auctioned
Rute:	Root
Sae:	So
Sal:	Shall
Sappy:	Wet

Schul, Schule:	School
Screed:	Harangue; a long lecture
Shivers:	Slivers, shards
Sic:	Such
Siller:	Money
Skeel:	Skill, ability
Slaistery:	Mess, dirty liquid
Slaked:	Smeared or streaked
Sleepit:	Slept
Soger:	Soldier
Soond:	Sound
Soopit / Soopin:	Swept / sweeping
Sough:	Murmur or whisper
Sowens:	A type of porridge made from husks of oats
Spearing:	Asking
Speeling:	Climbing
Sud / Sudna:	Should / Should not
Syne:	Since, ago
Sythe:	Sieve; the act of sieving or straining
Tak:	Take
The day:	Today
Tint:	Lost
Toon:	Town
Trow:	Believe, think
Twa:	Two
Unco:	Strange, unfamiliar, extremely
War:	Worse or were
Weel:	Well
Wimpling:	Twisting or winding
Winna:	Will not
Wonner:	Wonder
Woo':	Wool
Wook:	Week
Yearning:	Rennet
Yet:	Gate

Notes on *The Cottagers of Glenburnie*

p.47 Skaith of Scotland "Scotland's Scaith, or, The History of Will and Jean," a poem by Hector Macneill (1746-1818) first published in 1795, which was very popular in its day. It is a ballad about a young couple ruined by the man's growing taste for liquor; its heavy-handed moral is that "O' a' the ills poor Caledonia / E'er yet pree'd [experienced], or e'er will taste [. . .] Whisky's ill will skaith [harm] her maist!"

p.47 "Cheap Repository" A collection of moral tales, in prose and verse, written for a working-class readership by Hannah More (1745-1833) and others. They were published between 1795 and 1798 and promoted a conservative, more or less evangelical social agenda.

p.47 *Soi-disant* Self-proclaimed.

p.47 mode of criticism now in vogue Hamilton presumably has in mind, above all, *The Edinburgh Review*, founded in 1802, and which, under the editorship of Francis Jeffrey (1773-1850), quickly became notorious for the harshness of its reviews. Some of the best-known writers of the day – including Wordsworth, Coleridge, Scott, and Byron – were the subjects of attacks in *The Edinburgh Review*, but Hamilton herself was reviewed very positively. (See the appendix for Jeffrey's review of *Glenburnie*.) *The British Critic*, in a generally favourable notice, singles out this passage for comment, complaining about the "two peevish pages of remarks" Hamilton makes on the sort of "friendly criticism" that she has received from them in the past – then provides, in a note, a reference to the article to which it assumes she is objecting. (*The British Critic*, vol. 32 [Aug. 1808], 118.)

p.49 National happiness This was a view that was argued strongly in other literature of the day; Christian Johnstone's *Clan-Albin* (1815), for example, features a lecture on the subject by the novel's wise matriarch, Lady Augusta.

p.51 Englished That is, in an English manner, as opposed to speaking in Scots or with a Scottish accent.

p.51 as if she had been a lady Owning one's own carriage was a status symbol; a hack was a hired carriage. By riding "double," or behind someone else on a horse, Mrs Mason indicates not only her poverty but also her lack of any claims to social status.

p.51 respectful salute A greeting, usually a kiss.

p.52 sensible That is, in a manner apparent to the senses.

p.53 nursery of folly and impertinence A boarding school. Debates about boarding-school education for girls were common in women's writing of this period. The schools were attacked both by early feminists, including Mary Wollstonecraft (1759-1797), and by more conservative writers on education such as Hannah More, on the grounds that they taught girls little of use and focused on the acquisition of decorative accomplishments. They were also assumed to give middle-class girls an inappropriate taste for upper-class luxury and frivolity.

p.56 cousin-german First cousin.

Chapters II and III Hamilton's use of quotation marks has been modernised here for clarity.

p.60 meet with hardships In *Elementary Principles of Education*, Hamilton vigorously disputes the idea that children should be indulged while young as they will have to endure hard work when older; her argument is that such indulgence makes later self-control difficult or impossible (see page 228 in this edition). She also returns to this point later in *Glenburnie*, when Mrs MacClarty uses it to justify her indulgence of her children (pages 106-107).

p.61 half a-crown Two and a half shillings.

p.61 earnest Payment in advance.

p.62 I know that my Redeemer liveth Job 19: 25. This is also the text of one of the more famous arias in Handel's *Messiah*.

p.68 press-bed A bed that folds away into a closet or cupboard when not in use.

p.71 nothing for it but to frighten him The dangers posed to children by servants' attempts to scare them into obedience concerned a number of educational writers at this time, including Maria Edgeworth (1768-1849) and Mary Wollstonecraft; Hamilton refers readers of *Elementary Principles of Education* to Edgeworth's comments in *Practical Education* (1800) on mismanagement of children by servants.

p.74 Mrs Mason "Mrs" (as an abbreviation for "Mistress") was a courtesy address used at the time for both married and older unmarried women. At this point, Betty Mason would be unusually young to be addressed in this way, so the use of the title may be an indication of Jenny's attempt to be especially formal.

p.76 skreen Hamilton's original spelling

p.77 scarlet An expensive red cloth.

p.80 Merriton Hamilton spelled this word "Meriton" or "Merriton"; I have followed her usage throughout.

p.83 Lady Harriot Harriet (as the name is always spelled afterwards) is here named as the eldest child, although in the account of the marriage of Charlotte and Sir William Bandon that follows a few pages later, Harriet is mentioned in terms suggesting that she is the younger sister. Hamilton apparently returned to the original birth-order of the Long-lands children by the end of the novel when the elder, married daughter becomes, again, Lady Harriet Bandon. Hamilton's apparent indifference about keeping straight the names of the Earl's daughters implies her relative lack of interest in this plot.

p.85 settee bed A day-bed; a bed that can double as a settee by day.

p.92 her imagination was so warmed The idea that re-ligious enthusiasm is the result of an undisciplined imagin-ation, or of a state of mind in which the imagination has too few solid ideas on which to work, is one to which Hamilton returns later in the book, in the discussion between Mrs Mason and Mr Gourlay. It was also a subject that she thought worth exploring in much greater detail in the third and fifth essays in *A Series of Popular Essays.*

p.92 reprobation The state of being cast off by God.

p.99 her mind got a wrong bias from the first The discus-sion that follows sketches out, in brief, the basic thesis argued in *Letters on the Elementary Principles of Education.*

p.100 Irish car An open vehicle for the conveyance of passengers.

p.104 Rang the blest summons James Grahame, *The Sabbath* (1804), line 434.

p.105 sash window A window that opens by lifting the sash, or frame.

p.107 Pictish ancestors Hamilton is probably alluding to the work of James Burnett, Lord Monboddo (1714-1799), whose proto-evolutionary arguments in *The Origin and Progress of Man and Language* (6 vols, 1773-92), were mocked by many of his contemporaries, including Samuel Johnson. There was discussion among antiquarians in the later eighteenth century of the Picts and their habit of painting their bodies; see, for example, Hugh Blair's treatment of the subject in his much-reprinted *Dissertation on the Poems of Ossian* (1763) or John Macpherson's *Critical Dissertaions . . . on the Ancient Caledonians* (1768).

p.108 delf That is, Delft ware, decorative earthernware made in Holland.

pp.108-109 damask, huckaback Huckaback is a coarse cotton, as opposed to damask, which is a much finer woven cloth.

p.112 ticken Ticking; a type of cotton bed covering.

p.113 suthern wood Southernwood; a medicinal herb.

p.117 dimity A heavy cotton.

p.120 vallence Valance; drapery covering space between the bottom of a bed and the floor.

p.124 Train up a child Proverbs 22: 6.

p.126 honour thy father and thy mother The fifth commandment; Exodus 20: 12.

p.127 Jenny a pet name for Jean.

p.129 a pretender to superior taste The ideas about taste and morality explored in this passage are a précis of the concepts explored in the tenth letter of the second volume of *Elementary Education*, which included in this edition. Hamilton returns to this idea at the beginning of Chapter 17; she also develops her argument about the links between a "proper" taste – as opposed to mere connoisseurship – and religious feeling in Essay 3 of *A Series of Popular Essays*.

p.129 The eye is never satisfied Ecclesiastes 1: 8.

p.135n Horne Tooke John Horne Tooke (1736-1812) was a radical philosopher, one of the twelve men charged but acquitted in the famous treason trials of 1794. His *Diversions of Purley* (1786; second part 1805) a notoriously intricate study of grammar and etymology, features a twenty-five page (in the 1798 edition) discussion of the word "but". In the Scottish sense that Hamilton is using the term, it means the outer part of a house.

p.135 Sandy/Sandie the variant spellings of this name follow Hamilton's usage.

p.136 lashed like a dog Compare Scott's short story "The Highland Widow," first published in *Chronicles of the Canongate* (1827), in which the disgrace of English military punishments is so overwhelming to the Highland characters that it precipitates tragedy.

p.139 Lammas fair A traditional summer fair at the beginning of the harvest; Lammas was the first of August.

p.143 law of works Religious denominations influenced by Calvinism – including Scottish Presbyterianism – tended to be suspicious of the idea of salvation by works, or good deeds, insisting instead upon the transcendent importance of absolute faith in God. Mrs Mason's argument here is that the two can't be separated: proper faith manifests itself in charitable action.

p.143 Presenter A church official.

p.148 valley of the shadow . . . shall be lost See Psalms 23: 4 and Romans 9: 33.

p.149 gray hairs Genesis 42: 38.

p.149 heart to serve . . . walk in his ways Phrases used at several points in the Bible; see, for example, 2 Maccabees 1: 3, several verses in 1 Kings, and several verses in Deuteronomy. The deathbed speeches of Mr MacClarty, like exhortations of the minister and the serious reflections by Mrs Mason in the next chapter, are infused with biblical phraseology.

p.152 seditious import The chapter title alludes to the political debates of the 1790s and to the assumption by conservatives such as Hannah More that liberty and equality were more or less inherently dangerous concepts.

p.154 worldly cares Implicitly continuing the contrast with the Earl, who dies without providing properly either for Mrs Mason or his daughters, who are stinted of money until their youngest brother comes of age.

p.154 Candlemas February 2; like Lammas, one of the traditional Scottish quarter days, which were often used to mark the beginnings or endings of leases.

p.164 Chapter XIV this chapter has no title.

p.166 seven shillings The sum emphasizes both Mrs Mason's relative poverty and her open-handedness: she is paying the Morisons £18 4s a year out of a total income of £30.

p.168 gray hairs See note to p. 149.

p.169 as she has brewed Proverbial: she has to live with the consequences.

p.174 were married So-called "drapery misses," who bought fashionable clothes on credit in order to attract a rich husband who would then have to pay the bill were popular targets of satire in early nineteenth-century literature. Byron, for example, mocks the phenomenon in *Don Juan* (XI. 49; first published 1823).

p.176 Perth to Blair part of what was already a standard route for Highland tours; travellers made an arc across the lower Highlands, going from Glasgow to Edinburgh (or vice versa) via Loch Lomond, Callandar and the Trossachs, and the Taymouth area.

p.177 laws of this country Unlike English law, which after 1754 required couples either to obtain a special license or to post banns before going through a formal marriage ceremony, Scottish law recognized as legally binding any marriage in which a man and a woman declared themselves married before witnesses. (Hence its popularity in the later eighteenth and nineteenth centuries as a destination for eloping couples.) The chapter title points towards the distinction that Mr Stewart implies between a legal (but disreputable) marriage by declaration and the formal wedding ceremony that a virtuous woman would presumably seek. Mr Stewart's evident distaste for the legal status of marriage in Scotland was echoed by other voices throughout the century; one Sir John Carr, who visited Scotland in 1807, reported solemnly that Englishmen preferred not to attend the University of Edinburgh because of "the extraordinarily facility with which, in Scotland, the matrimonial yoke may, by very little stratagem, be imposed upon a young man" (*Caledonian Sketches, or a Tour through Scotland in 1807. New York*, 1809, 68). As late as 1870, the Victorian novelist Wilkie Collins published a thriller, *Man and Wife*, which attacked the Scottish marriage laws.

p.179 rose fever According to the OED, which identifies it as American usage, a form of hay fever.

p.180 close hanks Miser.

p.184 sat down to dinner The shift of the fashionable dining hour from mid afternoon to early evening was a subject of considerable comment in the later eighteenth century. In 1793, for example, William Creech noted, as one of a number of symptoms of the increased taste for luxury in Edinburgh life, that the dinner hour had moved from around two o'clock in 1763 to around four or five o'clock by 1783. (*Letters, Addressed to Sir John Sinclair, Bart. Respecting the Mode of Living, Arts, Commerce, Literature, Manners, &c. of Edinburgh, in 1763, And Since that Period.* Edinburgh, 1793, 32.)

p.187 cockpit That is, a place for cock fighting.

p.187 court calendar A list of aristocratic British families.

p.188 quizzing, or humming "Quizzing" and "humming" would involve a more or less teasing attempt to mislead a naïve or gullible listener with raillery or an invented story.

p.191 broken milliner A dressmaker who went bankrupt.

p.193 blazing ingle Allan Ramsay, *The Gentle Shepherd* (1725), I.ii.180.

p.194 the righteous man Psalm 37: 25.

p.194 three simple rules These "rules" were repeated and cited approvingly by a number of other writers at the time. Beatrice Grant, for example, made "the succinct, but excellent maxims in the Cottagers of Glenburnie" the basis of the conduct of the exemplary heroine of a didactic tale in her *Sketches of Intellectual Education, and Hints on Domestic Economy, Addressed to Inexperienced Mothers.* (2 vols. Inverness, 1812, 2: 133). Likewise, Ann Taylor (in *Practical Hints to Young Females* [1815]) cited these rules but attributed them to a manual of Lancaster's teaching methods.

p.195 holiday "Holiday" is here used in the original sense of "holy day."

p.195 17s in the pound That is, Morison still owes three shillings for every pound that he was originally unable to repay.

p.196 now the hurly burly's done *Macbeth*, I.1.3

p.196 *hic, hæc, hoc* The declension of the Latin demonstrative adjective meaning "this": it was one of the basic exercises in Latin primers.

p.198 point out the source of bigotry This, of course, is exactly what Hamilton sets out to do in her own voice in Letter X, volume 2, of *Elementary Principles* and (at considerably greater length) in the fifth essay in *A Series of Popular Essays.*

p.202 mere sound, without the sense Hamilton develops her reasons for her hostility to rote memorization of the Bible at much greater length in *Hints Addressed to the Patrons and Directors of Schools.*

p.203 sense of justice . . . injudicious management of parents This is the argument that underlies the chapters on benevolence (reprinted in this edition) in the first volume of *Elementary Principles.*

p.204n David Manson Hamilton's elder sister Katherine attended the school kept by David Manson (1726-1792) in Belfast. The book referred to here is *A New Pocket Dictionary; or, English Expositor* (1762). Joseph Lancaster (1778-1838), along with Andrew Bell (1753-1832), was one of the most important educational reformers of the day. Although their emphasis was slightly different, both Lancaster and Bell argued for a system by which elder or more advanced pupils taught lessons to more junior students, thereby both enabling a single schoolmaster to take on a large number of students and reinforcing the lessons in the minds of the student-teachers. Hamilton in fact had a number of reservations about this system – relying as it often did on rote – and in *Hints Addressed to the Patrons and Directors of Schools* recommended instead (or in addition) the approach of the Swiss educator Johann Heinrich Pestalozzi (1746-1827).

p.206 *witness to the truth* John 18: 37.

p.206 heritors The local landowners, who would have the right to appoint the schoolmaster.

p.206 Lady Harriet Bandon see note to p. 83.

p.210 stupidity Hamilton developed at much greater length this argument about the neglect of working-class girls' intellectual capacities in the first of her *Series of Popular Essays.*

p.215 flowering muslin That is, embroidering designs on muslin for women's clothing.

p.216 Extract of a Letter This letter started appearing as an appendix to *The Cottagers of Glenburnie* within two years of publication. There is no indication as to authorship in the editions in which it is included, but since it appeared during Hamilton's lifetime, it can be assumed that she approved its inclusion, even if she were not the author.

p.216 *Paris mud* A fashionable name for a shade of brown.

p.217 *Lichen Geographicus* The Linnaean name for a type of northern lichen.

p.218 tea-caddie A small box, usually with a lock, for holding tea leaves, which were an expensive commodity at the time.

Notes on *Letters on the Elementary Principles of Education*

p.224 William Ross William Ross, *The Teacher's Manual of Method; or the General Principles of Teaching and School-Keeping*. London, 1858, 189.

p.225-226 ancient Sparta According to the code of laws attributed to Lycurgus (c. 7th century B.C.) – the legislator mentioned below – sickly or disabled Spartan infants were to be exposed. There is scholarly dispute about whether or not Lycurgus actually existed.

p.226 doctrine of association Hamilton is here drawing on John Locke's arguments about the association of ideas, which she explains in detail in earlier letters.

p.227 painful sensations This idea was central to eighteenth-century moral and aesthetic theory; Edmund Burke, for example, uses it as one of the foundations of his arguments about the effect of the sublime.

p.229 everlasting happiness David Hartley, *Observations on Man, his Frame, his Duty, and his Expectations*. 1749. London, 1791, 219.

p.229 refined species of self-love The idea that self-love is the foundation of all affections was commonplace among the writers of the earlier eighteenth century; Alexander Pope, for one, provided a succinct and much-quoted summary of this concept in *An Essay on Man* (1733-34): "self-love and social are the same." The *Essay* was shaped by the thought of Pope's friend Lord Bolingbroke, who stated flatly that "Self-love made that of parents and children" [*Works*. 5 vols. London, 1777, 5: 54]). A number of the philosophers Hamilton most admired, including Dugald Stewart and Thomas Reid, disputed the idea that parental affections were selfish in their origins; see, for example, Reid's essay "Of the Particular Benevolent Affections" (Essay III, part II, chapter iv of *Essays on the Active Powers of Man* [Edinburgh 1785]), and Stewart's *Philosophy of the Active and Moral Powers of Man* [1828], in which he attacks the idea that the "benevolent affections" are a form of "self-love" (Cambridge, 1851, 59).

p.231 Pharoah's dream Genesis 41.

p.231n Zeluco *Zeluco* (1789), by the Scottish physician John Moore, was one of the most popular novels of the era. The novel traces the life of eponymous anti-hero, who is spoiled by his mother (whom in turn he neglects and mistreats until she dies broken-hearted); as an adult, he is both cruel to others and miserably unsatisfied with his own life.

p.233n Lord Kames Hamilton was using the sixth edition of *Elements of Criticism* (1785); the comment appears in Part II of Chaper 2, "Emotions and Passions as Pleasant and Painful, Agreeable and Disagreeable."

p.234 . . . clouds away James Thomson, *The Seasons* (1735), *Summer* 47-50.

p.234 the Polypus an octopus or squid.

p.237 altereth not Daniel 6: 12.

p.240 their *rights* Another allusion to the language of the Jacobin and anti-Jacobin political debates of the 1790s. Conservatives tended to be deeply suspicious of any talk of "rights," making Hamilton's use of the term a quiet move to bridge an ideological gap.

p.243 Ridicule is a sacred weapon According to Benger, Hamilton herself had been dangerously tempted in her younger days by her possession of "that quick sense of the ridiculous which often misleads its possessor" (1: 44).

p.244 These are the tares Matthew 13: 25.

p.244 "By far the greater part . . ." Dugald Stewart, *Elements of the Philosophy of the Human Mind.* 3 vols. London, 1792-1827, I: 30-31.

p.247 pride and prejudice The phrase is very common in eighteenth-century literature. Both Hamilton and Jane Austen might have taken it from Frances Burney's *Cecilia* (1783); it also appears in Robert Bage's *Hermsprong* (1796).

p.250 royal auditor Acts 24: 25. "The Apostle" is Paul, who was brought before Felix, the Roman procurator of Judea.

p.251n Ledyard and Park John Ledyard (1751-1789) was an American traveller who died in Cairo while on an African expedition sponsored by Sir Joseph Banks; Mungo Park (1771-1806) was a Scottish traveller who died while on his second journey into the interior of Africa. His

Travels in the Interior Districts of Africa (1799) was frequently reprinted in the early years of the nineteenth century, but only part of the passage that Hamilton cites here actually appears in his book (on page 263 in the second edition of 1799). She might have encountered the full passage in other travel books – it is printed in *Proceedings of the Association promoting the Discovery of the Interior Parts of Africa* (London, 1790), 53, and in John Leyden's *Historical and Philosophical Sketch of the Discoveries and Settlements of Europeans in Northern and Western Africa* (Edinburgh, 1799), 13-14. Thomas Gisborne also quotes this passage, citing the *Proceedings* as his source, in *An Enquiry into the Duties of the Female Sex* (London, 1798), 24.

p.252 believing wife 1 Corinthians 7: 13-14.

p.255n conduct of servants Compare Mary Wollstonecraft's worry that girls will acquire "nasty, or immodest habits [. . .] from ignorant servants" (*A Vindication of the Rights of Woman*, London, 1792, 287).

p.256 thousand decencies John Milton, *Paradise Lost* VIII. 611-12 (slightly misquoted).

p.256 sexual virtue Mary Wollstonecraft also attacks the idea that modesty is a "sexual virtue"; Hamilton had read Wollstonecraft and may here be deliberately quoting the title of the seventh chapter of the *Vindication*: "Modesty. – Comprehensively considered, and not as a sexual virtue".

p.259 venerable Reid Thomas Reid, *Essays on the Intellectual Powers of Man*. Edinburgh, 1785. Hamilton is merging separate passages that appear on pages 40 ("We take it for granted [. . .] set before his eyes"), 58 ("Another source of information [. . .] cause from the effect") and 58-59 ("Not only the actions [. . .] human understanding").

p.259 Mr Locke John Locke, *An Essay Concerning Human Understanding*. 1690. In *The Works of John Locke*. 9 vols. London, 1794, 1: 1.

p.261n Philosophy of the Human Mind Hamilton is quoting the first volume, published in 1792.

p.262 *nature of Angels* Hebrews 2: 16.

p.262 bury their talents Matthew 25: 14-28.

p.267 zenanas The women's quarters in East Indian households.

p.267 education to women so destined The argument

here is made as well, at greater length, in Hamilton's *Hindoo Rajah*.

p.267n Milton *Paradise Lost*, XI, 616-20; slightly misquoted.

p.270 To covet honour Shakespeare, *Henry V*, V.iv.3-4; slightly misquoted.

p.271 Doctor Akenside Mark Akenside, *Pleasures of the Imagination*, 1744. This was a blank verse poem in three books that remained popular throughout the eighteenth century.

p.273 Exhausted worlds From the prologue that Samuel Johnson wrote for Garrick's opening of the Drury-Lane playhouse (1747)

p.273 Kotzebue August von Kotzebue (1761-1819) was a German novelist and playwright whose plays were both popular and controversial in late eighteenth- and early nineteenth-century Britain. (He is probably best-known in British literary history for his offstage role in Jane Austen's *Mansfield Park*, in which an attempt to produce an amateur version of his *Lovers' Vows* causes havoc.) His memoir, *Sketch of the Life and Literary career of Augustus von Kotzebue*, was published in London in 1800, but the phrase that Hamilton quotes does not appear in it. Kotzebue does imply that his mother was responsible for cultivating his imagination, writing that "My tutors taught the parrot to prate, my mother taught the child to feel" (7). He also credits her with inspiring the taste for childhood reading that "called forth the first tears of sensibility" (8).

p.275 I have known a young person Possibly an allusion to Hamilton herself: Benger reprints some letters that the young Hamilton wrote to her brother Charles in which she chafes at her isolation from the world and comments that "the pleasures of imagination are [her] chief source of delight" (1: 97).

p.275n Reid *Essays on the Intellectual Powers of Man*, 429.

p.276-277 to the woes of imagination will sensibility be confined A complaint made by many writers of the day, including Mary Wollstonecraft. In the *Hindoo Rajah*, Hamilton contrasts the behaviour of two sisters, one of whom is a martyr to sensibility who flees in panic when confronted by an injured man; the other, less "sensitive," sister is able to offer practical help.

p.277n Alison Archibald Alison, *Essays on the Nature and Principles of Taste*. Dublin, 1790. The passage quoted in the next paragraph appears on page vii.

p.278 When Nature charms Samuel Rogers, *The Pleasures of Memory* (1792), Part 1, 19; slightly misquoted.

p.279 Adelin's lamp Aladdin's lamp, from the tale in the *Thousand and One Nights*. The spelling was corrected in editions published after Hamilton's death and may simply be a typographical error (although it was not corrected between the second and third editions). On the other hand, it might also suggest – as do the slightly misquoted lines of poetry – that Hamilton's references to imaginative literature tended to be made from memory.

p.281 a peal of thunder Compare Francis Jeffrey's later comment in his May 1811 *Edinburgh Review* article on Alison's *Essays*: "The noise of a cart rolling over the stones, is often mistaken for thunder; and as long as the mistake lasts, this very vulgar and insignificant noise is actually felt to be prodigiously sublime. It is so felt, however, it is perfectly plain, merely because it is associated with ideas of prodigious power and undefined danger; and the sublimity is destroyed the moment the association is dissolved. . . ." (Francis Jeffrey, *Contributions to the Edinburgh Review*. 4 vols in 1. Boston, 1854, 23).

p.284 St. Fond, Gilpin Barthélemy Faujas de St. Fond, *Travels in England, Scotland, and the Hebrides*. 2 vols. London, 1799; Wiilliam Gilpin, *Observations, Relative Chiefly to Picturesque Beauty*, 2 vols. London, 1789. Gilpin (1724-1804) was one of the most influential voices in the development of a taste for the picturesque in the later eighteenth century; he wrote a number of travel books (the one cited here is the one most focused on Scotland) as well as essays on the subject. St. Fond (1741-1819) was a French scientist, with a particular interest in geology, who travelled in Britain in the 1780s; his book includes vignettes of most of the important British scientists of the day.

Notes on *Memoirs of the Life of Agrippina, Wife of Germanicus*

p.290 one representative book "A Lady," *Roman History in the Way of Question and Answer*, London, 1825, 17; Sarah Trimmer, *A Description of a Set of Prints of Roman History*, London 1795, 41, 37.

p.291 Isaac D'Israeli Isaac D'Israeli, *Curiousities of Literature* 3 vols (London 1824), 3: 303.

p.293 Too classical for a female pen Benger 2: 58; the phrase appears in a letter to Dr S– dated 28 May 1803.

p.293 Two hundred pounds a volume Elizabeth Hamilton, unpublished letter to George Robinson, 29 November 1803. National Library of Scotland ms. 585, f. 49.

p.293 three octavo volumes Rev. of *Memoirs of the Life of Agrippina, The Scots Magazine*, vol 66 (Dec. 1804), 931, 935.

p.293 perspicacious and elegant Rev. of *Memoirs of the Life of Agrippina, The British Critic*, vol. 26 (July 1805), 33.

p.294 former work The reference, of course, is to *Letters on the Elementary Principles of Education*.

p.294 in order to the government of the passions The phrase appears as written in the original.

p.296 hope and fear . . . Slightly misquoted from John Home's play *Alonzo* (1773), I.i.255 57. Hamilton rarely quotes exactly in this preface, perhaps indicating that she is quoting from memory, but she is usually only a word or two off: the original, in this case, reads "But hope and fear alternate sway my mind." Dugald Stewart singled out this passage as an outstanding example of poetic allusion in the first volume of his *Elements of the Philosophy of the Human Mind* (1792; p. 303), a work that Hamilton had used extensively in her *Letters on the Elementary Principles of Education*.

p.298 peep and botanize Slightly misquoted from William Wordsworth, "A Poet's Epitaph."

p.299 built to themselves a name; perished with them Genesis XI.4 (slightly misquoted) and Psalms IX.6

p.300 invariably the same Compare Dugald Stewart's

statement "[t]hat the capacities of the human mind have been in all ages the same." He argues that the application of this idea "to the natural or *theoretical history* of society [. . .] is the peculiar glory of the latter half of the eighteenth century, and forms a characteristical feature in its philosophy" (*The Collected Works of Dugald Stewart*. 2 vols. Edinburgh 1854, 1: 69-70.) The passage is taken from *Dissertation Exhibitng the Progress of Metaphysical, Ethical, and Political Philosophy*, which first appeared in the 1815 *Encyclopedia Britannica*.

p.301 Tacitus Tacitus (c. 56- after 117) was one of the most important historians of the early imperial period of Rome. The main work to which Hamilton would be referring is *The Annals of Imperial Rome*, written sometime after 117, but she also drew heavily on *Germania*, which first appeared in 98. Hamilton used Arthur Murphy's four-volume translation of Tacitus, first published in 1793. Information on the tribes that she mentions – the Ubians and the Cattians – and the infighting of the chieftains Segestus and Arminius is mainly drawn from Tacitus.

p.301n Henry's Hist. of Britain Robert Henry, *The History of Great Britain, from the First Invasion of it by the Romans under Julius Caesar*. 6 vols. Edinburgh and London, 1774. 2: 378 (slightly misquoted). Henry is described on the title page as "One of the Ministers of Edinburgh," providing another example of Hamilton's tendency to situate her work in a strongly Scottish intellectual context.

p.302 outline of Roman history There were a number of abridgements and children's histories of Rome published during the eighteenth century; Hamilton was sceptical about the usefulness of such work, writing in *Elementary Education* that "the mere knowledge of dates and epochs, of the names of sovereigns, and the length of their successive reigns [. . .] will go a very little way towards intellectual improvement" (2: 225).

p.302 Suetonius Suetonius (c. 69-c. 122) wrote a gossipy, scandalous history of the first Roman emperors, *The Twelve Caesars*. The version that Hamilton used was *The Lives of the First Twelve Caesars*, translated by Alexander Thomson (London, 1796),

p.302 Dio Cassius, Paterculus Dio Cassius was a Roman historian whose life spanned the late second and early third century; his *Roman History* covers nearly a thousand years from the founding of Rome to 229. V[elleius] Paterculus was active in the early years of the first century and wrote a history from the beginnings of Rome up to the reign of Tiberius.

p.302 Mr Adams The reference is to Alexander Adam's *Roman Antiquities: or, an Account of the Manners and Customs of the Romans* (Edinburgh and London, 1792; second edition, enlarged). Adam was the rector of the High School in Edinburgh.

p.303n Currie James Currie, *The Works of Robert Burns; with an Account of his Life and Criticism on his Writing.* 4 vols. Baltimore, 1814, 1: 215; the book was first published in 1800. Hamilton sought out Currie's acquaintance, visiting him in Liverpool in 1802.

p.303n Johnson Samuel Johnson, preface to *A Dictionary of the English Language*, 2 vols, London 1755.

p.304 her son The infant Caligula.

p.304 late transactions A mutiny of the Roman troops, which was followed by riots sparked by the planned departure of the women from the camp. Hamilton, closely following Tacitus' *Annals*, describes both in detail in the previous chapter.

p.304 Ubiorum Oppidum That is, the town of the Ubians.

p.304 Agrippa The father of Agrippina, as indicated below; he was a favoured general and, eventually, the son-in-law of the Emperor Augustus.

p.305n German manners Hamilton's source for "German manners" is Tacitus' *Germania*. Her comments on the pleasures offered by invented speeches in histories are reminiscent of the more familiar observations on history made by Elinor Tilney in Jane Austen's *Northanger Abbey*.

p.306 complacency That is, she greeted them in a pleasant manner. "Complacent" did not then have its present negative connotations.

p.308 Here are fencers This scene is a variation of an episode in Hamilton's first novel, *Translations of the Letters of a Hindoo Rajah*, in which the fictional Rajah mistakes ladies dancing at an English ball for slaves hired to entertain the guests.

p.308 amusements of the amphitheatre That is, gladiatorial combats, including fights to the death.

p.310n says Tacitus Hamilton is quoting Arthur Murphy's translation of *Germania* (her italics); the lines of poetry are slightly misquoted from Thomas Gray's "Elegy: Written in a Country Churchyard."

p.313 Paulina Agrippina's companion; the character is Hamilton's invention.

p.316n Montesquieu Hamilton is quoting (with some variations) *The Spirit of Laws*, using a translation by a Mr Nugent (4 vols, London, 1758), book XX, chapter 2 (2: 2).

p.319 Varus Varus was the Roman commander who lost three legions in an uprising of the German tribes (in the year 9) along the Rhine. Tacitus gives an account of this catastrophic defeat in the *Annals*, including the roles of the German chieftains Arminius and Segestus.

p.319 Edar More usually Eder; a river in central Germany.

Notes on *Letters addressed to the Daughter of a Nobleman*

p.324 Agnes Porter Joanna Martin, ed. *A Governess in the Age of Jane Austen: The Journals and Letters of Agnes Porter*. London: The Hambledon Press, 1988, 257. (The letter is dated 5 April 1805).

p.324 Miss Ewbank Miss Ewbank of York, National Library of Scotland ms. 9481, f. 63. Miss Ewbank was a niece of the Rev. Andrew Ewbank of Londesborough and apparently the daughter of one of Hamilton's acquaintances (Hamilton inquires after her mother); she met Elizabeth Hamiliton on three occasions in 1805, at the house of a mutual friend, a Mrs Green. The conversation about the Lucans, which was with Mrs Green, not Hamilton herself, is described in an entry dated March 26.

p.325 Anne Grant Anne Grant, unpublished letter (to John Hatsell?) 29 December 1809, Edinburgh University Library, MS. La.II.357, f. 152v. The recipient of the letter isn't indicated on the manuscript itself, but references to his part in helping her extricate her son from the consequences of a mutiny at his military academy, makes Hatsell, who was an MP, the most likely addressee.

p.326 *British Critic* "Miss Hamilton's *Letters*," *The British Critic*, vol. 29 (April, 1807), 357.

p.326 expressions of tender familiarity Grant to Hatsell [?], f. 152v.

p.328 before you were born The person addressed is, of course, Lady Elizabeth Bingham.

p.329 born to be controll'd Edmund Waller (1606-1687), "Of Love" (slightly misquoted).

p.333 Nankeen, linsey-woolsey Nankeen is a light yellow cotton; linsey-woolsey is a plain, rough cloth woven of linen and wool.

p.333 one other little boy Presumably Lady Elizabeth's younger brother.

p.336 landau A travelling carriage with a removable top.

p.340 The man whose mind Thomas Blacklock, translation of the Third Ode of Horace. The translation appears David Hume's *History of England* (6 vols. London 1762, 6: 224). Hume notes (although the note does not seem to appear in editions later than 1770) that the poem was translated "at the author's desire," and as it was not printed in Blacklock's collections of verse, Hamilton's use of the quotation indicates that she was reading Hume. Blacklock (1721-1791) was a blind poet who attracted considerable attention among the Scottish literati in the later half of the eighteenth century.